Indiana Folklore
A Reader

Indiana Folklore
A Reader

Edited by
Linda Dégh

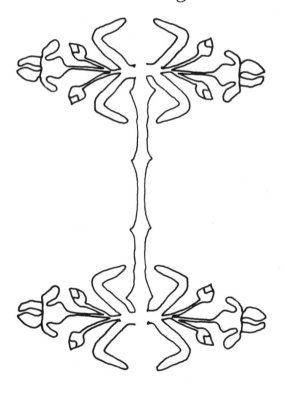

Indiana University Press   Bloomington

All the selections are from *Indiana Folklore: Journal of the Hoosier Folklore Society:* 1. Patricia Mastick, "Dry Stone Walling," IX:1 (1976), 113–33. 2. John M. Vlach, "Joseph J. Daniels and Joseph A. Britton: Parke County's Covered Bridge Builders," IV:1 (1971), 61–88. 3. Sandra K.D. Stahl, "Quilts and a Quiltmaker's Aesthetics," XI:2 (1978), 105–32. 4. John Gutowski, "Traditions of the Devil's Hollows: Relationships between a Place Name and Its Legends," III:2 (1970), 190–213. 5. Jeffrey Schrink and Frances Schrink, "Hangman's Crossing," XI:1 (1978), 87–97. 6. Barbara Ann Townsend and Donald Allport Bird, "The Miracle of String Measurement," III:2 (1970), 147–62. 7. Gilbert E. Cooley, "Root Doctors and Psychics in the Region," X:2 (1977), 191–200. 8. Sheryl Pisarski, "A Porter County Seer," IX:1 (1976), 93–111. 9. Sylvia Grider, "Dormitory Legend-Telling in Progress: Fall, 1971–Winter, 1973," VI:1 (1973), 1–32. 10. Linda Dégh, "The House of Blue Lights Revisited," II:2 (1969), 11–28. 11. Janet Langlois, "'Mary Whales, I Believe in You': Myth and Ritual Subdued," XI:1 (1978), 5–33. 12. Gary Hall, "The Big Tunnel: Legends and Legend-Telling," VI:2 (1973), 139–73. 13. William M. Clements, "The Chain," II:1 (1969), 90–96. 14. James Gary Lecocq, "The Ghost of the Doctor and a Vacant Fraternity House," VI:2 (1973), 191–204. 15. William M. Clements, "The Walking Coffin," II:2 (1969), 3–10.

Library of Congress Cataloging in Publication Data

Main entry under title:

Indiana folklore.

Bibliography: p.
Includes index.
1. Folk-lore—Indiana—Addresses, essays, lectures.
2. Indiana—Social life and customs—Addresses, essays, lectures. I. Dégh, Linda.
GR110.I6I52 398'.09772 79-2970
ISBN 0-253-10986-8 5 6 7 8 9 96 95 94 93 92
ISBN 0-253-20239-6 pbk.

Contents

Foreword   vi

I Old Crafts and Skills

1. Dry Stone Walling by Patricia Mastick   1
2. Joseph J. Daniels and Joseph A. Britton: Parke County's Covered
   Bridge Builders by John M. Vlach   22
3. A Quiltmaker and Her Art by Sandra K.D. Stahl   46

II Place Names and Oral History

4. Traditions of the Devil's Hollows by John A. Gutowski   74
5. Hangman's Crossing by Jeffrey Schrink and Frances Schrink   93

III Folk Belief, Medicine, and Magic

6. The Miracle of String Measurement by Barbara Ann Townsend and
   Donald Allport Bird   104
7. Root Doctors and Psychics in the Region by Elon A. Kulii   120
8. A Porter County Seer by Sheryl Pisarski   130

IV Horror Stories

9. The Hatchet Man by Sylvia Grider   147
10. The House of Blue Lights in Indianapolis by Linda Dégh   179

V Ghosts in the House and on the Road

11. "Mary Whales, I Believe in You" by Janet Langlois   196
12. The Big Tunnel by Gary Hall   225
13. The Chain on the Tombstone by William M. Clements   258
14. The Ghost of the Doctor and a Vacant Fraternity House by James
    Gary Lecocq   265
15. The Walking Coffin by William H. Clements   279

Bibliography of Indiana Folklore by Nikolai Burlakoff and Carl
Lindahl   287

Index   309

Foreword

The purpose of this book is to introduce the general reader to folklore as it is created, re-created, and circulated today among the people of Indiana. Folklore will not be presented here as something old and romantic, a voice from the distant past, as it was preserved and cherished by ancestral generations and left to us as a defunct and faded beautiful relic. Not that it is wrong to search for folklore before our time, to recapture past lifestyles from pages of old, written, or printed documents, or to discern origins and past facts of history from current collections. One can enjoy folklore testimonies of the "good old days" in which the folk was conceptualized as the population of the faraway rural countryside, well removed from urban sophistication. There is a wealth of materials to guide the searcher back to yesteryear and, indeed, to his roots, but this is not the presentation we wish to make with this collection of Indiana folklore. Rather, we shall emphasize the viability of folklore by offering a representative selection of materials which is the response of the people of today to the realities of the world in which they live.

Viewing folklore as the most natural, unselfconscious, and sensitive expression of the human mind, we must decode its symbolic language and learn how people feel and what they confess about themselves, their lives, their work, their hopes, and their fears. To help the reader understand the language of folklore it is not enough to publish a collection of texts, as told by individual informants. The folklorist must place each item into its socio-cultural context as close to reality as possible. The collector uses his tape recorder, camera, notepad and pencil to gather information; observes situations in which folkloric activities spontaneously take place; interviews several people to elicit individual variants for the same stories; and obtains explanatory and interpretive data to understand process of creativity. After careful transcription of the recorded materials, the folklorist can present his findings analytically, truthfully seen through the eyes of the folk, faithfully reporting what the folk tell him.

Except for some special and obvious cases, the articles follow this method of analytical presentation of materials collected among the Indiana folk over the last decade. Following this method, we address ourselves to the American folklore enthusiast who can conceptualize the folklore of Indiana as "a part of the main," a specific regional edition of American folklore. While the folklore of Indiana is distinctive, it is also, in a way, a representative American sample. As Anatole France once said: "The eternal stories which cross borders are differently colored by each people inspired by the distinctive feature of the skies, the mountains, and the taste of the waters." What are the specific colors of Indiana folklore which are different from those of its midwestern neighbors—Ohio, Kentucky, Michigan, and Illinois, or of more distant California or New York? One can only suggest which of the historically formulated or newly established elements are Hoosier attributes beyond doubt. There is still much work to be done to pinpoint the specifics within the general, to define the place of Indiana folklore within American folklore, and to identify its complex relations to that of other states.

To advance these goals, this book offers, in addition to enjoyable reading materials to the interested Indianan, a useful introduction and textbook to high school and college educators and students. Formal and informal classes that train amateur fieldworkers to explore their own heritage will not only help scholarly research but also benefit teachers and students as they become conscious of the humanistic values of folklore. Self-explored folklore can make people respect the quality of life and the wisdom of the common folk.

Most of the case studies in this collection were the products of close cooperation between my students and myself at the Indiana University Folklore Department. The courses—The Legend, Fieldwork, Survey of Folklore, and Indiana Folklore—were heavily dependent on field collection assignments in the different regions of the Hoosier state. Field explorations provided us with valuable materials upon which new in-depth research methods were probed. Additionally, colleagues, instructors, and archivists generously guided us to new collections to be used in our experiments.

The lack of dependably collected and annotated folk narrative texts, particularly legends, led to the establishment of *Indiana Folklore*, the biannual journal of the Hoosier Folklore Society from which the articles in this book were selected. Over the twelve years of its existence, *Indiana Folklore* has become the testing ground, the forum to publish materials to build on and help improve theoretical thinking. We have learned a lot but there is still much to learn. If we say we can draw a map of current and past haunted houses, cemeteries, and bridges in Indiana; if we say we have an idea how Halloween tricks have changed over the years, how preferred etymologies and uses of the name Hoosier by Hoosiers were formulated, what made Turtle Days of Churubusco famous, and why the Versailles Pumpkin Show got started, there are many more things we do not know. So many things that once were are no more, or have changed beyond recognition (if not to the sharp eye of the folklorist), and there are things which are being born, or are going to be born tomorrow.

It should be remembered that today's work could not have been done without the work of folklore's pioneers. The Indiana school of folkloristics was the first of its kind in the United States and became one of the most distinguished in the world. Its founder, Stith Thompson (1885–1976), was an English professor who was also an eminent folktale scholar and a classifier of narrative motifs and tale types. His international reputation prompted Indiana University authorities to name him Professor of English and Folklore, and to endow a folklore library and to launch a monograph publication series in 1939. The first group of professional folklorists in America graduated from Thompson's modest Bloomington workshop, while on a broader scale folklorists were trained in his Summer Institutes held every four years since 1942, with the participation of an international folklore faculty. With the support of students and interdepartmental cooperation a new discipline took shape.

The enthusiasm of Thompson and his disciples led them to look at the folk of Indiana as a primary resource of lore. Members of English composition classes were asked to collect materials, and soon a manuscript archive was instituted. With the support of the general public the Indiana team founded the Hoosier Folklore Society in 1938 and began the publication of the *Hoosier Folklore Bulletin*, its first official journal, in 1942, soon to be superseded by *Hoosier Folklore* (1946–50) and *Midwest Folklore* (1951–63). In the words of William Hugh Jansen, one of the founders of the Society, the journals "served a very great need and served it well. They encouraged collectors, showed them how to do field work, and made the field work available to other collectors. They brought folklore recognition to Indiana as a state, as a university, as a scene for rewarding collection. I am not one of those who believe that we must collect now before it is too late, but do believe that we must collect now so that we will have adequate basis for comparison with what has been collected in the past and with what will be collected in the future."

Indiana Folklore is carrying on the tradition in an era of plenty. Since the late fifties a folklore curriculum founded by Richard M. Dorson at Indiana University has matured into a training center for American students as well as folklorists from other continents. Generations of graduates have designed their own folklore education programs, carrying the gospel and broadening the scope of the discipline. Systematic and industrious collection developed the manuscript archive into the largest folklore treasury of the nation, and it is accessible to those who contributed to it and to whom it belongs: the people of Indiana.

So far we have not specified whom we mean when we speak of the lore-producing and transmitting folk. Certainly we do not think of a foggy, abstract entity, hidden impersonally behind texts, beliefs, and artifacts. We mean real flesh-and-blood people, whom we can meet any time and anywhere, who communicate their folklore messages to others within their social group. Although it might once have been the folklorist's assumption based upon insufficient information that folklore was communally created, there is no anonymity in folklore creation and there never was. People always were proud of their knowledge. It is individuals: men, women, children, adolescents who, sharing membership in different groups within the social network, tell or act folklore and find response by the appropriate group membership which individually also breeds folklore. In this complex relationship tellers, performers, and listeners alternate on the basis of an inherited, learned, and tacitly agreed upon traditional (or conventional) frame of reference in sharing and disseminating folklore.

Any group of people can have its own folklore repertoire: rural or urban, educated or uneducated, rich or poor. We can speak of the folklore of permanent or temporary groups based on age, social status, religion, or occupation which produce a set of folklore directly or indirectly related to the nature of the group. Functionally, we mean small groups within which folklore is passed on in face-to-face interaction. This does not necessarily exclude consideration of folklore that has been picked up and disseminated widely by the mass media or other channels, and after making this detour returned to the small group.

The collection in this book exhibits folklore in a wide variety of situations. We recorded teen-agers telling stories while on their way to a scary place to prove their courage; factory workers exchanging jokes while drinking beer in the canteen; church women trading folk remedies while making cookies for a bake sale; neighbors reporting on the sighting of a ghost in a large tenement. We observed the folklore behavior of young girls at slumber parties, boys' practical jokes in scout camps, farmers' ritual bargaining at barn auctions, old-timers' tall-tale telling at the "liar's benches," and the formulaic folk speech of wait-resses at McDonald's.

Like most other states, Indiana has developed a rich stock of organized community rituals. Nowadays there seems to be a notable increase in the staging of local festivals, centering around a specific feature which, in essence, serves as a reaffirmation of pride in local values and folk identity. Folklorists sometimes look with suspicion and disgust at the heavy commercialization of these events. They deplore the disappearance of homemade props and paraphernalia and their replacement with mass-produced, prefabricated objects. But we should not forget that we are living in a consumer-oriented world in which producers offer to fill our needs, even in ritual supplies, and that such a world has led to new development and variation of folkloric behavior more appropriate, timely, and convenient in the modern world. The peak season of celebrations is between late summer and the eve of winter, just as it always was among the farming folk, between harvest and Halloween. The fall fairs and family reunions in Indiana are often combined and highlighted by the celebration of Old Settlers or Pioneers Days, Fall Foliage Festivals, Great Pumpkin Parades, Apple Cider Harvests or by specialized Little Italy, Little Ireland, Little Switzerland Festivals, German Octoberfests (in September!), and others ending with All Hallow Eve's supernatural encounters. The scheme is the same: parades, floats, craft exhibits, carnivals, raffles, elections of a festival queen, sports games, contests, regional (ethnic) food specialties, hayrides, pole climbing, pancake eating, wine stomping, hog calling, tobacco spitting, and other features. The variables are infinite. So are the opportunities for the folk to get together and exchange folklore information, and for the folklorist to gather new field materials.

In five topical chapters this book describes fifteen folklore events. It begins with material life, crafts and techniques and continues with samples of oral history, magic belief, and medicine. The remaining two chapters include representative cases of legend telling among Indiana children, adolescents, and adults. The anthology is necessarily incomplete and disproportionate because of the varying quality of our resources. Legend and personal experience narratives are better represented than most of the other areas, and we were also able to choose from a rich store of material culture articles. In other areas we had to use the little we had, and there are still important and popular folklore forms missing. For example, we could not include articles on proverbs, riddles, ballads, jokes, life-cycle and calendar customs. This lack should alert the reader to the need of more systematic field explorations. The Indiana Folklore Bibliography at the end of this volume should be viewed as both a document of past contributions and an appeal for the filling in of gaps. Cooperation between laymen and scholars is a hope for the future. This book should mark the end of an era and be the prelude of a new beginning.

Bloomington, Indiana   LINDA DÉGH

I Old Crafts and Skills

Dry Stone Walling

Patricia Mastick

Early American masonry construction has received rather spotty attention, dwelling mainly on stylistic changes. This vacuum of complete data has left investigators such as Wilbur Zelinsky with numerous quandries as to the place of stone in American material culture.

> Why the contradiction in New England between the ubiquitous stone fence and the non-use of stone as a house building material? Why was stone an important house material in some parts of southeastern Pennsylvania where it was distinctly subsidiary as a fencing material? And why was stone employed so widely for underpinnings of houses and for chimneys in the Southern Piedmont and Appalachians and almost never for any other purpose?[1]

This problem of lack of sufficient data affects not only the kinds of research needed to solve the apparent contradictions presented by Zelinsky, but affects also the area of masonry building technology. Harley McKee notes that because stone buildings, unlike buildings constructed of less durable material, are available for architectural historians to study, they have received a good deal of attention. "The technology employed in their construction, however, is but sparingly mentioned in publications on American architecture."[2] It is this affliction, not unfamiliar to all forms of historical building construction research, in all geographical areas, which has hampered my own research on the technology of dry stone walling.

Dry walling is a masonry bonding technique which has been employed since the second millenium B.C. Masonry, though a term which is now used to refer to earth, stone, brick, and concrete, originally referred only to stonework.[3] It is for the construction of stone walls that dry walling, or laying up without mortar, has been used. Mortar in early American masonry constituted any bonding material which was used to watertighten walls, to fill voids between masonry units and to act as a plastic cushion to compensate for the gradual settling of the masonry.[4] The bonding materials used were clay (often called simply "mud"), several

1

forms of lime mortar, or natural cement mortar. Since clay was susceptible to erosion by strong rains, walls laid up in clay were often pointed, that is, the exterior parts of the joints were filled in with lime mortar to further protect them. Ultimately whether stone walls are laid up with or without mortar—in other words, dry—the selection and laying of stones so as to bond or interweave them is of utmost importance in securing the durability and longevity of any stone wall [see figs. 1 and 2].[5]

The stones used with either bonding technique have been acquired from several sources. Irregularly rounded boulders deposited by glaciers are found on the ground or just below thin layers of soil; it is this field stone which was used in early Connecticut buildings. Such rock deposits are also found in southern unglaciated areas in a more angular form. This type of stone is found throughout Kentucky and has to be constantly removed from the shallow fields. Natural erosion has also produced field stone broken off from mountains. This is characteristic of stones used in the Mormon Tabernacle in Salt Lake City, Utah.[6] Field stone can be used in its natural form, or can be shaped by breaking off unwanted bumps or uneven edges.

Figure 1: This double dry stone wall marks the border line between the property of Lawrence Brown and Jean Ferris on Maple Grove Road, Bloomington.

Besides the gathering of field stone, another source is that of quarrying. Stone could be most easily quarried from exposed ledges and outcroppings usually near creeks or streams. This simple quarrying has provided much of the stone, other than field stone, used in early American masonry construction. Commercial quarrying, which did not develop until a steady demand made it profitable, did not use these exposed sources of stone, but rather sought subterranean sources of superior quality.[7] Whether commercially or independently quarried, stone can be used in its

Figure 2: Corner of the garden wall west of the Ferris house.

uncut irregular form as it comes from the quarry or "can be roughly cut to
rectangular faces, more carefully shaped and selected to lie in horizontal
courses, or cut and shaped so that the edges of the blocks form accurate
rectangles. . . . The last type is known as ashlar; the others are all forms of
rubble masonry."[8]

In the United States, the use of stone has been primarily limited to
certain pockets of the country which have deposits of one of the more
common types of stone used in building construction: granite, marble,
limestone, sandstone, or gneiss. As Zelinsky suggests, there seem to be
contradictions as to its use in a given area. Using the distinctions drawn in
the preceding paragraph, we can begin to see in what kinds of masonry
construction dry walling has been utilized. Historically, it has been used in
all types of buildings—houses, out-buildings, public buildings—and in walls
or fences, separating buildings or areas of land. However, the technique of
dry walling has been most frequently used in the construction of stone
walls or fences. There are recorded instances of its use in the wall
construction of early colonial dwellings and in later foundations and
utility buildings, but these uses of dry walling are in the minority,
primarily because it has been considered essential to mortar a masonry
building to insure its permanence. Let us, therefore, consider the dry stone
wall or fence and its construction.

The appearance of stone walls in an area has all too often simply
been attributed to the abundance of stone. There are, in fact, many factors
involved. Many regional architectural surveys do mention that people
moved into an area because of an abundance of stone. Logan Esarey in his
guide to the study of Indiana local history offers an advertisement in the
Indiana Journal, 1828, for the sale of land "abounding with useful timber,
limestone quarries, and springs of never-failing water."[9] Hazel Spencer
Phillips notes that most early stone buildings in Ohio were built in Little
Miami Valley in Warren County because "material for such building was
available for the labor."[10] Norman Isham and Albert Brown also mention
that people moved to Middletown, Connecticut, in the early 1600s,
attracted principally by an enormous ledge of stone and that others were
attracted to hilly areas that had an abundance of field stone which they
used as building material.[11] James Thomas, Acting Director of Shakertown at Pleasant Hill, Kentucky, also suggested that the abundance of field
stone and quarriable areas near the site of the community was a
consideration in the Shaker's selection.[12] Hazel Phillips also mentions
Quakers and Shakers settling in stone areas of Ohio.[13]

H. F. Raup has called the presence of dry stone walls "indicators" of
poor, thin soils, and says that such walls are the result of attempts to clear

land for cultivation.[14] Thomas confirmed this belief by stating that the pastures around Shakertown had to be continually cleared because the fields were so shallow that erosion produced new field stone.[15]

It is Charles Stotz who ventures beyond the apparent reasoning of geographical fitness to suggest that in Western Pennsylvania even though much of the stone used in early buildings came from fields and outcroppings,

> the popularity of various building materials in each district was to some extent dependent on the origin and the previous building experience of its settlers. . . . It was only natural that immigrants to Southwestern Pennsylvania from these districts [stone areas of Eastern Pennsylvania, and Western Maryland] should utilize the vast deposits of stone. . .[16]

In this same vein, H. F. Raup concludes his article on fences:

> The type of fence is often a measure of the ingenuity of its builder, for he builds his enclosure at a minimum cost and for maximum protection. . . . The fence, then, is an increasingly significant element of material culture, indicative of its physical surroundings, having special social significance, and acquiring different forms which may stem from culture contact and tradition.[17]

It may be that for such related reasons stone walls did not exist in several regions of the United States where stone was readily available, such as Middle and Southern Appalachia. In the Northeast, as Zelinsky suggests, the stone wall may have been the end result of experimentation with several forms of fencing.

> When it was imperative to clear the stones away from a field so as to get at the soil, the rocks could be tossed into large heaps somewhere within the field or into ridges along its edges. The carefully constructed stone fence appears to have succeeded a period of experimentation in brush, stump and rail fences; and once the habit of building them was acquired, it may have become a regional cultural trait, but evidently not one that was clung to too tenaciously.[18]

The *Report of the Commissioners of Agriculture for the Year 1871* (just prior to the standardization of barbed wire) tabulated the percentage of stone walls in comparison to other forms of fencing in New England as varying from 32% in Vermont to 79% in Rhode Island; the report also indicated a "fair proportion" of stone walls in northern Virginia counties, but none south of Virginia or west of Pennsylvania.[19] James Thomas felt that the craft of dry stone walling was in Kentucky as early as 1790, with extant walls dating from the period of 1830-1840, the time when most of the original forty miles of stone walls were laid around Shakertown. Given this data, it is conceivable that the technology was spread from Virginia through the Bluegrass region of Kentucky to Southern Indiana. There are accounts of stone wall construction in the Bloomington area in the 1860s and 1870s.[20]

Thomas mentioned that a tremendous number of early stone walls in Kentucky were put up by slaves and are therefore often referred to as slave walls. Phillips also mentions that the Butterworths of Virginia built their stone buildings in Ohio with the help of freed slaves who came with them from Virginia.[21] In the 1840s, when cheap Irish labor became available, the Irish took over the construction of stone walls. In Southern Indiana there seems to be no one group such as the Irish involved in dry wall construction as was common in other regions. In the Bloomington area, walls were constructed by such people as George Wylie (Ben Owen's farm, Maple Grove Road), J. Adams (Maple Grove Road, 1878), and Old Man Ellett (Maple Grove Road). According to Levi Fyffe, who was eighty-one years old when Mrs. Richard Peden interviewed him in the 1940s, Perry Smith and Charles Lineback came up from Kentucky specifically to lay dry stone walls, particularly in the Maple Grove Road area.[22]

Just as there were many people involved in the construction of the walls on Maple Grove Road, so too does Haydn S. Pearson state that "thousands of teenage lads and young men took contracts to build long stretches. . . ."[23] This would indicate that many were employed as helpers to a few who, skilled in the craft, let out contracts.

> When it came to walls for barnyards, garden spots and perhaps a calf yard behind the barn, many good farmers wanted a wall that would stand undisturbed through the years. Thus in each community certain men made reputations as builders of good walls.[24]

Thomas reiterated this point of craftsmanship:

> You can find some areas of the Bluegrass where rock walls are better than others. I'm sure that has to do not only with the mason's talent but with the composition of the rock, the availability of the rock.

In Kentucky a distinction is even made between a stone mason who works with building stone—"somebody who lays a building foundation or a rock chimney"—and a rock mason—"somebody who lays a rock fence," according to Thomas. J. Geraint Jenkins quotes *Stephens Book of the Farm* as saying,

> We suspect that many dry-stone dykes are built by ordinary masons who being accustomed to the use of lime mortar are not acquainted with the proper method of bedding down stones in a dry dyke as firmly as they should be, and are therefore unfitted to build such a dyke. A builder of dry stone dykes should be trained to the business, and with skill will build substantial dykes at a moderate cost which will stand erect for many years.[25]

Jenkins distinguishes the British "waller" as someone who can work with the irregularly sized stone, "for he must size up the possibility of each stone knowing exactly whether it will fit into a particular gap."[26] Harry Chambers, retired Indiana University mason, also commented on this "eyeballing" process when interviewed at his home:

> You'd be surprised how many people will stop and talk to you and want to know where you got that stone, how come you can lay it up this way or that way. Now that's the secret about it. There are all kinds. I got a boy out there now—he took my job. I learned him. He's good I guess. He laid stone before he ever come to work there, but when it comes to building walls, he just don't know. He can't figure it and he can't get off and—anotherwords, he just lay a piece up there and forgets it. I always lay a little bit and then I'll get back and look at it so if I don't think it looks right, I'll take some of them out and put different ones in. That's the way they always had me to do.[27]

James Thomas admiringly spoke of the late Mr. Goforth, a third generation rock-fence builder, who also could "eyeball" a wall:

> He was really amazing because he could just walk up to a pile of stone and select pieces and talk to you at the same time and they would all fit. And I've tried to do it myself and it's been a hassle. It just doesn't work out that way when you are not used to it.

Some people even today are both stone masons *and* rock masons, but as Thomas says, "They prefer, of course, to do stone masonry work because they are people who can quarry and cut out a piece of stone and butch hammer it and cut it—can do it all." When I asked Harry Chambers which he preferred he told me that he really did not like putting up a dry stone wall. In the last two years of his employment at I.U. he put up only dry walls because the University could not afford to do it "properly," i.e., with mortar.

The problem of cost is certainly a factor which historically (as well as presently) entered into the decision of whether or not to build dry stone walls. Raup suggests that the fence can be seen as an index of wealth.[28] Even when stone was free—free for the hard labor of moving it—there was the expense of labor. Pearson mentions that men contracted to build dry stone walls at a cent per foot.[29] Judith Munn states that wages for stone fence building in Monroe County varied in memory: 25¢/rod, 80¢/rod, or $1.50/day. She stated that the perch (24¾ cubic feet) was also used to determine wages. Old Man Ellett built a fence across Stout Creek on Maple Grove Road and received $100 for his labor. Frank Sader who built the stone wall around the Maple Grove Christian Church after he returned from the Civil War (1868-78) was paid $275.00. Levi Fyffe stated that it took seven wagon loads of stone to make one rod of wall and "that was a day's work although one man was reputed to be able to do three rods"—or 5.5 yards.[30] In Scotland, according to Rainsford-Hannay, a man could build about six yards of four-and-a-half foot wall per day, and seven yards per day in limestone districts. In 1957 Rainsford-Hannay approximated the cost of reconditioning a stone wall 4½ feet high and 100 yards long, repairing 12 yards per day at a rate of one pound per man per day, or a total of 17 pounds.[31] Thomas stated that masons who laid up dry stone walls on his farm were paid stone mason's wages. "It about broke me but they did a tremendous job." Chambers also remarked at the expense:

> Now what people don't realize is the expense to that. That stone sells by the ton, see. And it doesn't take too much of a truck load to bring say 50 to 60 to 80 dollars, and if you build a wall right your labor is higher than the cost of the stone. So a wall, just a little wall, not over 20 feet long and maybe 3 feet high, cost 5 to 6 to 800 dollars. . . . People just think, oh you just throw a few pieces in here. But every time you pick up one [a stone] you're pickin up a dollar or two because that thing weigh maybe a hundred pounds. It don't take too much at 20, 25 and 30 dollars a ton—don't take very much rock to run you right up there.

Thomas' remark may be an interesting footnote on the decline of this "close-to-lost" art:

> The tendency in the eighteenth and nineteenth centuries was to

over-construct. They finally realized that labor and materials were something that cost money and time; so they finally devised ways of lightening up on their construction.

Even the rural trulli ceased to be built in the twentieth century because of rising cost of labor techniques which had been developed for the towns.[32]

When we speak of dry stone wall construction we must distinguish it from early and/or less complex rubble walls which are made from the clearing of debris from fields and piling this unwanted stone into loosely-packed fences or walls. "The stones, brush and trees that the pioneer cleared from fields could be heaped into an effective barrier against the cattle permitted to wander freely in the surrounding woods."[33] Pearson makes the following comment about stone walls in the Northeastern states:

> Through the 1700s and the first half of the 1800s, until man discovered how to make wire, two types of walls were common. The thousands of miles of wall that line roads, circle fields and climb hillsides follow a similar pattern. . . . The biggest rocks were laid on the surface, and smaller rocks placed on top of them. . . . As far as the stonewalls around fields, meadows, and pastures were concerned, men expected to 'run the fences' each spring and replace the stones heaved off by frost action.[34]

So, it is the intricate and laborious job of dry stone walling in which we are interested. Called a stone wall in New England, a stone fence in Pennsylvania and western New York, a rock fence in western Virginia and south, a stone row in northern New Jersey,[35] its construction varies more from region to region. Chambers felt that no two walls were the same, that everyone built a dry stone wall a little differently, depending on his skill and the material available.

Stone is rather difficult to transport, a good reason why individuals located as near to outcroppings as possible or used field stone near the site of walls. In the 1800s and up until the wide availability of trucks and tractors, oxen were used to drag the stones to the site. Both Phillips and Thomas mention the Shakers using ox teams to haul the quarried stone long distances, fifteen miles or more.[36] Stoneboats, sledges, and sleds were used to carry the material. Stones could be lifted onto the sled by means of levers. If the stones were too large for these conveyances, they were moved on rollers.[37] Pearson states that in the Northeastern states through the 1700s and early 1800s, rocks were moved "with a pair of patient, plodding oxen, a stone boat and crowbars. . . ."[38] Esarey mentions the use of a low sled and a yoke of oxen to move field stones from hillsides to fields' edges in order to build walls.[39] Levi Fyffe remembered oxen teams being used to move field stone on Maple Grove Road in the 1860s and 1870s. Both Fyffe and "Grandpa" Stanger, the grandfather of Bloomington resident Carr Stanger, recalled as small boys watching teams of oxen haul carts of shelfrock up Maple Grove Road to the Maple Grove Christian Church in 1868-78 to begin construction on the dry stone walls.[40]

Rainsford-Hannay noted that in Scotland, when possible, the stone was sledded downhill to the site of the wall and placed in easily accessible piles along the baseline of the wall construction.[41] Curtis Fields of Vermont, in his 1971 guide to dry stone wall construction, offers several methods of transporting stones. One method is to load the stone onto a stoneboat which is hitched to a jeep. When a stone is too large for the stoneboat, Fields suggests the use of a small log chain wrapped around it with a "hook and link" knot and then hitched to a jeep. Fields also gives detailed instructions as to the lifting of stones on to the wall once it has been started. He illustrates how a slab of stone can be rolled up a $2''\times8''\times8'$ plank or a descending series of blocks onto the wall. If the slab is, again, too heavy, he suggests the addition of rollers so that the stone can be maneuvered along the plank, pushed along with a pinch bar.[42] Chambers also mentioned using rollers and pipe, instead of planks, to move stones into position on a wall. On one job where the stones were enormous (15-20 tons per stone) he used a crane to move them into place. Chambers received the stone in truckloads. Much of the stone came from old buildings which had been torn down; the field stone was gathered from fields and creekbeds in Brown County. The University stores the stone on three acres of a farm which it owns so that it has a ready supply. Thomas stated that the Shakers made some dry stone walls out of quarried stone which they quarried probably from areas along the Kentucky River which bordered their property. One end produced sheets of stone, the other blocks. Wilferd Boruff of Bloomington recalled picking up stone along creek beds during the depression in order to sell to local farmers and contractors for 75¢ per week.[43]

Once the stone has been made easily accessible, Rainsford-Hannay states that the line of the wall should be marked out by pegs and later by taut string.[44] Fields also instructs one to chart the line of the wall by using a guide string stretched between two stakes or, for a curved wall, a rubber garden hose stretched along the ground. Fields mentions that some people can simply do it by eye alone, establishing the line of the wall by sight and proceeding without further preparation.[45] Chambers also stated

that he "eyed" the course of the wall, that it was something which you
learned to do when you fooled with walls long enough.

It is necessary that the wall have some type of firm foundation. The
walls at Shakertown were laid without foundations. Chambers said that he
did not always have to lay a foundation when the ground was firm enough,
but that if you did not have a solid foundation, it was best to provide one:

> [It is a] good thing to dig about 12 to 16 inches down in the
> ground, just as wide as you want to lay your wall, and put stone in
> there. Lot of times we use crushed stone. You fill that full of
> crushed stone, pretty well up, tap it good, and then start with your
> rock on that.

Rainsford-Hannay felt that the foundation "trench" should be dug out to
reach the firm subsoil, generally six inches deep and four inches wider than
the width of the wall.[46] However, Lawrence Brown, owner of the Tom
Owens farm on Maple Grove Road, found the foundation trenches to be
2½ feet deep. A yard stone wall near the Ben Owen house, now owned by
Jean Ferris, has a base of 2½ feet, yet the stone wall crossing Stout Creek
built by Old Man Ellett was up to 10 feet wide at the base.[47] Fields
provides that following advice:

> Excavate a section perhaps 6 feet long by some 40 inches wide [an
> extra 10 inches] and down to a depth that will provide a firm
> footing for the foundation stones. This depth will vary with the
> topography but it is important to be able to set the first tier solidly
> if the wall is to withstand the action of settling and heaving. Provide
> proper drainage for the first tier of stones by A) choosing flat stones
> of irregular shapes, leaving an inch or so of space between them, and
> filling such spaces with small stones from your random pile [of
> stones] ... B) laying flat stones over the interstices to prevent
> seepage of soil.[48]

Rainsford-Hannay states that the trench should be packed tight "with hard
flat stones, averaging the size of one's hand." If boulders are in the way,
they can be incorporated into the foundation.[49] These are the approxi-
mate sizes of the stones found in the foundations of ruined walls on Maple
Grove Road. Pearson also talks of trenches filled with approximately the
same size stones, though they are dug more deeply:

> A trench was dug, four feet wide and three feet deep to insure
> getting below the frost line when cold winters had sustained periods

of 20 to 30 degrees below zero. The trench was filled level with medium size stones plus plenty of smaller ones to fill the pockets.[50]

Obviously, there is great variety in the width and depth of the trench, the base of the wall, and the size of the stone used to fill the trench. Once the foundation is completed, if it is deemed necessary in the first place, stones are laid in an interwoven fashion in either a single (large stones used the full width of the wall), double or triple wall (double or triple rows of stone laid the width of the wall with their lengths extending into the wall) [see fig. 3]. Dry stone walls are totally dependent upon the strength of the bond created by interweaving the stones—a technique sometimes referred to as "breaking joint." When two stones are placed together, a crack or joint is formed. When another layer of stone is placed on top of this bottom layer, all joints should be covered by stones, the joints of this upper layer falling away from the lower layer's joints. Chambers describes it in the following way:

> If you lay two pieces of stone together, you got a crack right here between them. You goin' to have a crack, ain't no way around it. Well, when you lay your next course [layer of stone] on that, you don't want to have a crack in the same place. You want to try to break this stone over the crack. It might be a little one, might be a big one. Don't make any difference. Just so you break that joint right there. And so on and so forth on down the wall. Then when you come back you break the next joint. You don't never have two joints together. . . . And it's just kind of like brick; you don't never have rows running right straight up; you do, why it will fall apart. That ties it, see.

Fields provides a simple formula for assuring proper bonding: "one over two — two over one."[51]

Each course of stone will consist of a single line of stones as in the single dry walls of Shakertown; or a course will be laid in a double or triple line, with the length of each stone extending into the wall, the outside face maintaining an even line with the other stones. The interior space of the wall is packed with smaller stones or spall—broken chips—as previously suggested by Fields. Rainsford-Hannay refers to these small stones as hearting and contends that they should be laid so that they bind neighboring stones with the roughness of their surface and irregularity of their shape.[52] Jenkins also mentions the use of small irregular pebbles as filler for the internal space (or joint) in a double or triple wall. The

Figure 3: Gate pier of garden wall of the Ferris house. Note slab
used for bolt for locking.

external joints between stones can also be filled with small wedging stones
called pins so as to make the wall "rabbit-proof." This kind of
construction can be seen on the garden wall to the west of the Ferris
home.

Chambers spoke of tilting the stone, and though Fields does not
mention this, both Rainsford-Hannay and Jenkins do. In describing a dry
wall which he laid up into a bank near the Seventh Street and Union Street
tennis courts in Bloomington, Chambers said:

You have to lay it into the bank and you want to start out—you don't want it to come perfectly straight. Every layer you lay you lay in just a little bit and that way the pressure that keeps from pushing it out. Your bank will be pushing against it.

In building a free standing wall, in the limestone districts of Great Britain, the stones in a double wall were tilted outward slightly and downward so as to throw off the rainwater and prevent it from running down the wall. In Cornwall, according to Rainsford-Hannay, they were tilted inwards so that the rain ran through the center of the masonry.[53] Jenkins refers to an outward tilt which "causes rain which may have found its way through the wall to be thrown off to the sides."[54]

Both Chambers and Fields speak of laying walls in fairly long sections—six to twelve feet—so that the courses can be laid with some guarantee of straightness. "You don't want them [the courses] running up and down. It get to be like a washin' board," said Chambers. Fields quotes a folk saying to reiterate the importance of building a vertically straight wall: "Always lay a wall so that each stone casts a shadow."[55]

Starting either from a corner of the first tier of stone or from a scuntheon—a well-made pillar of well-shaped stones—stones are laid level in an even line, often by shimming them up with small, flat stones.[56] Stones of varying thickness can also be laid next to one another in a tier. For instance, the first stone might be very thick, six inches, and its thickness might have to be matched with a series of three thinner stones. But Chambers warns, "When you start off with a layer across your wall, you got to be sure you don't get something too thick, where you'll have the wall running this way [in a diagonal]."

Chambers sometimes breaks a stone if it is too thick. "A lot of times I'll take a rock . . . and split it right through the middle. Therefore, you got two pieces about so thick, but you ain't bothered the weathered edge really. . . . Some of them you split, some of them you can't." His comment about a weathered edge was a serious one which he again stressed:

If you're going to have 18 inch walls and you're going to have both sides showing, then you got to be kind of particular. . . . I have broken and cut them [stones] but a next thing I always have said is never put the side that's going to be to the weather, I mean outwards, never bother that; never scratch it, or knock any off of it; 'cause if you do then that takes the hard surface off and the weather will eventually cause that to crumble. You want all your old—what they call a weathered edge—to the outside. Doesn't make any difference about this inside part, cause it stays out of the weather anyhow. I never like to lay a broken part on the outside, always like to lay that on the inside. If I have to break them, I just turn them over.

When the stone needs to be broken, a three or four pound "rock hammer" is used to chip or trim a stone. James Thomas recalled that Mr. Goforth always had with him his rock hammer which he used for breaking field stone. Jenkins talks of a heavy waller's hammer used in the Cotswalds—short handled, weighing ten pounds and having two cutting edges, a sharp one for cutting stone and a blunter edge for cracking stone.[57] Fields uses two heavy hammers to split mica schist. He draws a line parallel to the grain and hits a heavy bevelled sledge hammer with another three-pound sledge hammer at each point along the line. As a crevice appears, he drives in a wedge or an old ax blade to open the crevice and then splits the stone by prying the crevice with a crowbar.[58]

Not only does "breaking joint" help bind the stone together, but in a double wall—or an area of a single wall which has been reinforced such as at creek crossings or passageways where walls have been tripled and doubled respectively—a builder will often put "tie stones" or "through-bands" in to further aid in reinforcing a wall. These stones, which run the width of the wall and ideally are even a few inches longer than the width of the wall, can be found at different heights, if used at all. Rainsford-Hannay specifies that they should be placed at no more than 21 inches from the ground, and a second one, called a "coverband," at about 40 inches in a 4'6" wall. Jenkins and Fields also mention them, Jenkins suggesting that the tie stones be inserted half way up the wall, and Fields suggesting their "occasional" placement.[59] How often they should be included along the length of the wall is not really specified, leaving Fields' "occasional" to be the standard. The throughbands of the Ferris walls, both field and garden walls, are approximately 1½ feet above the ground. The coverbands, which are flat, fairly smooth and continuous along the length of the wall, extend out a few inches on the field stone walls but not at all on the garden wall on the Ferris property. Interestingly, there were no coverbands on the field walls of the Tom Owen's farm.

Dry walls seem to vary in their dimensions depending on the purpose for which they were built. They range in height from the three foot walls of farms between Boston and Albany of the late 18th century to walls of the magnitude of Old Man Ellett's—12 feet high by 10 feet wide.[60]

Pearson mentions that Northeastern masons built walls five to six feet high and four feet wide at the base.[61] Thomas guessed that the walls around Shakertown were 40 inches high and varied in width.

> They are normally single; you can find double walls if you are going around a curve, or a termination where you have a gate post you can have a double wall. I've seen triple walls. It makes it stronger. Over at my place we have one that must be almost four feet square. I would say most of your rock walls are single, and double only where you have stress and triple where you have extreme stress points.

Thomas also mentioned that the walls taper, being wider at the bottom than at the top. Rainsford-Hannay also suggests that a good stone wall should be tapered from 26 inches at the base to 14 inches at the top on a 4'6" high wall.[62] Fields suggests that an effective width is 26 inches to 30 inches, that the wall does not taper, but rather remains the same width from base to top.[63] Chambers also does not vary the width of his walls, keeping them an even 18 inches wide, and anywhere from three feet to eight feet tall. The dry stone walls on Maple Grove Road varied in height depending on whether they were field walls, pasture walls, or garden walls. The graden walls are three feet high, increasing to 4'6" where they expand to meet the slope of the land. These walls taper from 2½ feet at the base to 1½ feet wide at the coverband. The stones used in the base courses are as thick as 8 inches and taper to the cope.

The field walls are higher, ranging from four to five feet, in order to enclose large animals. Thomas mentioned that in Kentucky in the mid-nineteenth century, all items of stock—cattle, pigs, sheep—were kept in the same field. Therefore, the fences had to be "cattle-proof, mule-proof, horse-proof, and everything else."

Another element which strengthens the wall is the cope or capstones, also called capping or coping, which are placed vertically on top of the coverbands or top course of stones which have been chosen for their flatness and large size so as to provide a level surface for the coping. The ability to lay cope stones so that they interlock with one another, according to Rainsford-Hannay, represents the supreme skill of a dry stone wall builder. He suggests that these stones should have been previously selected for their size—12"×12"—and their rough surface so as to grip neighboring stones, and set aside. A cope stone is placed at each end of the finished horizontal coursing; working from one end, the mason firmly beds each stone, packing it tightly next to its neighbor. Heavier cope stones are laid at intervals with thinner stones wedged in between.[64]

Thomas remarked that the coping provides additional weight. "Of course, it takes less labor in the top cap because you've got 12 to 15 inches in that cap or more, and that makes the fence high." Interestingly, a similar reason was offered for the use of a capstone on the apex of the Italian trulli, "to anchor it down securely."[65]

Harry Chambers mentioned yet another reason for the use of coping.

> Just lay them [capstones] in there any way, just so they are wide enough to cover your other wall, see. Then your water comes and hits—that way it don't run down your wall. It runs off of it, see.

H. F. Raup also considers capstones to be important for the protection of the wall:

> At Monterey, California, six-foot adobe walls are capped with heavy roof tiles to prevent winter rain from demolishing the structures. Such walls stand a century or longer with a minimum of repair, as long as the tiled coping remains in place. In most climates, particularly where frost action is severe, stone walls should be coped to prevent their destruction.[66]

Chambers beds the coping in cement mortar so as to increase its ability to shed water. Rainsford-Hannay, however, warns against this practice, stating that the dry wall will settle itself away from the cemented cope. He stresses that the most essential feature is the tightness with which the capstones have been placed, for animals like to rub up against them and nudge them, causing loose capstones to be dislodged.[67] Once the capping has been finished, the wall has reached completion and should remain a solid barrier, if well-made, against all obstacles except charolais bulls and straying cars.

Variation in dry stone walls can occur through the omission or inclusion of throughstones, coverbands or capstones, or the use of lime or concrete mortar as sealant under the capstones or as an addition to the exterior joints of an extant wall. There are other forms of variation as well. In some cases, the variation can constitute the addition of hedges as Rainsford-Hannay mentions in the Galloway Dyke, or as in Virginia, the addition of stakes and rider fences on top of a dry wall to increase its height.[68] Variation in the coarseness, or flatness of the stones used can produce very striking differences. The walls of Shakertown look very fragile in relation to the walls of Curtis Fields.

Chambers noted a difference in the walls which he had made of Brown County field stone, a dark colored, block-like stone, and the walls in front of Black's Lumber Company in Bloomington.

> They got an old gray-white shaly lookin' stone; it don't get very
> thick. It's real thin. It's kind of more of a slab. It has seams in it.
> Wherever they get it out of a creek, it comes out in little pieces,
> maybe awful big, but be awful thin. It's in layers.

When larger stones are used in the bottom courses and thinner stones
used in following courses, the result is a tapering effect with a feeling of
weightiness near the base, and refinement as the wall nears the coping.
What we are dealing with, in actuality, are aesthetic options, because
whether one chooses stones of generally similar size as Fields does, or
whether one varies their size in a descending manner, as was done in the
walls on Maple Grove Road, the practicality of the options is the same.
Thomas, in talking about the varying quality of dry stone walls in the
Bluegrass region, made an aesthetic choice almost unknowingly:

> One wall that comes to mind is on Highway 62, just outside of
> Midway. It's in front of a house built about 1820. The name of the
> farm is Stonewall Farm. It's the most beautiful wall you've ever
> seen. I believe it was quarried rock but I'm not absolutely sure, but
> it's all cut in nice rectangular pieces.

The Shakers, too, seemed to have opted for the finished, refined look of
ashlar. Their later dry walls, built in 1860 around the porch area addition
of the East Family House, have been finely shaped and fitted together.
Chambers, on the other hand, emphasized over and over again how much
he appreciated the aged, weathered quality of field stone and that he
preferred to work with field stone over quarried, cut stone.

Perhaps another aesthetic choice was made in the repairing of a
stone wall which runs parallel to the property line of Shakertown on
Morgan Lane. The course work has been done vertically instead of
horizontally. Thomas says of it:

> It's very unusual. I've seen this done in patches, what we call gaps.
> This could have been done because they found that the horizontal
> pieces didn't work on the slope and they probably repaired it every
> year and decided the heck with it; we are going to take this gap out
> and put in vertical coursework and see how it goes.

As the stone has now weathered to the extent that it is impossible to tell
in what chronological order the vertical to diagonal coursework was done,
it is hard to determine if, in fact, the patterns of diagonal, vertical, and
horizontal coursework were the result of aesthetic experimentation or

simply the coincidence created by continual patching of the wall. Rainsford-Hannay gives an example of vertical coursework done on an embankment on the Isle of Man. He calls it "an unusual but most effective use of thin slabs."[69] Obviously, for him, it does not come under the category of dry wall design.

As Rainsford-Hannay's comment points out, what is important is the effectiveness of the bond achieved, and this is as much dependent upon the availability of stone conducive to the construction of walls as it is upon the builder's skill generally and in relation to the particular kind(s) of stone available to him. Zelinsky notes that the stone wall is still to be found throughout New England and a small area of northern Virginia, and that "indeed, no other old fence type can be found with any regularity in New England."[70] Whether it has survived because stone lasts longer than other building material, or rather due to the fact that the walls were constructed with care and craftsmanship to last against clumsy animals, inquisitive children, and other marauding natural elements, there are few left today who know how to build using a dry stone walling technique, let alone build intricate dry stone fences.

NOTES

1. Harley J. McKee, *Introduction to Early American Masonry* (Washington, D.C., 1973), 9.
2. Wilbur Zelinsky, "Walls and Fences," *Landscape*, VIII, 3 (1959), 20.
3. McKee, 9.
4. *Ibid.*, 61.
5. *Ibid.*, 32.
6. *Ibid.*, 12.
7. *Ibid.*, 13.
8. A. L. Osborne, *A Dictionary of English Domestic Architecture* (New York, 1956), 60.
9. Logan Esarey, "Indiana Local History," *Bulletin of the Extension Division, Indiana University*, I, 7 (March 1916), 11.
10. Hazel Spencer Phillips, *Traditional Architecture* (Oxford, Ohio, 1969). 60.
11. Norman M. Isham and Albert F. Brown, *Early Connecticut Houses* (New York, 1965), 173, 176.

12. James Thomas, Acting Director of Shakertown at Pleasant Hill, Kentucky. Interviewed November 29, 1974.

13. Phillips, 57, 119.

14. H. F. Raup, "The Fence in the Cultural Landscape," *Western Folklore*, VI (1947), 2.

15. An interesting side note to this is the stone used in the building of trulli, dry stone walled shelters found in the Trulli state of Italy. Through the quarrying of stone, shallow fields were transformed into tillable land suitable for crops. As Edward Allen says,

> The thin topsoil would be carefully removed and piled to one side, laying bare the limestone bedrock beneath. Then the limestone would be broken out in chunks to a depth of two or three feet. The best stones would be saved for construction, and the rest replaced over the still unbroken strata of the limestone, with the coarsest pieces on the bottom and the finest on the top. Following this back-breaking procedure, red bolo soil from a nearby depression would be carried to the field in baskets and tamped over the loose layers of broken limestone to a depth of fifteen or twenty inches. Finally, the original topsoil would be spread back over the bolo, and the land would be ready for cultivation. The heavy but sometimes infrequent rainfalls would be absorbed eagerly by the shallow topsoil and thick cushion of bolo, and once these soils had reached saturation the excess water would filter into the loose bed of broken rock beneath, from which, retained by the impervious bedrock, it could be slowly reabsorbed by the soil and roots above when needed. This continuous bed of limestone fragments, in addition to acting as an underground reservoir, served to furnish continual chemical fertilization to the soil from beneath, to complement the organic fertilizer added from above (Edward Allen, *Stone Shelters* [Cambridge, Mass., 1969], 80).

16. Charles Morse Stotz, *The Early Architecture of Western Pennsylvania* (New York, 1936), 25-6.

17. Raup, 7.

18. Zelinsky, 20.

19. *Ibid.*, 17.

20. Judith Munn, "Dry Stone Walls," term paper for Folklore 220, 1971.

21. Phillips, 57-8.

22. Munn, 3.

23. Mamie Meredith, "The Nomenclature of American Pioneer Fences," *Southern Folklore Quarterly*, XV, 2 (June 1951), 141.

24. *Ibid.*

25. J. Geraint Jenkins, *Traditional Country Craftsmen* (London, 1965), 171.

26. *Ibid.*, 169.

27. Harry Chambers. Interviewed December 4, 1974, at his home in Bloomington.

28. Raup, 7.
29. Meredith, 141.
30. Munn, 16, 3.
31. Colonel F. Rainsford-Hannay, *Dry Stone Walling* (London, 1957), 43, 26.
32. Allen, 84.
33. Zelinsky, 15.
34. Meredith, 141.
35. *Ibid.*, 135.
36. Phillips, 118.
37. McKee, 18.
38. Meredith, 141.
39. Logan Esarey, *The Indiana Home* (Crawfordsville, 1943), 56.
40. Munn, 3, 18.
41. Rainsford-Hannay, 37.
42. Curtis P. Fields, *The Forgotten Art of Building a Stone Wall* (Dublin, New Hampshire, 1971), 28-33.
43. Munn, 6.
44. Rainsford-Hannay, 37.
45. Fields, 34.
46. Rainsord-Hannay, 37.
47. Munn, 16.
48. Fields, 35.
49. Rainsford-Hannay, 37.
50. Meredith, 141.
51. Fields, 36.
52. Rainsford-Hannay, 38.
53. *Ibid.*
54. Jenkins, 171.
55. Fields, 36.
56. *Ibid.*
57. Jenkins, 169.
58. Fields, 27.
59. *Ibid.*, 36; Jenkins, 171.
60. Zelinsky, 15.
61. Meredith, 141.
62. Rainsford-Hannay, 35.
63. Fields, 36.
64. Rainsford-Hannay, 39.
65. Allen, 81.
66. Raup, 6.
67. Rainsford-Hannay, note to figure 12b., 39.
68. *Ibid.*, 50-53; Meredith, 140.
69. Rainsford-Hannay, note to figure 15a.
70. Zelinsky, 18.

Joseph J. Daniels and Joseph A. Britton: Parke County's Covered Bridge Builders

John M. Vlach

In the history of American bridge building no type of construction had more public appeal than that of the covered bridge. These wooden structures, which first appeared in the Northeast early in the 19th century, can be found in almost all regions of the United States and recently have become revered as artifacts of bygone ages.[2] The attention received by covered bridges is well deserved, as they are extremely durable and lasting examples of traditional workmanship and skills which have been forgotten or replaced by changing technology. Though it would seem that bridges are outside the realm of folklore studies, the covered bridge at least is an exception. Regarding the folk nature of material objects, Henry Glassie has said: "To determine whether or not an object can be classed as folk, and in order to describe an object well enough for its historic and geographic connections to be accurate and completely revealed, any material object must be broken down into its components: fundamentally, it will have form, construction, and use."[3] This paper will examine these components, especially construction, as far as is possible with the covered bridges of Parke County, Indiana. The resulting analysis will attempt to show many variations and innovations in what at first glance appears to be a standardized and immutable form.

With 36 spans, Parke County, located 45 miles directly west of Indianapolis, contains the lion's share of Indiana's 130 covered bridges. The county also has the distinction of being the home of two of the state's foremost bridge builders, Joseph J. Daniels and Joseph A. Britton. Parke County hence is an opportune laboratory for studying the covered bridge in Indiana, having a dense collection of examples built by men who were considered highly skilled at their craft.

22

J. J. Daniels and J. A. Britton were truly remarkable and prolific carpenters. Together, they have been credited with 79 covered bridges in Indiana[4] and, respectively, with 12 and 16 Parke County spans.

Daniels, born in 1826, was the first of the twosome to establish his reputation. Daniels' father, Stephen Daniels, was a builder of railroad and turnpike covered bridges in southern Ohio. He had been a sub-contractor for Colonel Stephen Long, an army engineer who designed the Long truss which was awarded patents in 1830, 1836, and 1839. J. J. Daniels thus learned his skills from his father and probably was very experienced by the time he began his own career. He moved to Indiana and built his first bridge at Rising Sun in 1850.[5] This job was followed by two railroad bridges, one each at Evansville and Crawfordsville. After serving as a railroad superintendent he came to Rockville in 1861 and put in a bid on the bridge to be built that year across Sugar Creek at Rockport. Daniels won the contract and erected a bridge which reached 210 feet in one span (still one of the largest single span wooden bridges in the United States), which was so sturdy that it withstood the force of a tornado even though every shingle and piece of siding was torn away.[6] Daniels then made his home in Rockville and proceeded to build bridges throughout Parke County and the surrounding area. On several occasions, he submitted bids and won contracts as far south as Jackson and Lawrence counties. His competence as an engineer was esteemed throughout the county as he was called in to advise and consult in the construction of the county courthouse in Rockville.[7] Daniels built his last bridge, the Neet Bridge, in 1904 and he died on August 7, 1916, at the age of 90 years.

J. A. Britton's career was initiated in 1883, but he did not achieve real prominence until after Daniels' retirement. Britton's entry into bridge building is interesting as it was his second attempt at a profession. He learned carpentry from his father, who had worked on the old Armiesburg covered bridge, but he went on to establish a law career. He was admitted to the bar in Rockville in 1870 and later established a practice in Lawrence, Kansas. He returned to Parke County in 1879; here he took up carpentry[8] and began his first bridge at The Narrows across Sugar Creek. When Daniels retired, Britton no longer had any strong local competition for Parke County bridge contracts, and consequently he was awarded most of the bridges built there between 1904 and 1917. Britton shared his skills and knowledge with his sons. Together with them in 1915, he built the Jefferies Ford Bridge and his oldest son, Eugene, went on to contract bridge construction jobs of his own in other counties.

Clearly there was a transmission of skills in the careers of Parke County bridge builders. These skills included not only experience at fitting timbers with great precision but also a knowledge of basic engineering principles. Daniels was a capable draftsman and drew up extremely detailed plans to submit to county commissioners.[9] He also had a comprehension of engineering problems: in a plan for the Wabash Bridge at Bloomfield he computed both the bridge's dead load and the rolling load per lineal foot.[10] Through his father, Daniels probably had some kind of association with Colonel Long and thus was able to gain a basic awareness of formal engineering practices. This association was possibly crystallized later in Daniels' life since a copy of Colonel Long's *A Description of Col. Long's Bridges* was found among his personal papers. It is not known if Britton had any acquaintance with formal engineering practices but it is not unlikely that he might have read engineering treatises or observed and learned from Daniels' bridges. Britton began his career 22 years after Daniels had already developed a reputation. Thus, there may have been a transmission of skills and techniques between craftsmen as well as along family lines.

The type of bridge built in Parke County lends itself to individual-ized practice of construction skills. Thirty-five of the bridges in Parke County were built with Burr trusses with an arch added.[11] Theodore Burr, a native of Massachusetts, had received a patent for his design and it was used widely in the eastern United States (Fig. 4). This truss design was the major type employed in Indiana according to R. B. Yule:

> Recent newspaper and magazine articles indicate that the Long and Town Lattice types were much used in the eastern states but a personal examination of about 150 of Indiana's 202 bridges has failed to disclose the use of either. The Burr truss is most in evidence because it was the favored type of the state's three most prolific builders. There are a great

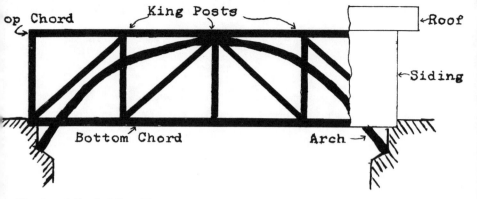

Fig. 4   A Typical Burr Truss

All drawings by John M. Vlach

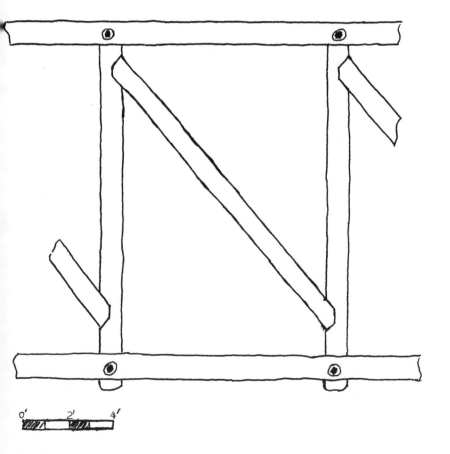

Fig. 5   Typical Burr Truss panel in Parke County

many Howe truss bridges in the eastern part of the state and quite a number of these were built by companies having headquarters in Ohio.[12]

Burr's description of his bridge in his patent application in 1817 reveals that the design particulars are ultimately to be determined by the individual builder.

> Both chord and crown plates may be of two pieces each embracing the king post between them, and put together by lockwork or they may be single and put together by tenons and mortises or partly on one plan or partly on the other as may suit the builder. When put together, put in the king posts or diagonal braces. They may be put into the corners where the posts are united to the chord and crown plates to correspond with the lines of the chords, plates, and king posts; allowing the angle to be partly on each as may suit; in equal proportions is best, or [they may be put in] by shoulders with tenons and mortises.[13]

The carpenter then had a degree of freedom in deciding the manner of construction; the result is that the bridge reflects the skills of the particular builder. The covered bridge thus had the potential to become a folk item by virtue of its construction, as traditional skills were applied to the task and a certain amount of variation was introduced into the final product.

There were sometimes distinct differences in the construction of typical Burr truss panels of Parke County bridges (Fig. 5). The choice of woods, the size of the timbers, and the means of joining them were consistently similar; but the builders showed a variation in the use of metal tensioning rods. These rods were long enough to span the width of the bridge and served a double function as they secured the king posts to the bottom and top chords (Fig. 6) in addition to tightening the sides of the truss against the cross braces (Fig. 7). Britton's style in this matter was unchanged throughout his career. He always placed 3/4 inch diameter iron rods at the king posts and fastened them with a nut and washer on the outside edge of the top and bottom chords. Daniels' first bridge in the county did not employ any iron rods, possibly because they were not readily available. But in later bridges, he utilized the long rods along with another piece of manufactured hardware, a metal brace holder upon which

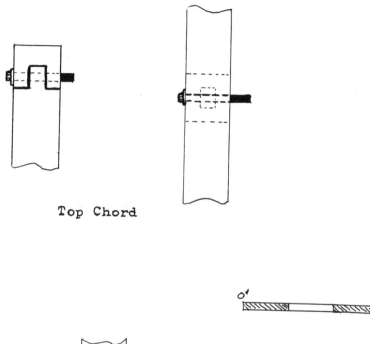

Top Chord

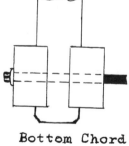

Bottom Chord

Fig. 6   Detail of Chord-King Post Joints, Showing Use of Tensioning
Rod

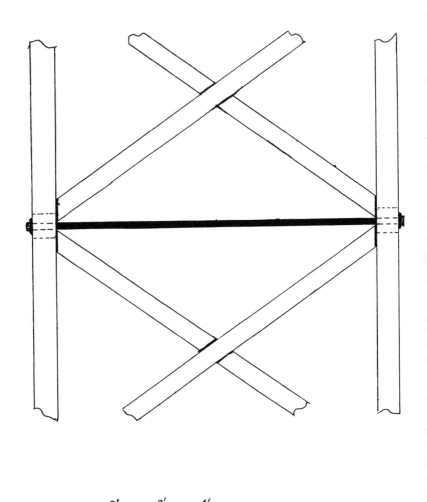

Fig. 7   Detail of Tensioning Rod and Cross Braces: Top View

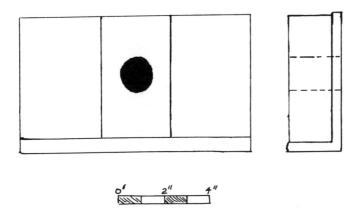

Fig. 8   Cast Iron Brace Holder Used by J. J. Daniels

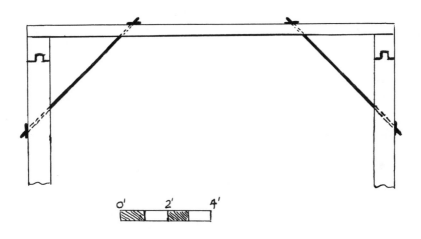

Fig. 9   Detail of Iron Rods in the Portland Mills Bridge

the cross braces rested (Fig. 8). This "shoe" facilitated the construction, as less carpentry was required in preparation for the placement of the braces. The oldest bridge in Parke County, the Portland Mills Bridge, had six inch by six inch timbers which were partially secured to the king posts by squared wrought iron rods (Fig. 9). The fact that this bridge predates Daniels' first Parke County effort and extensively incorporates metal for structural purposes is significant. This situation shows that as metal became available at least some builders were willing to experiment with its use. Daniels perhaps more than any other builder made extensive changes in his building style when he switched from totally wooden trusses to a more extensive use of metal products. Even though iron rods were available to Daniels in 1861, they apparently were not of a type which he wished to use. His motives for adaptation, a trait which is not universally found in bridge builders, will never be known. However, the changes which Daniels made show an attempt on the part of the craftsman to make his product acceptable to changing criteria.[14]

The diagonal bracing of the side panels is interesting. The king posts are notched and the braces are fitted precisely to give the bridge the strength to withstand heavy loads and stresses (Fig. 10). After the brace was set in place, two spikes were driven at both ends to prevent it from being dislodged. In Parke County, diagonal king post braces were always installed in the manner previously described. However, there is one example in a Brown County bridge where a protrusion or "shoulder" was left on the king post and the brace was allowed to lie against it (Fig. 11). It seems that the latter method is inferior to the plan employed in Parke County as much of the timber must be hewn away, using up much time and wood.

Another opportunity for a conscious choice in the design was provided in the construction of the bottom chord. This bridge member was composed of very large timbers, usually 40 feet in length. Since bridges were often more than 100 feet long, several timbers were joined and paired to span the distance (Fig. 12). The only exception to this design was the Jackson Bridge in which the bottom chords were composed of tripled timbers. Theodore Burr had specified that either lockwork or

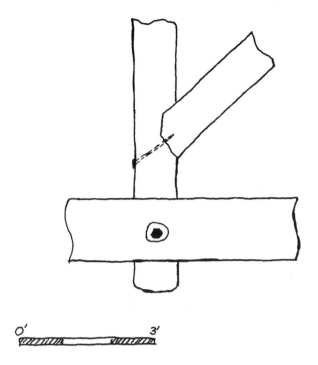

Fig. 10 Detail of King Post- Brace Joint

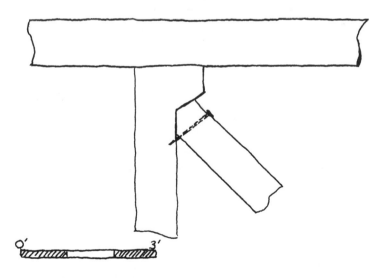

Fig. 11 Detail of Brown County Bridge King Post- Brace Joint

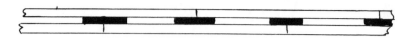

Fig. 12 Typical Layout for Bottom Chord

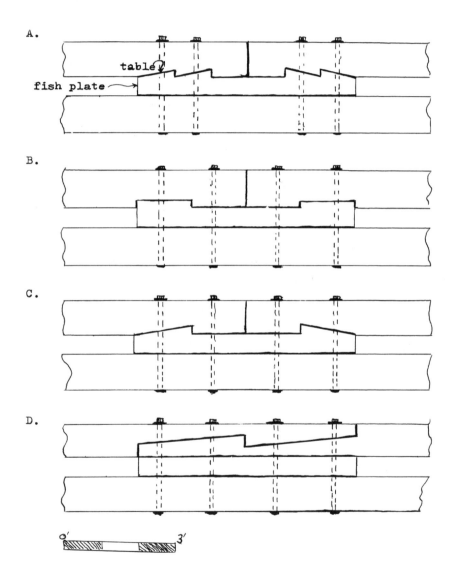

A.

table

fish plate

B.

C.

D.

0'   3'

Fig. 13 Bottom Chord Joints for Parke County Bridges

mortise and tenon joints could be applied to compose the bottom chord. In Parke County a system of splices was employed with several distinctive variations.

Four types of joints were used (Fig. 13). Three of them (13A through 13C) are known as eccentric tabled joints while the remainder is called a notched lap splice. The last type of joint was used only on the Crooks and Portland Mills bridges. The eccentric tabled joint holds the chord sticks in two ways. First, the tightened bolts secure the ends of the two pieces firmly to the middle of the parallel member. Second, the shear block, sometimes called a fish plate, adds frictional forces to distribute the load force away from the bolts to prevent them from bending. The fish plate also prevents the shear forces from splitting the chord timbers and creates a space into which the king posts are inserted. Thus this type of joint has multiple advantages.

Daniels consistently employed the type of joint shown in Fig. 13A. He called it a "double headed hook." It is a stronger type than the others because of the greater number of tables employed. The table shoulders receive the shear tension, and consequently more tables distribute the shear load more uniformly. Britton, in contrast, used all three types of eccentric tabled joints. His first bridges had squared, single tabled fish plates. Then, in later works, he employed tapered, single tabled fish plates and, finally, he used the "Daniels" type. Britton thus went through an evolutionary process in his choice of bottom chord joints. It seems that Britton may have learned how to strengthen his spans from the examples provided by Daniels' bridges. Certainly he had over twenty years to watch a master at work.

A great deal of skill is needed in order to properly fit a shear block. The pieces must be cut with the precision and exactness of a cabinet-maker.[15] Daniels and Britton, as well as other bridge builders in Parke County, were craftsmen of the highest order in cutting and fitting this type of joint. It is probably due, at least in part, to the loss of such expert carpenters that the construction of wooden truss bridges declined in America. Their skill was one which was learned through tradition and which was fostered by the builders' pride in their craft. The use of eccentric tabled joints and their subsequent demise serves as testimony to the passage of the bridge builder as a folk craftsman.

The arches which were added to the sides of the Burr truss provide further examples of the individual bridge builder's abilities. Burr had intended that the arch should be notched and fit to the king posts and braces wherever it crossed them. This direction was ignored in Parke County. The arch pieces, which were hewn from tulip poplar because it was easily worked with adze and broad ax, were fastened to every king post with two bolts. The individual pieces (usually 20 feet long) were designed to butt at a king post, where the ends were held by one bolt apiece and a three inch washer that overlapped onto the other arch piece (Fig. 14). The completed arch was supposed to have the appearance of a long graceful curve. Its height was determined by the length of the span, as short bridges had low arches and longer bridges had the arch reach almost to the top chord. Daniels' arches were always perfect symmetrical curves but Britton's early bridges were defective in this aspect. In The Narrows Bridge the arch comes to a distinct point at the center king post and in the Sim Smith Bridge the arch has angles at intervals along its length. Since Britton eventually acquired the technique of making perfectly curved arches, it seems that his early carpentry knowledge was deficient in some aspects of the bridge building craft. Britton, after 1900, when his skills had been sharpened by experience, would bevel the edges of the arches to give them a more finished appearance. Apparently no other builder considered this detail important. Perhaps Britton was attempting to compensate for his earlier shortcomings by increased perfection in later years.

When Daniels placed the arch of the sides of the truss, he did so after the false work under the bridge had been removed. The semi-completed span was allowed to settle and then the arch was added to secure the truss in its final attitude. It is known that Archibald Kennedy in neighboring Putnam County allowed the arch and truss to settle together but no record remains of Britton's technique.[16]

A distinct difference between Daniels and Britton developed in their choice of design in the arch-abutment connection. The arch rested on the sloped front of the abutment. Daniels' method avoided direct contact of

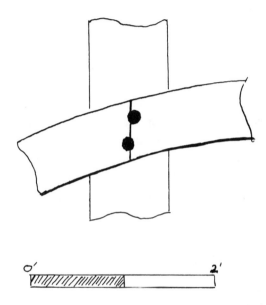

Fig. 14   Detail of Arch-King Post Joint

the arch and the abutment because he felt that the "stone 'breathed' moisture into the wood."[17] Daniels most often set an iron plate between the masonary of the abutment and the end of the arch. In the Mansfield Bridge, however, he bolted the arch ends to a six inch square post which was grouted into the abutment. Britton, seemingly unworried about moisture problems, grouted the arch directly into the abutment.

It should be mentioned that the techniques used with respect to the arch-abutment details did not change appreciably in the 20th century when abutments were made of concrete rather than cut stone. Both Daniels and Britton built their later bridges with concrete abutments. Usually it was not the builders themselves who were responsible for the construction of piers and abutments. This work was let out to subcontracters,[18] although Daniels did design the masonry work and the grillage of short walnut pilings which supported it (Fig. 15).[19]

Since covered bridges were almost totally wooden structures, they could and did float away during floods when the river levels would rise higher than the deck elevations. The Crooks Bridge now rests at its present location because of a flood in 1867 which deposited it there after carrying it 15 miles from its original site.[20] Daniels and Britton both realized that some security was needed to prevent such mishaps. Both men used a system of iron rods to tie the bridges to their abutments. Daniels employed two 1¼ inch diameter rods at each abutment (Fig. 16), while Britton linked 3/4 inch hexagonal rods, chain fashion (Fig. 17). The method used by Britton had been employed by Henry Wolf in 1856. Wolf had employed 3/4 inch rods which were fastened to the top chord and then ran along the outside of the bridge to be attached to the sides of the abutment. Perhaps Daniels thought that the linked rods were too flimsy and hence preferred to use the more rigid design. Britton did not copy Wolf exactly as he placed the rods underneath the bridge, out of view, and fastened them only to the bottom chord. This safety device can not be found in every bridge in Parke County. There is no explanation for their absence except that perhaps such precautionary measures were applied only where rivers and creeks had a tendency to flood.

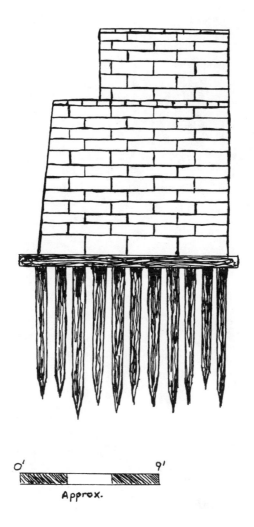

0'   9'

Approx.

Fig. 15 Abutment and Foundation designed by J. J. Daniels for the Newport Bridge, Vermillion County in 1868

*Fig. 16 Detail of Security Rod on the Bridgeton Bridge built by J. J.
Daniels in 1868*

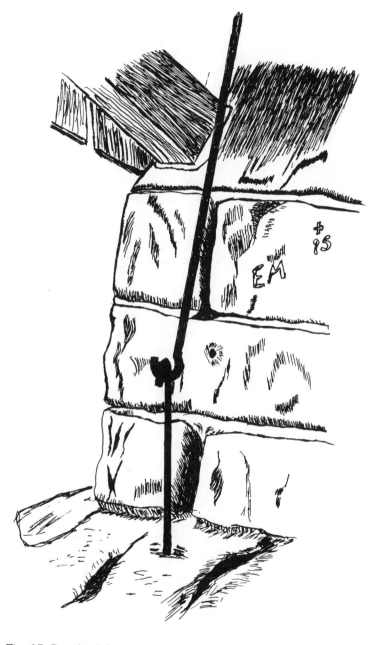

Fig. 17 Detail of Security Rod on The Narrows Bridge built by J. A. Britton in 1883

The sidings and roofs of the covered bridges, which provide their single most distinctive characteristic, never vary appreciably in Parke County. In fact, since the coverings were designed to protect the bridges from the rages of the elements, the present sidings are in most cases not the original ones. The materials used included wooden shingles for the roof[21] (later sheet metal was substituted) and yellow poplar, left unpainted for siding. Poplar was used for two reasons. First, it was a standard mill product and hence readily available in required amounts, lengths, and widths. Second, it could survive the elements well because when exposed it formed a pulpy surface coating that was resistant to weathering.[22] It seems that most sidings were nailed vertically onto the bridges. The Portland Mills and Jackson bridges are exceptions in that the siding is fastened in a horizontal fashion, not unlike that of a common frame house; in fact, the Portland Mills Bridge is covered with clapboards.

A noticeable external difference in the appearance of covered bridges can be found in the portal designs. Though limited by the square shape of the bridge, the roof lines assumed varied forms and are without discernible motivation for their use by the individual builders. Daniels' bridges show a domination of a shallow arched roof line with only two early bridges having horizontal portals. Britton first had a penchant for a very pronounced arching roof line in the portal construction. Later, however, all of his spans employed a New Hampshire barn portal[23] which compromises the squared and arch roof lines with angles. This type of construction yields the clearance of an arch but does not require the complexity of cutting out a curve (Fig. 18). Other bridge builders used all three portal types, but it seems that the earliest of them preferred the horizontal line style.

Though it is common for many of Indiana's covered bridges to have some distinctive portal decorations, only the Jackson Bridge in Parke County possessed any scrollwork. At one time the portal was worded with a quote from Andrew Jackson: "The Federal Union: It must be preserved."[24] This statement had great significance in 1861 when the nation was on the verge of civil war and the supportive scrollwork

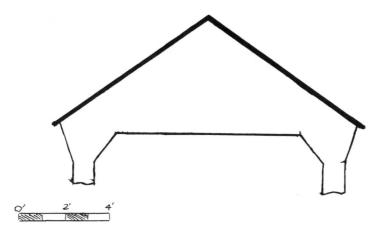

Fig. 18   New Hampshire Barn Portal

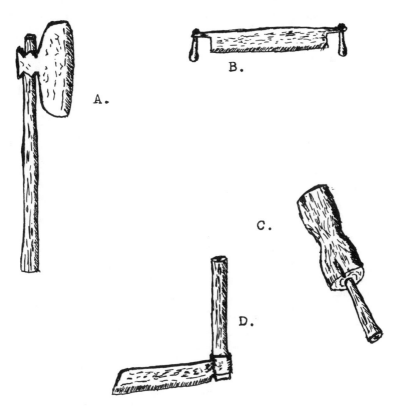

*Fig. 19   Some Bridge Building Tools: A. Broadax, B. Drawshave,
C. Froe Club, D. Froe*

"pillars" must have emphasized the seriousness of the sentiment. Today, however, the portal only shows the name, Jackson Bridge, as the quote has disappeared. The most common embellishment of the portals in Parke County is the listing of the names of the county commissioners who supervised the particular bridge's financing. Also, modern bridge devotees have made an attempt to capture some of the nostalgia of bygone days and have stenciled on the bridge portals the warning: CROSS THIS BRIDGE AT A WALK.

The folk-ness of the covered bridge is validated by the tools used in bridge building, all of which are common to traditional frame construction. Broadaxes and straight adzes were used to hew and trim arch pieces, to fashion fish plates, and to notch king posts. Precision cuts were made with buck- and scrollsaws and pieces were finished with drawshaves and mammoth bridge planes, often four feet in length. The froe and maul were employed in making shingles. When holes were required for bolts and oak pins, hand augers were used. A drilling machine of sorts was used when large diameter borings were needed in the bigger timbers. Bridge building tools show the affinity of covered bridge construction to the older knowledge of barn and house building (Fig. 19).[25]

The form of the covered bridge gains traditionality from its construction rather than from its design. It is the personalized details of workmanship which individualize the patented, semi-academic form so that the final structure becomes a representation of the bridge builder's own unique skills—skills which he inherited from his predecessors. Herbert W. Congdon, in a description of covered bridge construction, discussed the role of the master builder:

> An open field was usually close to the bridge. Here the timbers were laid on the ground. A sample "panel" or part of the frame was laid out carefully by the master builder, who was so concerned with accuracy that he marked his joints with a sharp knife, as a pencil line was too coarse. All his skill, all the secrecy of his craft went into this initial operation. Patterns or "templates" were copied from his sample with the greatest exactness, to be used by his men in cutting the joints.[26]

It is clear then that even the manner of assemblage of the bridge, like the construction techniques, gives tradition to the form. The work pattern in which a master craftsman prepared samples for a number of other less accomplished carpenters, was one which was often followed in New England, the Mid-Atlantic States, and the Midwest. Elmer L. Smith described the Pennsylvania bridge building process: "Local builders often laid out the bridge parts on a field near the site and made sure the truss joints fit exactly before assembling the parts over the creek. Such a system was very similar to a barn raising, a method almost all Pennsylvania Dutchmen were familiar with."[27] Again, this pattern occurs in Parke County[28] as the manner of bridge building. Thus a traditional erection method along with traditional craftsmanship contributes to the folk nature of the construction of the covered bridge.

The use or function of the covered bridge cannot really be employed to determine its folk nature, as the bridge has but one true function—to span a river or a stream. There is a widespread belief that young lovers used covered bridges as private refuges in which to engage in amourous activities. Doubtless, the covered bridges do deserve their nickname, "kissing bridges", as former kiss-stealers have owned up to their thefts.[29] However, it should be remembered that whatever was done in the covered bridge was accomplished while crossing the span.

The covered bridge is a bona fide folk item in the material culture of Indiana. Traditional building methods and tools were used in its construction, and the skills applied were ones which had been learned from other bridge builders; usually in a father-to-son pattern. The final structure always bore the mark of the individual craftsman, as he would choose any number of variations in design and apply many techniques depending upon his own expertise. This aspect most clearly indicates the creative element of the bridge building tradition and shows that covered bridges are indeed crafted items. The form of the covered bridge in Parke County is, in a strict sense, not traditional since the Burr truss was invented by a semi-professional architect. In another sense the final form of any particular structure is influenced by the construction techniques and the craftsmanship of its builder, so that it is possible for an item to achieve a folk status. In this respect, the bridges in Parke County are traditional in their form. Wooden bridges in general, and Parke County covered bridges in particular, are objects made and fashioned by the traditonal craft of the bridge building carpenter. J. J. Daniels and J. A. Britton, two outstanding builders in Indiana, deserve more of the folklorists' attentions for their creation of genuine folkloristic items— covered bridges.

Notes

1. I must express my thanks to Dr. Warren Roberts, who encouraged me in writing this paper, and to Dr. Henry Glassie, who read the manuscript and gave freely of his good advice.

2. Fred Kniffen, "The American Covered Bridge," *The Geographical Review* XLI: 1 (January, 1951): 119-122. Professor Kniffen reconstructs the diffusion of the construction of American covered bridges in a map (p. 119) and shows that Indiana's bridges were part of a major national trend in building activity.

3. Henry Glassie, *Pattern in the Material Folk Culture of the Eastern United States* (Philadelphia, 1968), p. 7.

4. *Indiana Covered Bridge Topics* I: 1 (December, 1945): 3.

5. R. B. Yule, "The Covered Timber Bridge in Indiana," *The Indiana Historical Bulletin* VIII: 7 (April, 1931): 368.

6. *Parke County Memorial* (Rockville Chautauqua Association, 1916), p. 17.

7. *Rockville Tribune*, August 8, 1916. This source is an obituary clipping from the covered bridge files of the William Henry Smith Memorial Library, State Library, Indianapolis, which hereafter shall be abbreviated WHSML.

8. *Indiana Covered Bridge Topics* IV: 3 (June, 1949): 4.

9. Many drawings can be found among Daniels' papers in the WHSML.

10. "Plan for Wabash Bridge at Bloomfield," drawn by J. J. Daniels and among his papers in the WHSML.

11. In one case, the Philips Bridge, the arch is omitted due to the shortness of the span. One other Parke County bridge, the J. H. Russell Bridge, is a queen post truss.

12. R. B. Yule, "The Covered Bridge in Indiana, Part I: The Early History," *The Highway* XXIX (October, 1938): 221.

13. Llewellyn Nathaniel Edwards, *A Record of History and Evolution of Early American Bridges* (Orono, Maine, 1959), p. 51.

14. Henry Glassie, *op. cit.*, p. 11. Glassie indicates that construction, more than any other of the components of a folk item, will be highly variable because of

the accompanying technology. Possibly, with the growth in the popularity of iron bridges, Daniels was influenced to incorporate changes into his bridges. He did have in his possession a plan for a prefabricated metal arch bridge produced by the K & F and Z. King Company of Cleveland, Ohio which had received patents on October 1, 1860 and September 25, 1868.

15. Robert Flectcher and J. P. Snow, "A History of the Development of Wooden Bridges," *Transactions of the American Society of Civil Engineers* XCIX (1938): 341. The article mentions that the fish plates in Colonel Long's bridges were specified to be made of cast iron; however, oak was suggested as a substitute.

16. R. B. Yule, "The Covered Bridge in Indiana, Part II: Construction Details," *The Highway* XXIX (November, 1938): 259.

17. *Indiana Covered Bridge Topics* V: 2 (March, 1950): 4.

18. R. B. Yule, *loc. cit.*.

19. An example of the details of abutment construction can be found in the plans for the Vermillion Bridge among Daniels' papers in the WHSML.

20. Bryan Ketcham, *Covered Bridges on the Byways of Indiana* (Oxford, Ohio, 1949), p. 112.

21. "Specifications for a Wooden Truss" filed September 26, 1900 with John S. Whitaker, Auditor, Morgan County by J. J. Daniels stipulates that #1 red cedar shingles will be used for the roof.

22. R. B. Yule, *op. cit.*, p. 261.

23. Eric Sloane, *American Barns and Covered Bridges* (New York, 1946), p. 102.

24. *Parke County Memorial* (Rockville Chautauqua Association, 1916), p. 17.

25. Henry C. Mercer, *Ancient Carpenter's Tools* (Doylestown, Pennsylvania, 1960). This work gives ample testimony to the traditionality of the broadax (pp. 85-86), the adze (pp. 92-95), the drawshave (pp. 97 and 100), the froe (pp. 11-13), the bucksaw (pp. 145 and 147), and the auger (p. 178).

26. Herbert W. Congdon, *The Covered Bridge* (New York, 1946), p. 83.

27. Elmer L. Smith, *Covered Bridges of Pennsylvania Dutchland* (Witmer, Pennsylvania, 1963), p. 33.

28. Collected from J. A. Britton's grand-daughter by Janette Belue of Pittsboro, in October, 1970.

29. Collected by Janette Belue of Pittsboro, in October, 1970.

A Quiltmaker and Her Art

Sandra K.D. Stahl

Quiltmaking is one of the folk crafts that lends itself to a wide range of investigative approaches. Nevertheless, classic studies of the craft are generally historical and descriptive while more recent publications extend this established approach only through greater attention to practical instructions in quiltmaking. The study that follows does not depart radically from this earlier research, but it does consider an aspect of quiltmaking generally absent from earlier studies—the role of personal aesthetics in quiltmaking. I was fortunately well-acquainted with Mrs. Bessie DeVault of Darke County, Ohio, who is recognized as an excellent quilter in her community and among others who know her. Questions on personal aesthetics could profitably be addressed, I think, to someone with such a reputation for fine quilting.

Mrs. DeVault was born October 8, 1903, in Middleton, Michigan, to Frank and Nettie Huffman. (For a photograph of Mrs. DeVault, see Figure 1). In 1916, she moved with her parents to her present residence in Darke County, Ohio, just outside of the state-border town of Union City, Indiana. She attended Manchester College and, upon receiving her B.A. degree, began a thirty-eight year teaching career in Darke County. I first met Mrs. DeVault in 1960 when she was married to my maternal grandfather, Charles W. DeVault.

As with many American families, quilting was a long-standing art among women in her family. She learned to quilt by observing both her mother and her grandmother. Before she started school, she had pieced her first quilt. This was a Single Irish Chain (Figure 2) made of four-patch squares in the Irish Chain pattern. Such four-patch patterns (or sometimes nine-patch) are usually the "starters" little girls learn on.[1] As they shared the same residence for so many years, she and her mother worked many quilts together and shared patterns, materials, techniques, and ideas about quilting. Altogether, over two hundred quilts have been made in the house since 1932 (when they started keeping a written record)—some by Mrs. Huffman, some by mother and daughter together, and some by Mrs. DeVault alone.

Fig. 1. Mrs. Bessie DeVault in her home, May 1975.

Fig. 2. Corner detail of Single Irish Chain (84" x 76"); dark squares are red print.

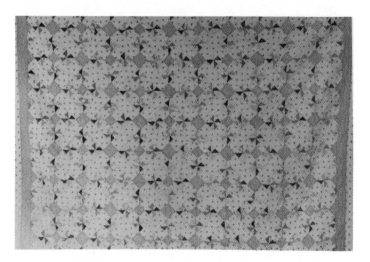

Fig. 3. Flying Star quilt (80" x 68"), made by Mrs. Huffman before 1894 for her mother-in-law; solid squares and border and binding are of pink; darker pinwheel pieces are of navy blue and red.

Though they shared many ideas and techniques, both Mrs. Huffman and Mrs. DeVault displayed independent aesthetics. For example, compare the quilts shown in figures 3 and 4; both are variations of the Flying Star pattern. The quilt in figure 3 was made nearly eighty-five years ago by Mrs. Huffman. The pattern is set horizontally and vertically; a print background is used; there is an internal border; it is a fairly small quilt (80'' x 68''), and it has a solid color binding. The quilt in figure 4 was made by Mrs. DeVault. The pattern runs diagonally with the border; the background is solid white; there is no internal border; it is a fairly large quilt (98'' x 90''); and it has a solid white binding. Some of these differences suggest important aspects of Mrs. DeVault's personal aesthetics which will be dealt with later in this study.

The quilts discussed here are some of the thirty to thirty-five quilts Mrs. DeVault now has in her home; many other quilts have either been given to friends or relatives (happily, I am one of these lucky ones) or sold as special orders. Aside from the quilts they made themselves, Mrs. DeVault and her mother often quilted quilts for other people who wanted to piece their own quilts but needed someone else to do the quilting. Back when her mother was doing quite a bit of such quilting, the charge was one dollar per spool of thread used (100 yards to the spool). An average quilt would require around 600 yards of thread, so obviously the dollar-per-spool charge long ago succumbed to inflation. Today, Mrs. DeVault says she would not quilt for less than six cents per yard of thread. For a quilt like the Rose of Sharon, which requires at least 800 yards of thread, she would be paid forty-eight dollars just for the quilting, but, as she says, "it takes three weeks to do it!" Though she has many requests for such quilting, she prefers not to quilt other people's quilts mainly because they underestimate the value of the time spent in doing it: "The people that pay you, say forty-eight dollars for that quilting, —some of them are making almost that much a day. But they have a fit about paying you forty-eight dollars to quilt the quilt." I asked Mrs. DeVault what she would consider a fair price for a quilt made on order and from scratch. She said that it would depend on the materials and the work involved. For example, about the Lincoln quilt (Figure 5), with all the tiny squares and eight-point stars, she said, "I don't think I'd want to make one of those for less than four hundred, five hundred dollars." And, after seeing an ordinary quilt sell at the Goshen auction for $2125, I think $500 for the Lincoln is a very modest price.

We can, I think, have some idea of Mrs. DeVault's relationship to quilting from the above sketch. Her interest in quilting is reflected not only in her own work but also in her frequent visits to auctions and museums where quilts are displayed. She often attends the annual quilt auction at Goshen, Indiana, as well as others throughout Indiana and Ohio, and she is always eager to meet any fellow quilters and examine their handiwork. She receives regularly the "Quilter's Newsletter" and "Nimble Needles' Treasures," two interesting and helpful quilting publications. In these and during her visits to auctions and museums she always keeps an eye open for new patterns, new ways of treating old patterns, and striking color combinations. At home she files such patterns (often sketched on paper bags or whatever else is handy) in a "scrap-book" that now contains over 800 patterns. She has helped two sisters-in-law learn the techniques and tricks-of-the-trade in quilting and said that she would be glad to work with anyone else interested in learning to quilt. Asked if she thought quilting was a dying art, she replied that it seemed to be dying out ten to fifteen years ago, but now it seems to be picking up. Altogether, she has the positive, enthusiastic attitude that makes her a craftswoman rather than a mere hobbyist.

Perhaps some background material on quilts and quilting might be useful before dealing with more specific aspects of Mrs. DeVault's work. Americans have been making quilts for over 300 years, which is to say, since colonial times.[2] However, though quilts have flourished impressively here, they by no means represent the mythical American inventiveness. Rather, the art of quilting came along with the early settlers. Marie D. Webster argues that patchwork and quilting were introduced to the American continent by the English and Dutch. "No evidence," she says "has been found that Spanish or French colonists made use of quilting."[3] However, Webster's book was written early in the century. Lord and Foley in a more recent publication suggest that as early as the eleventh century the fashioning of quilts was practiced throughout Europe so that immigrants from any European country would have been acquainted with the art.[4] Webster herself deals extensively with the practice of patchwork and quilting in the middle ages and in antiquity.[5] Her argument, then, is not that other settlers did not know about quilting but simply that there is no evidence that they used quilting. A helpful overview of quilting as a traditional American craft can be found in a recent article by Andrea Greenberg.[6]

In any case, it is fairly well agreed that prior to 1750 most quilts made in America were pieced quilts rather than applique. This means that early quilts usually involved two distinctive kinds of needlework. The "patchwork" involved sewing together various patches or pieces of material, and "quilting" involved the fastening together of (usually) two layers of cloth with a filler in between.[7] Several reasons have been suggested as to why, despite the rather elaborate, time-consuming process involved, quilts became so popular in America. Mrs. DeVault suggests four very sound reasons. The first is "practical necessity," that is, for warmth. Layers are warmer than one heavy blanket, and of course homes years ago did not have gas or oil or electric heat. And, second, they made the house "more pleasant." Jonathan Holstein says it more formally:

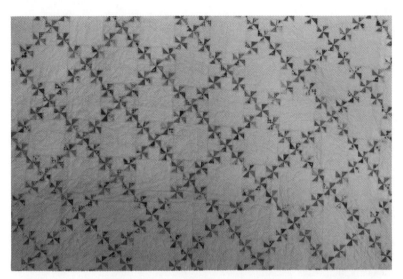

Fig. 4. Flying Star quilt (98" x 90"), white border and binding; all pinwheel pieces are of light blue, red, or pink prints.

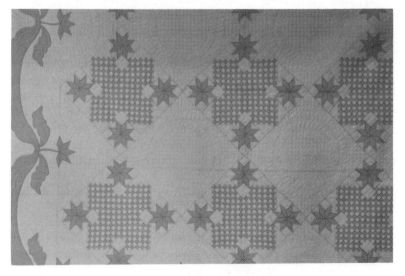

Fig. 5. Lincoln Quilt (96" x 94"), in yellow and white.

Besides their utilitarian function they were the main and often the only outlet for women to express their love of color and pleasing form, the only bright patches of color in many simple homes. Into their quilts these women poured all of their feelings for their world, for their sense of order and beauty.[8]

A third reason is that quilting used to be quite a "social event." Mrs. DeVault says she never took part in a quilting bee herself, but her mother did. They used to have quilting bees along with corn huskings; some of the women would quilt while some fixed the food for the big suppers. Maria Webster mentions quilting bees that lasted as long as ten days. Sometimes as many as twelve quilters could sit around one quilt.[9] Today, Mrs. DeVault comments, it would be too hard to get that many people together in a community who have the time or desire to quilt. A fourth reason for the popularity of quilts is that it is a good way to make use of scraps and partially worn-out garments. Mrs. DeVault and her mother always kept two bags for scraps, one for wool and one for cottons. Besides, many scraps evoke pleasant memories associated with the particular material preserved in a quilt. The red patches in her Single Irish Chain (Figure 2) were scraps from aprons Mrs. DeVault's mother had made for her when she was four; like rag rugs, quilts can sometimes create a very personal kind of nostalgia.

The patterns for the early patchwork or pieced quilts were handed down from one generation to another. Usually, pieces of stiff paper cardboard or tin were used to cut these early patterns, and worn patterns had to be replaced or repaired to insure exact measurement of corners.[10] The patterns were shared not only generation to generation but also "horizontally" with many quiltmakers knowing and using the same designs other quilters knew throughout the country. "Given that frame-work, however, each woman had total freedom in her choice of colors, size and arrangement of blocks, contrasting border materials and the like, so that no two quilts are ever alike."[11] We have already seen the variation in the Flying Star quilts made by Mrs. DeVault and her mother. Another interesting comparison can be made between two Eccentric Star quilts both made by Mrs. DeVault. The earlier quilt is an example of the Eccentric Star using print scraps for the design. Later the same pattern was used with no variation other than in the use of solid inner star and co-ordinated print outer stars. Otherwise the quilts are nearly alike, but the variation in material used makes quite a difference in the appearance of the two quilts. Quilts made by two different quilters over the same pattern might easily vary even more.

The quilt patterns themselves are interesting and would certainly merit the more rigorous attention of historical-geographical study. And the names given to the patterns reflect the psychological and social complexities of the American people fully as well as any other of the oral genres. The individual blocks that make up a pieced quilt are often "geometricized abstractions" of the things or ideas their names reflect.[12] Often varying ideas or things have been abstracted and represented by the same design; that is, many patterns have two, sometimes four to six, names. The Eccentric Star, for example, is known to Mrs. DeVault by such other names as Circle Star, Dutch Rose, Carpenter's Wheel, or Octagonal Star. A sense of the variety of patterns can be drawn from the very interesting Sampler Quilt (Figure 6) containing fifty-six separate pieced block patterns. The names of the patterns as Mrs. DeVault remembers them (she made the quilt in 1955) are as follows, from left to right on the print:

Row one
1. -?-
2. Home Treasure
3. Queen Charlotte's Crown
4. Prairie Queen
5. Wheel of Fortune
6. Aunt Sukey's
7. Pinwheel Square
8. Aunt Patty's Favorite, or Snowball

Row two
1. Rolling Star
2. London Roads
3. Good Cheer
4. Devil's Claws
5. Bay Leaf
6. Steps to the Alter
7. Optical Illusion
8. Imperial T, or Capital T, or Friendship

Row three
1. Lincoln's Platform
2. Pond Lily
3. Jacob's Ladder
4. Broken Heart
5. Pieced Star, or Mosaic
6. Baseball, or Snowball
7. Pinwheel Star, or Rolling Pinwheel
8. Yankee Puzzle

Row four
1. Next-door Neighbor
2. Eight-pointed Star
3. Washington Sidewalk
4. Lover's Knot, or Rose Dream
5. -?-
6. Irish Puzzle
7. Aunt Lida's Star
8. Flock of Geese

Row five
1. Duck and Ducklings
2. Nosegay
3. Hen and Chickens
4. Album, or Five Patch, or Building Blocks
5. Wonder of the World
6. Clay's Choice
7. Swastika, or Milky Way
8. Eight Hands Around

Row six
1. Path through the Woods
2. Key West
3. Snowball
4. Single Wedding Chain

5. Feathered Star
6. Centennial
7. Falling Star
8. -?-

Row seven
1. Crazy Ann
2. Old Maid's Ramble
3. Drunkard's Path
4. Starry Path

5. Sugar Bowl
6. Susie's Fancy
7. Domino
8. Fly Foot

Some patterns use similar pieces but differ remarkably in design; compare number eight, row three and number eight, row four, for example. Others are similar in design, varying only in color emphasis and slight piecing changes; for example, compare number seven, row four with number two, row seven. I asked Mrs. DeVault why she thought the patterns were given the names they have, and she replied that people named them after "things they knew." As an example she cited the Drunkard's Path; someone must have thought the design resembled the path a drunken man would take staggering down the sidewalk. And it does seem a logical abstraction.

There are certain matters of terminology that should be dealt with more thoroughly before moving on to a consideration of the aesthetics of quilting. Most sources are generally in agreement over the use of the greater number of terms used in reference to quilting. The word *quilting* itself was dealt with earlier; basically it means to fasten together through some kind of needlework two or more layers of material with filler in between. The terms for finished quilts are somewhat more confusing. Jonathan Holstein says: "There are three main types: plain, applique, and pieced. Plain quilts carry the design in the quilting stitches."[13] A *plain quilt* is more often called a quilted counterpane;[14] it is usually white and often decorated by padded quilting. I will not be dealing with this type of quilt in this paper as Mrs. DeVault does not make counterpanes. Of the other two types, a quilt is usually considered *pieced* if its top is composed of pieces sewn together (not on top of each other) and quilted. The top for an *applique* is a single full-size piece of material to which the design is then sewn. A problem arises in the use of the word *patched* quilt synonymously with applique quilt.[15] The use of the word *patched* is understandable in that a patch of material is placed on top of another, larger piece and sewn down. However, the word *patch* itself is used interchangeably with the word *piece,* thus causing confusion with

Fig. 6. Sampler (100" x 86"), border and rectangular pieces in light green, various colors in pieced designs.

Fig. 7. Debutante, or Debutante's Pride Quilt, (108" x 88"), in blue and white with geometric rose in pink and green.

the components of the pieced quilt. For the purposes of this study, I think the safest thing would be to use the terms *pieced* and *applique* as Holstein has suggested and let the term *patch* enjoy its ambiguity.

Some examples would probably help to clarify the difference in types. The Sampler Quilt (Figure 6) is an example of the pieced quilt—though usually a single pieced pattern is repeated over the entire top of the quilt as in the traditional Fan pattern. (See the illustration in Figure 14a). Usually the pieced pattern is contained within a single *block,* and with the addition of each block the design is simply repeated until the top is completed. Sometimes the blocks of pieced quilts are grouped through a process of turning so that a repeated design is made up of perhaps four separate blocks that differ from each other only in terms of relative position. The Debutante quilt (Figure 7) is an example of this more complex pieced quilt structure. An idea of the actual manipulation of blocks involved in producing the design can be drawn from the illustration in Figure 8. Even in this instance the group of blocks is repeated without variation over the top of the quilt. Less frequently each block of a pieced quilt may contain only a part of a larger design covering the whole top of the quilt as, for instance, in the popular Star of Bethlehem pattern. All of these patterns demonstrate the angularity of design usually associated with pieced quilts.

Another type of quilt not classified probably because it is a mixed breed is the combination pieced and applique quilt. As might be expected, there are two ways such combinations might be accomplished. The Rose Garden quilt (Figure 9) is an example of a pieced quilt in which some of the blocks contain appliqued designs. That is, the top is composed of alternating green nine-patch squares and white squares that either contain no design or contain an appliqued flower design. The opposite type would be that represented by the Dresden Plate (Figure 10), the Chinese Star, or the Double Wedding Ring. Here the patch is first pieced and then appliqued to the quilt top. And, of course, the applique quilt itself is represented by such designs as the Iris Quilt (Figure 11) in which more delicate and less geometric designs have replaced the angular, repetitious designs associated with the pieced quilt.

A few other terms might be mentioned simply for the sake of comparing some varying terms used by Mrs. DeVault. (For a comprehensive listing of terms generally agreed upon, see Ruth Finley, *Old Patchwork Quilts.*[16]) In reference to the pieced quilt, the terms piece (or patch) and block have been mentioned. The process of sewing the blocks together to form the top is usually referred to as *setting together;* Mrs. DeVault more often speaks of *joining the blocks.* Her phrase is preferable since it avoids confusion with the term *putting together,* which refers to the combining of the three layers of the quilt. This in turn should be distinguished from the term *putting in,* which refers to the process of placing the as yet unquilted quilt in the frame. This

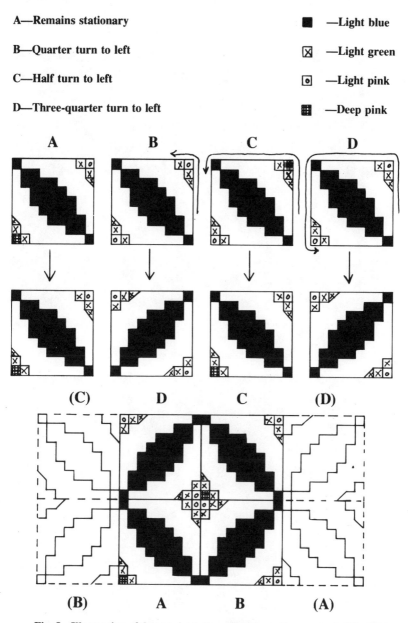

Fig. 8. Illustration of the manipulation of blocks to form repeated design in the Debutante quilt. Each block (A, B, C, or D) contains seventy-nine squares plus four triangles, making an equivalent of eighty-one squares per block; there are 6608 pieces in the pieced top excluding border pieces. The four-block patch formed by turning the blocks is repeated on the quilt top to form the Debutante design.

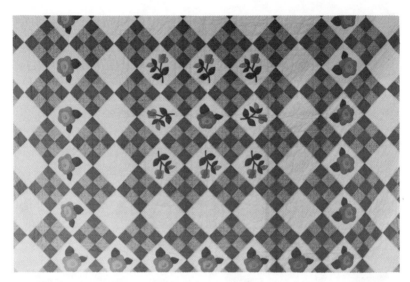

Fig. 9. Rose Garden (92" x 92"), in green solid and green print nine-square patches with appliqued flowers in rose, yellow, and green on white.

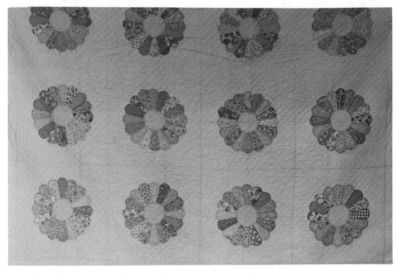

Fig. 10. Dresden Plate (96" x 82"), in multicolor prints with solid yellow center pieces, on white.

Fig. 11. Corner detail of Iris quilt (98" x 86"), with borders and flower leaves of green and flowers and buds in solid blue, purple, lavender, rose, pink, and yellow.

Fig. 12. Detail, Crazy quilt comforter in solid color fabrics with wool yarn knotting and embroidery floss decorative stitching.

unquilted quilt contains the three layers usually known as the *top*, the *fill* (or *filler*), and the *back* (or as Mrs. DeVault terms it, the *lining*). These three layers are usually fastened together by the process known as *quilting*, that is, sewing running stitches taken through all three layers.

Sometimes, instead of being quilted, the layers are *tacked* or *tied* (or as Mrs. DeVault says, *knotted*) with short pieces of wool yarn, or sometimes embroidery floss, that bind the three layers together. This process is usually used with thicker bedcovers, usually referred to as *comforts*[17] or *comforters*. Many such comforters were made in Crazy Quilt designs with yarn tying the layers together and fancier stitches added to the top itself:

> The outlines of the pieces were usually gone over afterwards with colored silkateen or crochet cotton, in fancy stitch—sometimes in an amazing repertory of fancy stitches. There were probably more Crazy Quilts in wool than in cotton; cotton was cheap—wool was not, and every fragment was put to use.[18]

Figure 12 shows the combination of tying the embroidery stitches. It also suggests another reason why wool was used; it wears better. Witness the worn places in the thinner fabrics. Mrs. DeVault does not like to see fabrics mixed on a quilt, and this is a very practical reason for obeying her aesthetic inclination.[19] Obviously, she did not make the comforter. But in deference to the person who did, my great-grandmother Henricks, it has served and still serves its purpose well.

Quiltmaking requires a number of materials. Cloth is probably the most obvious necessity. Along with wool, many kinds of cottons have been used in American quilts; most popular of these are calico, cambric, chambray, chintz, cretonne, gingham, longcloth, muslin, nainsook, percale, prints, Turkey red, and more recently, cotton blends, such as cotton-polyester, or cotton-dacron.[20] As mentioned earlier many of these cloth pieces came from scrap bags in which salvagable materials are kept. More often, modern quiltmakers buy material especially for a quilt, particularly if a large quantity of a particular print or solid is needed. Plain white or pastel cotton is usually used for the back or lining. The filler is usually cotton or dacron batting, though carded wool batting was often used in earlier times especially among people who raised their own sheep.[21] More recently, dacron is usually used even though, as Mrs. DeVault says, you pay double the price you would for cotton batting. The reasons, she suggests, are that cotton sometimes mats and that dacron, being light, "fluffs so pretty."

Other items needed are scissors, thread, needles, a thimble, pins, pencils, straight-edges, and sometimes even a sewing machine. Some of these items should be qualified. For sewing, Mrs. DeVault prefers a number seven *between* needle though regular quilting needles are available. In making blocks she uses the plastic-headed straight pins because they are easier to pick up. Though some people do make an entire quilt on a sewing machine (Mrs. DeVault has made some doll and crib quilts this way), usually the only use for a sewing machine in quiltmaking is its occasional use in sewing together pieces to make up the blocks.

Also among the materials used in quiltmaking are the patterns themselves. Like tale types and Child ballads, the patterns themselves move about in ever-changing forms in the minds (or sketches) of the quiltmakers. But to be worked with, the patterns have to take a tangible form, usually as a piece of stiff cardboard cut to a specific size and shape. Quilt patterns can be bought, borrowed, handed down, modified, or made up. They come on filler wrappers, in quilter's magazines; or they are sketched from the patterns in other quilts or even other items that carry interesting designs.

It is interesting to see how quilt designs are modified by tradition or the individual quilter. The Flower Garden is a very well-known pattern; Mrs. DeVault says that between herself and her mother they have made at least twenty. Recently while visiting in Illinois, Mrs. DeVault saw a quilt in which the hexagon-shaped block of the Flower Garden pattern was modified to a diamond-shaped block. She sketched the pattern later from memory, adding one piece to each ''end'' of the inner, solid-color hexagon and four extra pieces in the outer print trim, thus making a diamond-shaped block. The usual Flower Garden has one row of white pieces between each block. With the modified pattern, however, Mrs. DeVault used two rows of white with a row of small solid-color, diamond-shaped pieces in between and a solid star where the blocks meet. (Mrs. DeVault is shown working the quilt in Figure 1.) No one knows for sure how such a modification entered tradition in the first place (I have seen a similar pattern, without the green row, in a newsletter since then under the name Diamond Mosaic), but the process may have been similar to that described above.

An even more striking modification was involved in developing the Mountain Trail pattern (Figure 13). This design was developed by Mrs. DeVault's mother sometime before 1935 and named Mountain Trail by her father. The photograph shows the entire central design; this pattern is repeated twice in larger designs surrounding this smaller one. Mrs. DeVault says that her mother created the pattern by rearranging the old Fan pattern in the block and turning the blocks to form the winding design. The Fan pattern is usually a simple quarter-circle in a square block; see Figure 14a. In a Fan quilt this pattern is usually repeated unchanged over the entire surface of the quilt. To make the Fan pattern useable in the Mountain Trail, Mrs. Huffman reduced the pattern in the block so that measurements on either side of the pattern in each block would be equal, as in figure 14b. The blocks could then be rearranged to form the winding pattern shown in Figure 13 and 14c. Again, one can only guess how many patterns have been developed by such experiments and then handed down to join tradition.

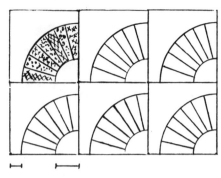

Fig. 14a. Illustration of Fan pattern. In the traditional Fan pattern the distance represented by A is less than that represented by B. The single-block design is repeated over the entire quilt top.

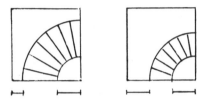

Fig. 14b. Comparison of Fan and Mountain Trail blocks. The distances C and D in the Mountain Trail block are equal to each other and to distance B in the Fan block. The sides of the Mountain Trail block are thus divided into thirds.

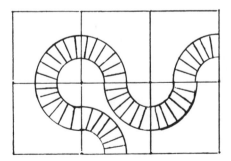

Fig. 14c. Detail illustration of Mountain trail pattern. The basic block can be turned to form the winding pattern. Notice that the lower middle block can now accommodate two designs and allow for the overall pattern connections.

Another kind of pattern needed in quiltmaking is the quilting pattern. Earlier patterns were either cardboard stencils or metallic markers. Chalk dust (usually blue) or cornstarch was used to mark the pattern on the quilt top.[22] The designs for quilting are somewhat less varied though not nearly so much so as earlier supposed.[23] For many years quilting patterns, like quilt top patterns, could be purchased from companies selling cotton batting, or from quilt pattern catalogues.[24] Besides these, quilters usually make their own patterns, often copying designs from other items such as the designs on furniture, pottery or china, mantel pieces, or coverlets.[25] Mrs. DeVault's quilting patterns (for examples, see Figure 15) include commercial patterns (Figure 15—lower left corner), standard homemade patterns (Figure 15— lower right corner), and patterns made especially for certain quilts (Figure 15—upper corners). The pattern in the upper right corner of Figure 15, for example, was made especially for the border of someone else's quilt which was quilted by Mrs. DeVault.

Perhaps the only other material necessary for quiltmaking is the frame itself. The description of the frame is fairly well agreed upon by most sources. Elizabeth Wells Robertson describes it as follows:

> The frame consisted of four poles or pieces of board, usually pine, about two or three inches wide, one or two inches thick and nine feet long. These strips of wood had pieces of heavy homespun muslin, or ticking, tacked along their entire length. They were fastened at the corners with metal clamps.[26]

Such frames could be supported by four kitchen chairs or suspended by ropes from the rafters; these "temporary" support arrangements were particularly popular at quilting "bees." More common among modern American quiltmakers is the use of the self-supporting frame with a ratchet adjustment for altering the tension of the material and for rolling the quilt as the work proceeds.[27] Such self-supporting frames, Averil Colby suggests, have never been made or sold commercially though working drawings were sometimes supplied by filler companies when requested.[28] Mrs. DeVault usually uses one of the self-supporting frames her father made many years ago. The "small" frame—the one she usually uses—consists of two octagonal poles (known as "rails" or "runners"),[29] each one hundred inches long, with muslin tacked on to hold the quilt; two I-shaped supports twenty-eight inches from the floor with holes (twenty-seven inches apart) in the upper bars ("stretchers") to hold the runners; a flat, one hundred inch board to complete the tressle support; a rachet at the end of one runner; and two wooden pins to hold the three pieces of the frame support together. Occasionally Mrs. DeVault uses a quilt hoop (similar to a large embroidery hoop) for quilting doll or crib quilts, but she never uses it for full-sized quilts.

As suggested earlier in relation to patterns and materials involved in quiltmaking, the personal aesthetics of the quilter helps her decide which patterns to use, how to modify them, or what fabrics or colors to work with. The process of quiltmaking often involves even more subtle aesthetic judgments, the kind that can be made only when the quilter has perfected her art to the point of being able to achieve the results her aesthetics envision. In other words, the more skilled craftsman will make higher aesthetical demands of himself than a less skilled craftsman. And, likewise, he will recognize in other people's work failure or success in meeting these demands. It is reasonable, then, to expect to abstract certain aesthetic values held by a skilled craftsman simply by watching or discussing his actual procedures, noting what in fact *is* the process in the hands of a skilled craftsman.

I asked Mrs. DeVault a number of questions about the process involved in making a quilt. Deciding on a pattern and material is part of the process. Of course, if the quilt has been ordered or is to be a gift, often such specifications have already been made. Otherwise, it is often just a matter of trying something new. A Lennox Plate quilt (Figure 16), for example, was on display one year at the Columbus State Fair. Mrs. DeVault saw the pattern there for the first time and thought to herself, "I believe that would be pretty in some other color." In this case the color was yellow; she included a half-plate internal border and a solid yellow trim, and produced a very nice quilt. Sometimes treatment of the pattern is important along with color choice in making what a quilter considers a good quilt. For example, Mrs. DeVault made a Lone Diamond quilt (Figure 17) in medium blue and white with the points of the triangles touching the solid blue corner pieces. A friend of hers had used the same design with the triangles reversed (base toward the corner pieces) in the Sawtooth pattern and had made the quilt in a much darker blue. The two friends compared their quilts, and this, reports Mrs. DeVault, was the result: "She said, 'Well, it's all right, yours is pretty, but I still like mine the best.' And I said, 'All right, yours is pretty, but I still like mine best.'" Mrs. DeVault conceded that "it's just a matter of choice," but obviously a good quilter will defend her own choice simply because her whole system of aesthetic evaluation was involved in the choice of pattern, material, and color in the first place.

Another important part of the process is the cutting and sewing of the pieces that make up the top of the quilt. Accuracy is very important here especially in complicated piecing patterns, such as the eight-point stars in the Lincoln quilt (Figure 5). Appliqued designs require greater care at this stage than most pieced patterns. Mrs. DeVault feels that on a properly appliqued quilt the stitches used to sew on the design should not show. To accomplish a successful "hidden stitch" takes quite a bit of practice, but it can be done. Mrs. DeVault was simply mystified by a quilt on which the quilter had

Fig. 13. Mountain Trail (96" x 86"), in multi-color prints on white.

Fig. 15. Quilting patterns.

evidently taken the easy way and stitched in large, very visible stitches right on top of the appliqued design. You can see how successful her own hidden stitches are on the close-up photograph of the Rose of Sharon (Figure 18). Once the top is finished, the quilt is ready to be put into the frame. First the back or lining is sewn onto the muslin strips on the rollers (poles) of the frame—they are removable. Some people use pins to tack down the quilt, but Mrs. DeVault avoids pins as much as possible in the quilting process because they sometimes "catch" and cause holes in the quilt. After the lining is attached to the rollers, it is stretched its full length on the floor or a large table and the cotton or dacron batting is spread over it. Finally, the top is placed on carefully and the three layers are basted together. The quilt is then rolled tightly and put into the frame. One person can put the quilt into the frame, but it usually "rolls" more evenly if two people do it. Once in the frame, the quilt surface between the two poles is made taut by setting the cog at the end of the take-up pole and stretching the ends toward the end supports by pinning hand towels to the edge and looping them around the cross bars of the end supports, as in the picture of Mrs. DeVault (Figure 1). These towels must be relocated each time a new section of the quilt is rolled up for quilting.

When Mrs. DeVault puts a quilt in, it has usually already been marked for quilting. She likes to mark the quilting design while the quilt is laid out on the floor or table just prior to putting it in the frame. This way she feels she can see the whole design and judge its effect more accurately. Some people mark the quilt after it is in the frame, and most quilters will do some "by the eye" quilting, especially if the quilting design is to follow the pieced or appliqued pattern.[30] See, for example, the quilting on the pieced triangles in the Lone Diamond (Figure 17) or on the appliqued roses on the Rose of Sharon (Figure 18). Other quilting designs are the various patterns discussed earlier or simple straight-line patterns such as the single diagonal or squares. Varying patterns are used on different parts of the quilt,[31] as can be seen on the Rose of Sharon or Lone Diamond quilts where there are squares, circular feathered designs with squares inside, curved feather designs, and "by the eye" quilting within the appliqued designs. Mrs. DeVault explained that her consistant use of the square straight-line pattern rather than the use of the diamond pattern is a matter not only of preference but also of practicality. The squares can be drawn and sewn diagonally across the weave; this makes the stitching easier because the needle always goes between two naturally separable threads in the material. With diamonds, on the other hand, the quilter cannot avoid sewing on the straight of the weave at least some of the time, and this makes the stitching harder. Mrs. DeVault says that the first quilt on which she did the quilting entirely by herself (when she was around nineteen) was the most difficult because she had tried to quilt with the weave on the straight-line patterns. Her mother explained why she was having such difficulties, and it is a lesson she was glad to take advantage of on all the rest of her quilts.

There are some other points of process that are worthwhile noting about Mrs. DeVault's work. Any good quilter would be dismayed as seeing stitching knots exposed on a quilt.[32] Mrs. DeVault's methods for ''hiding the knot'' are interesting. There are two knots—the knot that ends a thread and the knot that begins a thread. The easiest way to hide the knot that ends a thread is to conceal it in a seam, if one is handy. Usually, however, some kind of tying back is necessary. Mrs. DeVault does not trust the simple technique of sewing ahead and starting behind the stitches with the next thread. Rather, she works the needle between the layers of material back a couple stitches, passes the needle through the stitches while yet between layers and brings the thread forward, thus forming a knot. The knot that begins a new thread is hidden simply by making the usual sewing knot, taking one stitch, and giving the thread a sharp, quick tug. The knot is pulled through the first layer but catches inside the quilt rather than pulling through on the other side.

Another problem in the process of finishing the quilt is the formation of the binding around the border. Mrs. DeVault says that the binding should be cut on the bias or it will not fold neatly. Also, it should be doubled material and sewn down on the front side first. On the back, the same care must be taken with sewing down the binding as is taken in appliqueing designs on the top of the quilt. Mrs. DeVault usually uses a plain white binding so that the back of the quilt can be used as a counterpane spread.

Perhaps now we can deal with some more general aspects of Mrs. DeVault's aesthetics. Her favorite quilt is the Lincoln (Figure 5), and it is not hard to see why. It is, as she says, the most ''tedious'' quilt she has made. Each block contains 256 tiny yellow and white squares and there are nine blocks on the quilt. In addition there are all those difficult eight-point stars, so the piecing is definitely a tedious task. But the finished quilt is certainly worthy of the quiltmaker's highest regard. Other favorites are the Rose of Sharon, the Lone Diamond, and Lennox Plate.

I asked Mrs. DeVault which quilt she felt represented her best quilting job. She felt that the Lone Diamond (Figures 17 and 19) showed the best quilting because in it she had taken the tiniest stitches, this, she says, because the cotton batting was thinner. On counting, I found approximately twelve top stitches to the inch. These tiny stitches are part of her definition of good quilting; another part of the definition is evenness of stitches. Besides the stitches themselves, the distance between lines of stitching is important.[33] As usual, Mrs. DeVault backs her aesthetic preference for close quilting with a practical explanation. The closer quilting helps to hold the cotton filler in place and keeps it from lumping together. We can see her aesthetics in practice by looking at the quilt in Figure 20. She bought the top for this

Fig. 16. Corner detail, Lennox Plate (97" x 82"), in multicolor prints and solid yellow, on white.

Fig. 17. Center detail, Lone Diamond quilt (86" x 86"), in medium blue and white.

Fig. 18. Corner detail, Rose of Sharon quilt (96" x 84"), with deep pink binding and border design, green flower leaves, and deep and light pink flowers, on white top.

Fig. 19. Corner detail, Lone Diamond.

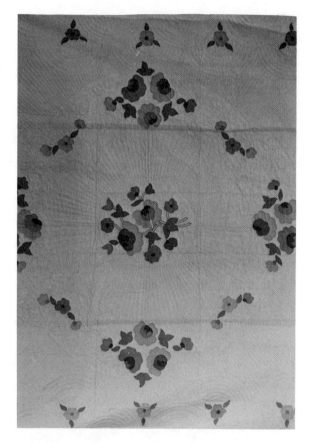

Fig. 20. Mount Vernon quilt (94'' x 80''), in solid blue, pink, rose, yellow, red, and orange, on white top.

Mount Vernon quilt in a store years ago because the cost was about the same as the material would be anyway. The pieces were already cut and the quilting lines were already marked. When she finally decided to put the quilt together and quilt it, she added at least two lines of quilting between all of the lines already marked on the top. Obviously, the "authority" of the purchased instructions was disregarded in favor of sound, traditional aesthetics—to the advantage of the quilt, I am sure.

A good quiltmaker can also be detected by her borders. Mrs. DeVault feels that borders (unless they incorporate the design) should be all one piece of material on each side with the corners mitered rather than formed by the extension of one border piece. Furthermore, the border quilting patterns are always continued into the corners (as in Figure 16) rather than abruptly broken to accommodate the turn.[34] She frequently adds a wider border at the head and foot of the quilt to meet her own aesthetic-practical requirements: "To me a quilt ought to be about eighteen inches longer than it is wide—if you want it to come up over your pillows." Most of her own quilts are twelve to fourteen inches longer than wide, but the beds she uses them on have foot-boards and no overhang is needed at the foot. Another practical concern that to some extent directs her aesthetics in relationship to borders is the fact that borders usually wear out first on quilts, and molded borders, she believes, would fray even sooner. And the molded border would be harder to repair than a straight solid border.

She evinces a number of general aesthetic opinions that direct both her own work and her response to other quilts and quilters. Several statements reflect the high value she places on the quilting as opposed to the quilt design itself. It is not that she is unconcerned about the quilt design or the piecing or appliqueing; it is simply a matter of trusting that the quilting itself, as the most demanding skill of the whole process, reflects in its quality the quality of the other skills involved in quiltmaking. She says, "I think if you see the wrong side of the quilt on a bed, it can tell you something about the other side." In other words, if it is a good quilt, you can tell by the quilting. Even "the most unattractive pattern, if it's well done, can still be beautiful."

Though she claims "there's not too much about quilts I don't like," there do seem to be a number of things she does not like to see in other quilts. For one thing, she has justified contempt for machine-made quilts: "To me, quilting is hand quilting." But she will make some allowances for machine-piecing: "I wouldn't discount a quilt if it was machine-pieced, if it was done neatly." Other things she dislikes seeing are uneven stitches, large stitches, or appliqued designs quilted at the edge of the design (this, she says, is impractical anyway; it gives you two more layers of material to sew through; the stitches couldn't possibly be small enough with all that material; better to quilt on the top itself, around the design). She also dislikes quilts on which different kinds of material are mixed and quilts on which colors are improperly chosen. She consistantly avoids solid black or dark colors, and she dislikes the use of any color that strikes the eye as too intense, usually certain reds, blues, or greens.

Considering her obvious appreciation for the hard work put into any good quilt, I asked her if she took any special precautions in storing or cleaning her quilts. One precaution she always takes is to keep the quilts turned upside down on the beds as long as company is not expected. The least bit of sunlight fades the colors over a period of time, and of course there is nothing wrong with seeing the "counterpane" back of a well-made quilt. Quilts should be washed in cold water with a handful of salt to set the color (her mother always did this, too). They should be dried on a line as dryers would probably shrink them. Quilts should be stored in covered chests or linen closets, wrapped in blue tissue paper, sheets, or plastic bags. Whenever a quilt is taken out of storage and then returned, it should be refolded with the folds opposite to the previous fold so permanent creases will not develop.

I posed one last question out of curiosity. I wondered if she knew why she and her mother like to try new patterns, modify old ones, try new color combinations, and make up new quilting designs. Her answer was, of course, traditional enough: "Well, variety is the spice of life." But though her feeling for the tradition of quiltmaking allows for, in fact invites, such variation, still her personal aesthetics demand a rigid consistency in the high quality of craftsmanship. It is this obvious appreciation for the skill involved in quiltmaking (particularly that required by the most difficult part of the process, the quilting itself) that underlies Mrs. DeVault's personal aesthetics. It is this appreciation for the difficulty of the craft that directs both her own quiltmaking and her evaluation of examples of the ongoing tradition around her.

Notes

1. Eleanor Driscoll, "Quilts in Moore County," *North Carolina Folklore* 4:1 (1965): 11; see also Marie D. Webster, *Quilts: Their Story and How to Make Them* (New York: Doubleday, 1915), p. 76.

2. Jonathan Holstein, *Abstract Design in American Quilts.* (New York: The Whitney Museum, 1971),p.7.

3. Webster, p. 60.

4. Priscilla Sawyer Lord and Daniel J. Foley, *The Folk Arts and Crafts of New*

England (Philadelphia: Chilton Books, 1965), p. 127.

5. Webster, see Chapters Two and Three.

6. Andrea Greenberg, "American Quilting," *Indiana Folklore* 5 (1972): 264-279.

7. Webster, pp. xvi-xvii.

8. Jonathan Holstein, "American Quilts as Visual Objects: A Personal View," *Historic Preservation* 24:1 (1972): 30.

9. Webster, p. 67.

10. Ella Shannon Bowles, *Homespun Handicrafts* (Philadelphia: J.B. Lippencott, 1931), p. 161.

11. Holstein, "American Quilts," p. 33.

12. Ibid.

13. Holstein, *Abstract Design*, p. 7.

14. Carrie A Hall and Rose G. Kretsinger, *The Romance of the Patchwork Quilt in America* (New York: Bonanza Books, 1935), pp. 14-15.

15. Ibid.

16. Ruth E. Finley, *Old Patchwork Quilts and the Women Who Made Them* (Philadelphia: J.B. Lippencott, 1929), pp. 42-43.

17. Webster, p. 91.

18. Earl F. Robacker, "Piece-Patch Artistry," *Pennsylvania Folklife* 13:3 (1963): 4.

19. "Whatever the material used in the creation of the quilt block design, it was considered best not to mix cotton with wool, or either of these with silk, not only because of possible incongruous effect but because one would likely wear out before the other." — Robacker, p. 3.

20. Elizabeth Wells Robertson, *American Quilts* (New York: Studio Publications, 1948), pp. 32-33.

21. Bowles, pp. 157-158.

22. Robacker, p. 7.

23. "Patterns of quiltings are not as plentiful as designs for the patchwork tops of quilts; only about eight or ten standard patterns being in general use." — Webster, p. 102.

24. Mrs. DeVault owns one such out-of-print catalogue, *The Lockport Quilt Pattern Book,* published by the Lockport Cotton Batting Company, Lockport, New York, 1942.

25. Robertson, pp. 146-149.

26. Ibid., p. 55.

27. Averil Colby, *Quilting* (New York: Charles Scribner's Sons, 1971), p. 32.

28. Ibid., p. 34.

29. Ibid., p. 33.

30. Webster, p. 103.

31. Bowles, pp. 159-160.

32. Robertson, p. 56.

33. Robacker, p. 7.

34. "The continuance of a border pattern on the corners without a break is a test of skill, as the tidy manoeuvering of a pattern, such as a twist or running feather, is not easy." — Colby, p. 64.

II Place Names and Oral History

Traditions of the Devil's Hollows

John A. Gutowski

Two separate localities in the Fort Wayne region bear the identical place name, Devil's Hollow. One lies behind the Cedar Canyons sector of Perry Township, a few miles north of Fort Wayne. The other can be found along Liberty Mills Road, five miles west of Fort Wayne in Aboite Township. Both have achieved notoriety as parking spots ideally suited for amorous escapades and as settings for the stuff of legends: supernatural intrusions, tragic misfortunes and miscellaneous teenage hijinks. Nonetheless, the Devil's Hollow legends are remarkably dissimilar. Perry Township features a well-constructed local legend type, while Aboite manages to sustain only the fleeting migratory legends. The similarities, differences and general confusion surrounding the tangled traditions of the two hollows require explanation. An examination of recently collected texts in light of their place name significance as well as legend formation processes will best serve this purpose.[1]

Most of the following material was gathered by students enrolled in my introductory and American folklore courses at Fort Wayne during the 1970 spring semester. The impetus behind this collecting activity was provided by an *Indiana Folklore* subscriber, John Martin Smith, a lawyer, devotee of local history and associate editor of *Vanguard,* the Auburn-Dekalb County historical magazine. Through a letter to the editor of *Indiana Folklore,* Mr. Smith informed Linda Dégh of the Perry Township Devil's Hollow traditions and indicated his willingness to assist in their exploration. Professor Dégh promptly forwarded me this lead whereupon I suggested the tracking down of the Devil's Hollow legend as a potential collecting enterprise for interested students. Some became involved with the project, especially when controversy arose due to the discovery of another legend-producing Devil's Hollow. With instructions to obtain texts, background and contextual information from tradition bearers in Allen and Dekalb Counties, eight students contacted twenty-three informants who produced sixteen legend texts and a number of illuminating facts. Our presentation includes twelve of these texts plus two others from the Indiana University Folklore Archives. Four substantially identical texts from the same informant, Mr. Smith, have not been included, while in one case, where a peculiar variation exists, the texts of a single informant, Mr. Hoffer (B_1, B_2) have been retained. For the reader's convenience, this investigation is divided into five sections: I. nine traditions localized in Perry Township, II. analysis of Perry texts; III. interviews with Perry residents; IV. five texts localized in Aboite Township with brief commentary and summary of interview data; V. concluding remarks about the historical priority of the place names, their connection with the legends, and the probable origin of the local legend type attached to Perry Devil's Hollow.

I. Perry Township Texts

A

To the best of my memory, the area itself is physically suited to fit into the story, especially the house up on the hill where the light is always burning and the fence around that and the bridge just down the road. Supposedly the man who lived there murdered his wife and then committed suicide by hanging himself near the bridge. And the significance of the fence is that it is built in an unusual pattern with every space between the posts having a different pattern to it. And the story is that no two of them are alike and that it does contain a message of some sort, being his suicide message or an explanation for his murdering of his wife. Several of us did one time more or less concentrate on the fence and did conclude that that part is true, that each section of the fence is in fact different from any other section. In the fence itself, toward the east part of it, the part toward the bridge, I recall a spring or artesian well which was—the fence was built right over it—then above that was a little wellhouse, an additional post maybe. Oh, two or three feet back each way from the fence with a little roof over it like you'd imagine a wellhouse would be, and this had some significance in the story, I just can't recall what it was. The light itself always burns. It was in the window which would face the bridge and it was left burning constantly. I been down there every time of the day and night from during the day until as late as five o'clock in the morning and the same light was always burning. As I recall it, having been down there, there were seldom any other lights. Occasionally you'd see some other dim lights in the background, but it usually was that one light burning. This added to the credits of the story, the fact that you could always say that that light was going to be burning when you'd take somebody down there. And sure enough, it was. I can't recall that I ever heard any explanation or reasons as to why the guy murdered his wife or why he committed suicide or why the light was left burning—just the fact that it was.

Collector: Has anybody ever talked about this old man—anything strange or unusual about him?

Informant: No, not that I recall, just a man murdering his wife and hung himself from the bridge.

Collector: Do you recall a name?

Informant: No.

Collector: You mentioned earlier that you had gone there several times, with groups of people, especially girls, what for?

Informant: Yes, I graduated from high school in 1957 and I would imagine that I first heard the story approximately three years prior to that time and from that point on I would guess that I was down there an average of at least once a month. And the circumstances would usually be: a group of kids, usually two or three carloads of guys and two or three or more gals just riding around in a car—not necessarily dates, but just out having a good time, maybe going out to a drive-in, driving around the square like we used to do—then somebody would say, 'let's go to Devil's Hollow.' And especially if one or more of the gals had never been there, it was a fun place to take them and tell them the story, build them up before they got there, and then they'd see the whole thing which was rather spooky and for a minute they'd get scared and this was the fun of going out there. The bridge, I recall, if you'd go slow or stop rather quickly, it would kind of creak and moan and you'd say, 'Do you hear any moaning up there on one of the beams?' And this sort of thing. I don't know if anyone really believed it, but is sure was a good story. And you could—especially on a kind of a dimly moonlit night—the place was terribly spooky, and you could imagine you could see all sorts of things. Of course, if you'd suggest to somebody that they saw something out there in the woods or on the bridge, they'd take a quick glance and, yea, they did see it [laughs].

Collector: Did you play any tricks on anybody there?

Informant: Yea, one time I recall, one of the fellows got out of the car and talked a couple of the gals into getting out and I believe it was at the point where the wellhouse was—and the excuse was 'Let's go get a drink or look at the well or something'—and it had been prearranged with the fellows that the driver would take off, but let the other fellow jump back in the car before he did. And this is what happened, the fellow got out and jumped back in the car. The car took off and left the girls standing there, and they just became hysterical—terribly frightened. And we went up somewhere west and turned back, came back rather slowly without the lights on. Then they saw us and as we got close, the one gal saw us, and literally ran toward the car, jumped up on the hood and more or less clawed at the windshield. She was just so scared she had to get back in the car one way or another.

Collector: Did you usually plan these things ahead of time?

Informant: Oh not necessarily. It oftentimes would just be a casual thing. It seemed like you were just plain bored. You were out driving around—been around the square forty times and you had two hamburgers and five cokes—so what else was there to do? And so somebody would say, let's go to Devil's Hollow. And so a lot of times it would be a spontaneous thing. Sometimes just a carload of guys would go if there was someone who hadn't been there before. It wasn't nearly as much fun with a carload of guys as it was with some giggly, screaming gals.

Collected by John Gutowski from John Martin Smith, 30, in Auburn, May 4, 1970. Informant first heard the story around 1954-55.

B₁

As you come over the bridge, you see this light on all the time in this deserted house. A family lived in the house. The man threw his wife, there might have been a baby or child too, I can't remember exactly, he threw them off the bridge and later hung himself on the bridge. It all happened in one evening. They had left the light on when they did this, and the light has been on ever since. That's about all I remember about it.

Collector: Do you know the names of the people who did this?

Informant: No.

Collector: Do you recall anything about the fence?

Informant: The fence was a code of some kind, supposed to spell out some kind of message.

Collector: Do you know whether or not the man had a hook?

Informant: Never heard of it. There is something about a weapon or something he had used to kill his wife. It may have been left on the bridge. There was something about a weapon but I can't remember it. Used to scare everyone or something like that.

Collector: Can you tell me anything about the fences—what it looked like?

Informant: Well, it was a rail fence. All different designs. Similar to Chinese writing. Every section of the fence is different.

Collector: How about the light?

Informant: It's always on, day or night. Just shines right down the road. Every time I've been there the light is always on.

Collector: Didn't you ever go up there to see if anyone was living there?

Informant: [laughs] Nope. Never went up there. Neither did anyone else as far as I know.

Collected by Philip Dawson from Max Hoffer, 30, in Waterloo, April, 1970. The informant first heard the story around 1955-1956 in Auburn, his hometown. The collector, having obtained one version (E) with the hook motif, has assumed, over-zealously, that the hook will appear in others. The effect of his suggestive question is noticeable in the following text. (B₂).

    FA IU:70/301

B_2

Devil's Hollow, as I heard and recall it—there was a family, I believe a husband, wife and a child who lived in this house up on the hill right on the curve there. He was a little mentally unbalanced as you would say and he killed his wife and child and then hung himself on the bridge. There was a light up there in this house and it was there and it never went out, but, of course, none of us ever went up to check. And then there was the story about the fence, there is supposed to be a message in the fence, the way the cross-bars are and such. This fence is supposed to hold a story, as to what happened—like a suicide note was in this fence. Also, I heard the story he was supposed to have buried his money near the fence. I also heard that he had a hook on the stump of his arm and that when he had hung himself, he had fallen or something and the hook got caught and it hung on the bridge. A story about a German officer that moved in there was also told and that people came up missing and such.

Collected by James Ellowsky from Max Hoffer, 30, in Auburn, May 7, 1970. This text collected one month later than B₁ demonstrates the influence exerted by the previous collector's suggestion of the hook motif. The hook has now become a part of Hoffer's story, a development that would not have occurred were it not for the unwarranted and folkloristically unacceptable asking of a leading question.

    FA IU:70/301

C

Well, as I remember it, the first time I heard about Devil's Hollow was when I was a sophomore in high school. I can't really remember who told me about the story but I think it was from some girls who lived in the area. Now the story was told to me in this way: I heard that an old man and his wife lived in this house overlooking Devil's Hollow. Anyway, one day his wife passed away and he really felt bad about it. In fact, he never really could believe that she was dead and so, hoping that she or her spirit would return, he always kept a light in the window overlooking the hollow. Well, anyway, I think a year must have passed before he really believed that she had left and he became very depressed—so depressed, I guess, that he shut himself away from his neighbors. One day the neighbors saw him constructing this odd fence around the house. You know it wasn't just an ordinary fence but one which consisted of rungs running on a horizontal, vertical and diagonal plane. I guess a lot of people asked him why he was constructing it, but he refused to tell them. Anyway, shortly after he finished, he went down to the iron bridge at the entrance of the hollow and hung himself. The sheriff, upon investigating the suicide, never found a note of explanation why he had taken his life. However, all the people I know told me that the message didn't have to be written since it was contained in the strong fence around the property. They also said that there was never any money found in the house and the fence was supposed to have given some sort of clue where it was buried.

Collected by James Ellowsky, 26, from himself. The collector-informant first heard the story in 1960 from a friend in Fort Wayne.
·FA IU:70/301

D

It was a good place to chase out parkers. Devil's Hollow was very hilly, beautiful roads. It has recently been built up with large homes. Everyone was always afraid to be there, especially at night and on a full moon. There's stories of people going there and never returning. I think I heard it first in grade school as a child of the war era. A Nazi was reported to live in Devil's Hollow. He carried on Nazi work in Devil's Hollow: sabotage, things like that. Everyone thought he was still there. One part of the house was at the top of a hill. The road went around the house at the base of the hill, a winding road.

This was where the German was supposed to live. Everyone was afraid to go because they were afraid of Nazis at the end of the war. This was in the early 1950's. Afterwards, in high school, stories started about supernatural things, especially when there was a full moon. Ghosts, skeletons, strange cries. Anything with the supernatural and strange noises are connected with Devil's Hollow. Stories about werewolves, vampires, things like that.

Collector: Have you ever been to Devil's Hollow?

Informant: I've been there but I don't actually know if I have seen the house.

Collector: Do you really believe the story about the Nazi?

Informant: I believed that the Nazi lived there and feared it. The supernatural things were logical but questionable.

Collected by Philip Dawson from Charles Louis Quinn, 28, in Auburn, April, 1970. The informant also mentions that his grandmother once possessed phonograph records of local Ku Klux Klan songs and chants which may have contained references to Devil's Hollow. However, he was unable to locate the records.
FA IU:70/295

E

My father told me all about Devil's Hollow and he knows it exactly the way it happened, because he was about twelve years old at the time. It's about this guy everybody thinks is crazy who lives in the big house at the top of the hill in Devil's Hollow. One day someone found his wife's body at the bottom of the hill near the river. Since everyone thought the man was crazy anyway, he was accused of killing her, but was set free because there wasn't enough evidence. A day or two later someone saw the man's hook (which he had in place of a hand) hanging from the bridge over the stream. Some people have seen his hook in the stream since then or in the woods. It was sort of glowing and floating, just floating around.

Collected by Philip Dawson from Rex Surface, 19, in Fort Wayne, April, 1970.
FA IU:70/295

F

This experience happened at Devil's Hollow about ten years ago. I took my girlfriend and one of my boyfriends and his girl out on a drive and the four of us were driving down the road near a familiar place called Devil's Hollow. We had heard a lot of stories about this place and we had heard a lot of different rumors going around concerning an old man who lived in a house around Devil's Hollow. So, curious young people that we were, we were about sixteen years old, we decided that we would investigate personally and see exactly what was upon that hill. You could just see the house from the road and there was a winding lane that went up to the house. It was at that time, if I remember it, a type of gravel road, just a lane, like an old lane, but very rarely used. But we drove up this lane in the car and then we were confronted with a gate. There was a fence that went 'round the house, it was a wooden fence, an old wooden fence and the only thing I can remember about the fence was that it was relatively high, about four feet high. It was not one that you could step over pretty easy, you would have to climb over it, you would have to make an effort to get over the fence. It looked like it was dead around there. It did not look like there was anybody that lived there at all. We sat in the car for a few minutes and talked and made threats about going in there, and dares, and finally, the other guy and myself got out of the car. We were going up to the house and look around a little bit. So we got up to the gate and the gate was locked with a lock and we started to climb over it and as we started to climb we heard this gunshot from somewhere and we don't know if it came from the house or if it came from down the hill across the road from some guy hunting or if it came from the supposedly old man that lived in isolation inside of the house. But, anyhow, wherever it came from, since we had been talking about this place, it scared us and so we immediately ran back to the car and we climbed back in the car, backed her out and got out of there as fast as we could.

You see, we had heard rumors about a guy that had died and supposedly some type of a ghost or something was still alive there that actually could do things. There was still something there that was doing things even though the man who had lived there was supposedly dead. I can't remember too well how the man died, I would probably say that the man committed suicide by hanging himself with a rope from a tree. That is how I would say I remember it, although I cannot verify it.

Collected by James Ellowsky from Dennis K. Kruse, 23, in Fort Wayne, May 3, 1970.
FA IU:70/301

G

Devil's Hollow used to be a place where all the guys used to take the girls. It was kind of spooky, and they'd all get scared. One night we were at Dunn's in Waterloo when we overheard some guys asking the girls if they wanted to go there. Two other guys and myself got into the car and beat it to the hollow before they could get there. I put on an old trench coat and hat. We hid the car off the road aways. I hid in the ditch. Then I saw their car coming down the road. As it slowed down a bit, I jumped out and grabbed hold of the car door handle and it opened. One girl in the front seat, June Deitrick, screamed and tried to get away. That scared me. I jumped back and they sped away. We went back to Dunn's to hear what they had to say. June had cut her shin quite bad, but boy were they scared. They were telling everybody about the guy down in Devil's Hollow who tried to get them. I've never told them that it was me.

Collected by Sharon Zonker from George Kandel, in Butler, February 26, 1970.
FA IU:70/297

H

I can remember the place you speak of, Devil's Hollow. It was always a real spooky place. The fog and all of the tree branches hanging over the road. I remember going through there at night with horse and buggy with my parents. It was spooky then. Even the horses seemed to get spooked. I can't recall any story about a man hanging himself, though. That must have happened recently.

Collected by Sharon Zonker from Mrs. John Springer, 65, in Auburn, February 26, 1970.
FA IU:70/297

II. Analysis of Perry Texts

The preceding narratives show a kinship with a number of currently popular legends, most notably: the haunted bridge complex,[2] "The Hook"[3] and "The Warning Light."[4] Further collecting should establish the localization of other migratory legends and legend motifs as one informant (D) suggests. At this point a composite of all the versions reveals a fairly stable outline:

1. The focal character is an old man (crazy man, Nazi or man with hook for a hand) who lived in the hilltop house;

2. The old man murdered his wife (and child) or engaged in sabotage or abduction;

3. Because of his guilt, grief (or for no reason) he committed suicide by hanging himself from the bridge (tree);

4. Prior to his suicide, he left a light burning in the house, then built the strange fence whose design contains his suicide expalantion or reason for murdering his wife or a clue to the hiding place of his money;

5. Since then, the light in the house continues to burn, the man's glowing hook can be seen or his groaning can be heard on the bridge.

Texts A, B_1, B_2, and C conform closely to the above outline. As the most complete, coherent and elaborate texts they possess sufficient stability to warrant their independent existence as the "correct type" of the Devil's Hollow legend. Despite variation relative to the suicide motive, each of these highly localized texts builds its plot around the four outstanding and observable features of the site: the house on the hilltop, the eternal light, the mystical fence and the bridge. These four core elements structure the narrative by requiring an explanation of how each relates to the old man's suicide. Unlike other bridge-suicide legends, which report what has happened since the tragedy, this tale reconstructs the major events prior to the suicide as suggested by the notable physical features.

Variation in the other texts (D, E and F) stems primarily form the narrators' inability to logically incorporate all four of the structural elements. After mentioning the old man in the house on the hill, informant Quinn (D) is free to attribute sabotage activities to the alleged Nazi mainly because the other structural elements—the light, fence and bridge—do not control his narration. The notion of Nazi sabotage in Indiana exists primarily on the rumor level and is therefore understandable in view of the proliferation of such rumors throughout America during World War II.[5] Surface's narrative (E) comes closest to the localized type by including the death of the wife followed by the husband's suicide, reference to the house on the hill and to the bridge where the suicide occurred. The glowing hook motif, here an incidental addition, has an analogue in one variant of "The Hook" where the metal object is seen floating in a lake.[6] The legend reported in the last paragraph of text F is vague and fragmentary; while, interestingly, the disclosal of a personal experience, more important to the narrator, does utilize the fence and house.

The connection between supernatural legends and teenage rituals involving dating, parking, tests of daring and verification of the legend is already well established[7] and further supported by our informants. Smith (A) strongly emphasizes the necessity of visiting the locale, and indeed, the existence of the localized type seems to presuppose that each narrator has surveyed Devil's Hollow at night to confirm the story.

The well-plotted prank mentioned by Kendal (G) points to a form of legend ritualization which few investigators have reported.[8] Essentially, Kendal relates the personal experience of a Devil's Hollow prankster in action—an action which appears to be a dramatization of the core incident in "The Hook." Kendal does not say that he intended to enact the hook; however, given the Devil's Hollow traditions and atmosphere, one suspects that consciously or unconsciously "The Hook" has influenced his prank.

III. Interviews with Perry Residents

In an attempt to determine the possible sources of the legend, and any relevant historical factors contributing to its formation, long-term residents of the Devil's Hollow area were contacted. Since some preferred to remain anonymous, all names have been withheld in this section. The results of these interviews indicate unanimity concerning three topics: (1) ignorance of Devil's Hollow as a place name for their locale, (2) indifference toward the legends and rumors which none have heard and (3) an overall annoyance toward the provocations of the youths. A recent arrival to the area was surprised that the place was a legend topic, while a life-long resident, who has lived near the bridge all his 84 years, had heard no stories about murders or hangings and doubted that they ever happened. Another individual queried about Devil's Hollow produced a most emphatic and revealing reply:

For one thing this isn't Devil's Hollow. The real Devil's Hollow is in Aboite Township near Hamilton Road. I don't know how they ever got the idea this was the place. The only spooks you're going to find around here are the two-legged kind, human ones. Farmers around here get mad at the kids making all kinds of noise and have started shooting at them. Those are your real spooks.

Collector: How about the fence? It's supposed to have an incrypted message.
Informant: The same man that built that fence built the house. He just built that fence as cheaply as he could, from nature. There's no incryption, just a man's imagination and that's all.
Collector: In some of my stories, my informants said that there was always a light shining down at them. What would be the reason for the light?
Informant: You have these kids throwing beer cans and yelling up at the house, and the old woman would yell back at them. She keeps that light

shining on the road so she can see who's down there.

Collected by Philip Dawson, April 1970.
    FA IU:70/301

An informant who assisted in building both fence and house had no knowledge of Devil's Hollow but did possess some illuminating background information. He states that the current resident of the house bought the property in 1937, built the cabin-house in 1939 and has resided there continuously until today. The person whom he helped to build the house and fence died in April of this year. The informant allowed student collector Barbara Barrett, to borrow a 1939 photograph of himself and the deceased standing in front of their newly constructed fence. (A sketch of the fence in the photograph has been included on page 207 to illustrate details no longer present in the fence.) Asked if the fence contained any symbols the informant answered: "Naw. We just made designs out of the logs so it'd look nice." The informant had no explanation for the stories other than one dealing with the present occupant of the house: "It's really funny. She never liked kids and I suppose she would be frightening, especially in the evening."

Renewed attempts to interview the occupants of the house have met with little success. Early in the spring, one of the student collectors was able to exchange a few remarks with a couple who were working outside on top of the hill. The woman had little to say aside from denying any knowledge of local legends. Her companion, presumably the deceased, commented that he had rebuilt parts of the fence several times and changed the design with each reconstruction.

No tragic accidents or suicides have occurred in Devil's Hollow; the same two persons have dwelt in the house since 1939; and the fence has undergone continuous alteration. Therefore, the search for any historical basis to the legend leads nowhere. The explanation of the narratives lies in the concrete existence of bridge, fence, house and light, which, understandably, burns at night. The added stimuli of environmental sounds, the abundant wildlife, occasional gunshots, the woman's yelling at troublemakers and her flashing another light on the road all contribute to the general atmosphere and challenge of Devil's Hollow.

IV. Aboite Township Texts and Interviews

I

There is a place west of Fort Wayne, on the Liberty Mills Road called Devil's Hollow. It is said that once a woman was murdered there and if you go there on a moonlit night you will see her ghost among the trees. Devil's Hollow is an area arched by trees and it nearly always had a fog hanging over it.

Collected by Geneva Flora from Walter Stanley, 42, in Fort Wayne, April 3, 1970.
FA IU:70/299

There is a place near Fort Wayne, off of Highway #24, called Frank's Place. It is told that some time ago a woman killed her husband in their house located in that area. She is said to have hung him in the house. Ever since then the house and the entire area is said to be haunted by his ghost.

Collected by Geneva Flora from Charles Brinneman, 24, in Fort Wayne, April 2, 1970. Although the informant locates the tragedy in Aboite Township, the house and the reference to Frank's Place indicate that he may be referring to the Perry Township Devil's Hollow.
FA IU:70/299

K

A young man and his girlfriend were parked one night in Devil's Hollow. A man walked up to their car and grabbed the doorhandle. When they heard the man, they turned to look and noticed that he had no head. They quickly turned the car around and sped away. As they did they heard a strange noise. When they got home they saw the man's arm hanging on the car door.

Collected by Geneva Flora, from William Klage, 22, in Fort Wayne, April 2, 1970. FA IU:70/299

L

The hook: an escaped killer with hook on arm attacks couple in Devil's Hollow.

Collected by Bob Schneider from Mike Foster in Fort Wayne, April 25,1965. FA IU:674

M

The hook: an escaped convict attacks couple parked in Devil's Hollow.

Collected by Fred Tone from Tom Tone in Fort Wayne, December 5,1966. FA IU:678

All we can conclude on the basis of these meager variants is that the hook along with revenant motifs have been localized in the general area of Devil's Hollow. Without a cluster of permanent landmarks, a differentiated and consistent tradition apparently has not materialized.

Interviews with Aboite residents conducted by Barbara Barrett and Linda Weatherwax have turned up anecdotes, personal reminiscences and vague recollections, the most prominent being that Devil's Hollow was formerly a hideout for thieves and bandits, a meeting place for both the Ku Klux Klan and bands of beer-drinking Germans. One informant remembers that the area had been called Devil's Hollow around 1900. None mentioned the existence of a Devil's Hollow in Perry Township.

V. Conclusion

Knowledge of a Perry Township Devil's Hollow seems restricted to those conversant with its legend. On the other hand, denizens of both Perry and Aboite as well as Fort Wayne proper, with or without the knowledge of any legends, agree that Devil's Hollow is situated in Aboite

Township. Current Fort Wayne newspapers lend additional support to Aboite's legitimacy. The *News Sentinel* of April 3, 1970 reports a late proposal to reconsider Allen County's future park site and to relocate in Aboite Township. The article's headline reads: "Devil's Hollow Area Pushed as Park Site." Also, the Fort Wayne *Journal Gazette*, February 8, 1970, features a local history article detailing the story of Gloyd's Grist Mill on Cedar Creek that is at the bottom of Perry Township's Devil's Hollow. Forest J. M'Comb, author of the article, writes of the original settlers, their descendants and matters of local color. He even includes a traditional lying tale, type 1920B "I Have Not Time to Lie." M'Comb names the district "Dutch Ridge," but not once does he employ "Devil's Hollow" nor does he relate its suicide legend. To my knowledge the earliest printed occurrence of Devil's Hollow can be found in Griswold's 1917 Pictorial *History of Fort Wayne, Indiana* (pp. 692-93). In the section on Aboite Township, Mrs. Samuel R. Taylor specifies the two areas under consideration but reserves Devil's Hollow for but one:

> Approached by the Liberty Mills road, which turns due west from Upper Huntington road, is a locality which is surpassed in wild romantic beauty only by the gorges of the Cedar Creek region in Perry Township. The road as it reaches the Aboite river valley, dips from the straight line of the prairie into the sinuous windings of picturesque "Devil's Hollow" and leads through a landscape which abounds in unique topographical features charming to the eye, and of deep interest to the scientist.

The weight of the evidence clearly favors Aboite Township as the original and most familiar location for Devil's Hollow. But only as late as 1939, the year the house and fence were built and the earliest possible origin for the Perry Township local type, could the place name have been appropriated in order to enhance the mysterious aura surrounding the suicide legend site. Thus the combination of environment and narrative have preceded the Perry place name; conversely, in all probability, the migratory legends attached to Aboite's Devil's Hollow have been stimulated primarily by its place name.

If the distribution of Perry Devil's Hollow texts were exhibited graphically, one would observe clusters up to fifteen miles north of Perry township (the Dekalb county towns of Auburn, Garrett and Waterloo) and another concentration in Fort Wayne up to about fifteen or twenty miles south of Perry Township. The western boundary would end at Aboite Township, while the eastern limit is uncertain. Perry township, of course, would be excluded from the distribution. Though the number of texts does not suffice for any definite conclusions concerning origin and dissemenation, there is some likelihood that the legend arose among the populations of the Dekalb county towns and was later transmitted to the Fort Wayne area. Young people from Dekalb would be more inclined, more often, to travel past Devil's Hollow en route to the varied attractions of metropolitan Fort Wayne. The place name itself may have been learned while in Fort Wayne in connection with Aboite Township then later applied to Perry, because of its suitability to the horror story.

Absence of both place name and localized legend within the Perry community itself can be comprehended in light of the legend formation process. The legend's structural elements, the house, light, fence and bridge generate neither question nor mystery for the community. No speculation about the peculiar fence is required since local residents have observed its construction for decades. The light in the hilltop house needs no explanation since neighbors know that the same couple has resided in the house for decades. What constitutes a "spooky" atmosphere for outsiders doubtlessly represents scenic beauty in the minds of the insiders.

Notes

1. The place naming of other popular haunts has been discussed by Linda Dégh in a recent article which emphasizes the importance of place naming upon the legend formation process. See Linda Dégh, "importance of Collecting Place-Name Legends in Indiana," *Indiana Names* I:2 (1970) 34-40.

2. Linda Dégh, "The Haunted Bridges Near Avon and Danville and Their Role in Legend Formation," *Indiana Folklore* 2:1 (1969): 54-89.

3. Linda Dégh, "The Hook," *Indiana Folklore* 1:1 (1968): 92-100.

4. Magnús Einarsson-Mullarký, "The Warning Light," *Indiana Folklore* 1:1 (1968): 42-48.

5. For a detailed account of these rumors see David J. Jacobson, *The Affairs of Dame Rumor* (New York, 1948). Jacobson's chapter eight, "Little Alf's Stamp Collection," pp. 286-453 contains abundant examples of World War II espionage rumors.

6. FA IU:677.

7. Linda Dégh, "The Haunted Bridges Near Avon and Danville and Their Role in Legend Formation," *Indiana Folklore* 2:1 (1969): 77-81.

8. A similar incident dependent upon local folk belief rather than the dramatization of a migratory legend is reported in an unpublished paper by Donald Bird, "The Legend of Ghost Hollow, Hartsville, Indiana." In this case a man frightened travelers through "Ghost Hollow" by donning a cow hide with tail and horns, placing a small candle in his mouth then lighting it.

Drawing by John M. Vlach

Drawn from a 1939 photograph, showing the rail fence and its makers.

Hangman's Crossing

Jeffrey Schrink and Frances Schrink

In spite of the nostalgia that has taken a firm grip on this country and its inevitable accompanying commercialism, one is hard put to find evidence of the historic past of Seymour, Indiana. There are no signs at the edge of the city proclaiming that it is the site of the world's first train robbery: only a sign proclaiming that it is the "City of Progress." Even the history books tend to ignore or give sparse attention to Seymour's past.

The people of Seymour are, for the most part, friendly people who go quietly about their business, not bothering anyone and not wishing to be bothered. Although the city has grown to nearly 16,000 people, serious crime is still a rarity. When a rape or murder occurs, the city literally buzzes with excitement, and normal activities are held in abeyance until the perpetrator is caught. In these respects, Seymour is no different from a hundred other towns and cities in southern Indiana.

One of the few reminders of the past is a location west of Seymour, which carries the strange and frightening name of "Hangman's Crossing." Although no sign or monument marks the spot, the locals have referred to it by this name for over 100 years. A great deal of mystery surrounds the location. If one were to ask the average citizen of Seymour about the significance of the location's name, the citizen would likely reply that the notorious Reno brothers were hanged from a tree just a few feet north of the railroad tracks. He might even point to the last remains of a tree stump and identify it as the fateful tree. The average citizen would be wrong on all counts. Certainly many citizens of the area know the real story of the location because their ancestors took part in the incident which led to its naming and the story has been handed down by word of mouth, perhaps losing precision with each generation. Nevertheless, the majority of Seymour citizens either possess inaccurate information or know nothing about the location at all. This lack of knowledge, of course, does not lessen their inclination to tell anyone who will listen all about the location and its significance.

There is nothing prominent about the location which would cement it in one's mind or which would suggest its historic past. A person could drive by it a thousand times and still have trouble describing it. It is just a typical railroad crossing in a partially rural area of south-central Indiana. The wooden railroad markers are weathered and in need of paint, and the entire area is overrun by weeds, some of them waist high. It is obvious that no effort has been expended to make the area stand out.

Second Street, the pride of Seymour, is a beautiful broad street where it bisects the city from east to west. But, as it leaves the city to the west, it becomes a rough, narrow, twisting, blacktopped road which gradually angles toward U.S. Highway 50. A mile or so out of Seymour, Second Street Road abruptly turns south, crosses the Baltimore and Ohio Railroad tracks, and connects with U.S. 50, which is only a few yards away at this point and also runs east and west. This crossing is Hangman's Crossing. Although there is an auto sales company, a furniture store, and a development of houses across the highway to the south, the west and north are still open farmland. The city looms ever closer from the east. For some unknown reason however, the city has expanded much faster in the other three directions. It is almost as if fate is saving this location from the city.

To understand the meaning of the location one must go back to the years immediately following the Civil War when the city of Seymour and Jackson County, in which Seymour is located, were teeming with crime and violence.[1] During the last half of the 1860's, Seymour was as wild and lawless as any of the more famous western towns such as Dodge City and Abilene.[2] Rape, robbery, burglary, murder, counterfeiting, con games, and gun duels were common daily occurrences. The untrained and undermanned law enforcement agencies of the area were unable or unwilling to handle the situation. The guilty were seldom arrested or convicted of any misdeeds. Decent people did not venture out at night, except in emergencies, because of the ever present danger.

Much of this violence was directly attributable to the Reno Brothers and their gang. There were five Reno brothers, but only four were criminal: Frank, John, William, and Simeon. The fifth brother, Clinton, was known as "Honest Clint," and was not involved in his brothers' criminal activities. A sister, Laura, was said to be as good with a gun as her criminal brothers, but apparently was not criminally involved with them.

While most Hoosiers may not realize it, the four criminal Reno brothers, on their farms just north of Seymour, collected what may well have been the first organized gang in this country:

> Americans, disturbed by the rising menace of organized crime, may be interested to recall that the beginning was a century ago this month. And Hoosiers might ponder that the start was made in Indiana, when four young deserters came home from the Civil War to launch a reign of terror in southern Indiana.[3]

Through the threat of violence and connections with certain elected officials, they had managed to build up a system of immunity in the city and county.[4] At its peak, the gang may have numbered as many as two hundred. Their immunity did not extend beyond the county, so on the night of October 6, 1866, when they carried out the world's first robbery of a moving train,[5] it was the beginning of the end for them. On that evening, it is alleged that John and Simeon Reno and a gang member named Franklin Sparks boarded the Ohio and Mississippi train in Seymour. As the train moved out of town to the east, the three gang members, wearing paper masks, forced their way into the Adams' express car and overpowered the messenger. Taking some $10,000 which was readily available, they rolled the unopened safe through the door and leaped from the train near what is now the Seymour post of the Indiana State Police. They were soon forced to abandon the unopened safe because of the approach of a posse. Interestingly, the original indictment for the robbery is still on the records at the Jackson County Courthouse in Brownstown. No one was ever brought to trial on the charges.

The Adams Express Company immediately secured the services of the Pinkerton Detective Agency to hunt down and capture these innovative bandits. Employing tactics such as paid informants and "mug shots," which were far advanced over those of local law enforcement agencies, the Pinkertons soon kidnapped John Reno and spirited him off to Missouri where he was tried and convicted of an earlier robbery and sentenced to the Missouri State Prison. As fate would have it, John was destined to be the only one of the criminal brothers to die of old age. Only the security of the prison walls saved him from the angry citizens of Jackson County. He was also the only one of the brothers to be given the luxury of a trial.

The gang's most successful train robbery occurred on the night of May 22, 1868. On that date the gang allegedly robbed the Jeffersonville, Missouri, and Indianapolis train at Marshfield, some fourteen miles south of Seymour. During the course of the robbery a messenger was thrown from the speeding train and killed. The robbery netted an incredible $96,000, three times more than Jesse James ever managed in a train robbery.[6] Following the robbery, Frank and some of the gang went to Canada, while Simeon and William went to Indianapolis, apparently to elude the Pinkertons.

Some of the gang remained behind and decided to carry on as usual. On July 10, 1868, they fell into a trap while attempting to rob a train at Shields, about half-way between Seymour and Brownstown. The outlaws were badly shot up and had to flee. Three of the outlaws were soon captured and the other three bandits got away.

On the night of July 20, 1868, the three captured gang members—Roseberry, Clifton, and Elliott—were put aboard a train and sent to

Brownstown for arraignment. About three miles outside Seymour, however at the railroad crossing now called Hangman's Crossing, the train was stopped by a band of masked vigilantes, numbering between fifty and two hundred. Apparently, the prisoners at first thought it was a rescue party and were exuberant, but they soon realized their mistake. The three outlaws were taken from the train by force and hanged from a large tree. Stories differ concerning the discovery of the bodies. One source says a German farmer named Borcherding "looked on approvingly" during the hangings and then notified authorities the next morning.[7] Another account says he "went temporarily insane the next morning, when he saw their black faces and protruding tongues."[8]

The other three members of the unsuccessful train robbery attempt— Moore, Sparks, and Jerrell—were captured a few days later in Mattoon, Illinois. Incredibly, just five nights after the first hangings, at a place in the road just beyond where the earlier hangings occurred, several hundred vigilantes wearing red masks stopped a wagon carrying the remaining outlaws and hanged them from the same tree as the others.

Whether by accident or design it is an ironic twist of fate that the tree was located within both hollering distance and sight of the railroad tracks which carried the first train the Renos ever robbed and the last train the gang attempted to rob. Whatever the reasons for picking the tree near the crossing, much circumstantial evidence and considerable public sentiment point to the railroad interests as supporting the vigilantes at least financially, and possibly taking an active physical part in their activities.[9]

The particular type of tree which was selected for the hangings was not a very likely candidate for such heavy duty. It was not a spreading chestnut tree or even a majestic oak tree. Rather, it was a beech tree, a type common in the Seymour area. Beech trees normally do not have long, strong limbs and would not appear to be well suited for the grisly task of hanging. This particular beech tree, however, was apparently very large and well suited for the business of execution.

Following the hangings, a carnival atmosphere prevailed; "a train was chartered in Seymour, and nine whole car loads of curiosity-seeking people jammed the scene, having arrived there in excursion fashion . . . "[10] The desperate souvenir hunters cut the ropes up into small pieces and even stripped the leaves and twigs from the limbs of the tree.[11] Such activities continued over the years, and it is reputed that in 1875, Nellie Jonas, a sister of John Moore, had the tree girdled to kill it and then had it burned.[12] By this time, it was literally covered by carvings and initials made by the throngs of people who had visited the scene.[13]

Sometime after the hangings, a letter was printed in the *New Albany Weekly Ledger* which said, "People at a distance must not condemn us; under the circumstances, others might have done even more."[14] Reportedly, the letter was mailed from Seymour and was signed by T.H.C., who could have been Travis Carter, a prominent citizen reputed to be the leader of the vigilante committee.[15]

These gruesome hangings gave the name to Hangman's Crossing and locked it in the minds of the residents. To this day there is no need for a sign to remind the citizens of the location of Hangman's Crossing.

The play was not ended. On the night of December 11, 1868, the vigilantes commandered a train, rode it to Jeffersonville, and then seized a second train to New Albany where William, Simeon, and Frank Reno and a henchman named Anderson were being held in the jail. The vigilantes broke into the jail and promptly hanged the three Renos and Anderson and then reboarded the train and departed. Frank and Anderson had only recently been extradited from Canada and thus were technically under federal custody. In the history of the United States, Frank Reno and Anderson are the only prisoners ever lynched while in federal custody.[16] Considering the widespread rumors of such a raid which circulated for days before it transpired, it appears the federal government was remiss in its duties.

Since England had agreed to the extradition of Frank Reno and Anderson only when their safety was assured, these lynchings created an international furor. Great Britain recalled its ambassador to the United States. Quickly admitting its guilt, the United States offered a humble apology through Secretary of State William Seward. To prevent such occurrences in the future, Congress enacted a special law guaranteeing that the federal government would safeguard all prisoners extradited from foreign countries.

Hundreds of newspapers across the nation devoted space to the story. Many foreign newspapers condemned the actions. For example, *The Montreal Herald* stated:

> The American government was strictly responsible for the safety of these men and should be strictly held to account. Extradition must cease if men are sent over the border to be torn to pieces by unauthorized rabble.[17]

Several of the local newspapers probably better reflected their readers' sentiments by praising the action of the vigilantes. For example, the Seymour *Democrat* seemed to express sarcasm and threats:

> Retribution is not always swift, but it is always sure. Right or wrong, the Renos met a fearful doom. The New Albany tragedy will give our legislators

something to think about. . . . The people will assume their delegated powers
if those powers are misused. Give us a better criminal code, or the Vigilantes,
like a nightmare, will haunt all lawyers and judges for all time to come.[18]

Regardless of what the newspapers said, the vigilantes' actions were
not of the type to inspire legends. In every case the Southern Indiana
Vigilance Committee waited until some law enforcement or detective
agency captured the bandits and then it stepped in and executed the unarmed
prisoners. Law enforcement agents were shot or otherwise injured in several
cases. The vigilantes also did not concern themselves with technical matters
such as degree of guilt. In a manner which can only be described as guilt by
association, they summarily hanged the three Reno brothers and seven of
their gang members. There was some sentiment at the time of the hangings
that at least William Reno had an alibi for the time of the big train robbery.[19]
However, the ropes made no such distinction. Then, once the core of the
gang was destroyed, the vigilantes went on a rampage of their own threatening and frightening relatives and friends of the former Reno gang. Appeals to
the governor were of little avail, although he did offer a weak threat to do
something if the vigilantes did not desist.

While one may criticize the vigilantes' methods, no one can question
the results. Prior to the hangings twenty or more unsolved murders might be
recorded in a single year. Following the hangings, murder became a decided
rarity. Whether this resulted from specific deterrence (killing the killers) or
general deterrence (frightening potential killers) would be a matter for
speculation. The fact that there were never any arrests or trials for the
lynchings suggests that support for the vigilantes' actions extended well
beyond the immediate community. Certainly the Reno gang's success in
escaping conviction in the courts had not gone unnoticed by the state's
populace, nor had the extreme violence attributed to the Reno gang.

Thus, less than two and one-half years after the world's first train
robbery, the gang was gone; but the tragedy remained. The state was
deprived of the right to try these outlaws, and the hangings prevented the
Renos from talking about where they hid their money or about their sus-
pected connections with important people at the local and state levels.[20]
These lynchings, like the killings of John Wilkes Booth and Lee Harvey
Oswald, left many questions unanswered. All that is known for certain is that
a prominent Seymour citizen named John Pfaffenberger, a business partner
of John C. Grubb (a bondsman for the Renos), was arrested some years later
while trying to pass some of the stolen bonds at a Cincinnati bank,[21] but
nothing ever resulted from his arrest.

The money from the train robberies and other criminal activities was
never officially discovered. Rumors of citizens finding money around the

Reno farm house are still quite common. One persistent story purports that a farmer while digging postholes found a box containing thousands of dollars of the robbery money which he used to purchase extensive rich farmland north of Seymour. All the stories are unsubstantiated. The father of one of the authors lived in the old Reno farm house as a boy and remembers hearing stories of huge caches of money buried around the yard and of underground escape tunnels, but the most he and his brothers and sisters ever found were a few spare coins. The house no longer exists, although a few pictures of it are available.

Despite the fact that their daring exploits made the headlines all over the United States and in many foreign countries, the Reno brothers are not well known. The reasons probably lie in their comparatively short reign, the fact that they did not go out in a blaze of glory, and because the local citizens were reticent about the entire matter, either out of embarrassment over the Renos' reign of lawlessness or fear of prosecution for their own activities in either supporting or actually participating in the lynchings. Whatever the reasons, less industrious outlaws like the infamous James gang have been credited with inventing and perfecting the art of train robbing. The truth of the matter is that a member of the James gang served time in the Missouri State Prison with John Reno and had his imagination fired by Reno's tales.[22]

Thousands of travelers from throughout Indiana and the rest of the United States daily speed by Hangman's Crossing on busy U.S.Highway 50 without realizing the historical significance of the location. Perhaps the people of Seymour in the past did not need a sign to remind them of what transpired at Hangman's Crossing over a century ago; but in the future when the city of Seymour overruns the location, one wonders if this important story will be lost to future generations, like so much of America's past.

Presently the exact location of the tree is shrouded in mystery. Perhaps because its location was so obvious at the time,the Seymour *Democrat* did not even bother to give its location, being content to state merely that it was located "a short distance from the Railroad."[23] Another early source, however, provides more detail as it noted that the first three victims were walked "down a country road about 200 yards."[24] The same source in speaking of the second hanging observes that about 100 yards further down the lane was a small bridge and then a sharp turn in the lane.[25] This description is especially helpful in locating the hanging site because a bridge and a sharp turn in the road still exist. Volland offers little assistance concerning the location of the tree but he does provide in his discussion of the second hanging some general description of the area by noting that "the tree was near a worm or snake fence made of rails, with just enough room for the wagon to get between."[26]

Shields also provides a description which is helpful in locating the tree. He states that the tree was located about a quarter of a mile south of Hangman's Crossing on the property of a German named Borcherding, and that it stood on the right side of the road near a tiny stream which went under the "Old Brownstown Road."[27] Unfortunately, the phrase "right side of the road" is not too helpful because one does not know where the author was standing or which way he was facing when he described the location. Most likely, however, he was facing south away from Hangman's Crossing. Shields further notes that the tree stood almost at Borcherding's front door.[28]

In a recent account, Boley states that "The tree, no longer there, was at a spot now in the middle of U.S. 50."[29] This description does not fit well with any of the others. Either Boley did not realize that the old Brownstown Road went south from Hangman's Crossing rather than following the present U.S. 50 or he based his comments on descriptions other than those previously discussed. Most of the available evidence points to a location just south of the Crossing on the west side of the road, while all of the accounts agree that the tree was located quite some distance from the Crossing.

Even more interesting than the vagueness of the location of the tree is the disagreement concerning the hangings themselves. The Seymour *Democrat* states that the victims were all hung from one limb of the beech tree.[30],[31] Horna and Swiggett note that "three ropes were flung over the same branch of a huge tree.[32] However, another source notes that the first three victims were "strung up to 3 different limbs,"[33] and that the last three victims were hung "upon the same 3 limbs."[34] Shields rather vaguely refers to "its branches" when discussing the hangings.[35] Obviously, some of the early descriptions were based on accounts by individuals who did not visit the location, or at least not until after the bodies were cut down.

The physical destruction of the tree and the lapse of nearly 110 years have greatly altered the site of the hangings. The remains of the roots of the beech tree may still exist far below the surface but no evidence remains for the human eye. Grass covers the entire vicinity and children play peacefully around the general area where the bodies must have fallen when they were cut down. A small stream winds its way past the spot, living and dying with the annual spring rains and summer dry spells, as it has since well before the hangings. A few houses are scattered down both sides of the road. Several of the houses are set back from the road as if in quiet respect for the dead, but most of the houses crowd the road as if oblivious to the past. Perhaps some day the few old houses along the historic stretch of road will be razed and a housing development will spring up with a beautiful paved street and broad sidewalks and the last memories of the actual hanging site will be lost forever. No doubt the descendants of the Reno gang members and vigilantes hope this will be the case so the story will finally die.

At the time of the Reno rampage there were quite a few individuals in Seymour and Jackson County with the name Reno. Today one searches in vain for the name of Reno in Seymour. No Reno appears in the city telephone book. Nor does one find a reminder of the family members in the city cemetery. All the Reno brothers and various other family members are buried there, but the markers were long since removed to frustrate the curious sightseers and souvenir hunters. It is almost as if the train robberies never happened and the Reno gang members were never hung. But they did, and Hangman's Crossing stands as the last reminder of the Reno incident. Little matter that the hangings were all carried out elsewhere, and that all that really happened at the Crossing was the illegal seizing of the first three victims.

As a great philosopher once said, "Those who do not know history are doomed to repeat it." Heaven forbid that such a thing should ever happen again. In spite of the mystery surrounding the incident, perhaps Hangman's Crossing will defy all of man's and nature's attempts to obliterate it, and will remain as a sober warning for all times of the depths to which man can descend. Perhaps this is the real reason that people have not let the story completely die. Still, it would be nice if someone some day had a historical marker placed at the Crossing to make the remembering a little easier and more accurate.

It is evident that much mystery has already replaced fact concerning the circumstances surrounding the naming of the Crossing. Nearly everyone in Seymour seems to have had a distant relative who observed the hangings and passed down first-hand accounts of the rise and fall of the Reno gang. In listening to locals tell of the hangings one has the feeling that literally thousands of citizens must have been hiding behind every rock, bush, and tree in the vicinity when the hangings took place. One wonders who remained at home to watch over the babies and to care for the ill and infirm. Surprisingly, none of the locals' ancestors seem to have taken part in the actual hangings; they were just spectators. Apparently, the vigilantes were imported from out of the area or were locals who were destined to have no offspring. The majority of these local tales do not correspond with the few sketchy historical facts or even with any of the other local tales. Such diversity makes it difficult to determine which stories have validity and which ones do not.

When a retelling of the story is historically appropriate, such as the 100th anniversary of the hangings, local newspapers dig through their old files and develop written accounts which look remarkably like the last ones they printed. The accounts are usually quite general and ignore specific details. Many of the local citizens dust off their own "true" accounts of the

Reno rampage and the hangings and bandy them around, ·and like Pin-
nochio's nose they seem to grow with each exaggeration. After a few days,
however, they are put back to rest until the next appropriate occasion. Then
only the inconspicuous Hangman's Crossing remains as an ominous reminder of the tragic events of so long ago.

NOTES

1. Rodger Birchfield, "Reno Outlaw Gang's Cell To Be Seymour Attraction," *The Indianapolis News*, 13 February, 1969.

2. Robert W. Shields, ed., *The Life of John Reno of Seymour, Indiana: The
World's First Train Robber*, (Seymour, 1940), II.

3. Ralph Donham, "Organized Crime Began With Reno Gang," *The Indianapolis Star*, 20 December, 1964, Sec. 2, 4.

4. David Dressler, "Brothers in Crime," *Colliers Weekly*, 121 (1948), 30.

5. James D. Horan and Howard Swiggett, *Gold, Guns, and Gallows*, (Fort
Wayne, 1951), 10. Reprint from *The Pinkerton Story*, G. P. Putnam's Sons (New
York, 1951).

6. Birchfield, 14.

7. Cleveland Moffett, "The Destruction of the Reno Gang: Stories from the
Archives of the Pinkerton Detective Agency," *McClure's Magazine*, IV:6 (1895),
552.

8. *The Indianapolis Daily Sentinel*, 24 July, 1868, 4.

9. *The Indianapolis Journal*, 14 December, 1868, 4. Cited by Robert F.
Volland, *The Reno Gang of Seymour*, Unpublished Master's Thesis, Indiana University, 1948, 282.

10. Volland, 198.

11. Anonymous, *The Reno Family and the Seymour Tragedy: The Only True
History of the Affair By One Who Knows and Was on the Ground*, Unpublished
manuscript, 1869, 8.

12. *The Seymour Democrat*, 9 February, 1882, 2.

13. Robert W. Shields, *Story of the Reno Gang*, (Seymour, 1939), Preface.

14. Volland, 207.

15. Volland, 207.

16. Volland, 307.

17. *The Indianapolis Journal*, 18 December, 1868, 4. Cited by Volland, 291.

18. *The New Albany Ledger*, 19 December, 1868, p, 1. Cited by Volland, 286.

19. Anonymous, 32-33.

20. Volland, 295.

21. Volland, 306.

22. James D. Horan, *Desperate Men: Revelations from the Sealed Pinkerton Files,* G. P. Putnam's Sons, (New York, 1951),66.

23. *The Seymour Democrat,* 22 July, 1868.

24. Anonymous, 6.

25. Anonymous, 7.

26. Volland, 206.

27. Shields, *Story of,* Page of Contents.

28. Shields, *Story of,* 35.

29. *The Seymour Tribune,* 15 March, 1976, 10.

30. *The Seymour Democrat,* 22 July, 1868.

31. *The Seymour Democrat,* 29 July, 1868.

32. Horan and Swiggett, 24.

33. Anonymous, 6.

34. Anonymous, 7.

35. Shields, *Story of,* 37.

III Folk Belief, Medicine, and Magic

The Miracle of String Measurement

Barbara Ann Townsend and Donald Allport Bird

Before modern medicine brought new methods of caring for children and diagnosing their problems, many mothers watched their babies with anxiety and sometimes fear. One chronic ailment that could beset children was short growth, sometimes called "flesh decay" in some parts of Indiana.

Measuring with a "raw" or red yarn both for diagnosis of certain diseases and for curative powers has been known since Pliny and continually reported from Europe since the 1st century. Various methods and usages have been practiced in Germanic countries.[1] It was thought that ideally a man's length from head to foot should be equal to the width of his outstretched hands. If a discrepancy occurred, the man's balance supposedly was upset by some illness such as headache, jaundice, loss of weight, dizziness, rickets, or even bewitchment. While *Handwörterbuch des Deutschen Aberglaubens* provides us with elaborations of further techniques, diagnostic powers, and a bibliography of the custom,[2] it does not refer to curative powers associated with short growth measurement of sick children—a belief and practice that has been collected in Indiana. Quite to the contrary, this source mentions beliefs that the measuring of a child would harm it, stop growth, or at best determine only whether it would live or die.

From various 19th century sources, it appears that in Britain children were measured by undyed yarn, red yarn, or string. This practice was often used as a curative charm and was accompanied by ritualistic phrases and gestures. Thompson F950.3 and Baughman F950.3 (a) "Child does not grow (who has "short growth") is measured with a string, thread or yarn and the string is disposed in various ways," has been reported for some time in many parts of Europe and America. Baughman further notes that the custom was collected from different parts of the United States as early as 1898 and also cites an Irish, Welsh and Herefordshire source.[3] *Hoosier Folklore* (March, 1948)7:15-19, the predecessor to *Indiana Folklore,* printed several reports of short growth measurement collected more than 22 years ago.

In Indiana, as well as Europe, there were probably several reasons for the condition that many parents called short growth. Sometimes it was a failure to grow at the expected rate. Poor diet may have been a factor. Sometimes the child suffered from a weakened condition brought about by a series of diseases. Any child whose growth or general health did not seem to be what his parents hoped it would be could be diagnosed as having short growth.

Seeing their children in such a fragile state of health, parents had to have a remedy—something they could put faith in. Mrs. Dresier was groping for such help in Terre Haute when she saw her baby Theodore, born on August 27, 1871, "puny beyond belief, all ribs and hollow eyes and ailing and whimpering." The measuring practiced on him while an infant was recounted by Theodore Dreiser in 1931. In this autobiograph- ical account we witness a fusion of the German diagnostic concept of measurement with the curative powers reported in various British sources.

> She grieved and grieved over my impending fate, and as she herself later told me finally resorted to what can only be looked upon as magic or witchcraft.
>
> Opposite us, in an old vine-covered, tree shaded house falling rapidly into decay, lived an old German woman, a feeble and mysterious recluse who was regarded in the neighborhood as, if not a witch, at least the possessor of minor supernatural and unhallowed powers. She may have practiced illegal medicinal arts, for all I know. At any rate, in cases of illness or great misfortune, she was not infrequently consulted by her neighbors. One night when the family feared that my death was imminent, my mother, weeping, ordered my eldest sister to run across the street and ask this old woman to come over. But, knowing of my father's strict religious views, she refused. She did say, however: 'If your mother wants my help, tell her to take a string and measure your brother from head to toe and from finger-tip to finger-tip. If the arms are as long as the body, bring the string to me.'
>
> This was done, and the measurements proving satisfactory, the string was taken to her, whereupon she smiled and sent for my mother.

'Your child will not die,' she announced. 'But for three nights in succession, you must take him out in the full of the moon. Leave his head and face uncovered, and stand so that the light will fall slant-wise over his forehead and eyes. Then say three times: ' "Wass ich hab, nehm ab; wass ich thu, nehm zu!" '

As a result of this remarkable therapy, I am reported to have improved. In three months I was well.[4]

Originally the cure was probably a German import, established and modified by Pennsylvania Germans. Moving to Indiana, the same pattern was reinforced and has persisted from Dreiser's childhood. Like the old German woman in Terre Haute, there were, and are, many other women in Indiana who feel they possess the power to measure. This custom has recently been collected in Hartford City, Fort Wayne, Muncie, New Castle, Anderson, Winchester, Peru, Mishawaka, and elsewhere. These accounts closely follow other oral texts previously printed in folklore publications. The following are interview texts collected from Hoosiers:

A

We visited Mrs. Lee Nelson twice. She lives on Commercial Street in Hartford City. She was born near Dunkirk, Indiana, and is now eighty-four years old. We asked her whether there were still people wanting to have their children measured, and she said that she still measures quite a few children. Besides measuring, she knows many of the old-fashioned cures and feels that a time will come when people will go back to old values. Mrs. Nelson is an intelligent woman. Her three daughters are college educated and have taught school. We do not have Mrs. Nelson's story in her exact words because it was difficult to get the story. Part of the story had to be told to my husband out in the kitchen because the method cannot be told by a woman to a woman.

Stella Nelson does measure children for the short growth. It has to be done three mornings in a row before the sun comes up. A different string is used each morning. The child must be naked and on his stomach. Then a string is laid from the crown of the child's head to his heel. This measurement has to be seven times the size of the child's foot. The string is made into a loop and put over the child's head. When the loop gets to his shoulders, she says, 'Father, Son, and Holy Ghost.' She repeats this when the string reaches the child's hips and repeats it again when the string is around the child's legs. She does this three times each morning for three mornings. The strings must be put someplace where they will deteriorate quickly. She says that when she measures someone, it makes her feel weak afterward.

An account by Barbara Townsend of an interview March 8, 1970, with Mrs. Lee Nelson of Hartford City.
FA IU:70

B

My mother had me measured. Her name is Oma Casterline, and she lives at 539 West Franklin. I had my boy measured. His name is Jimmy Allen Carpenter. He was about two years old when he was measured, and he is thirty-five now. His legs were that big around. [She showed with her thumb and index finger.] I think the trouble was with the milk. I took him to Mrs. Lee Nelson. You have to go three mornings before the sun comes up. You have to strip the child off and measure from the crown of the head to the heel, and you have to measure the bottom of the foot from the heel to the toe. She puts the child through the string, and she says something. She says something from the Bible, but she doesn't say it out loud. Then you throw the string where it will decay the fastest. I tied his string around the tire of the car. That will make it wear out fast.

We noticed he was so thin. Mom said, 'He's got the short growth.'

The person who does the measuring is not supposed to charge anything for doing it, but she can accept a gift. I just laid down something on the table.

She measured from the crown of his head to his heel. Then she measured the foot and tied a knot. Then she doubled back on the string to see if it was seven times the length of the foot. If it isn't, the child has the short growth. His was an inch and a half short. Then she took the string and made a loop that she put over his head three times while she said some words. She might have said, 'Father, Son, and Holy Spirit.' I'm not sure because she didn't say it out loud.

Old lady Overmeyer used to measure. She was Ed Overmeyer's mother.

I was measured when I was less than a year old because I was so puny. We just about lost Jimmy. I can't believe that we let him get in such a shape.

Collected from Gretchen Carpenter of Hartford City by Barbara Townsend of Muncie, February 15, 1970.
FA IU:70

C

I don't know whether other families did it or not, but my Mom and my aunt did. If a baby wasn't doing well, they'd measure it for short growth. And that had to be passed on from mother to son and the same way. I know Aunt Allie's next to the oldest boy, he was just a little bittie guy and Aunt Allie had had all great big ancestors, and she just knew that that baby had short growth. Don't ask me what short growth is; I don't know.

And so, her oldest son, I was there when he measured him with a string some way and tied it this way. He measured some more and tied a knot, measures his foot and tied a knot. It was pure short growth. The measuring was to cause the baby to grow faster. I think there was words said, but I never heard them.

Collected from Lottie McFarland Stone of Fort Wayne by Beulah E. Roddell also of Fort Wayne, July 1966.
FA IU:Folk Medicine File

D

When Carl was little (he hadn't started to school yet), he was sick most of the time. I took him to a relative of old Mrs. Leonard's on Perkins Street. I took him three days in a row before the sun came up. She put him on the floor on his stomach naked. Then she put the string from the crown of his head to his heel. You don't pull the string tight. You let the string lie on the curves of the body and go over one hip. The length of the child has to be seven times the length of his foot. If it isn't, the child has the short growth. Then she had him stand up, and she tied the ends of the string together and put it over his head. She said some words, but I don't know what they were. She did that three times. We used the same string each morning. Ma wrapped the string around the axle of the buggy and put the wheel on. That made the string wear out. That woman said that it was a good thing that I took him when I did because he was the next thing to having TB. It took him a long time to begin to get better. He was about eight years old before he really started to grow and do well.

Collected from Mrs. Adam Townsend of Hartford City by Barbara Townsend of Muncie, February 15, 1970.
    FA IU:70

E

Mrs. Jones took this child down to Shed Town in Muncie. This place has been done away with long ago. The boy's name was Robert Truitt Jones. He lives in Muncie now. His mother is in the county home. He was just a young baby, and he just did not thrive on anything. His backbone was almost through his skin. This woman took a string, and she tied so many knots in it. And she made a circle with it. As she put him through this circle of string, she said something. I think she said something out of the Bible. She took him through the loop three times.

Mrs. Jones took him to be measured in the morning. I don't think the woman had had her breakfast yet. After he was measured, he picked up. He grew up to be such a "no good" that his mother often said that she wished she hadn't had him measured. Doctor Boze [sic] came out to see him, and he gave him some tablets. We didn't know if it was the tablets or the measuring that helped him.

It was just a bunch of shacks out in Shed Town, but she was clean. She was spotless clean. I was just past sixteen years old. I think she laid him down and measured him. I think she checked on the size of his foot. He had to be seven times the size of his foot. I don't know what she did with the string.

Collected from Mrs. Frank L. Taylor (Mary Taylor), formerly of New Castle but now residing in Franklin by Barbara Townsend of Muncie, March 3, 1970.
    FA IU:70

F

Short growth (child is cross and won't eat)—Take one thread and measure the child, then take another thread and measure his foot. Tie the two pieces of thread together with another piece of thread. Pass the child through the circle, made by joining of the threads, a certain number of times. Then fold the thread and place it on the hinge of a gate. Leave it there until it rots, and then after that there will be no danger of short growth.

Collected from Mrs. Roscoe Whitezel, 83, of Peru by Karen McCoy of Anderson, May 9, 1965.
    FA IU:70

G

My mother was of Pennsylvania Dutch extraction, and she believed that it would help my sister Mary to be 'measured' for what was at that time called 'short growth.' Mary Dutro Peters was not a very healthy child. She remembers one trip when my mother drove with horse and buggy and took her to see the 'seventh daughter of a seventh daughter.' This lady's name was Mrs. Cass Holder, and she lived approximately seven miles southwest of Winchester, Indiana. Mary does not remember exactly how old she was, but we think that she was very likely four years of age. Mary remembers that Mrs. Holder removed her clothes and took twine string and measured a length of it from the top of her head to the tip of her toes. The string was fastened at both ends in some fashion, and Mary had to slip this string (like a hoop) over her body each morning until the string wore out. Mary does not remember how many times she went to see Mrs. Holder. My father did not believe in these superstitions, and he called them 'the work of the devil.' He thought that she was never helped by this treatment. My mother died when Mary was six and I was three, so I never heard her speak of the results of the 'measurement.' I have heard that if the child is very ill and the string should wear out very fast, one should place the string in a door jamb, so that each time the door was closed, the string would wear a little. I have also heard that sometimes these ladies who did the 'measuring' would place the string on an old-fashioned grind-stone and turn it vigorously so that the string would wear out very, very quickly.

Collected from Ruth Dutro, a high school teacher from Hagerstown by Kristin Townsend of Muncie, March 10, 1970.
    FA IU:70

H

The following information was given to me by Arthur Kennedy, who came to the Masonic Home from Muncie, Indiana. He is now dead, but I took these notes before he died. A yarn string was used to measure the child's foot in some manner. A loop was formed with the string and passed over the child's body. This was accompanied by quoting certain scripture and concluded with invoking the Holy Trinity. The string was then hung on a door and forgotten until it disintegrated. The power to measure children must be passed from a female to a male or a male to a female, never from male to male or female to female. The string could be wrapped around an egg. I do not know whether the egg was cooked or not. It was then placed in the hot ashes of the fireplace. It meant one thing if the egg broke and kept the string from burning and something else if the string was burned without breaking the egg. In order to be measured, the child had to be nude and placed on his stomach. Measuring might have to be repeated several times before a child was healed.

Bertha Wilson of Anderson, was measured in the Alexandria area. She was measured because she did not grow and thrive. The doctor had told the family to get rid of all the cats because they were draining her health away. It is not known whether the measuring or the removal of the cats had anything to do with her survival, but she did live to have eight children. She died in 1953. Being measured did not make her grow tall. She was less than five feet tall, but she did live to be an old woman.

Cecil Warnock of Marion, Indiana, was also measured.

Collected by Barbara Townsend of Muncie from Charles Funkhouser, Chaplain of the Masonic Home, Muncie, March 3, 1970.
   FA IU:70

I

I remember when I was young, my sister Doris became very ill and the doctor's medicine didn't seem to do any good. My grandmother Tipple, while she was visiting said to my mother, 'That child has flesh decay'. I can't think of the lady's name, but they took her [Doris] to Hillgrove [Ohio] where this lady lived that practiced 'measuring'. As I recall, this was done with a continuous piece of string measuring each member of the body: length, width, and diameter. Each measurement was subtracted from the original length of the string in a cumulative fashion, making the final length the length of the members of the body. When this was done, my Mother was instructed to take the string home and bury it in the ground under an eave spout. She also said to my mother, 'When this string rots or decays your child will be on her way to being healed'. Whatever happened there I don't know, but nevertheless her health improved noticably. It took several months to get back to full strength, but I noticed an immediate improvement. I believe to the extent that my mother had faith in this method of healing that all of this came about as she believed. I believe to this day, if a person would have the conscienceness [sic] of accepting this belief and would feel in their hearts that it would work, it would work.

FA IU:Folk Medicine File

Collected by Mark Tipple from Lloyd E. Tipple in 1967, both of Winchester. The following background material is provided by Mark, Lloyd Tipple's grandson:

Lloyd E. Tipple, was born in Darke County, Ohio, to Roll and Bessie Strader Tipple. His mother, Bessie, was his source for all of the cures he told to me. She was a very religious and superstitious person taking much faith in her folk cures and signs. She obtained this superstitious nature from her husband's mother and father, Andrew and Anne Sullenbarger Tipple. My great grandmother and great grandfather moved from Lancaster County, Pennsylvania, to Lancaster County, Ohio, shortly after the Civil War. After a short stay in Lancaster County, Ohio, they moved to Darke County, Ohio, where my grandmother and grandfather lived beside my grandfather's parents for seven years. My grandmother was of English background, but was influenced greatly by her husband's parents, who were of Pennsylvania Dutch ancestry.

My father was raised in a family which lived by superstitions and folk cures. His family was very large and money was very scarce so a doctor was hardly ever called. His mother had to be both mother and doctory [sic]. During the different seasons of the year, she would gather and save the plants and materials she might need to make up her medicine. She even had a special cabinet containing all of these dried leaves and barks, and she took this doctoring seriously. Also, my father's father took much faith in different signs when planting his crops and when buying or selling anything.

I can remember these folk cures coming up in the conversation ever since my early years. My father comes up with some of these cures or superstitions whenever someone mentions an ailment his mother used to cure. Sometimes my grandmother's cures wouldn't work, then she would take other steps, like taking my father's sister to a 'measurer'.

FA IU:Folk Medicine File

J

When I was a little girl in Toledo, Ohio, I visited my grandmother in North Baltimore [Ohio]. She said I had the 'undergrowth' and she took

me to a lady who 'measures'. The lady put a string from the top of my
head down to the soles of my feet. Then she rolled it into a little ball and
gave it to my grandmother. She said to take it home and boil an egg in my
chamber lye [urine], hard boil it, and then bury the string wrapped
around the egg in an ant hill. When they were both gone [rotted], I would
grow.

Collected from Mrs. Lucille Wittenberger, 72, Peru, By Bonnie Sims also of Peru, July
2, 1966.

FA IU:Folk Medicine File

Anglo-American, Slavonic and German Variants
Collected Outside Indiana

(1) Our earliest source is Father Strange, *Life and Gests of St.
Thomas Cantilupe, Bishop of Hereford* (Ghent, 1674). He describes the
measuring of the subject's length and circumference with two threads and
the placing of them at the altar to cure madness or disease. (2) A short
growth cure more similar to the Indiana variants was practiced by a
farmer's daughter in Donegal and reported in the Irish *Folk-Lore Journal*
(1887) 5:69. (3) Sidney Hartland, *The Legend of Perseus* (London: David
Nutt, 1894-96), p. 225., writes of a ritual that measures a saint's body and
binds the thread around the body of the patient. (4) F. S. Krauss,
Volksglaube und Religiöser Brauch der Südslaben (Munster, 1890), pp.
51, 139., records a patient measured by a thread which is then worn and
details a wife-beater cured by being measured with a thread previously
used to measure a dead man of the same name. The author notes that
sometimes the thread is worn as a charm, and a woman close to the author
"drives a roaring trade in magic threads, with which she measures her
patients." Although the above versions do not necessarily deal with child
short growth measurement, it is interesting to see how the custom overlaps
various functions and age groups. (5) F. Howard Gore, "The Go-Backs,"
JAF (1892) 5:107-9., notes a Virginia mountain custom which measures
the height and feet of the child and then places the measuring yarn upon a

gate hinge. (6) Emma G. White, "Folk Medicine among the Pennsylvania Germans," *JAF* (1897) 10:79., records a similar placing of the measuring string on a gate. Prior to this, the child has been passed backwards three times through a warm horse collar. The correct verbal formula must accompany the ritual. (7) Mrs. George A. Stanbery, "Grandmother Harper's Cure for the Decay of the Flesh," *Folk-Lore* (1897) 8:185., details that a child must be brought three successive mornings and stripped of clothing. A linen string measures the foot length 7 times and then the body length from crown to head and down the back of the tip of the heel. If the child is less than 7 lengths of the foot "the child is affected with decay." In this event a string loop is formed by holding the ends together between thumb and forefinger. The loop is passed 3 times from the child's head to foot and the string is then wound around the hinge of a door or gate; as the string is worn away the child will be restored to health. While Mrs. Harper recommends placing the string on a wooden hinge, she observes "I presume an iron hinge would answer the same purpose." (8) Ann Whitney, "Items of Maryland Belief and Custom," *JAF* (1899) 12:273., provides a "cure for flesh decay or wasting disease in a baby." The 7th son or 7th daughter must measure a baby 3 days in succession before sunrise or after sunset and repeat a charm—unintelligible to observers—over the child. The string is doubled after the 3rd session and tied to the hinge of a door or window, "and if it rots out in a certain time the body will recover; but if the child is 'foot-and-a half gone,' there is not possible cure." (9) In the 20th century, Henry M. Wiltse, "In the Field of Southern Folklore," *JAF* (1901) 14:205-208., records a distantly related cure for phthisic. A sourwood stick is cut to the exact height of the child and then hidden. The child grows as the stick decays. (10) In Ella Mary Leather, *The Folk-Lore of Herefordshire* (London, 1912), p. 221, a woman strips the patient, measures 3 times around the body and over the heart with a green tape to discover heart fever. (11) L. Winstanley and H. J. Rose, "An Old Wife's Tale," *Folk-Lore* (1926) 37:170., records the curing of a sick boy by making "ready a length of wool [which may be dyed] to measure the sick boy," and wisely note that such a practice is not confined to Wales nor to healing specific sicknesses.

Indiana Variants

(12) C. O. Tullis, "Measuring for Short Growth," *Hoosier Folklore* (1947) 6:112., appeals to readers for contributions about the child measurement ritual he observed in Kokomo and Marion. (13) Harry Gray, *Hoosier Folklore* (1948) 7:16., answers Tullis' request. Gray, from Hot Springs , Arkansas, notes that in the second decade of the 20th century "it was common practice for parents of an undersized child to take the child to someone who practiced measuring for short growth." If its length was not 7 times the length of his foot, the child had short growth. The string was tied to a yard gate which, when wearing out, would permit the child to grow. (14) W. I. Feagans, "Measuring for Short Growth," *Hoosier Folklore* (1948) 7:17., also replies to Tullis. One method "used extensively at the present time in Pulaski, County," involves a piece of wrapping thread held over the child, cut to his exact length, and then buried under the home's eaves. As the string rots, the child grows. In a variant, the string is "tied around a water pump cylinder rod within a few inches of the top," but "in both methods the measuring must be done just at the time the sun is peeping over the eastern horizon on any morning except Sunday morning. Monday and Friday mornings will be the most desirable. It must also be done on a clear day. Not everyone has the power to do this—only people who have never seen their father; and the power has to be given to them by someone else who has had the power. They cannot accept pay as this will break their power." (15) Ernest W. Baughman, "Measuring for Short Growth," *Hoosier Folklore* (1948) 7:17-19., notes a practice observed in Muncie in the early 1940's. The child has short growth if the distance from the head's crown to his heel was less than 7 times the distance from the heel to the end of the big toe. A tight forehead skin might also signify short growth. Before measuring, one must repeat 3 times, "In the name of the Father, Son, and Holy Ghost, Amen." Measuring must take place upon a naked child 3 times on succeeding days, and then the string must be burned. Another variant is similar to (6) above. A third variant stipulates that the magical cure is transmitted from a man

to a woman or visa versa, the string is tied, the child slipped feet first 3 times through the string, and a "pow-wowing," the use of carefully guarded word charms, commonly practiced in Indiana, follows. Then the string is allowed to wear out on a door hinge. (16) In April, 1965, Kenneth R. Barker collected from Sara L. Manges of Mishawaka, an account of her taking her child to a Mrs. Lago to be measured. She wound the string around an egg, placed it into the ashes to cook, thus burning the string. (17) **FA IU:Folk Medicine File.** Beulah E. Roddel of Fort Wayne collected a similar account from Mrs. Chloe Cook, also of Fort Wayne, on July 1966. (18) **FA IU:Folk Medicine File.** She was measured by her grandmother when the informant was six weeks old. (19) A similar account was collected by Jerry Hasch of Columbus from John Hershal Oltman of Edinburg, December 1966. The informant was cured of short growth by his mother.

The Indiana form of the Old World cure is based upon the belief that disease may be transferred to an object. The custom is related to the animistic belief that a body disease may be healed by, or transferred to, a bush or tree: Baughman F950.3 (b) "Person bores hole in tree exact height of child, puts lock of child's hair in the hole, plugs up the hole. As tree grows, the child will begin to grow." Indiana variants of this related form not considered in this article, place the measuring string, instead of a child's lock of hair, into the tree.

While there are variations in the measurement custom, the ritual maintains a cohesive structure. Details omitted in some accounts that appear in others, may indicate narrative omissions rather than contradictions among variants.

The power of short growth measurement is transmitted, as in other healing beliefs, from one sex to the other sex (H,15), mother to son (C), seventh daughter or a seventh son (G,8), or by one who has never seen his father (14). As in other rituals, the magic must be performed before the sun rises (A,B,D,E, 8, 14), after sunset (8) or associated with a full moon

(Dreiser account). To have short growth, the total length of the child must be less than 7 times the length of his foot (A,B,D,E,7,13,15). The measurement or string is usually manipulated in some manner 3 times, and the string is almost always looped, joined, rolled, or knotted with accompanying word formula (A,B,C,D,E,H,6,8,15). In variant 15 one can observe the influence of Catholicism upon the custom; the names of the Trinity must be repeated three times.

The underlying idea of short growth measurement is that the disease absorbed by the string must deteriorate before the child can recover. This has, of course, variants more culture bound than the above structure. The manner of discarding the string appears to take on new forms easily. The string is placed where it will deteriorate most quickly: buried (I), burned (15,16), placed on an altar (1), tied or placed on a window, door or gate hinge (F,H,5,6,7,8,13,15,17), twined around a grindstone (G), placed under the house eaves (14), put in fire ashes (16), carried or worn on the sick person's body (2,4), wrapped around a buggy axle (D), tied around the tire of a car (B), or tied a few inches from the top of a water pump (14). The adaptability to modern living, from altar and buggy axle to the automobile tire and water pump, is clear. Mrs. Harper reflects such an attitude for, although she places the string upon a wooden hinge, she takes care to note, "I presume an iron hinge would answer the same purpose."

Measuring by any of the methods given here would be ridiculed by any medical doctor. Probably the main reason for its success in so many cases was that waiting for the string to deteriorate gave the body time to heal itself. The cure is important because people believed in it. One must realize, in perspective, that these were people who did not have penicillin, sulpha drugs, or vitamin pills. They did not have bottle sterilizers, special formulae, or a scientifically prepared variety of baby foods. When their children were sick, they needed help, and that is what measuring promised. Those who believed in the early cures were important people, those who made Indiana what it is today. It will be interesting to determine when this generation of elderly people is gone, whether measuring for short growth—a persistent part of culture for at least 2,000 years—will disappear, or, as seen by our example of past adaptability, the string custom will merely assume some unforeseen twist.

Notes

1. Theodore Zacharias, "Etwas vom Messen der Kranken," *Zeitschrift für Volkskunde* 21(1911):151-59. We choose to focus on the German and English variants of short growth measurement since the Indiana versions root from them. Yet, this practice has been reported in other Old World countries as well.

2. Hanns Bächtold-Staubli, ed., *Handwörterbuch des Deutschen Aberglaubens* (Berlin and Leipzig, 1927-1942) 5:1852-61.

3. Ernest W. Baughman, *Type and Motif-Index of the Folktales of England and North America* (The Hague, 1966), p. 236. See also Wayland D. Hand, ed., *The Frank C. Brown Collection of North Carolina Folklore* 6(Durham, North Carolina, 1961), p. 31, item 165; Madge E. Pickard and R. Carlyle Buley, *The Midwest Pioneer: His Ills, Cures, Doctors* (New York, 1946), pp. 9-10; and Vance Randolph, *Ozark Superstitions* (New York, 1947).

4. Theodore Dreiser, *Dawn* (Greenwich, Connecticut, 1965), pp. 9-10.

Root Doctors and Psychics in the Region

Elon A. Kulii

My aim in doing fieldwork in the Calumet Region of Northern Indiana was to determine the extent to which blacks from the rural south retained hoodoo beliefs and tales after they migrated to Gary, East Chicago, and Hammond. Although I had worked with this belief system in the rural area of North Carolina back in 1973,[1] I was totally inexperienced in collecting in an urban center, and even somewhat reluctant about going to Gary since I had heard many of the gang stories about it that flowed in the oral tradition. After the first three days in the field, however, I felt completely at home.

As time went on I discovered numerous accounts of hoodoo, especially after I recognized that hoodoo itself was not always the term familiar to the folk. Often an individual would initially deny knowing anything of hoodoo tales and beliefs, but would make a statement such as "I don't know nothing about hoodoo but I have heard something about rootworking." Responses of this sort prompted me to use several other folk terms to describe hoodoo (conjuring, fixing, tricking, rootworking, witchcraft). One excellent example of this unfamiliarity with a given term was illustrated in my interview with Mrs. Alma B. of East Chicago After introducing myself, I asked her if she was familiar with stories dealing with rootworking. She immediately said, "No," so I further added, "You know, people fixing people." Then she said, "Oh, you are talking about voodoo or hoodoo! My God! Why do you want to know about stuff like that?" As the conversation progressed she recounted a legend that involved a typical theme in the voodoo system—the idea that menstrual blood can charm males:

There was this young couple who was the ideal couple in the town. Everytime you saw one, you saw the other. They just seemed like they loved each other to death.

120

Well, one day the husband came home from work and started playing with his wife. She accidently tripped over a throw rug and the steak she was wearing fell from between her legs and she was in her cycle, menstrual cycle. And he got the gun and blew her brains out. He told the judge what happened but the judge still gave him time.

The core belief in this account is that menstrual blood when mixed in with a man's food will cause the man to fall madly in love with the woman from whom the blood has issued. And as Mrs. B. later pointed out, this lady would let the steaks soak in the menstrual blood so that the spell would be strong.

This particular theme, of menstrual blood being used by women to woo reluctant males, definitely does not originate in the urban setting. Harry M. Hyatt in his monumental *Hoodoo-Conjuration-Witchcraft-Rootwork,* has recorded similar accounts concerning this love potion:

> 3881. "...a drop of blood if she's ministratin!"
> 3882. "...take dere monthly due an'...prepare it in the man's meals. Well it's no way in the world dat he can git away."
> 3884. "...give him yore periods once a month. Get it as natural an' as fresh as yore kin. An' even aftah yo' quit him fo' a yeah or two, des jis hang to yo."[2]

The *North Carolina Folklore Journal* cites similar tales dealing with menstrual blood.[3] The point is that as this belief migrated to the city, the ritualistic employment of it magnified somewhat. In the south, one could guarantee the desired effect by adding the blood to the man's food without actually wearing the meat for an extended period of time.

Quite often an urban informant would become very hesitant about relating a story of this nature and would ask me if it was okay to speak into the taperecorder. I had great difficulty assuring one of my informants, Mrs. Mary M., that it was all right to talk about the use of menstrual blood in fixing a man:

Mrs. M.: And she would get people to give her taboo [menstrual] blood to keep her husband, you know. And she would—I can't tell you all the bad—[pause]
Cooley: I really really would like to know—
Mrs. M.: I can't tell you all this bad stuff, man that's terrible! If I tell you that—
Cooley: Well, I'll tell you what. I'll ask your son to step out for a minute. I would like to get the complete story—
Mrs. M.: [Laughing.] Well, now I can't tell you stuff like that—
Cooley: I sure enough would like to know—

Mrs. M.: Anyway—and then before you prepared a meal you get this steak. That's terrible—
Cooley: Okay, just tell it.
Mrs. M.: And wear it between your—oh—I can't say that. Well, between your vagina, I'll say it like that.

Finally after getting over the taboo and saying vagina, Mrs. M. related numerous hoodoo tales and later sent me to see a relative of hers who was familiar with the tradition.

The differences and similarities between the southern root doctor and his urban counterpart are worth mentioning. Instead of calling themselves root doctors, these urban professionals adopt the names "psychic," "spiritualistic reader," and "prophet". This metamorphosis in name has several explanations, but the one that seems closest to the truth asserts that the title root doctor simply carries too many negative associations. Consequently, most urban root doctors work under the guise of another name. Furthermore, they associate themselves with a particular church or at least assume the title of minister. The church also shields them from possible legal repercussions, especially if they are not licensed as a psychologist or a minister.

These psychics and prophets perform many of the same feats as their southern counterpart. Notice how Robert E. describes a well-known prophet in Gary:

Now he not only calls himself just healing people, he gives out numbers or some type of name where people go spend up their money playing the policy racket trying to catch money. And uh, see when he calls himself healing the people, they might heal one or two. But you see he's not actually healing them because the demons did get in the man to make him fool people.

Another informant told how a spiritualist reader found out that a certain man "had snakes and stuff inside his body." This particular prophet later stated that he does not believe in hoodoo but "you can't tell an individual that he has not been fixed if he believes that he has." He simply points to verses in the Bible that tell of God's omnipotence, especially over demonic forces. He prays for them and they get better.

One of the most popular psychics in the Calumet Region is the Reverend Kirby Jeffries (Fig. 1), who has a daily radio program with a wide listening audience. Although some members of the folk view him as a voodoo priest, he says "I am not a voodooist. I know something about it, I study it, I might draw some power from there, some knowledge from

there, but it is not that I am stepping over to become a voodoo priest." He further elaborates on the snake that is common to the system of hoodoo:

> If there is a thought which is sent to you, or someone has said something to you, or a sickness is with you, if a person is a strong enough psychic, he can cause that thought or substance within you or whatever the case may be, to materialize as a serpent and take it out of you. But he does it with his thoughts, but it doesn't have to be done that way. The person who did it may have sent it with a thought of it being a serpent and it will materialize within you as a serpent.

Again he also states that "lizards, snakes, and that kind of thing are lesser forces. When you get high enough along, you don't have to deal with lizards or snakes. . . . The higher up you go, then you begin to deal with higher forces such as the goat. . . ."

Thus according to the Reverend Jeffries the duties of some psychics and some hoodoo doctors overlap. As with the hoodoo doctor, the psychic

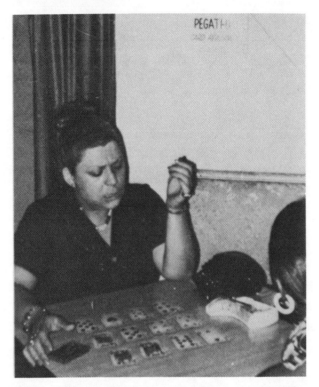

Figure 2. Pegatha, the witch, is an associate of Rev. Jeffries.

seeks to help a person who has become sick by supernatural means (Fig. 2). Although the psychic and the hoodoo doctor are familiar with the snake, they differ notably in their attitudes toward reptiles. In most cases when the hoodoo doctor puts a lizard or snake or some other small creature within the body, sickness and suffering immediately afflict that person. Jeffries states that the psychic can use the snake to cure a person.

Just as the hoodoo doctor is considered to be superior to the medical doctor, so are the psychic and the reader. According to Mrs. Carol H.,

I saw once a lady there in Gary; she supposed to cured a cancer in her breast. The reader prayed over the lady and she said that this was an open meeting and we sat there and we watched. She lay a white towel over the left breast; now I didn't see what was in that towel but when they got through praying and talking and doing this unknown tongue, the towel was red. When she went back to the doctor he said nothing was wrong.

The spiritualist and the root doctor acquire their powers differently. The southern root doctors receive their powers from an older root doctor who is well-versed in this art. Their relationship is similar to that of teacher and student, as Zora Neale Hurston and Norman Whitten have pointed out.[4] In the south, this information is perpetuated and communicated by word of mouth to the incoming layman.

According to various urban psychics, they are born with their powers, although generally they fail to recognize their full extent until a later stage in life. Often they are plagued with dreams and visions that come true. Hosea W., a psychic from Gary, states that he was amazed by his dreams because he would always see the people from his dreams in real life. Later he began to meditate more and also began to record his dreams immediately upon awakening in the mornings, and, as a result, he cultivated and enhanced his powers.

The paraphernalia of rootworking consists of candles, sprays, oils, incenses, roots, stauettes and many other items. In the Calumet Region, stores that sell occult items are generally referred to as spiritual or candle shops. One of the most striking shops in the region is Solomon Turner's "Religious Candle Shop" (Fig. 3). According to Turner he received the idea for this kind of shop and everything to put in it from a dream.

In Gary, I noticed several stores that were not religious candle stores but which included a section catering directly to the rootworking belief-practice system. These stores sold oils, sprays, roots, and so on that would purportedly cure persons who had been fixed. The Apollo Drug Store on Broadway (Fig. 4) and Melnics T. V. Store, also on Broadway, are two businesses that recognized how profitable selling hoodoo items can be.

The testimonies that were collected came from the upper as well as the lower economic levels within the community. Mrs. Ella B., a public school teacher in Gary, related to me the following account of a fellow teacher:

This one concerns a lady who was, rather is, a teacher at one of the high schools. She was a firm believer in voodoo and was a person who many of her co-workers seemed to wonder why she was able to do many of the things she did. So she would come to school with rollers in her hair. Brew coffee during class time. And she used to tell us that she could do what she wanted to do. And she would go to Louisiana and she would make things right (keep the principal from firing her).

Although city dwellers were initially suspicious towards me as a stranger, they seemed to be fairly open about their knowledge of voodoo. In fact, I interviewed several teachers and only one refused to be taped. Southern blacks, on the other hand, appeared to be quite friendly towards strangers but more hesitant and hostile about sharing what they consider "taboo" knowledge.

Figure 3.   Turner's Religious Candle Shop sells candles (top shelf) and numerous oils and powders (second and third shelves) for use in hoodoo.

Figure 4.   The Apollo Drug Store contains medicines for physical and supernatural ailments.

In trying to explain why blacks in the "sophisticated" urban setting continue to keep the hoodoo belief-practice system intact, we must look at the social climate. William Lessa and Evon Z. Vogt say that witchcraft

> is far more than a grisly aberration of human spirit; despite its macabre elements, it has positive functional value. All societies have the problems of providing an outlet for aggression engendered by the conflicts, antagonisms, and frustrations of social living; witches exist as convenient scapegoats for such aggressions.... Like magic, witchcraft may also explain unhappiness, disease, and bad luck. Similarly, witchcraft has its dysfunctional aspect. Witches do real harm, cause real fears, and promote dangerous conflict.[5]

Now if witchcraft is an outlet for conflicts, antagonisms and frustrations, how is it related to modern city living? Numerous blacks have traveled to urban centers to escape the southern economic slavery system, thinking that all their problems and worries would vanish upon their arrival in the city. But there they experience an entirely different kind of slavery—menial jobs. Thus many urbanized Afro-Americans face almost constant tensions, uncertainties, and frustrations.

Often the mere setting of the city presents psychological hazards. One city dweller has commented:

> First of all, overcrowding exacts its toll. As more of us opt for city life, we find ourselves getting in each other's way more often. Ubiquitous waiting lines test our patience. Commuting has become a jangling endurance contest. Thin apartment walls make us privy to our neighbor's most intimate activities. Even relatively spacious suburban lots don't really provide us with the privacy we'd like to have.[6]

Malinowski states that in a situation where "there is danger, uncertainty, great incidence of chance and anxiety, even in modern forms of enterprise, magic crops up."[7] Voodoo as a belief-practice system is a convenient tool through which frustrations and tensions are filtered; it performs a function similar to that of the slave songs and spirituals that kept the black man going in his deepest turmoil. A person who is being knocked by the system is given encouragement by the spiritualist. In order to keep his sanity, the black American (probably unconsciously) channels the mental and social pressures of the urban setting into the hoodoo belief-practice system.

Another point this study discloses is that while numerous informants were unable to recount specific examples of hoodoo, they knew the nature of the system. The general conceptualizations that came forth in the interviews are given in the following diagram:

I_1 Inflictor of the spell

I_2 Victim

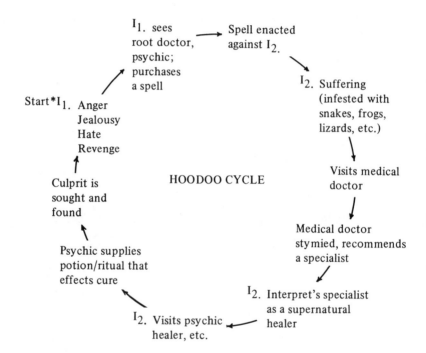

So long as the frustrations of the blacks continue, they will most likely persist in using this supernatural belief-practice system as a mechanism to vent their hostilities and aggressions.

NOTES

1. Gilbert E. Cooley, "A Study and Collection of Recent Black Folklore" (Master's thesis, Greensboro, North Carolina: A & T State University, 1973).

2. Gilbert E. Cooley, "Root Stories," *North Carolina Folklore Journal* 23 (1975), 39.

3. Harry M. Hyatt, *Hoodoo-Conjuration-Witchcraft-Rootwork*, Vol. 3 (St. Louis: Western Publishing Co., 1973), 2520-2521.

4. Zora Neale Hurston, *Mules and Men* (New York: Harper and Row, 1970), 229-304; Norman E. Whitten, Jr., "Contemporary Patterns of Malign Occultism Among Negroes in North Carolina" in *Mother Wit From the Laughing Barrel*, ed. Alan Dundes (Englewood Cliffs, New Jersey: Prentice-Hall, 1973), 411.

5. William E. Lessa and Evon Z. Vogt, eds., *Reader in Comparative Religion: An Anthropological Approach* (2nd ed., New York: Harper and Row, 1965), 246.

6. Carole Ritter, "Is Our Environment Driving Us Bananas," *The Plain Truth: A Magazine of Understanding*, November, 1976, 10.

7. Lessa and Vogt, 105. Cf. Theodore Rosenthal and Bernard J. Siegel, "Magic and Witchcraft: An Interpretation from Dissonance Theory," *Southwestern Journal of Anthropology* 15 (1959), 144.

A Porter County Seer

Sheryl Pisarski

Throughout time, people have been interested in knowing what their futures hold for them. There are many persons today who are considered by some to be able to predict coming events. Some of these "seers" are quite well known, such as Jeane Dixon;[2] others are well known within a given area, but are not known to the world in general. The woman with whom this article is concerned is one of the latter. Mrs. Weeks[3] considers herself as being "gifted," emphasizing the fact that she is not a "fortune-teller." She is very serious about her abilities, and shuns anyone who does not feel likewise.

As can be seen in the interview with Mrs. Cade, the image connoted by the term "fortune-teller" is often that of an over-dressed gypsy in a small, dark tent, crouched over a cystal ball. Association is usually made with cheap carnivals where these same mysterious women read palms, spout generalizations, and charge exorbitant prices for their services. Such is not the case with Mrs. Weeks. In fact, these side-show theatrics are precisely what Mrs. Weeks discredits and labels "fortune-telling" herself.

Mrs. Weeks and most of her clientele live in or near Valparaiso, a small, rather conservative city of 20,000 persons, located in the north-western corner of Indiana about fifty miles southeast of Chicago. It is interesting that in a conservative area people would consult a seer. Hopefully the following interviews will provide some insights into why this is so.

Mrs. Betty Weeks, The Seer

Mrs. Weeks is originally from Iowa, and she is part Blackfoot Indian. She is sixty-six years old and lives in Valparaiso; she finished high school, and has traveled a great deal. She has no special religion, considering herself to be "God's child." She does not consider reading for people to be an occupation. Mrs. Weeks insisted that the collector come to the interview alone; after the collector explained what she wanted to do, Mrs. Weeks was extremely co-operative.

*(When and where did you first learn the technique of fortune-telling?)**
I will start at the very beginning so you can understand the situation better. First of all, I am not a fortune teller. Fortune-tellers, if you even want to call them that, are regular people who tell other people lies and stories just to make money. Whenever I hear the word fortune-teller I get very upset. They should do something to those people who call themselves fortune-tellers. You see, I am a gifted person. It is a very rare thing and since it has happened to me I want to share my good fortune with other people by reading for them.

Now, let's see, I'll tell you how it all began. My mother was a Blackfoot Indian. I was ten years old when I had my first experience. It was a very warm day and my mother was very tired and she wanted to lay down for a little bit, which was very unusual for my mother. She was very sad and I knew something was wrong. Well, I was outdoors playing and I saw my Uncle George and I said to myself, "Something is wrong with my Uncle George." Well, I dashed in the house and woke my mother up and said, "Mother, something is wrong with Uncle George." She said, "Yes, I know. We are going to receive news that he has passed on." I said, "How did you know?" and she said, "Because I've had several unusual things happen to me today. For one thing his picture on the wall fell but the hook didn't fall down—just the picture did.[4] I've also had certain dreams about him for the last week and he's been around me constantly."[5] Then I said to her, "Well, how come I knew something was wrong with him?" Then she said, "Well, I'll have to explain to you what this means but please remember that I don't want you to practice this now 'cause you're too young." So she explained to me that I was gifted the same as she was and the same as her sister and her mother who lived to be over one hundred years old. Now I'm the last one in the family. So my mother said to me, "Whenever you get a feeling about something disregard it now 'cause I don't want you to practice it until you are older." She didn't want me to do it now because she thought it was harmful when you are little. She told me that I shouldn't use it until I was older, about seventeen or maybe eighteen. Then she told me, "Now remember what I said about just forgetting any strange feelings you get."
Even though she discouraged it when I was young I still used to get

*Questions in parentheses are those of the collector.

the most powerful feelings sometimes that you wouldn't believe. I could almost always tell what my mother was gonna do but I didn't say anything to her because she is very stern and she would have punished me and that I didn't like very well. So, I started practicing it when I got older, around seventeen years old, but I didn't go into it strong because you see, everyone was against people in my days about this ESP thing.[6]

My mother's sister went to Boston to start classes about it and everyone was against her. She said that they treated her like she was a witch from the New England days in Salem.[7] It was horrible and terrifying.

But you know, I really don't understand that because they had it in Biblical times and everything seemed good then. But these days the reverends and priests are against people foreseeing things. If they knew about me while I was in their church they would say that I am the devil. For this very reason I cannot go to public churches—I would be cursed if I did.

Yet, it is wonderful to foresee things in a way and yet in a way it's not. You see, I cannot foresee a thing for myself, my husband, or my two children. You see you have to pay because you can't have everything. It's wonderful but yet you know I am disturbed constantly. I'll be disturbed about you for a long time because I'll start thinking about you and then I'll start seeing things for you and if they are good things that's terrific, but if they're bad things, then I get terribly disturbed. Some people I don't dwell too far into their mind because I'll tell you why. Some people are too emotional and you can't tell them some things for they take and make harm out of it [nods her head]. But you know I'm really glad about the open minds of today. They're using it more and more today.

I'm gonna tell you something now that you may not believe but I swear to you that it's the truth. It was way back in the beginning of November of 1963 that I had strange feelings all the time. I would have people come to me for readings[8] and I found that I couldn't read for them because something kept upsetting me but I couldn't figure what was bugging me. Then whenever I saw President Kennedy on the television or heard him on the radio a strange sickness would come over me. Finally I couldn't stand it any longer and I told my husband and two children, "Something tragic is going to happen to President Kennedy while he's in Dallas. I don't know what it's going to be but I fear that the end result will be death." My husband and children were horrified. I also told my husband's sister and mother and they were horrified also. Sure enough just less than a week later he was shot and killed.[9] I also told them about the Watergate affair[10] before any of it happened and sure enough everything I said came true. Now you don't think that is scary? Believe me, it is.

You're probably wondering why I don't tell other people so I can help these things from occurring but the plain truth is that I can't. People would think that I was a crazy old woman trying to get attention or cause trouble. I might as well just keep still if they're gonna think I'm crazy. This is where it's bad to be able to foresee into the future. I see too many things that I wish I wouldn't—it upsets me too much. Not only that, I have to keep all these things to myself which is even harder to do, especially when I know they're gonna do terrible harm. I remember I told somebody who I thought was my friend something important like I just said and she spread the word that I was some maniac woman who was spreading nasty rumors. What can you do [shrugs her shoulders]?

(*Do your neighbors know that you are gifted?*)
Oh, yes, a few of them know about me. My close friends come here about once a month and have me read for them. They seem to be great believers in me for which I am very happy.

I'll tell you something that is very interesting. The women, you know they're really funny. Oh, land of days [throws her arms up]! They come running here to me asking about their husbands. They want to know if their marriages are doing all right and if their husbands are satisfied with them as wives. I swear there are some women friends of mine who cannot make a big decision in their family without coming to me first.

Sometimes it makes me feel like George Washington or something because you know he had a Indian chief friend who passed away and every time Washington had a great decision to make he would sit in front of the fireplace and would get messages from the Indian.[11] Now that's not in history, yet it's the honest to God truth. Don't believe it if you don't want to, but it's not a lie. Sounds silly, doesn't it?

(*Are most of the people who come to you for readings from around this area?*)
Oh, heavens no! You know I've had people from every country in the world here except two and they're right here in the United States. You probably already guessed it—Alaska and Hawaii. I've had people direct from Poland and all over—pretty exciting. About three weeks ago I had a lady here straight from the Philippines who had come to America for a vacation. Well, anyway, through certain people she heard of me and then she came to me to ask when would be the time to fly back home, and she also told me that she had found a boyfriend here and wanted to know if it would work out between them or not. The only problem is that I wish I knew more languages because that sometimes limits me from communicating with some people. That is about the only problem that ever arises though.

You know, I just remembered something else that I predicted that I'm pretty proud of. It was while the war was going on and I said that Red China and Russia would resolve friendship and everybody, and I do mean everybody, told me that I was a really crazy case. They said that there was no way that would happen but it did happen and people couldn't believe it. You know many people started believing me after that incident. Now I started saying that Japan and China are going to be allies. Now they're building up for a war and people say to me, "No way, no way." I'm afraid it's true.

(*You said that the churches wouldn't accept you?*)
Yes, under the circumstances that is true. My husband is Methodist and so are my children, but I am God's child. I attend no church because of what I have said. I have my own little church right here in my own home. I know this shouldn't be said but, one day a priest came into my home for a reading. Now imagine that! I cannot attend their churches but they can come to my house for a reading. Some future day I'm gonna build me my own church and I'm gonna let anyone on this earth come to it who wants to.

(*Do you find that some people are harder to read for than others?*)
Oh, definitely! Some people come here and their minds have a big block in them and then that makes them hard to read. I can read everyone but some are definitely harder than others. When someone has a mental block I just start talking to them about the opposite of what they're thinking and eventually the block goes away. Men are much easier to read for than women because they are much more open and aren't hiding things. I get much more women than men because they have more time than the men, but I do get a great percentage of men. They are usually concerned because their wives and them aren't communicating anymore. They also come to me about their jobs. They like to know if they'll be getting raises or promotions and things like that. It's also very funny, but most men who come to me beg me not to tell anyone they were here and not to give out their names to anyone. They are very worried about one of their friends finding out about them coming to me. Most women don't worry about that at all.

(*What do you feel about these so called fortune-tellers at carnivals and fairs?*)
Oh, that's so disgusting! Now that in the true sense is called fortune-telling. Lies, lies, lies. It angers me so much I can't stand it. Of course there are a few, and I do mean only a few, who actually are gifted, but nine out of ten aren't. They make things up and this of course worries the people. Now I'm not going to do that with anyone. If someone comes here and they're very upset I won't read for them. I'll tell them, "Well, just talk to me like a friend, have a cup of coffee and then you can go home and come back when you're not so upset."

You know there's something else that bugs me. That's when I tell somebody something and they say it another way jumbling the whole story up. Many of the people who come here write down the things I say. I have a typewriter they can use if they want to type the stuff out so they won't forget it. But one thing you have to understand is that things don't happen overnight. You have a pattern and every year that pattern changes. You don't have the same pattern constantly.

You know I have an art teacher in Chicago, a lab technician in Indianapolis, and a police woman in Washington, yes, Washington, who call me every week for decisions. They never miss a week and they really rely on me.

Now sometimes I have people who come here and they're contrary to me and I won't take them back and I tell them so. I'll tell you something that happened a few years ago which is very sad but unfortunately true. I had a lady come here who had called up and made an appointment. Well, she came over and she was one of these who said, "Oh, I'm not gonna believe a word you say." When I asked her why she even bothered to come then she answered, "Just out of curiosity, I guess." I told her that was all right. Then I told her that her husband had been having a pain, because you see I could feel the pain suddenly from my foot clear up to the side of my arm [motions to her arm].[12] I told her that he'd been having the pain for at least three months now. She said, "No, no, no, my husband has never been ill, he has no pain." I said, "All right, all right." Then I said to her, "As soon as you arrive home you're gonna get a telephone message, and on the way home you're gonna stop and purchase something which looks like a pair of shoes. She said to me, "No, no, no, I don't need no shoes and I'm not gonna get no phone call." Then I told her something that I don't usually predict because it's against my principles, but she made me so angry that I did it anyway. I knew I shouldn't have been that way, but I didn't like her so I didn't care. I told her, "In about four months or so your husband is gonna come home from work and he's gonna sit at the table in the kitchen, and you're gonna have your back to him working getting dinner ready, and you're gonna turn around and your husband's gonna be slumped over the table, and he's gonna be dead." I knew I shouldn't have told her that because it upset me terribly. She got rather angry and got up and left.

Later on that night I decided I wouldn't take any calls from anybody because I was too upset and tired. I told my husband that if anybody calls to tell them to call back later. So later on that night that same woman called me up and told my husband to tell me that on the way home she bought a pair of shoes, and that as soon as she got home she got a call from her sister in Ohio saying she was coming for a visit, and that her husband came home from work and she asked him what was the matter with him, and he said that he had a pain and that he had had it for a couple of months now. My husband relayed the message to me and asked me what it was all about. I told him it wasn't important. You see I never tell my husband anything about my customers because it's just between me and them and not my personal family life. I don't want my family to get upset too.[13] Well, anyway, I thought to myself, "Oh, dear God, now that other thing's gonna happen for sure." I felt terrible, I really did. I still knew I shouldn't have told her those things but she made me so angry because she kept contradicting everything I said. You know I even went back fifty years, yes, fifty years to tell her something she wanted to know.[14]

About five or six months later she called me up and told me that her husband had died a couple of months earlier.[15] She had told me that she wanted to come over and talk to me and I told her that I didn't think so, that it wouldn't be a very wise thing to do. Well, as far as I know she's doing pretty well these days working somewhere.

(*Do you have many teenagers come to you with their problems?*)

Many parents bring their children to me so I can help them with their problems. They're going more and more for ESP these days, which really helps. Many of them don't come here but they correspond with me. I have this one boy whom I'm working on right now who won't come to me but does correspond with me. He's from around here and I guess he has something on his mind from childhood that I can't quite get to. I'm working really hard on him right now because I guess he's in pretty serious trouble, but I don't think I should talk about that.[16]

I'll give you another example on something like this. Once I had this mother come to me telling me about her son and how she had no communication with him anymore. She said that he hardly had anything to say anymore. I said to her, "Let me have his picture and I'll try to concentrate on it." She gave me the picture and I concentrated on him every night for a week trying to get to him, and later his mother came back to me and said, "You know he's gradually been changing. He's talking more and is finally beginning to open up to me." She was so happy and it made me pretty happy too. She also said that her son said to her that he always had a feeling that somebody was watching over him trying to tell him what to do. I was trying to build something around him like a shell or something to protect him.

(*About how many people do you average a week for readings?*)

Oh, each week varies tremendously. Winters as a rule aren't usually busy, but this last winter I was swamped. The reason why is because so many men are getting laid off this spring and the wives would come here and would want to know if their husbands would be one of them. I didn't have one week last winter where I didn't have somebody each day to read for, which is really hard considering I read each person for at least two hours. I don't think I'm going to read for anybody this summer because I'm gonna study cards so I can start working with them.

Oh, I have another interesting story that happened to me soon after I moved into this house. One night I went to bed early because I wasn't feeling too well. I was restless the whole night and I couldn't understand why. Finally it was about five o'clock in the morning and I sat up in bed because I heard a noise. I couldn't believe my eyes because my father was standing at the end of the bed and he said to me, "I am departing from this world and I just wanted to tell you good-bye until we meet again." I got out of bed to go to him but he had already disappeared. This upset me the rest of the night because I didn't know what to do. When I got up the next morning I told my husband that my father had passed away last night and he asked me how I knew, and I told him that I couldn't explain it. Well, anyways, about ten o'clock that morning I got a phone call from my mom's sister saying that my father had passed away about five o'clock that morning. The funny thing is that the very same thing happened to my mother when her father died.[17]

(*Do you do any advertising at all?*)
No, because I don't need to [laughs]. I already have enough people come to me as it is. Could you imagine how many people I would get if I advertised? Besides, the people who come from advertisements are the ones who really don't believe in it, and I don't want those kind of people in my house anyways. I'm willing to help anyone who has real faith in me.

Mrs. Edna Jacobs, A Believer

Mrs. Jacobs is fifty-four years old and lives in Valparaiso. She is a native of Indiana, and is of German ancestry. She was raised as a Protestant, and completed the eighth grade. Mrs. Jacobs was worried at first, wondering how the collector obtained her name. After being told this information, Mrs. Jacobs became more friendly, and stated frequently that she firmly believed in Mrs. Weeks' abilities.

(*How did you first hear of Mrs. Weeks?*)
The first time I heard of this woman was about four years ago through a mutual friend who had went to be read by her. I didn't even want to hear about it then because I thought it was so absolutely silly and dumb. Well, a couple of years later a couple of my friends were talking about that same lady again and about how wonderful she was. I said to my friends that they were crazy and that I would prove to them how crazy it was by going to her to be read and proving her wrong. So, one of my friends made an appointment for me and I decided to go see her.

(*What was your reaction toward her?*)

Well, you see I had made up my mind even before I saw her that I wasn't going to believe her no matter what she said. As soon as I walked in the door I told her that too. She just looked at me and asked me why I was bothering to come to her and I told her because of curiosity. I think that she was slowly growing angry at me. I know now that I was being very hard to get along with and I really didn't care at the time. I was so convinced that this idea was the most far out idea I had ever heard of.

Well, after a little while we were both beginning to get a little hostile towards each other and you could tell there was anger in the air. Finally, she began to predict things for me and the results weren't very good. She told me something about buying a pair of shoes and getting an unexpected phone call. Well, naturally I told her I didn't believe her. I didn't need no dumb shoes and I wasn't gonna get no dumb phone call. Well, she talked some more and got a really serious look on her face and told me, "Soon your husband is going to come home from work and you'll be in the kitchen doing something, and you're gonna turn around and he's gonna be dead." Oh, I forgot to tell you that she said that my husband had been having a pain for a couple of months now. Well, I didn't believe her because my husband never mentioned no pain to me. Well, anyway, I got very mad. I thought that this woman had no right to say such things. Well, to get my mind off her I stopped at the store on the way home and there was shoes on sale, so I bought some, but I didn't think it had to do anything about what she said. Very simple. After I got home my sister from Ohio called me up and asked me if she could come over and visit me this weekend. I asked her why she decided to come this weekend and she said, "Well, Bill [her husband] has to work all weekend and the kids won't be home so I just thought I'd come and see you." I said that would be just fine. But you know I still didn't think much about anything that was happening. I just thought it was all a coincidence. A couple of hours later my husband came home and went to lay down before dinner. I went to ask him what was the matter and he said, "Oh, nothing. I've just got a pain that I've had a couple of months now. I must have sprained a muscle. It'll go away soon." I asked him if he wanted to go to the doctor and he said no. I didn't know what to do so I called Mrs. Weeks back up, but her husband told me she wasn't taking any calls. I told him to tell her that all those things did happen to me.

Well, the days went by and my husband was feeling much better. I began to hope that everything would work out. Well a couple of months later my husband told me that he was still feeling fine but I noticed that he never looked well anymore, and that he always looked strained and tired. Still, I put it out of my mind and convinced myself that everything would be all right. But as fate would have everything did not work as I had hoped it would [closes her eyes]. One evening he did come home from work, and I turned and the exact thing she predicted had happened. Lord only knows that I prayed to God that it wouldn't happen. Well, I called up Mrs. Weeks and told her and she said she was sorry, and I asked her if I could talk to her and she said she didn't think so. I realize now that everything could have been prevented if I had only been more concerned with the situation. I should have made my husband go to the doctor anyway, but I doubt if he would have listened to me.[18]

(*Are you ever going to go back to her again?*)
Well, I thought about it and decided against it. I'm sure she would let me but I just don't think I should. You see I can't stand to listen to things like that. I'm afraid something bad would happen again and believe me, I couldn't take that. I've had enough bad experiences for a while.

Mrs. Martha Cade, Another Believer

Mrs. Cade is another strong believer in the powers of Mrs. Weeks. She is forty-two years old and is a resident of the Valparaiso area, and was born in Illinois. She is a Methodist, and completed high school. Mrs. Cade's daughter was also present during the interview. At first Mrs. Cade was somewhat reluctant, but became more open as the interview progressed.

(*When and where did you first hear about Mrs. Weeks?*)
I first heard of her from one of my friends. She came over one day for a cup of coffee about a year ago, and she told me that she had went to a fortune teller the day before. She started telling me all these weird things this woman said were going to happen and then she told me that a couple of the things had already happened. I thought, "Oh, this is really crazy and a waste of money and time." My friend said to me, "Why don't you go to her once just for the heck of it and listen to her cause she's really interesting." I said that there was no way I was going to one of those nuts; besides my husband and kids would have thought I had really gone crazy and they would have never let me hear the end of it. Well, anyway, my friend was really bugging me to go.

Well, finally after bugging the heck out of me I told her I would go if she called up and made an appointment for me. She called and made an appointment for me for the following week. I didn't mention it again to anybody and then I told my husband about her the night before I went. He thought it was rather funny and told me to tell him if she dressed up like a gypsy and had a crystal ball. Real funny.

On the day I was supposed to go I thought, "Maybe I'll call her up and tell her I can't make it because I'm sick." You see I was chickening out.

Well, I finally decided to go just to see what it was like. I went in her house, which was very nice and quite different from what I expected. She took me in the kitchen and we had a cup of coffee and just talked for a little bit. After I was talking to her for a few minutes I wasn't embarrassed any longer. You know she was very fascinating, and before I knew it I had been talking to her for over two hours. I thought that I would stay there for about fifteen minutes and then I wouldn't be able to stand it any longer and would have to leave. It didn't work out that way though.

(Did anything she predict for you actually come true?)

As a matter of fact just about everything she said came true. When I first went in she said to me, "Well, I can tell you have three children and two of them are boys. The boys are very jealous of each other and one is away at school and the other one is at home working." I told her that this was true because my two sons, Mike and Tim, are very jealous of each other.

She told me something really big that happened too. You see I had an accident at work and hurt my back, but after a few days I felt pretty good. Well, when I went to her she said to me, "I know you've had an accident recently and this accident will be the cause of you having a big operation soon that will be out of state and will keep you out of work for a long time." I thought that this was silly but when I went back to the doctor about a month later he told me that he was going to put me in the hospital for some tests. Sure enough after I had the tests he told me that I had to go to Chicago for an operation on my back. Well, I went to the hospital and had my operation and didn't get to go home for almost three weeks. I still haven't gone back to work and I really don't think I ever will.

She told me some other things that came true also. They were just minor things but they did actually happen.

Oh, I just remembered something else she told me that was going to happen. She told me that I had a child that died when it was very young. Well, I did have a daughter that died when she was barely three days old. You know I kept looking for some kind of clue that would lead me to find out how she knew all these things about me but I couldn't find one. She couldn't have found out all this stuff about me before I came to her because she didn't know my name. She also told me that my daughter was around twelve and was a surprise arrival for us. Well, this was true also. I suppose there might be some sort of conceivable way she could have found out all this stuff but I just can't imagine what it would be.

There is one thing that she told me that there was no way on earth she could have found out about though. She told me that before I was married I had always wanted to be a clothes buyer. Well, before I got married I was applying for jobs as a clothes buyer, but after I got married I gave it up. Like I said before there is no way she could have known that.

She told me a few things that never did happen but her percentages were far better on the things that did happen. She told me that there would be a divorce in my family but as far as I know there hasn't been one yet. She also told me that someone very dear would be dying in my family, but I can only pray that doesn't happen. She also told me that my husband would be getting a promotion and I sure wouldn't mind if that happened. Now those kind of things I don't mind listening to. Who wouldn't?

(*How exactly did she read for you?*)
Well, I've heard that she has read some people's hands but she didn't read mine. The way she read me was quite interesting. We would just sit there and talk about any odd thing and then out of the clear blue sky she would say to me a prediction or something from my past.

Oh, she was so dramatic, she acts things out. I mean if you have a pain she actually gets the pain too. She told me the last time I was there that she was going to start reading cards soon. I would still prefer the way she does it now because it seems more real. With the cards it would seem less fascinating because I just love to watch her reactions when she gets a feeling now. Besides, I don't see how anybody could really find anything out just by using cards.

(*Are you going to consider going back to her for another reading?*)
Oh, I definitely think I'll go back to her sometime later on during the year. I really enjoy listening to her. You know, if I had never gone to a fortune-teller before and someone told me that they went to one and actually believed in her I would have told them to go see a psychiatrist instead of a fortune-teller. But I guess I can't say this anymore, can I? How can you not help but believe in someone who has made unbelievable predictions about you that have really come true? I just don't know what to say, I really don't. I guess I would have to say that as long as I don't find out a way that she is faking or finding out things before seeing me then I really have to believe in her, right? I know it's crazy, but what else can you say? She's helped me a lot, she really has.

Mrs. Myra Williams, A Third Believer

Mrs. Williams was amused that she had been selected as a subject to be interviewed. She was very co-operative, and indicated that she believed very strongly in persons' abilities to foretell the future. Mrs. Williams lives in Valparaiso, is forty-eight years old, and was born in Georgia. She is a Baptist, and she completed high school. She seemed delighted to have been interviewed.

(*How did you first find out about Mrs. Weeks?*)
Well, you have to understand that I don't want to give out any names of the person who told me about the woman but she's a friend of

my sister-in-law's. My sister-in-law is a great believer in this sort of stuff so she talked me into going to this woman one day. I went to her with no opinion at all. I didn't think it was stupid or crazy, but then again, I really didn't believe in it either. I wanted my sister-in-law to go with me but she said that this woman demands that you come alone. She doesn't like to have an audience other than herself and you. I guess that's maybe so she can think better or something. This was about two years ago the first time I went to her. I've been to her three times since that.

Well, the first time I went to her she only made a few predictions and only one of them came true. I guess everyone is entitled to mistakes though. The second time I went to her she made about four or five predictions and three of them I know actually happened. None of the predictions were very important except for one. She told me that my son, who was nineteen at the time, would be getting married within the next year. I told her that I didn't think this would happen since he wasn't dating anyone at the time. Well, within the next couple of months he met this girl at work and soon they were announcing that they wanted to get married. I'd say she made a pretty good prediction there.

Since then I've went to her two more times and again most of her predictions have come true. She told me that I would be a grandmother by last summer, and believe it or not my son's wife had a baby girl at the end of July. Now some people might say that is really just a coincidence but you know that is very improbable. I don't think any guess could be quite that accurate. Oh, I forgot to tell you she told me that the baby would be born in the middle of the summer, probably in June or July, and it was born in July. The last time I went to her was just a couple of weeks ago and she told me that I would be a grandmother again by the summer of 1975, and as far as I know my son has no plans on having any more children.

Oh, by the way in case you're wondering, I didn't tell my son or his wife any of this. I'm afraid if I tell them what she said they just might have a child just to prove that she was right. I'd rather just be the only one to know; that way if it really does happen I'll know the prediction really came true. I didn't tell my son about what she said about him getting married either. I also didn't tell him about what she said about me becoming a grandmother the first time around either. Like I said I want to make sure that it all comes true by itself. It's kind of neat to know about these kind of things before they really happen. I wish she could tell me if they would be boys or girls though.

(*Do you believe in her?*)

Yes, I really do. I really do think she knows what she's talking about. At first my husband thought it was ridiculous but the last couple of times he has showed great interest in what she has said. Even my son doesn't think it's as ridiculous as he first thought it was. He can't really afford to, considering everything she's predicted about him has come true. I plan on going back to her again simply because I don't see any reason not to. I'm not no crazy old woman who believes in magic or nothing like that, but I don't see any reason why I shouldn't believe in her, and that's all I can say.

Mrs. Sarah Brock, The Skeptic

I was referred to Mrs. Brock by Mrs. Williams. Mrs. Brock was extremely reluctant to speak about Mrs. Weeks. Mrs. Brock is thirty-seven years old and was born in Chicago. She was raised as a Lutheran, and completed one year of college. She was extremely skeptical of me as well as of Mrs. Weeks' ability to predict the future. She made me prove that I was a student at Indiana University before she would consent to the interview.

(*Where did you first hear of Mrs. Weeks?*)
One of my friends, Myra Williams, who gave you my name, told me about her just this last summer. I also heard about her from a few of my other friends since then.

(*What was your first reaction about her?*)
Well, naturally when you hear something like that you automatically think, "Wow, that woman's crazy." I thought here was another woman just trying to make an extra buck. The thing that really shocked me is that people actually are believers in her. I couldn't believe people could actually believe in things like that—you know, a nineteenth century sort of thing. I guess things like that really happen though.

(*Have you ever been read by her?*)
No, not really. Several of my friends have and they tell me she's very good—doesn't act phony. They all pretty much believe in her and many of them have proof of instances where she has been very accurate in her forecasting. Sometimes it really does make me wonder if maybe she is for real after all.

(*Do you believe in her now?*)
You know I really doubt if I could *truly* believe in that sort of thing, though I'm not saying she is a fake. Maybe she has helped a lot of people and maybe she has been right about several things, but I just can't get used to something like that. Maybe I'm just scared about something like that, I don't know.

(*Would you ever consider letting her read to you?*)
Well, I've thought about it and I've decided against it. For one thing,
I see no reason to do it. I don't need that sort of thing right now. Maybe
when I'm older with nothing else to do.

(*What do you think of your friends letting her read for them?*)
I really don't care one way or another. Many of my friends think
that she has really helped them, so in that aspect maybe it is worth it. I
can't really see anything wrong with it as long as you don't become totally
dependent on her. I guess if that's the sort of thing you like then all I can
say is more power to you .

In the preceding interviews, we find a woman who claims the ability
to predict the future, three women who strongly believe in her powers,
and a fourth woman who seems to be somewhat skeptical. Through
personal experience with Mrs. Weeks, the believers have chosen to accept
her claim that she is gifted. Of particular interest is the conversion of Mrs.
Jacobs, from disbelief to full acceptance, since both Mrs. Weeks *and* Mrs.
Jacobs relate the incident.

It is certainly clear that some of Mrs Weeks' accurate predictions
could have been coincidental or simply lucky guesses. However, as the
informants themselves have stated, many of the things which Mrs. Weeks
told them were things which she could not have known by any normal
means.

NOTES

1. This article was originally turned in as an undergraduate term
paper in F391, Folklore of Indiana, at Indiana University. Notes have been
added by the editor.

2. For further information concerning seers, see Ruth Montgomery,
A Gift of Prophecy, The Phenomenal Jeane Dixon (New York, 1965);
Thomas Sugrue, *There Is a River, The Story of Edgar Cayce* (New York,
1942) (Cayce was a famous early twentieth century seer); William A.
Owens, "Seer of Corsicana," *Publications of the Texas Folklore Society* 29

(1959); and Gopalan V. Gopalan and Bruce Nickerson, "Faith Healing in Indiana and Illinois," *IF*, 6, 1 (1973), 33-99, especially 55-68.

3. In order to protect the privacy of the persons who were interviewed for this project, all names which have been included are pseudonyms.

4. Related to motif D1649.1, Magic object keeps falling down.

5. Related to motifs D1812.0.1, Foreknowledge of hour of death; D1812.3.3.11, Dream gives advance notice that another person has died; E545.3, Dead announce own death; and E723.4.4, Wraith of dying woman goes to see children for last time before death.

6. ESP, or Extrasensory Perception, refers to abilities which some persons are supposed to have which enable them to do things which most persons are not able to do, such as foretelling the future (clairvoyance) or moving objects without touching them (telekinesis).

7. Sources containing more information on the treatment of women accused of being witches in Salem, Massachusetts, include Marion L. Starkey, *The Devil in Massachuestts, A Modern Enquiry into the Salem Witch Trials* (New York, 1949), and George Lyman Kittredge, *Witchcraft in Old and New England* (New York, 1956), especially the chapter "Witchcraft and the Puritans," 329ff. Kittredge also includes another useful chapter related to the present study, entitled "The Seer," 226ff.

8. By "readings" Mrs. Weeks is referring to sessions in which persons come to her in order for her to give them advice, reveal their futures and so forth.

9. Ruth Montgomery, in chapter one of *A Gift of Prophecy,* tells the story behind Jeane Dixon's prediction of John F. Kennedy's assassination; it is amazingly similar to that of Mrs. Weeks.

10. The Watergate Affair was a scandal which began in 1972 when a group of men broke into the Democratic Party national campaign headquarters in the Watergate building in Washington, D.C., apparently attempting to obtain information to help the Republican Party in its 1972 campaigns. The affair resulted in the resignation of President Richard M. Nixon, in August, 1974 (just prior to the initiation of impeachment proceedings against him), and has, as of yet, not been completely resolved.

11. We have not been able to verify Mrs. Weeks' statement concerning Washington's Indian counselor; however, according to the thesis of the Spiritualist Church, everyone has an Indian spirit guide.

12. This is related to motif D1500.3.1.1, "Saint causes pain of sick man to be transferred to himself."

13. It is interesting to note that Mrs. Weeks, like doctors and lawyers, has a set of ethics underlying her practice. Consultations with her clients are kept confidential.

14. The revelation of the past by a seer is a traditional means of gaining a person's belief (and respect). According to Basil Ivan Rakoczi, in

"Divination," printed in *Man, Myth, and Magic* II (New York, 1970), 652-60, divination "is primarily concerned with the future, but it sometimes necessitates a turning backward of the vision in order to learn from the forgotten past."

15. Related to motif D1812.0.1, Foreknowledge of hour of death. Also present are motif M341, Death prophesied, and the related motifs following it in the *Motif-Index*, particularly M341.1, Prophecy: death at (before, within) certain time; M341.1.2.3, Prophecy: death within two months; and M341.1.5, Prophecy: death within certain period.

16. See note 13, above.

17. Related to motifs D1812.3.3.11, Dream gives advance notice that another person has died; E545.3, Dead announce own death; and E723.4.4, Wraith of dying woman goes to see children for last time before death.

18. Mrs. Jacobs, interestingly, is here relating precisely the same predictions and their outcomes which Mrs. Weeks mentions above. Both Mrs. Jacobs' and Mrs. Weeks' accounts of the events coincide exactly.

IV Horror Stories

The Hatchet Man

Sylvia Grider

Considering its long standing and not altogether unmerited reputation as the "party dorm" of Indiana University, it is not surprising that McNutt Quadrangle has become the repository of a fairly stable core of urban, collegiate legends, among them "The Roommate's Death" or, as it is commonly known at McNutt, "The Hatchet Man." The following text is an interesting variant from which to begin our consideration of what has become the standard McNutt legend:

The Legend of the Roommate's Death

A1

It happened over a vacation, Thanksgiving, I think. Two girls stayed in the dorm by theirselves. At the time a sex maniac was supposed to be loose, raping girls. The two girls were told to stay in their rooms and not to let anyone in. Well, one girl decided she wanted to go out. She told her roommate that she would be back in a little while. She said she was taking her key and told her roommate not to let anyone in. Well, her roommate was going to wait for her friend to return, but it was late and she fell asleep. The next day there was knocking on the door. It was some policemen. They told her they had found a girl outside the door—dead. Supposedly, when the girl was coming home she saw something that frightened her very much. She was so scared that when she got at the dorm

147

all she could do was scratch on the door. Her fingers were all bloody and down to the bone. She died of fright. This was supposed to have happened at McNutt here at Indiana University. Now, during vacation, all girls staying on campus have to stay in one dorm.

IUFA: 1969 Collected by Debbie Sumerlot from Debbi Crissinger, both students at I.U.

The etiological nature of this story is no longer applicable because, as of the 1972-73 school year, girls are allowed to stay in their own dormitory rooms during Thanksgiving and spring break instead of all moving into one dorm during the holiday. Girls who are afraid to be alone in the buildings can, however, make arrangements to move into the other dormitories temporarily.

This variant is unusual in that it leaves out the violent murder of the girl, the most popular element of the story, and has her die of fright instead. IUFA 1967 and 1968 both have similar modified endings. In nearly all other recorded versions of this legend, the main element of shock is the girl inside awakening the next morning to find that her roommate has been brutally butchered, decapitated, or stabbed. The following text of a stabbing murder is representative of this motif of the story:

A2

The story I heard was there were two girls staying on campus over the Christmas vacation. They were going to be all alone in the dorm. At the same time, numerous murders were occurring. The girls were told to stay in their rooms and keep the doors locked. They decided they wanted to go to this fraternity party. Between the dorm and the fraternity there was a wooded area. After the girls got to the party one of them got scared and decided to go home. She left for the dorm. The other girl was afraid something would happen to her friend, so she decided to leave. The first girl heard heavy breathing right behind her, when she was walking home.

She started running as fast as she could. As soon as she got home she locked her door. She waited up for her roommate to return, but fell asleep. The next morning she was going down to fix breakfast and her roommate was lying in the hallway. Her hands were all bloody and she was dead from a slit throat. Apparently when she left to follow her roommate the murderer had seen her. She couldn't yell because of her throat, all she could do was scratch on the door.

IUFA: 1970 Collected by Debbie Summerlot from Susi Gadjwerisc, a student at Purdue.

S1118.2 Murder by cutting throat.

Stories such as this are widely reported from dormitories and sorority houses throughout the I. U. campuses and, furthermore, all over the country.[1] The legend took a peculiar form as it was told among one group of girls living in McNutt Quadrangle during the 1971/72 school year and on into the following fall.[2]

McNutt Quadrangle, named after the influential and popular Indiana governor, Paul V. McNutt, was formally opened in 1963. It houses close to 1,350 students and staff, thus making it the largest of the eleven residence halls on the I. U. Bloomington campus. The dormitory has been co-ed from its very beginning, housing boys in the north building and girls in the south building, with both groups sharing the dining hall and central administration building. In the fall of 1972, the co-ed policy was liberalized to the extent that boys and girls shared both buildings but lived on separate floors.

It is difficult to pinpoint exactly when, or even how, McNutt gained its now almost universal campus reputation as the "party dorm"; but, apparently, this developed after 1968, when McNutt and the other campus residence halls gained open-visitation rights. "O. V." generally means that boys and girls can visit in one another's rooms during designated hours. Panty raids and impromptu pep rallies traditionally start at McNutt too. Because of the great number of athletes housed there, many students also refer to McNutt as the "Jock Quad." Such nicknames accrue to college dormitories across the country. College students capitalize on and isolate what is to them the most distinctive feature of a housing unit, not necessarily intending to be slanderous or pejorative, in much the same manner that the *blason populaire* emphasizes a folk characteristic from a racial or ethnic stereotype.[3] Other examples of this tendency on the I. U. campus are the designation of the high-rise unit for married housing, Tulip Tree Apartments, as the "Fertile Crescent"; Forest Quadrangle, the only all-women's unit remaining on campus as the "Virgin Forest"; or the dormitory for graduate students, Eigenmann, as the "Zoo" or "Animal Farm." Dormitories are not the only structures to which students have attached nicknames. The new and unpopular Metz Carillon, for example, is rapidly becoming known among some people as "Hell's Bells" and the impressive Indiana University Musical Arts Center, I. U. M. A. C., has already been metamorphosed into "Big Mac."

McNutt was the topic of a feature article in *Life* magazine in 1967[4] and there is a persistent but unfounded rumor that McNutt was "once" cited in *Playboy* as one of the best dorms for partying in the country, "partying" being taken in the sense of drinking and sexual activity. Although *Playboy* has done such campus surveys of "where the action is and where it isn't," I. U. and, certainly, McNutt have never been mentioned.

The popular legend-cycle of urban ghost-stories or scary stories easily fits into almost any dormitory situation, but the cycle has stayed reasonably stable at McNutt. "The Hook," "The Boyfriend's Death," "The Killer in the Back Seat," "The Mysterious Hitchhiker," and "The Fatal Fraternity Initiation," as well as many others, are regularly reported there. There is initially strong peer-pressure exerted on incoming students to get into the swing and activity of college life, whatever nebulous concept that may entail. One way to most effectively accomplish this is to get acquainted with the other residents as quickly as possible. This get-acquainted period is especially critical at McNutt because of its size and extremely high turnover rate; usually around 60% or more of the residents each year are incoming freshmen. Rumors of the infamous parties, which may or may not actually take place, increase the pressure.

Another obstacle to the dynamic of the getting-acquainted process is the layout of the room arrangement on the individual floors of the dorm. The narrow corridors and isolated rooms make it difficult for people at one end of the hall to come in contact with those at the other end.[5] Therefore, situations which attract groups from all over the floor to one particular room or area of the hall become an integral part of the group dynamic which determines how well the residents on a particular floor get to know each other and work together throughout the rest of the school year.

Among girls, the two most common informal means of getting acquainted with other girls are these: on a one-to-one basis individuals first inquire where others are from and then proceed to ask, "Do you know (person's name)?" This quickly establishes acquaintances in common and, from there on, entrée for longer and more specific conversations and inquiries. The next step in the process is for a group of girls who have met superficially in this manner to get together, almost invariably late at night, just to talk. Such group conversations among new friends lead to descriptions of what they have heard about college life, expressions of fear and apprehension about their college futures, and then, finally, to the almost universal opener, "Did you hear the story about . . .," the contact form generally employed to introduce the telling of the first scary story as though it were true. The tensions and fears derived from the newness of the situation of being in the dorm and, often, away from home for the first time are released in the screaming and giggling which ensues and mutual support is drawn from this new group of friends sharing and releasing the same emotions.

Such precisely was the situation surrounding the advent of the Hatchet Man on DeJoya III, a predominantly freshman floor at McNutt. In the fall of 1971, all but one of the fifty-six girls on this newly-formed academic unit were new to I. U. Most of them were from Indiana but only a few of the girls had known one another in high school. The "Do you know . . .?" ploy was the primary vehicle for establishing preliminary acquaintances and as early as registration week the girls were gathering in rooms late at night to exchange gossipy experiences and relieve their boredom. These storytelling groups usually consisted of from six to eight girls at a time who seated themselves on the floor around a lighted candle and dramatically told these urban legends, as well as recapitulations of plots of scary novels and TV programs, such as Rod Serling's *Night Gallery*. "The Roommate's Death" and "The Baby Sitter and the Killer Upstairs" became the most popularly retold and appreciated stories. The girls could identify with their protagonists most readily because nearly all of them had baby-sat at one time or another; furthermore, all were presently in a large dormitory, and on the top floor at that. A good example of the baby-sitter story is this version:

The Legend of the Baby Sitter and the Killer Upstairs

B

This is a story about a baby sitter and a terrifying experience that she had. There was a young girl about high school age who went to baby-sit one evening. She arrived at the house early in the evening so that she had to cook dinner for the children, play with them a little bit, and then later on, about 7:30, she put them to bed. So she went downstairs and was just sitting around reading and watching television and the telephone rang. And she went to answer it and there was this male voice on the other end saying, "At 10:30 I'm going to kill the children and then I'm going to come after you." And the girl thought it was a crank call and she was a little scared but she just put it off as a joke that someone was playing on her and she hung up. About half an hour later the phone rang again. And the same male voice said, "At 10:30 I'm going to come in and I'm going to kill the children and then I'm coming after you."

At this point the girl was getting a little more scared because she thought the man might be, you know, a maniac and might actually come and do something. But she decided that she would still go on and just sit around and wait. And she thought about going upstairs and looking in on the children because she hadn't been up there for awhile but she decided against it, just . . . she didn't think anything was wrong. And the third time, about half an hour later, the telephone rang. And this male voice said, "It's getting closer to the time and I'm going to come after the children and I'm going to get you too."

And at this point the girl got very upset and she decided that she would call the police. And she called the operator and told her the story of what had happened and the operator said, "All right, you know, we'll take care of it if he calls back again just keep him on the line and we'll put a tracer on it."

And the girl sat around; she was very nervous but decided that it was the best thing that she could do. Pretty soon the phone rang again. She ran to answer it. And it was the man. She tried to talk to him a little bit more and tried to get some information out of him but all that he would say was, "I'm going to come in at 10:30 and I'm going to kill the children and then I'm coming after you." And the girl hung up the phone and was just terrified but could do nothing but just sit and wait. And the phone rang again. And she answered it and the operator was on the other end and she said, "Get out of the house immediately; don't go upstairs; don't do anything; just you leave the house. When you get out there, there will be policemen outside and they'll take care of it."

The girl was just really petrified and she thought she should check the children or something but decided that if the operator told her to get out she should get out. So she went outside and when she got out there she was talking to the policemen and they told her that when they traced the call it was made on the extension from the upstairs line and that the whole time the man was talking to her he had been in the house and that he had already murdered both the children who were found torn to bits in the bedroom. Had she waited any longer she would have gotten it too.

Collected by Sylvia Grider from Melissa Warner, 21 February 1973. Melissa was a resident of DeJoya III and told this story many times while living there.
S 139.2 Slain person dismembered.

These legend-telling sessions lasted over a period of several nights and involved at one time or another some fifteen to twenty residents of the floor, including the Resident Assistant as a spectator. These girls were one of the first groups on the floor to become really well acquainted. One of them became the most active tradition-bearer who ultimately carried the story over to the incoming residents of the floor the following fall.

The contrived, intentionally scary legend-telling sessions lost their primary function as soon as the girls had become well acquainted. Then they began to use them to try to "initiate" or scare for fun new participants in the sessions. They came to an abrupt end as the result of an elaborate hoax which terrified one of the girls who had been part of the initial group from the very beginning. The following complete taletelling session, ensuing discussion, and interpretation of that whole episode *post facto* was recorded from the girls involved by Julia Brooks, a Folklore graduate student, on the night of 16 November 1971. The session started with this fully developed narrative of "The Roommate's Death" because the girls had been told earlier that this story was of the most interest to the collector:

Informant #1: O. K. This was a small college and at Christmas and Thanksgiving vacation, ah, everybody goes home except these two girls who happened to live clear across the United States. And they don't wanta go home, so they're gonna stay in the dorm. And since everybody's gone they move in together, into the same room, and it's very lonely up there. But they're friends, and they're gonna stay and have a good time with each other. One girl goes out and the other girl is in the room alone, you know, and she's spending the evening there. And she's catching up on her term papers, and she, ah, you know, goes to sleep. She thinks this other girl's on a date or something. It's night and she hears these noises outside, you know, like very vague noises—a struggle, or like somebody moving in the hall. And she isn't really sure what's happening, so she doesn't bother. She's a very calm person. And so, pretty soon it gets louder and the door is being pounded on. She's going crazy because she doesn't know what's going on. And it's just the loneliness; there's nobody there who can help her. And so she stays in there, you know, and it pounds again. And she's not gonna open it up because she doesn't know who's gonna be there. And she hears this scratching noise and just a raking and scratching and a little more pounding; not much, and it's getting weaker, and then scratching and scratching. And she's just sitting there, listening to it. And ah, ah, she just prays for it to go away, go away. And she didn't call anybody or anything because there's nobody to call. So she just stays there and finally she falls asleep from exhaustion. She tires herself out completely, ah, sitting up in bed. She realizes when she wakes up she has fallen asleep; it's nearly morning again. And she doesn't know what to do. She's afraid to open the door; she's afraid to do anything. So she opens her window and looks out. And so she watches for awhile and pretty soon a custodian walks by. And she yells at him, gets him to come up there. And he opens the door and shows her. And its her roommate, and *she has a hatchet buried in her head!*

Informant #2: Blaaach!!

Informant #1: And her fingernails are just—they're just worn to the bone because she was scratching to get in.

Informant #2: Uhhhhh . . . .

Informant #1: And the blood that has come from her head wound . . . there's tracks where a man had been standing there. Standing there waiting for her, the roommate, to open the door to see what was there, and to get her too. And the tracks just lead off and get fainter and so that he's gone.

Informant #3: Did you say that was true?

Informant #1: Yes, I think it is, it happened at Hanover.

Informant #2: Oh no, I don't believe that story.

Informant #1: At Hanover, it's in Ohio, on the Ohio River. I know this one is true because the guy it happened to was my teacher. He was parking with a girl; he's a real Romeo. And he was out parking in the country with a girl, you know, in college. And he was making out with her, and really going to it, you know, and then a car drives up behind him. He thought nothing of it because, you know, who cares? And this car didn't go on by or didn't do anything. It just kinda sat there in back of them and kept its lights on. And pretty soon they thought, "Well, this is strange; what are they doing?' And so, finally, the car drove up beside them and said, 'Pull up and follow us.' Well, this is strange, you know, but they put their clothes back on, ah, got arranged, drove off, and they followed right behind this car for awhile and finally the car signalled a stop. They put the lights on and came back and told them that they came along and this man was on top of their hood, waiting there. And it was very . . . you could see . . . tell that this man was deranged, because, just because of his attitude and the way he was, ah, acting. Not too many people would be sitting on top of your car.

Informant #4: How did he get there without them knowing it?

Informant #1: Have you ever been out parking? [laughter]

Informant #4: Did the man leave when the car started up?

Informant #1: Yeah, well, see, this other car stopped back there but they didn't want to rush him into anything, you know, or make him do something drastic. They just stayed there in case he did do something . . . in case they needed help. And, finally, the man saw them, and went away, and they didn't know for sure; they couldn't see if he was just standing in the woods or whether he was still threatening them. So that's why they said to drive on. Ah, they didn't want to scare the . . . either . . . too much.

Informant #2: Gosh.

Informant #1: The first time I heard that story about the Hatchet Man was at Purdue. I was in Purdue at a summer clinic, so just half the dorm was being used. The building was in eight parts, attached underground in the basement, and you had to go a long way through the basement from our section to get to the vending machines. And it was late one night and we were starved. There were three of us, and we went on down, past the furnace room and empty places that seemed to echo. And we kept to a walk because we knew if we started to run we'd get scared and go back without any food. We were the only brave ones and we had to get food for everybody else. So we went on and got the food and we were coming back, you know, and we heard some noises, real noises, you know? And we ran all the way back up the stairs. Later we realized it was just our imaginations, probably, but we were very nervous. Later on that night someone told the story and none of us could sleep much after that.

Informant #4: I don't want to believe the stories but I'm afraid not to.

Informant #2: Yeah, just look at all the strange things that happen all over all the time, like in Ann Arbor. Those people being chopped up all over the place. And how about the "Clam Story," you know?

Informant #1: Oh, the Clam Man. It's supposed to be a true story too. The people that told it were telling about the actual place and you find evidences. It's down off the Wabash in Lafayette and, ah, there's a camp down there. Anyway, deep in the woods, and you have camping in tents. Well, it seems that the two directors of the camp had been hearing complaints from the people about a man, not connected with the camp, just moseying around the facilities, not the major areas, you know, where the dining halls were, but the trails. And they'd go out overnight and such, and everybody was free to wander and they began to wonder who he was. So they decide maybe it was someone just squatting, or just kinda living there. They also found a lot of clam shells and a little fireplace like. So they started to say, 'Well, the Clam Man's been here tonight', and bring up the story. Then they thought, 'Well, this is silly, you know, to make up a story about it. Let's go see if he really is around here'. So they took a boat down the Wabash and they weren't really trying to find him you know, just discovering all the backwaters and eddies. Then they came up to this pretty-hidden backwater, stagnant, you know, like nobody had ever been there. They turned in, and they heard dogs. Three scrawny dogs came running out, barking at them. And they don't know what's gonna happen. They saw a little shack, not a shack but just an old lean-to, more or less, and some logs, a sort of pier with an old boat tied to it. They paddle up there and this shaggy old man comes out of the lean-to and tells them where to go, fast. And they go and fast! And he is there, a hermit that lives there, the Clam Man.

[Finally, the conversation shifted to the description of how this group had contrived the actual scaring episode which had resulted in the hysterics of Informant #2 a few weeks earlier.]

Informant #3: I got Carole so scared. She was on this ghost kick. This is how it all got started. We decided my room had ghosts, for some reason, because of the way my room is placed. There's that overhead duct and I get noises from the floors below and things like that. And when I sit at my desk you can hear when someone uses the phone right below us. You can hear them pick up the phone, dial the number, and you can hear their side of the conversation. And it's really kind of eerie. If the phone box is open and the windows and door are open, the breeze coming through there makes my room perpetually cold. [Informants #2 and #3 live next door with a connecting, shared telephone box.]

Informant #2: Yeah, and I could feel that breeze with the door shut and I could hear drawers banging around. I'm not insane. I mean I can hear noises in there.

Informant #3: Ha, ha. She can hear all these noises. She was positive there was a ghost, absolutely positive. And she started telling me this. I do not believe in ghosts. But she had me convinced and I started thinking about it. I'd just broken up with this guy and I thought, 'Wonder if he's killed himself and he's coming back to kill me?' [general laughter] I was really shook up. One night I got really frightened so I hit back at Carole. She had a friend who's a ghost hunter, or something like that. Ha, ha, ha. Anyway, he came and looked over my room and Carole wasn't there. When she came back we had this story cooked up—he had contacted the ghosts in the other world and originally, many, many years ago, on this exact spot at McNutt, there was this old house, an old farmhouse. And there'd been a fire and three girls were trapped in the upper room of this old house. And they were burned to death. And there's ghosts, their ghosts, in my room because my room was the upper corner in this building. And eventually, like, these girls, what they were trying to do, they were trying to get in touch with this world so that they could get, you know, passed on to the . . . you know . . . the afterworld. Because their spirits were caught here on earth so fast, that what they needed to do was recreate the scene or something like that, so their spirits could go on. And from then on they would be doing things to get in touch with me, you know, like banging on the door, and making telephone calls, and things like that. Now we're all frightened at that, at least Carole is frightened. I'm pretending to be scared. He said things would happen, like glasses, ah, would fly around the room.

Informant #2: He never said that would happen.

Informant #3: Didn't he say things would fly around the room?

Informant #2: No, he said pictures would fall off the walls.

Informant #3: Well, I had a picture that fell off the wall that day and I turned a table the other way so the lamp was turned around and Carole suddenly realized that the lamp was turned the other way and I claimed I hadn't touched it. So after he left Carole was scared half to death. She's laying in here in bed and she's been talking to me a few minutes before and I'd gotten a glass of water to make some coffee and I'd set it on top of my dresser. I said, "I'm gonna study for awhile and don't you worry now, I'm right here." I waited for awhile and she was relaxed and I cautiously got up, poured the water from the glass down the wall, and pitched the glass against the wall. It just shattered! And I yelled, "Carole!" at the same time. She leaps out of bed, starts banging on the door, screaming, "Let me out, they've come, they've come, oh help, help!"

Informant #2: I didn't do that bad, now hush. I've got a good story, about that frat man, remember? It's real scary at the end.

There was this young fraternity man on a train and he was really a fraternity buff. He'd researched, he really was nuts, he'd reseached all the fraternities, and he knew everything about the history of all of them, every one that had ever existed. Well, he saw this old man sitting across the aisle from him. He was wearing a fraternity pin that he'd never seen before, never heard of the fraternity, and he couldn't understand how he'd let one slip by him. So he says, 'Ah, excuse me, sir, but I've never heard of that fraternity before. Is it still in existence? I wonder why I never heard of it?' And he said, 'No, it's not in existence anymore'. And the young man asked him why, and he answered that it was a long story. The young man said, 'Well, I've got plenty of time'. So he said, 'Well sit down and I'll tell you'. So he told him this story:

This was a really big fraternity. We were in a small college, and it was the best on campus. It was really great. We were especially famous for our initiation ceremonies where we'd take young pledges out to this old haunted house pretty close to campus and make them go up one by one to the second floor, without a light except a candle. And they were the only persons in the house. All the rest of us would be out in front. So, ah, we sent the first fellow up; he got to the second floor. We saw him go up there and then we saw the candle go out and then nothing else. So we sent the second guy up. We thought he was just pulling a joke on us. These pledges get kinda feisty at times. Well, his candle went out too. And we didn't hear anything out of him. We still thought it was a joke, we thought they'd planned it. We sent the third guy up and the same thing happened. So we began to think something strange was going on, so we took some flashlights and went in the house and searched it from top to bottom; couldn't find a thing. There wasn't a trace of them anywhere until we were going out. And we saw this closet all boarded up and they were all in there, dead. Well, our first reaction was to try to hide it, but of course that was impossible. There was no way we could hide that. It caused a pretty big furor on campus, and they made us disband the fraternity. The really bizarre part of the story is that every man who belonged to this fraternity has either died under really strange circumstances or has gone crazy. And since I'm not dead, ROWERRRRRR!!!

[At the climax to the above story the narrator screamed or snarled and lunged at the audience, and although they had heard the story before, they all, including the graduate-student collector, screamed, thus ending the storytelling session in a burst of embarrassed giggles. After the laughter had subsided, Informant #2 made this concluding remark]:

Informant #2: Did you hear that Jeane Dixon predicted there would be hatchet murders on the I. U. campus this year? Well, I heard it's been predicted for the last six or seven years and they use it when they want to scare somebody to death. This year they got me!! Ha, ha, ha.

[At this point the telephone rang, Informant #3 answered and called, "For you Carole, Hatchet Man." That was the end of this session.]

Analysis of the Legend-Telling Session

The above extended transcription is important because it incorporates all the features of the typical legend-telling session, if there is such a thing, among college girls: dramatic emphasis, audience reaction and participation, stories interspersed with conversation, flowing transition from story to story, and definite closure of the session. Although this particular episode was in part contrived because the girls had been called together for the specific purpose of relating the stories so that the collector could record them, they almost immediately forgot about the tape recorder and the artificial session and the tales became "real." It is especially significant that throughout the evening, it was Informant #2, the girl who was frightened by the glass-throwing episode, who responded most to the stories, although she had heard them all many times before. She also turned attention away from herself by telling her favorite story, "The Fatal Fraternity Initiation." Of further interest is the fact that Informant #2's fright did not directly involve any of the features of the story of "The Roommate's Death." Finally, the girls never told the story as though it had actually happened at McNutt. In the above version, as well as others in the Folklore Archives, Hanover College is mentioned as the site of the murder,[6] possibly because of Hanover's proximity to Cragmont Hospital, from which it is implied that the lunatic has escaped.

The story was initially told as an integral part of the whole cycle of scary stories but because the unknown protagonist, the Hatchet Man, was more easily personified than of the characters in the other legends, he developed an existence independent of the actual narrative. The motif of murder by burying a hatchet in the girl's head (S 139.2) is especially persistent and has given rise to the whole series of later changes in the function of the story as well as the transformation of the name of the story from "The Roommate's Death" to "The Hatchet Man." In an article on esthetic response to folklore items, Robert J. Smith chose as his example an abstract of the Hatchet Man narrative which he called "The Scratching on the Door" and discussed the phenomenon of this change in focus by pointing out that, ". . . the greater part of the response to a folklore genre that contains a cognitive element is directed not toward the performer but toward the referent of the performance. The referent, of course, is not present, and overt expressions of feeling toward it are not necessarily made."[7] The referent is the Hatchet Man himself.

The actual terrifying of one of the girls forced the temporary reduction of the narrative to the status of a joke based on shared experience and understanding and thus reduced the impact of her brief hysteria. The fact that the Hatchet Man was not actually the character who frightened her indicates how easily such motifs shift from their original narrative context. Such transformations and shifting is not at all uncommon, for as Linda Dégh states, "The legend of 'The Roommate's Death' and its kin is a complex that varies, blends and merges to generate new forms. Its constituent elements are violence and horror, and the natural concern of man for the tragic face of life, all satisfied and inspired by daily news and crime fiction prevalent in our modern society. Horror though is pacified by humor; rendered harmless as it is used as a practical joke."[8]

The process by which the anecdote of the Jeanne Dixon prediction that a certain number of girls would be beheaded or similarly murdered at some particular college and the narrative of "The Roommate's Death" became associated is also fairly clear when one considers their point of similarity, the murder by butchering of girls in a college dormitory. The longer narrative and the Jeanne Dixon anecdote serve as justification, substantiation, or reinforcement of one another, apparently regardless of which one is told first.

The name Hatchet Man *per se,* but not the full narrative, became a catchword, even a motto, and eventually a mascot for a large number of girls on the floor. Those who had not heard the full narrative were told an abbreviated summary of it by way of explanation of what had really happened the night they heard all the screaming. There was even talk of having special T-shirts made up with a bloody hatchet as the design but this never materialized. Admonitions from the Resident Assistant regarding procedures for reporting obscene or threatening telephone calls often elicited the response, "Oh, it's just the Hatchet Man." Instead of knocking, for awhile, the girls scratched on one another's doors before entering. The epithet shifted form again during this process when the girls began leaving humorously threatening notes on one another's doors, as well as in the community bathroom, dealing with the possible future exploits of their mascot. In dormitories it is common for the room doors to serve as message centers and bulletin boards to display items of interest to the residents within. These various notes about the Hatchet Man have a general Big-Brother-is-watching-you quality. Placed chronologically, this random sampling of the notes emphasizes a progressive personification and positive attitude toward the character of the Hatchet Man:

C1

M. Don't you hate . . . being afraid of getting a hatchet in your back when you bend over to wash your face in the bathroom? Heh. [signed] C. A.

C2

C. A. Aren't you afraid now that you know . . . someone like me could easily slip through the phone box with a hatchet? So some night when you are alone, asleep, you could be hatcheted while you slumber peacefully. You won't even have a chance to scream. Hugs and kisses. [signed] M.

C3

Toots: Did you know that the McNutt Hatchet Man is moving to Harper III? You better watch out because the Harper Hatchet Man is watching you. Signed, a friend [Harper is a building in Foster Quadrangle, the dormitory across the street from McNutt.]

C4

Dear Miss Smith, It has come to my attention that someone has been impersonating me. Let me make one thing perfectly clear, *I am* the Hatchet Man. My calling card is enclosed, and, as is custom, whoever holds that card is the next to die. See you in the graveyard. Heh, heh, heh . . . [signed] The Hatchet Man [See Fig. 1]

C5

I'll bet that's something you *really* didn't want to see! [See Fig. 2]

C6

C. A. The next time, this hatchet will be in your head. [See Fig. 3]

C7

Patti: Ta-Dah!! Yes, believe it or not, I finally made it. I would have dropped by sooner, but I had a date with the Hatchet Man and you know how those things are. I'm still looking for something cute to give you, but I'll think of something. I was going to buy you a football player, but I didn't have 57¢ . . . Your Pixie

The last item represents the last appearance of the Hatchet Man game on DeJoya III that year. This note was left on a door just before Christmas break when the residents were having their gift exchange with secret pals, or pixies, on the floor. After returning from the Christmas holidays, the girls completely lost interest in this elaborate joke-network. Furthermore, the main recipient of the notes, the girl who had been so badly scared in the first place, moved to another dormitory, a move totally unrelated, however, to the Hatchet Man episode. As far as is known, she did not take the tradition with her. The total lack of any further interest was evidenced when, in February of that year, a girl was actually stabbed to death in a dormitory in Oregon State University. This news item was reported on WFIU, the I. U. radio station, on 8 February 1972:

Figure 1*

*All sketches by the author.

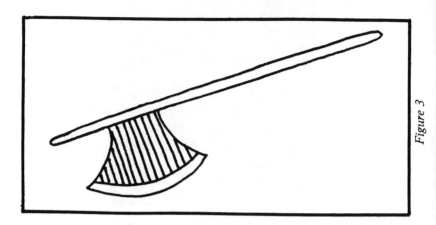

Figure 3

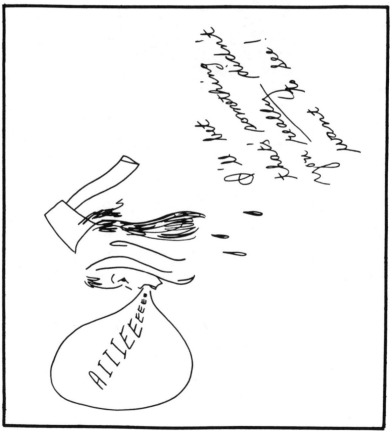

Figure 2

> A freshman co-ed was murdered at Oregon University last night. Nancy Wyckoff was found stabbed to death in her third floor dormitory room. A policeman described the scene, 'Some girls heard screaming, then heard some hurried footsteps running away. They ran into her room and found her dead, stabbed to death.'[9]

Although the Resident Assistant heard this radio report, none of the girls heard it, or, if they did, nothing was said of it. The following news item from the *Amarillo* (Texas) *Daily News* of 12 February 1972, was posted by the R. A. on the bulletin board and received absolutely no comment from any of the girls who saw it. They had scared themselves badly enough with the telling of the legend at the first of the year and apparently refused to accept the reality of what they themselves had safely relegated to the thoroughly tolerable status of a joke and a game:

Lock Doors, Travel in Pairs, Coeds Told

> Corvallis, Ore. (UPI)–Oregon State University co-eds were warned to lock their dormitory doors and travel in pairs on the campus Wednesday because of the stabbing death of a pretty California student.
>
> Police searched for a young man with 'short brown hair' whose description was given by two co-eds previously attacked.
>
> Nancy Diane Wyckoff, 18, of Glendale, Calif., was stabbed in the heart in her co-educational dormitory room early Tuesday. Her body was found lying near the murder weapon, an eight-inch knife.
>
> Previously, two other girls were struck by heavy objects, one in the basement of a dorm, the other on campus.
>
> University President Tobert MacIvar imposed stringent security measures and ordered 20 campus police in on the investigation with Oregon state police, Corvallis city police and Benton County sheriff's officers.
>
> 'There have been no arrests', an official said. 'We are checking all possible leads'.
>
> Security patrols had already been stepped up following the attacks on Connie Kennedy of Portland, Ore., and Elizabeth Anne Gleckler of San Mateo, Calif.
>
> Both girls described their assailant as between 17 and 20, white, and with short brown hair.
>
> Miss Wyckoff had not been sexually assaulted. The slaying took place in Poling Hall, a five-story dorm which houses women on the third and fourth floors and men on the others.
>
> Nancy Lundeen of Lake Oswego, Ore., who lived down the hall, discovered the body after hearing 'a couple of terrifying screams'.

The fall of 1972 saw nine residents returning to DeJoya III from the previous year; the rest of the residents were almost all incoming freshmen. These freshmen went through their own process of getting acquainted, but the returnees from the previous year provided them a focus and source of stability and information that they themselves had lacked because they had all been new to I. U. and the dormitory. The telling of these urban legends was not needed as much as a vehicle for getting acquainted; instead, the former residents, one of whom had figured prominently in the Hatchet Man cycle of notes the previous year, entertained the new girls with anecdotes of what had happened on the floor the year before. Some of the new residents, taking these reminiscences as their cue, created their own "Legend of the Evil Eye" (Motif D 2071) patterned on the Hatchet Man and for awhile left notes on one another's doors emblazoned with a stylized drawing of the Evil Eye. Examples of the notes concerning the Evil Eye are:

D1

Bye! Did you ever stop to think it could have been you this time? Don't *ever* leave your door unlocked or turn your back for even a second.

D2

The Evil Eye is upon you. [See Fig. 4]

D3

The 'Eye' was here. *Beware* [See Fig. 5]

D4

And night began to fall. The fear of what might be chilled her. *Alone,* or was she? Her footsteps echoed down the empty stone walk. She stopped.

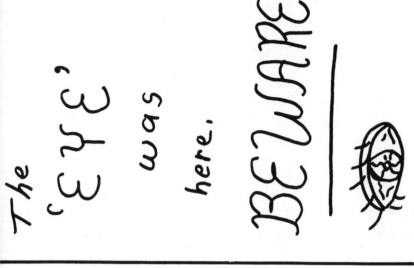

Figure 5

Figure 4

The breathing she had heard behind her grew closer. The next morning the rising sun began to illuminate the countryside. In unknowing cheerfulness it illuminated something soft and white. It would be hours, though, before anyone would find her body. She had become another victim of . . . . . . THE EVIL EYE!

This contrived story and associated gestures and symbols never achieved the high status that the Hatchet Man had enjoyed. There was really no genuine narrative and the elements of the story were quite flexible. The brief and limited popularity of this pseudo-legend lay in its external manifestations. An elaborate game developed of leaving notes on doors and making a cross with the arms in front of the face to keep from getting struck by a glance from the boy who was supposed to have the Evil Eye. Such a glance from him was supposed to be a "zot." "Toz" ("zot" spelled backwards) was the spoken charm the girls made up to help ward off the Evil Eye. As had been the case with the notes about the Hatchet Man, none of this game was ever taken seriously by any of the girls but it nevertheless performed the function of helping the girls get acquainted. In fact, many of the girls saved the Evil Eye notes that were left on their doors as scrap-book mementoes of those early days of their freshman year at college.

Continuous visits at the first of the semester by girls who had lived on the floor the year before reinforced the revival of the Hatchet Man, especially when these former residents began leaving calling cards and notes on the doors of their friends, notes cryptically signed with the initials "T. H. M." or just "H. M." These initials thus reduced what was left of the legend to the absolute minimum. Some of the new girls also briefly picked up on this communication code. Again, random samples of the notes are illustrative:

C8

Did you ever stop to think that if there's not a man in your bed, he may be in your closet? Sorry I missed you. [signed] H. M.

C9

Dear Sylvia, Just wanted you to know I was alive. [signed] H. M.

C10

Hi Sue. XXXXXXXXXXXXO [signed] The Axe Man

[This note was apparently left by someone not totally familiar with the tradition of accepted nomenclature. This is the only known example of the linguistic shift from "hatchet" to "axe."]

C11

Hi! Sylvia Gridder. [signed] The Hatchet Man. Willkie token only.

[Many of DeJoya III's 1971/72 residents moved to Willkie Quadrangle on the other side of the campus where they lived together as a group but did not actively take the traditions of the Hatchet Man with them, although a few did continue to tell the legend there occasionally.]

C12

Sorry I missed you. [signed] T. H. M. [See Fig. 6]

The final appearance of any such signs concerning the Hatchet Man was a series of notes left on the door of the most active tradition bearer in the days preceding her birthday in early September. These signs had a facetiously ominous tone which mixed implications of the Hatchet Man actually coming to visit and the revealing of his true identity on her birthday. In addition to the "unmasking" of the Hatchet Man, the girls also gave her a small mallet for her birthday. (They couldn't find a hatchet.) On her birthday the following elaborate sign appeared on her door:

Figure 6

Figure 7

C13

Happy birthday to you,
Happy birthday to you,
Happy birthday dear Marilou,
Happy birthday to you.
For your birthday we have decided to reveal the true identity of the Hatchet Man. See other side. [See Fig. 7]

The association of the Hatchet Man with George Washington and the cherry tree shifted the humor of this personification into the realm of the pun and thus provided the absolute finale of the whole process which had started with the full legend narrative.

In the course of slightly over a year, among this particular group of co-eds, there was a total shift of emphasis from a fully developed legend to a set of out-of-context initials. The legend, for the time being, has passed out of their active oral tradition. It is likely, however, that any one of the girls who knows the story will tell it in future taletelling sessions or under different circumstances, because they nearly all still regard this as the epitome of the scary story; and all of the notes and associated paraphernalia have only enhanced the story's popularity.

When asked, almost any of the girls will retell the legend of the Hatchet Man out of context but as a complete narrative. A few of them even admit to having told the story at the first of the year in order to scare their new friends in the dorm. The following two more recent examples, collected from the same informant, demonstrate how the narrative core of the story has stabilized and how the narrative itself has become much more structured and elaborate, possibly as a result of all the attention that has been paid to this particular story over the past year and a half. The informant calls the first example her "dormitory version" of the story because she had learned it another way before moving onto DeJoya III. The second text is the story as she originally heard it.

A3

The time is Christmas vacation, which is a very desolate time in the dormitory. And there are two girls who are roommates and they come back to the dorm early before anyone else is in the area. And they're sorta joking around, you know, about how funny it is to be the only people in this great building with all these empty rooms around them. And they're just sitting around talking and doing things and they had their radio on and they hear that a man, a murderer has escaped from a prison and that he is armed and dangerous and people in the area should be on the lookout for this person and they shouldn't go into any desolate areas or be out late at night or do anything that might open them to this man. And the girls hear this story and they think, "Oh, I doubt if anything's gonna happen; maybe we should just, you know, lock the door and stay inside and not worry about it too much."

So they were sitting inside and one of the girls got hungry. And she said, "I'm gonna go downstairs to the Coke machine and get a Coke and something to eat." And the other girl said, "Oh, I'm not too sure. Maybe we should just stay in here at least until morning; it's kinda late." The other girl said, "Oh, no, you're just being ridiculous; there's nothing that's going to happen."

So she went downstairs. Time went by. First it was five minutes and then ten minutes and then the other girl was getting a little bit worried because there was no reason why her roommate should be gone so long just to go downstairs, three flights. And she was waiting. Sat around, and after about forty-five minutes she heard a noise. And it was just this drag and then a "klunph" and a klunking noise like a chain being dragged up stairs, a similar noise to that. And she could not figure out what it was and she was absolutely petrified. She just waited and waited and she kept hearing this noise. She couldn't decide what to do. She was too scared to go outside and she didn't know who to call because there was no one in the area and there was no one she could . . . no other human beings around. And she decided she was going to turn on the radio and just make some noise and try to block out this sound. And she tried but she just could not stand it. And after she heard this klunking noise and then she didn't hear it for awhile. And it went away and she thought, "Oh, great, this is all over with."

And then she heard another noise. A sliding noise. And then scratching began on her door. And she just thought that this was too much. That if somebody was pulling a joke on her she didn't like it. She thought it was her roommate. After awhile . . . that it was somebody doing . . . she was trying to scare her a little bit. So she started asking her, saying, "C'mon, just cut it out." She heard nothing. The noise just went on. She kept getting more scared and more scared. And finally called the police. And they thought, you know, that she was probably just exaggerating and was a scared girl but they said, "O. K. we'll come and check it out for you." And, uh, after about fifteen minutes they arrived and she heard noises coming up the stairs and a lot of voices outside and somebody told her, "Everything's all right. We're gonna be in there in a few minutes. Just stay inside and we'll come in and get you, take you out of there."

And the girl was just thrilled to hear a human voice because she had been alone for all this time and she was so scared that she threw open the door. And when she opened the door she saw the body of her roommate lying on the floor and she had had her legs cut off and had dragged herself all the way up the stairs trying to get back to her roommate and she had been scratching on the door and had died while she was waiting outside.

Collected by Sylvia Grider from Melissa Warner, 21 February 1973.
     S 139.2 Slain person dismembered.

Melissa perfers to tell the story with this ending, instead of the girl having a hatchet buried in her head, because of the added dramatic device of the thumping and dragging sound, a motif found in published versions of the story from other informants.[10] She still regards this as *the* story of "The Hatchet Man" because the man supposedly used a hatchet to cut off the girl's legs, even though this fact is never mentioned directly in the narrative.

A4

This story took place out in the countryside. There were two young girls whose parents had gone out of town for the weekend and they were staying alone in the house and just having a pretty good time. They were a little bit worried because, uh, recently a convict had escaped from the local prison and they had heard on the radio that the man was armed and he was dangerous and the people in the area should watch out. And they decided that they weren't going to worry about it too much. They would just lock the doors and stay inside.

And they sat around during the day and then one of the sisters decided that later in the evening she wanted to go out for awhile. And the other sister, who was a little bit more scared by the story, and was a little uneasy about it, didn't think that her sister should go but couldn't really talk her out of it. And so they decided that she would go out and the other sister would stay home.

So the girl went out and she was gone for several hours and her sister just watched television and had a snack or two and then it started getting later and later and she was getting a little bit worried but decided that her sister had just had a good time and decided to stay out later. So she went to bed.

And after she had been in bed for awhile she heard noises outside, like scuffling noises and then a fall, and then she started hearing a dragging noise. And she was getting really scared because she didn't know what was going on but she was too scared to open the door and see. And she heard this noise for a long time, just a dragging noise. Coming up toward the door and then she was sitting outside. She finally got up nerve enough to get, to go right to the door, and she heard a scratching noise. A very faint scratching on the door, that she couldn't really place, like an animal, a cat or something scratching on a tree or a similar noise to that. She was just absolutely terrified and kept hoping that it would stop but it just kept going on and on and on.

And she decided, after a certain number of hours, that she just couldn't stand it any more and she called the police. And they said that they would come out and check what was happening. And it took a little while since they were out in the country but about half an hour later the police came and they said, oh, you know, "We're out here. It's O. K. Just don't come out. We're going to come in and take you out." And the girl was so thrilled to hear another person's voice that she opened the door. And when she opened the door she saw her sister's body lying outside and she had been stabbed in the back and had just dragged herself up and couldn't scream or anything because she was so weak but had been scratching on the door for her sister to let her in. That's the way I first heard the story.

Collected by Sylvia Grider from Melissa Warner, 21 February 1973.
S 115 Murder by stabbing.

The above two texts indicate that there was no shortening or devolvement of this legend narrative through repeated re-telling. The functional shift of emphasis to written notes was rather the conscious attempt of some of the narrators to personify and thus neutralize the terrifying force, in this case, the murderer. The primary element of fear in this story is not the Hatchet Man himself but rather an over-identification of the audience with either the murdered girl or the guilt-ridden roommate who doesn't open the door to help her. The simplest way to reduce the tension and fear resulting from this identification with the heroines of the story is to reduce the status of the unknown assailant by identifying and drawing attention to him and away from the girls. To turn this identification into a joke reduces the fear element of the story to an absolute minimum. The name of the Hatchet Man was finally shortened in the written notes to its mere initials: T. H. M. or just H. M., the ultimate reduction. It was this naming and identifying which underwent shortening and change and not, in any case, the actual narrative.

Notes

1. Published accounts and interpretations of this legend include: Linda Dégh, "The 'Belief Legend' in Modern Society: Form, Function, and Relationship to Other Genres," *American Folk Legend: A Symposium.* Berkeley, 1971, 55-68; "Folk Narrative," *Folklore and Folklife: An Introduction.* Chicago, 1972, p. 75; "The Roommate's Death and Related Dormitory Stories in Formation," *Indiana Folklore,* 2:2 (1969): 55-74; Daniel R. Barnes, "Some Functional Horror Stories on the Kansas University Campus," *Southern Folklore Quarterly,* 30:3 (1966): 312-331; Jo Ann Stephens Parochetti, "Scary Stories from Purdue," *Keystone Folklore Quarterly,* 10:1 (1965): 49-57.

2. A special word of thanks to those girls on DeJoya III who contributed the most to the life of the Hatchet Man, both by their storytelling and cooperation: Nancy Jo Johnson, Patricia "Trish" Lootens, Suzy Slavich, Carole Anne Smith, Marilou VanLaningham, and Melissa Warner.

3. Alan Dundes, "A Study of Ethnic Slurs," *Journal of American Folklore,* 84:332 (1971): 186-203.

4. "Who Says College Kids Have Changed?" *Life,* 62:20 (19 May 1967): 90-100.

5. Helen Mamarchev, "The College Student and his Environment," unpublished MS, 1972; Joy M. Menne, and E. Robert Sinnett, "Proximity and Social Interaction in Residence Halls," *The Journal of College Student Personnel,* 12:1 (January, 1971): 26-31.

6. Dégh, "The Roommate's Death and Related Dormitory Stories in Formation," pp. 59, 61.

7. Robert Jerome Smith, "The Structure of Esthetic Response," *Journal of American Folklore,* 84:331 (1971): 77.

8. Dégh, "The Roommate's Death . . .," p. 74.

9. Collected by Julia Brooks from Larry Pensinger, WFIU reporter, 8 February 1972.

10. Dégh, "The Roommate's Death . . .," pp. 58, 59.

The House of Blue Lights in Indianapolis

Linda Dégh

Ma'gnús Einarsson-Mullarký in his assessment of twenty variants of *The House of Blue Lights* story [*Indiana Folklore* (I, 2, pp. 82-91)] had noted that there is a "strange discrepancy between the richness of descriptive detail, relative variety of motives and emphases and the lack of textual development." None of the texts presented by Mullarký appear to be as fully developed legend narratives but all of them seem to emphasize one or two of the constituent elements of a strange subject heard of or experienced by the tellers. The core of the account (dead wife in glass casket surrounded by blue lights) is more or less consistent, nevertheless its significance might be overshadowed by other recurrent though quite colorless, nonfitting, nondramatic motifs. Is this a legend at all or just a local gossip passed on by juvenile adventure-seekers? Do the story components tend to crystallize through oral transmission, relinquishing the meaningless, incoherent details? Or do they remain rather on the rumor-level, because live facts prevent them from uniting into a perfect fictional narrative?

In view of the lasting popularity of the legend and its current use in tests of courage, among high school students, the variants Mullarký had in hand were too few and too reticent to throw light on the scope of the total content. Nor was there adequate factual information available to substantiate the existence of the mysterious *House of Blue Lights* that generated this visionary rumor. In possession of the essential facts of reality, we hope to link together the seemingly meaningless motifs of the story and to show the interrelationships of the content elements in the story through the presentation of twelve recently collected texts. None of these versions to be printed here in full deviate essentially from the twenty discussed by Mullarký, but some of them bring us closer to the historical reality from which the legend has evolved.

179

Thanks to the generous help of several Indianapolis residents who provided us with important printed documents as well as detailed verbal information, we hope to show an immediate relationship between facts and fiction. Folklorists are seldom in this favorable position to follow up the steps of legend formation at the close range where events and stories they stimulate, maintain and shape can both be called contemporary. In the case of *The House of Blue Lights* story we were able to consult people who know well the former owner of *The House of Blue Lights*. These informants were his neighbors, friends, business acquaintances and relatives whose names they requested we withhold. Their factual information as well as their personal opinion, their communication of local rumors and gossip will be the basis for our consideration of the twelve new versions.

The Factual Background of the Story

On March 19 and 20, 1964 all Indianapolis daily papers reported the death of Skiles E. Test. He was the owner of *The House of Blue Lights*. The obituary in *The Indianapolis Star* (March 19, 1964, p. 14) is worth quoting:

> Skiles E. Test, 74, 6700 Fall Creek Road, president of Indianapolis Motor Inns Inc., died last night in Methodist Hospital. A resident of Indianapolis most of his life, Test was a member of the family that owns the Test Building on Monument Circle. For 10 years he was a member of the board of the Indianapolis Transit System. He was a member of the Columbia Club. Test lived on a farm, where he had kennels for St. Bernards. He liked cats and dogs and found refuge for any strays on his farm. In 1960, Test put in trust 20 acres of farm land for Lawrence Township schools. It is at the corner of 71st and Johnson Road. Private services will be Saturday in Flanner & Buchanan Fall Creek Mortuary. Survivors are the widow, Ellen, a daughter Louellen Test, Burlingame, Calif., and a brother, Donald N., and sister, Dorothy Hiatt, both of Indianpolis.

The auction sheet, reproduced here gives an idea to the reader about the wealth of Skiles Test in terms of farm equipment and household goods. Other than a side remark in paranthesis: "Several hundred tons of junk", there is no indication to the strange possessions known to the legend tellers. However, directions to the auction site include not only the streets leading to the location of the estate but also identifies the site as: "Known as *The House of Blue Lights*", which means that the farmhouse was generally known by this name to Indianapolis residents. *The Indianapolis Star* offers further clues to the legend in its account of the three day auction on May 24, 1964 p. 14. Photographs show the lined-up cars whose owners had to walk more than a mile to *The House of Blue Lights*. The auction, indeed, has a key role in the legend formation.

An estimated 30,000 people, mostly sightseers, picked their way through the assorted items yesterday, on the final day of the auction of the estate of the late and eccentric millionaire, Skiles E. Test.

Besides setting some sort of an attendance record of some 50,000 persons for the three-day auction, one auctioneer said buyers paid higher prices than he ever had seen at an auction.

Household goods, furniture and collections of art works were the chief articles on sale, and housewives and amateur bargain-seekers far outnumbered professional antique dealers and scrap collectors.

Homeowners carefully examined e v e r y imaginable kinds of table, sofa, bed spring, and women's jewelry, while c h i l d r e n and teen-agers stalked the grounds of the estate looking for headstones that would identify Test's fabled cat and dog cemetery.

The thirsty crowd emptied the concession stands' stocks of chilled soft drinks and the operators started hawking warm drinks by mid-afternoon. "Anyway, they are wet," one salesman said.

Auctioneers estimated that about 90 per cent of the crowd that pressed around cases of antique jewelry, and lounged on assorted furniture, left empty-handed.

By 3 p.m., more than two-thirds of the late Mr. Test's enormouns stockpile of aspirin tablets, catsup, office equipment, artwork and household furnishings had been carted away.

Garnett E. Eaton, 3920 Eisenhower Drive, an associate of chief auctioneer Earl Cornwell, said that the buyers paid higher prices than at any auction he had handled.

Just about everything sold well, with antique furniture the most popular items, Eaton said.

Sheriff's Detective Sgt. Jack T. Bevan, head of the security and traffic detail, made the attendance estimates. "They were lined up like at the Speedway when we opened the gates at 6 a.m.", Bevan said. Traffic moved steadily in and out of the 20-acre field converted into a parking lot off of 65th Street and past the Test home onto Johnson Road.

The now-shabby house, called the "House of Blue Lights" because Mr. Test strung blue Christmas tree lights among surrounding trees, was partitioned from the crowd by a 12-foot-high metal fence.

> Mr. Test, owner of the Indianapolis Motor Inns Inc., died last
> March 18.
> Bevan said there were some reports of pilfering but that no
> major items were stolen.

Piecing together our bits of information concerning the Man and the
House (reproduced here from a photograph taken in 1953) and the motifs
included in the variants of the legend, it becomes quite clear that the
floating stories are not too distant from the facts.

The Test family was prominent in Indianapolis and Skiles Test grew
up in Woodruff Place where his family lived in one of the largest houses
that still stands. One of our readers tells us of an old man who said the
first car he'd ever ridden in was a National owned by Skiles Test as a
young man. The son of an affluent family, active in Indianapolis business
life, Skiles Test became a noted personality himself. He was a man of
many skills. He operated the Circle Motor Inn and also ran a farm of 700
acres where he grew corn and wheat, raised cattle and operated a dairy
farm. The farmhouse, though modest from the outside, was well-equipped
for modern living. The Test farm had its own power plant and a system
that pumped and circulated water day-round for a swimming pool. The
swimming pool was quite an attraction when it was built about
1922-1923; it certainly was unique in the area. To entertain his family,
Skiles Test also made his own fireworks. However, his family life was not
happy and two marriages ended in divorce. Reacting to a comment about
the wife's casket in the window surrounded with blue lights, an informant
once replied: "Which wife? He had three and two survived him!" It was
said that he remarried one woman who had divorced him earlier.

Between his unsuccessful marriages Skiles Test lived alone on his
farm and found consolation in raising pets and tending his delicate hot
house plants. He had dogs and cats and also a rabbit at one time. "Outside
he did raise St. Bernard dogs. They were registered, thirteen of them in a
pen, he had wire fence and fairly close there was a heated house where he
kept cats—said one friend.—Whoever wanted to get rid of a cat, he took it
in and if they were sick or had a broken leg, he had the vet take care of
them and he healed them and when they died, they were put into a casket

and buried. If you go in from the North, the cemetery is to the South. I do not think you [can] find it today, you know; people took curios, took what they could grab." Another friend said Test also had kept Great Danes and very small dogs in addition to the cats. "He had at one time a hundred and fifty cats and had little houses for them at a separate place, an acre was fenced in for them. The vet came once a week."

Another informant suggested: "In front of the house there was an animal graveyard for forty years. Family pets were buried there."

"Mr. Test was very fond of flowers,,"—said a neighbor—"and he enclosed a portion of the steps with glass and grew flowers and shrubs on the heated porch and he had blue bulbs in there. In fact, the blue effect was done by the thick glass.

However, the "blue lights" were given also another explanation equivocal with the newspaper article. A nephew had this to say: "One year he had set up some lights at Christmas time. He left them there afterwards, and they were blue lights. This was before 1941, let's see, thirty years ago. The power and light company had a competition on Christmas decoration in order to promote electric sale."

A former neighbor thought: "There were some lights outside on the phone pole. At Christmas time he had decoration in front of the house. Some might have been blue." Another informant said that "the blue lights were strung in the trees in the yard" and another thought "they were daylight bulbs which have a blue tinge."

It is rather unusual to put fences around one's property and doing so, Mr. Test unwittingly attracted the attention of adventure-seeking youngsters in the area. What might be inside, to be concealed from observant eyes? Mystery? Crime? Extravaganza? On the part of Skiles Test, it was quite understandable that he wanted to protect his property from intruders attracted by the kennels, the animal cemetery, the flood lights and the swimming pool.

A nephew stated that "He was always bothered by young people who climbed the fence and there was a constant feud between my uncle and the fence-climbing children. He raised the fence higher and locked the gate at night. He had to make sure nobody falls into the swimming pool at night."

Another informant spoke about the tricks played by kids: "They threw cats over the fence between the dogs and this was the dirties tricks: they threw broken glass into the swimming pool. But Mr. Test was a lovely man. He liked children if they came, he showed them around what they wanted to see but those youngsters came only by night and trespassed so he had to watch out and keep them out. He was the kindest man that ever lived."

This statement was affirmed by another: "Kids wanted to come in and chase around and he didn't want them without permission and put a fence and a gate that was locked. The 'haunted house' idea, you know. They came all hours at night but never during the day. He even had to ask for protection from the sheriff's office."

Informants are unanimous in stating that the rumors of the *House of Blue Lights* started sometime between the two World Wars. People in their forties already have heard the story and many of them visited the premises when they were in high school. Mr. Test was divorced for the first time around 1936, and he lived alone in the house for a period of time. The extraordinary aura of the house was coupled with the fact that its location and environs made it seem similar to the "haunted" houses.

"It looked isolated and ghostly when the moon shone at night", said a sometime frequent guest of the house, "Set on a hill, you could not see it from the road, from the thick woods." Now the area is populated with many new homes. The family plans to tear the house down and make a public park on the estate of eighty acres for the neighborhood children who have no playground.

The latest addition to the towntalk, that Skiles Test was a great hoarder and an eccentric, came from the well-publicized auction, which was indeed an outstanding social event. "The auction was like a state fair" said one relative.

An informant who had been to the sale spoke of the guards who kept the crowd out of the house. The huge barn or barns were open for the visitors. This was the unique opportunity to match rumor with reality. It was well known to close friends that Mr. Test bought many things in quantity. In addition to his family, a housekeeper, a cook and a man who ran the farm, there was a time when he had quite a number of families on the farm. However, he bought staples beyond reasonable need. He stored catsup, he bought boxes in 1924 and still had much of it in 1964. Numerous drums of oil for use in farm equipment, trays of nails, staples and the like arranged by size as in a store were also noted by observers.

The Legend Variants

1.

A long time ago, around the 1930's, Mr. Test's wife died. To keep himself from being lonely, he kept her in an open coffin in one of the tower rooms. The room itself was filled with flowers and were kept fresh. In the summer time, he used to move the coffin into the garden. That's why blue lights were seen outside as well as in. He used blue lights so that she would rest more peacefully.

Informant: John Earl, of Indianapolis; colleced by Diana Dean, Indianapolis, July 18, 1967. FA IU:1274.

2.

The wife of Mr. Test had been a very beautiful woman. When she died, he was very saddened and completely withdrew from the world. He decided to keep her near him always, so he had her placed in a glass coffin and kept it in the living room. Blue had been her favorite color, so he surrounded the coffin with blue lights—and then eventually the whole house. He would sit for hours just staring at the coffin.

Told by Steve Koers of Indianapolis; collected by Diana Dean, Indianapolis, July 18, 1967. FA IU:1272.

3.

It's a house on Fall Creek, the "House of the Blue Lights" situated on a woody hill. It's on the corner of Fall Creek and Road 100. The man's wife died supposedly a long time ago and instead of burying her he put her into a big glass coffin and put blue lights all around her and keeps her in the house with him. A glass casket. You can see the blue lights through the house.

Told by Russ Jens, 19, of Indianapolis; heard when attended North Central High School. He had gone to this house. Collected by Stephen M. Dickhous. FA IU:1718.

4.

The legend that I most vividly recall was the story of "The House of Blue Lights" in the Geist Reservoir area in Indianapolis, Indiana. I heard the story while on camping trip in the area with fellow Boy Scouts at the age of sixteen.

After drinking a few beers that someone managed to sneak past the scoutmaster we began to tell stories about the surrounding area. Most of us were sixteen and had recently received our driver's licences. We were therefore eager to learn of good places to park with our dates. The story telling settled down to 'serious business' when the subject of the "House of Blue Lights" was mentioned.

So the legend went, an old man in a very exclusive neighborhood near our campsite was said to have the body of his wife displayed in a glass-enclosed casket. The casket was supposed to have been surrounded by eerie blue lights that were visible from the yard of the home. Young people on dates often were asked to leave the neighborhood by security police who assured them that there was no lady in a glass coffin. The eerie mood set by the storytelling on a date was always effective in evoking the proper mood for love-making when we later (after learning the story), took our dates into the area to park.

It was disappointing to many young people in the Indianapolis area when Skiles Test died; his was the "House of Blue Lights." When the house was inspected after Mr. Test's death it was found that there was no glass coffin surrounded by a bank of blue lights. However it was odd that there was found numerous cat graves in the yard, boxes of shoes, food, etc. The eccentric old man evidently bought everything in bulk, and did indeed exhibit some strange habits.

Written report of Edward S. Marcus, student from Indianapolis, 1969. The camping trip took place in 1964.

5.

On the northwest side of Indianapolis there is an old mansion built in the thirties. The owner's wife died about fifteen years ago. The rumor was that on the sunporch he had her casket. The only lights on the porch were blue lights which were visible from the garden, about fifty yards away and during the colder months when there weren't any leaves on the trees you could see the lights from a country road. It was a great fad of teenagers to get to the porch or rather to try to get to the porch. They were usually hampered by four big dogs. I almost got there but the dogs got too close. Recently the house was sold. While it was being advertised in the papers it was billed as the "House of Blue Lights." I first heard this story in 1955 or 1956.

Told by Richard L. Mills of Indianapolis to Kathy Mills in Bloomington, July 15, 1966.

6.

This is a story which is frequently told around the high school groups in Indianapolis, Indiana. There is a big estate in town owned by a millionaire who died a few years ago. The house is up a long drive and is surrounded by a tall fence. Inside the fence were dogs which were to keep out strangers. The fence had blue lights around it, and many times the initiation into clubs or just to see inside the house kids would climb the fence and try to look into the living room which was lit up with blue lights. The owner was suppose to have put his wife in a glass casket after she died so he could look at her. He was to have had the casket surrounded with blue lights. He was supposedly to have had her there for several years. I heard after he died that he had been a little crazy, no doubt, and that he thought there was going to be another war; so he had bought several items in large quantities like nails and canned foods etc., preparing for the war. The place was to have had several hundred cats around too, and I heard that he had a special cemetery for them and buried each one in its own casket. I don't know how much of the story is actually true but I believe parts of it are true and could be traced back through newspapers; like the last part of the story preparing for a war and other things. I couldn't say for sure though on the part about his wife, but, the story has been widely spread in Indianapolis.

Collected by Philip Harping of Bloomington Campus, I.U., submitted May 5, 1968. FA IU:69/172.

7.

Mr. Test kept the house closely guarded at all times to keep people from seeing his wife in her coffin. There were pits dug all over the grounds to trap anyone that wandered around there. Vicious dogs attacked any prowlers, and Mr. Test was known to have taken shots at people. He could be seen wandering through his house carrying a blue light with him all the time. His wife was kept in a closed casket above the ground in the garden. The dogs were kept in huge pens most of the time, but if anyone fell into the pits, he released them to attack.

Told by Rick Haberman of Indianapolis to Diana Dean, July 18, 1967. FA IU:1273.

8.

There was an eccentric, old, rich man who had a farm and it is a wooded farm. He has blue lights all around the farm and the fence surrounding it. He has blue lights in his house and blue lights in a big swimming pool outside and a blue flood light in his backyard. The real story is, that he had killed his wife at some time, whether by accident or intent and keeps her body in a casket in the bottom of the swimming pool.

Told by Denny Miller, 19, student from Indianapolis; collected by Tommy Prinz at Foster Quadrangle, IU, Bloomington, May 8, 1968.

9.

The story goes that there is an old man who lives on the northeast half of Indianapolis, Indiana. When the old man was younger he was given a bad deal with the firm with whom he was associated. As he lived to grow older he became more and more like a hermit. After his wife died he put her in a glass coffin and surrounded it with blue lights.

Told by Mike Jordan, 20, Indianapolis to Raymond E. Clift, 1968. FA IU:1743.

10.

The reason for the blue lights was for the orchids that Mr. Test grew in a green house on his property. He had been a very wealthy man and had hidden his money throughout the house. After his death, the lawyers found it hidden in all sorts of pockets throughout the house. Perhaps some of the money is still there, but the general public has lost interest in the house. His wife is definitely buried in Crown Hill Cemetery, complete with large tombstone. The lawyers, though, found an empty coffin sitting in one of the tower rooms, empty and dusty, never used.

Told by Jeff Salberg to Diana Dean, both of Indianapolis, July 18, 1967. FA IU:1271.

11.

"The House of the Blue Lights" refers to a large estate on the north side of Indianapolis. Guards were said to take care of the place but they were never seen. The guy who lived there would buy things by the case. People disappeared periodically from the area so police were posted to watch it. Then the man living there disappeared too. Four years later a policeman was found shot in the head on the road near the property. It finally got to a point where no one would go near the house. They finally found him dead and arranged to auction off his furniture. About 200,000 people showed up. It was the largest turnout ever at an auction. The strange happenings at the house attracted many curious people.

Told by Keep Morse, 24, from Indianapolis to Dorothy Deal at IU dormitory lounge, December 19, 1967. FA IU:68/138.

12.

There was a home in Indianapolis years ago. There was an old man who lived all by himself. When he died they found all kinds of junk and garbage and things in his garage and basement. He had a high fence there and it was lit with lights to keep people away. After he died and the electric power was turned off many of the children in Indianapolis would go back to this house that looked "haunted" house and even now they say that when they try to climb over this fence, blue lights would come on.

Told by Rita Jackson, 20, who heard it from schoolmates while attending school in Indianapolis. Collector: Stephen Joseph Daily, Kokomo, December 23, 1968.

Analysis

In the light of the historical factors behind the legend, the first thing one is struck by is the accurate retention of the facts found most outstanding by all those who described the personality and household of the late Skiles Test. Both who furnished background and folklore information, elaborated with the same details: the blue lights, the swimming pool, the dogs, the cats, the animal cemetery, the fence and the iron gate, the household goods stored in large quantity as they were on display at the auction. All these facts combined show the eccentric personality of the man. What the common talker found worthwhile to remember when voicing the judgement of his society concerning actual points of interest, the folklore informant deemed also worthwhile to pass on.

The prosperous Test family, the deeds, the fate of individual family members was—no doubt—a point of interest to Indianapolis society. As a rule, not only local gossips spread the latest events about people in the limelight; no social evening can pass without some entertaining story about prominent people. Skiles Test was certainly interesting enough to talk about at different stages of his life. After his death the auction opened new insight into his personality, when finally the "secrets" of his farmhouse, the topic of tea party talk, became public. Fifty thousand visitors of whom very few were professional antique dealers or buyers came to inspect the place. Most of the visitors came to get some curio of no value as proof of their visit to the premises and to refreshen their data on the subject for social get togethers. This far, Skiles Test's personality was cast as that of a withdrawn eccentric who preferred the company of animals to that of people, who kept his privacy secure by fences and gates, who did not like to waste, bought on sales and kept good in quantity even if they were of no further use to him. How did his public image evolve underscored by the typical colors of folklore?

The twelve variants that correspond to those analysed by Mullarký change greatly the features of the owner of the *House of Blue Lights*. In most of the versions [(1), (2), (3), (4), (5), (6), (7), (9)], he is characterized by his tender love to his wife whom he did not want to part with when she died. He dedicated his whole life to her, setting up a permanent catafalque where her glass casket is being placed. He sits by her keeping vigil over her eternal dream. The beloved one is surrounded by flowers (1), and by blue lights, blue being her favorite color (2). As far as color symbolism goes, in addition to the references given by Mullarký (ibid. pp. 84-85), one might include love magic: the touching of blue cloth in order to induce the sweetheart to appear (Brown Collection 6: item 4203 and 4275). The bier is placed in the "tower room", (1), in the living room (2,6), on the sunporch (5), above the ground in the garden (7), the coffin is even moved to the garden in summertime (1). In this pattern it seems natural that the house owner, who loved his wife that much, lost contact with the outside world and became a hermit, displaying strange habits. He withdrew from the world when his beautiful wife died (2), and in his bereavement became a maniac, (7).

Is it not in accordance with this dramatic story that he became violent when prowlers tried to spy on him? The old man protected his beloved wife by keeping four watchdogs (5), by building a fence with posts illuminated by blue floodlights, surrounding the fence with mean dogs (6), and even trapping intruders and shooting at people (7). The versions in which the man killed his wife, seem to be a negative replica of the main pattern. Although no malice is shown in the killing [the woman

"There is a big estate in town owned by a millionaire who . . . was supposed to have put his wife in a glass casket after she died . . ."

went crazy in Mullarký's version E, and (8)], it was "neither by accident or intent"; in our version, the man does not display the body but hides it under the swimming pool. This corresponds also to Mullarký's "Related text": it is obvious in both stories why the killer wants to keep out visitors. This is a complete and very logically structured legend in itself.

However, there are other, rather discordant elements in the story. Some of them appear at random, others de-emphasize the main story and eventually discard it. In one (6), for example, another story is included about a crazy man who bought large quantities of everything because of the fear of another pending war. Another variant (9) tells principally of the reason the old man became a hermit. It seems that his keeping the dead wife in a glass coffin is a consequence of his disappointment with the outside world.

The last three variants are rather distinct in their content and aim. Although they contain most of the usual details, what they really have in common is the mysterious house with blue light fixtures. One variant, (10), explains that the lights come from a greenhouse, where sensitive plants are grown. But this explanation is only a side remark, as is the mention of the wife buried in the cemetery—it really means that the informant had heard about the glass casket, but suspects otherwise. This is the story of a miser, who hid his money, a hoarder who even bought his coffin. There is also a note for treasure hunters: It is worthwhile to search the place; the lawyers might not have found everything.

The House of Blue Lights of variant (11), is a real mystery house, where weird things were going on. It was guarded but the guards were never seen. People had disappeared near the property and a policeman was once found shot. The owner of the house disappeard too, but was later found dead. No one dared near the house until the auction. The mystery—crime? supernatural?—is left open to conjecture.

There is only one ghost story among the versions (12). The weird old man who was a hoarder (his possessions turned out to be "junk and garbage" after his death), he used blue lights to keep people away. The lights (as in *HDA* 2:1395) would come up after his death if someone would enter. This haunt corresponds to variants C and (12), in Mullarký's article.

The application of the blue light motif shows diversity. Most commonly they surround the glass casket (1), (2), (3), (4), (5), (6), (9); otherwise in (6) and in (12) the fence is lighted; in (7), the man carries the light; in (10), the greenhouse, in (8) the fence, the house, the swimming pool and the backyard; only (11), does not specify. It seems to be certain, that the once existed blue lights around the farmhouse were the principal reason to suggest a mystery house to the fertile imagination of young people; these blue lights remained the central motif of the legend.

As far as the form of the legend is concerned, it remains imperfect and fragmentary, as already stated in the above. The variants are closer to the memorate than to the more elaborate fabulate; they often stay on the rumor—level. There are two reasons to account for this and for the lack of development into a lengthier narrative, despite the fact that stories about the *House of Blue Lights* had been reported since the mid-thirties.

(1) The facts originated too close in time to let fantasy develop freely. The folklore-generating facts of the story did not penetrate folklore at the same time as the historical events occurred at different times over a lengthy period of time. These facts are so different in their quality and value as folk narrative elements that they keep the story rather incoherent—although they could have been easily shaped into different stories. Consequently, in this case, the period of thirty—to thirty-five years was too short to develop a legend because the real facts kept accumulating until the last few years.

(2) The story enjoyed a steady popularity among Indianapolis high school students for over thirty years, concurrently as it entered adult society in and outside of the city. From the Folklore Archives at Purdue University Jo Ann Stephens Parochetti quotes versions in her "Scary Stories from Purdue" [*Keystone Folklore Quarterly* X. (1965) 49-54] from Indianapolis and one from Franklin, 20 miles south of Indianapolis. The folk legend material was both reaffirmed and watered down by historical factors known about the "House of Blue Lights." Among the generations of high school students, the farmhouse became one of the mystery houses so typical in the life of American adolescents. In the Indianapolis area this house became the object of maturation test, a part

of an initiation ritual. In possession of a new operator's license, the aspirant could drive to this "scary", desolate place, challenge the danger, enjoy the fear and the frustration of imagined horrors and vicariously gain admission into the adult world. Some of the tellers referred to the ritual related to this legend (3), (4), (5), (6), (8), (11); others yielded information only by specific questioning. Function left its imprint on the form of the story: it consists of two parts: the story of the strange occurrences in the blue light house and the account of personal experience of the teller (or his acquaintance) visiting the house. Since both story and visit are common knowledge to all respondents, relation does not need much elaboration. The telling in itself is also being utilized as a ritual, to rouse fear at specific get-togethers. Also its function in dating, to make girls draw closer to the protective male, preparing the atmosphere for love-making, is noted by an informant (4).

V Ghosts in the House and on the Road

"Mary Whales, I Believe in You"

Janet Langlois

Discussion of the interrelation of myth and ritual had remained on an abstract, if not sacred, plane for me until October 14, 1972. On that day, I wandered through the booths at the annual Psychic Fair in Indianapolis and met another fair-goer, Gia, a twelve-year-old student at Holy Angels, an experimental Catholic elementary school for black children on the northwest side of the city. Talk turned to things occult. Gia told me of revenant nuns, of disembodied footsteps in the convent and of spirits conjured in mirrors. With her permission, I taped a repeat of our conversation:

JL: Now tell me again about Mary Whales. . .
G: There was one time—six years ago she died, Mary *Whales,* that is and she got ran over by this truck when she was on the corner of Crown Hill Cemetery.
JL: And this is in Indianapolis?
G: Uh-huh. And so then these two, a young couple, was just driving along and everything. And she was hitchhiking 'cause she was on her way to a party and it was raining that night and so, you know, she was kinda wet and she was bleeding, and she had scratches on her face, so they thought it would be nice to pick her up and things. And so, they, they picked her up. And she told them, she gave them this address. And so (pause) they took her there. And when they got there, she was gone! And they went into this house where they had took her (pause) the girl got out of the car and the boy did too and they went in this house and her mother was in there and sister. And they were talking and things. And then she looked at the picture and she said, "Who? We picked a girl up that looked just like her tonight."
       And her mother said, "Naw, it couldn't have been her. She's been dead for six years."
       . . . And then them kids at school, they talked about it and stuff and got everybody believing it and so, then we went into the bathroom and we tried it.
JL: Tell exactly what you had to do to call her.
G: Ya, you had to, you could call her ten or a hundred times and call her name and say, "I do believe in Mary Whales" and she was supposed to come.
JL: And come in the mirror? That's right?

196

G: And come in the mirror. And I was back in the corner all by myself. They, they, we said it up to a hundred times and we waited and waited and I closed my eyes and we still waited. And then Leslie said, ''Cut on the light!'' and they said, she said, ''I saw her, I saw her and you didn't get to see her!''

        And so, I went home and I just got through watching a scary movie and I did it in the mirror myself.

JL: And you called her a hundred times?

G: All by myself, I called her a hundred times, and I was saying, ''I do believe in you.'' And I was by the light switch and she came and her eye started bleeding and then I cut on the light real fast.

        And then, all that night, I had a dream about her and I dreamed that she was right by my bed. She was about ready to touch me. . .

(From text 11a.)

Gia's narrative includes:

1.   A LEGEND VERSION. Mary Whales is, of course, ''the Vanishing Hitchhiker,'' perhaps the most-popular and best-documented revenant in American legendry,[1] localized to the corner of 38th Street and Northwestern Avenue at the entrance to Crownhill Cemetery, not many blocks from Holy Angels school.

2.   A REPORT OF AN ASSOCIATED GAME. I have labelled calling Mary Whales in a prescribed litany in the contexts mentioned here (the group experience in the girls' restroom and the individual experience at home) a ''game'' for want of any classification by Gia herself.

3.   A REPORT OF A DREAM EXPERIENCE.

The relation of legend and game, however ephemeral or unique it might be, reminded me of the relation of myth and ritual. Jan Brunvand's statement that ''it seems reasonable to think that the tale-game relationship— psychological and structural—might easily result in as many articles and theories as the myth-ritual relationship has''[2] encouraged me to play with this analogy. If the two types of narrative do have a similar association to stylized behaviors, regardless of secular and sacred distinctions, then questions that have been asked about myth/ritual might help me in understanding this legend/game.[3] With this thought in mind, I took up Gia's offer to visit Holy Angels and subsequently interviewed students in groups and individually, as well as participated in the calling of Mary Whales.[4] Of the eighty students interviewed, approximately a quarter of them knew about the ''Mary Whales thing'' and about half of those twenty—a core of ten students,—actively participated in the legend/game.

My participant observation and directed interviewing created artificial contexts for legend transmission and game-playing. At best I heard reports of earlier natural contexts in which students told stories "made up on the basis of the modern atmosphere of violence, horror and fear learned from overhearing adult talk, reading newspapers and fiction, listening to radio news and watching TV horror shows."[5] Furthermore, my presence rekindled interest in Mary Whales, which several students told me had been "dying down." For instance, Anna, who had known the legend but not the game at our first interview (text 1), was able to give me a detailed account of the game and of her participation in it at our last interview (text 8). A comparison of Gia's first conversation with me (text 11a) and her last (text 11c) also shows influence of other tellers during the period of my interviewing. I feel that the artificial contexts induced certain students to create their own secondary natural contexts for speaking and playing which they again reported to me. My data, then, are several orders of reports.

The question of the "primacy" of myth or ritual is a useful springboard for evaluating the different attitudes of the interested students towards the legend/game. The Anna of the first interview is representative of those students—all girls—who reported that Mary Whales was "the Vanishing Hitchhiker" but who did not know about the game or, if they did know about it, had never participated (texts 1-4). For them, legend-telling appears primary in the sense that it was an experience sufficient in itself and not a secondary justification of on-going behavior.

Carol, a non-participant in the game, reported a *result* of the game—that Mary Whales had scratched the face of one of the game-players (text 4). This result and the mechanics of the game itself were reported by those students—all boys—who had no idea who Mary Whales was (texts 5-7). For them, the game-playing appears primary in the sense that the stylized behavior and its consequences are sufficient in themselves and the origin legend is not necessary for interest to be maintained. However, no boys interviewed had actually called Mary Whales in a group situation (text 7). They had only heard of others doing so:

> Girls always do, did it.
> You know, Leslie and them was doing it?
> Almost every day.
> (From text 6.)

For the girls always doing it, the myth or ritual question takes on the "chicken or egg" form revealed in this discussion between participants:

Frances: She was supposed to be a lady who on her way to a dance or something.
Anna: A prom.

Frances: She be, she had on a white dress.

Anna: Uh-huh. And she died or something on the way there or something.

Theresa: And the first time I heard about it was from a boy named Larry. And he asked us if we ever, you know, cut out the lights and did that. And I said I never heard about it. And then they brought it up in school and we started trying it.

. . . .

Anna: They say she'll do something to you.

Frances: Right.

Theresa: She'll scratch you.

. . . .

Frances: The first story I heard is about the time that—somebody says it's in the newspaper but I didn't hear it from the newspaper, I heard it from somebody in the school that said that she was on the corner. And if you stop for, if you, if you pick her up, she'll disappear or something like that.

Theresa: She'll take you to this house or something.

Frances: And leave a wet spot.

Theresa: And she'll tell you to go in the house and do something and when you come back, she won't be there but a wet spot will.

Anna: Uh-huh.

Theresa: And if you, if you stop and say you not going that way, you'll get killed or something. And that happened one time. One time she, one time somebody picked her up and they went to a house, they went to a house. And they went in there, and they said, ''That's the lady we had in the car'' and she said that was her daughter. She'd been dead for five, ten—I don't know how long.

                              (From text 8.)

In terms of time, Frances hears the legend first and Theresa the game first (and from a boy). In terms of interest, legend-telling and game-playing appear so inter-related that the "primacy" question becomes irrelevant.

And so I moved on to another myth/ritual question: What is the formal or structural relation between the legend and the game as expressed by those who participated fully in both (texts 8-11c)? The legendary Mary Whales, as victim of traffic accident, has been killed, her face has been scratched (text 11a). As revenant, she disappears when the unsuspecting couple (or single driver) attempts to take her home where they subsequently learn from her relatives about her death and recurring attempts to return. Future drivers will either have the same experience if they pick up the hitchhiker or they will have an accident if they don't (texts 8,9,11c).

The ritual Mary Whales, however, appears in the mirror through the actions of the game players, who know the circumstances of her death previous to their interaction with her. She victimizes participants by scratching them on the face.

The double inverse relationships are a structuralist's dream:

LEGEND:
1. Mary Whales is passive: is killed, is scratched.
2. As revenant, she disappears.
3. Participants are passive.

GAME REPORT:
1. Participants active.
2. Revenant appears.
3. Mary Whales is active: scratches.

Since I've already suggested that neither the legend nor the game is primary for this particular group, it is not possible to establish in which direction the transformation goes.

And *why* is there a transformation at all? What are the reasons for the apparent incongruity between the pathetic revenant and the malevolent spirit? Leslie, whom both Gia (text 11a) and the boys (text 6) mentioned as instrumental in calling Mary Whales in the mirror, gave me the first clue: "There's a whole bunch of them. Oh, just like Mary Whales" (from text 12). There's Mary Lou, Mary Johnson, Mary Weathersby, Mary Worthington and Mary Worth.

Analysis of the sparse reports of these other Marys (texts 13a-13d) suggests "missing links" in the circular movement from legend to game[6]. For instance, boys calling Mary Worth did not know who she was but only that she "comes leaping out of the mirror screaming and lashing out with her long, sharp fingernails and scratching the chanter's face to shreds" (from text 13a). Girls calling Mary Worth in southeastern Wisconsin say that she is a woman whose face was marred once and who "will shatter the mirror, trying to mar your face as hers was" (from text 13b). Other callers say that Mary Worth is a witch—sometimes a witch burned at the stake after being convicted at the Salem with trials (from text 13c) and sometimes an African mulatto connected with African cult life (from text 13d). Girls who called Mary Worth at slumber parties in Kokomo said that she was a woman who had been killed by her jealous lover (no text available). The jealous lover motif occurs in versions of the Chicano legend, "La Llorona,"[7] which report sightings of the Weeping Woman searching eternally for the children she has murdered, often through jealousy, before her own death.

The legendary "La Llorona" and "the Vanishing Hitchhiker" have much in common: both are women revenants who have died in tragic circumstances; both are doomed to wander in endless patterns; and both, often dressed in white and associated with water or rain, confront unsuspecting persons. The structural similarities between the two have been seen not only by me but also by East Chicago residents who conflate them into the "Cline Avenue Ghost."[8]

But the way the two differ is significant as well. "La Llorona," as murderess, had an active malevolent aspect in life. And she has a malevolent aspect in death as well for she can appear as a hideous horse-headed monster dangerous to those whom she encounters. She can also scratch.

There is a ritual "La Llorona" too. Bess Lomax Hawes is the only folklorist, to my knowledge, who has published an account of girls calling the Weeping Woman. She quotes an excerpt from *New Yorker* author Renata Adler's conversation with two "habituees of Los Angeles' Sunset Strip" who recall their life in a juvenile home:[9]

> "They spoke of the ghost story the Mexican inmates used to tell—about La Harona [sic], a woman who, crazed by syphilis, killed her children.
> 'They said if you shouted "La Harona!" five times, she would come to you,' Meg said, 'and a lot of kids in my unit wanted to test it.'
> 'I was so terrified I cried all night,' Dot said.
> 'They said she came through mirrors.' Both girls still seemed terrified at this thought."

I am suggesting that the Mary Whales complex in northwest Indianapolis forms a set with the Mary Worth and "La Llorona" complexes elsewhere. The malevolent aspects of the revenant, expressed in both legend and game for "La Llorona" and for Mary Worth, are only expressed in the game for "the Vanishing Hitchhiker" although the threat of a traffic accident if the hitchhiker is not picked up hints at malevolence in the legend too.

When Gia told me that she called Mary Whales "to see if it was true or not" and that she was going to stop calling her because "she's gonna get us for messing with her" (from text 11c), the logical explanations for the disparity between the legendary and ritual Mary opened into the socio-psychological ones. Gia expressed an attitude towards the dead that is close to being a cultural universal: fear.

As I mentioned earlier, the couple who do a good deed for the revenant in the legend are passive participants in the invasion of the supernatural into their everyday world.[10] On the other hand, the girls calling Mary Whales actively participate in this process. Reports of the intentional traffic with the dead, typical of American teenage legend-telling and game-playing,[11] often include pain or death for the participants. The death of the girl who sticks a knife in a grave in the "Graveyard Wager" and the death of the boys who try to spend the night in a haunted house are just two examples. And so it is fitting that the woman in the mirror scratches while the woman on the street does not.

Given these odds, it is a wonder the legend/game occurs at all. Why? To help me approach this question, I looked to Clyde Kluckhohn's statement about myth/ritual: "That is, they are symbolic representations of the dominant configurations of the particular culture."[12] Remembering Melford Spiro's critiques of symbol studies which are not based on theories of symbolism or sufficient data,[13] I'll still venture a few thoughts. Hawes suggests that girls at the Las Palmas Juvenile Home in Los Angeles tell the "La Llorona" legend as "*signalling* the basic realities of their situation"[14] [italics mine]. Like the Weeping Woman, they are in a state of disequilibrium, of uncertainty, and their life histories—as Hawes poignantly comments—will probably correspond to events of the legend.

The girls isolated in the L.A. detention home are only the most extreme example of adolescent girls in groups separated from other human beings. Girls at slumber parties and in school restrooms are other examples. If "La Llorona" and "the Vanishing Hitchhiker" do form a set, then it is possible that telling the legend of Mary Whales also signals a state of uncertainty for the girls at Holy Angels.

It is precisely to alleviate such uncertainty that rituals are performed. Kluckhohn, following Malinowski, states that both "rituals and myths supply, then, fixed points in a world of bewildering change and disappointment."[15] Clifford Geertz states that ritual molds cognitive and affective states into tangible form.[16]

Anthony F. C. Wallace says that the goals of all ritual are to effect a transformation of state of the participants.[17] Such a transformation does take place for the girls who call Mary Whales in the mirror: both revenant and participants move from a passive to an active role.

The use of the mirror in this symbolic transformation is double. In the first place, it literally reflects the identification of the participants with the revenant. In normal situations, when any of the girls looks in the mirror, she sees herself; in reports of the game-playing, she sees Mary Whales, or, at least, expects to. In a sense then, Mary Whales becomes the girl's own reflection.

In the second place, the mirror connects this particular legend/game with the other narratives told by students at Holy Angels. Gia's statement that "I just got through watching a scary movie and I did it in the mirror myself" implies a relationship between the T.V. screen and the mirror that Dr. Linda Dégh makes explicit in another urban setting:

> Television, however, opens a window into the unknown world in the intimate surrounding of their comfortable home. . . . The traditional realm of folk-belief is reaffirmed through science fiction, modern ghost stories and supernatural mysteries.[18]

window = mirror = T.V. screen

entrance
of the
unknown world

The majority of stories students told in the group sessions clustered around this entrance of the unknown into their known world. In some cases, revenants and their sinister counterparts—human intruders—enter homes literally through windows and doors (texts 14-15). In other cases, the T.V. screen's metaphorical extensions are closets and windows (texts 16-17). Again, calling Mary Whales has the important difference that the girls are *in control* of the entrance while, in other cases, they are not.

A final myth/ritual question—the old one of individual or group origin—is mirrored here. Gia's report of her dream experience (text 11a) signals that she may have qualities similar to the religious innovators documented by Kluckhohn and Wallace.[19] Her account of the game "The Old Man With The Blue, Blue Shoes" substantiates the anthropologists' findings that a new myth/ritual complex grows out of an individual's creative use of existing behavior and out of participants' further augmentation and renewal.

It was something about an old man and he always wore blue shoes. . . and things. And if you call him back: "Old Man in the Blue Shoes," he'll come (from text 12).

We was, we were all girls and we was up there all alone—we was at a slumber party—and that was when this Mary Whales thing was *real big*, and everyone was standing around. . . I didn't know it was going to work because I made it up! and everybody, and everybody said, "Gia, don't you see it?" And I said, "Where, where?" And it was a blue figure! And I kept it to myself that I made it up (laughing) (from text 11c). . .

Whatever the relation of legend to myth and of game-playing to ritual, I find that the analogy of legend to game as myth to ritual generated exciting possibilities for understanding a not-so-simple game once played by not-so-simple children.

Wayne State University

TEXTS

1.
Anna L., 12, questionnaire, Holy Angels, February 8, 1973.

Q. Have you heard about a dead girl called Mary Whales or Mary Worth?
A. Yes, I've heard about Mary *Whales*. Well, to tell you the truth, I don't know much about her. All I know is that she stood on corner when it rained and she had a long white dress on. And when someone stopped to give her a ride she would disappear in the back seat and just leave a wet spot with blood on the seat and she wouldn't be in car anymore.

E332.3.3.1 Vanishing Hitchhiker (c) ghost. . . leaves wet spot on automobile seat; E422.1.11.5.1 (c) Ineradicable bloodstain after bloody tragedy, at scene of bloody accident; E422.4.4 Female revenant in white clothing.

Q. Where did you hear her story and who told you?
A. Well, I heard her story when I was in third grade, I'm in seventh now. When I heard it I was with a group of girls down in the Tramm lavatory. Everyone told me about her because they all knew about her and I didn't. Well, I've heard about her at least 20 times!
Q. Have you heard of calling Mary Whales or Mary Worth in the mirror from anyone?
A. No, I don't recall hearing about her in the mirror from anyone.
Q. Have you called her in the mirror yourself?
A. No, I haven't called her in the mirror myself.

2.
Michelle B., 13, questionnaire, Holy Angels, February 8, 1973.

Q. Have you heard about a dead girl called Mary Whales or Mary Worth?
A. Yes. The paper said that she was pick up at the cemetary. A man was in the car. He ask her where she was going. She told him to go to a house. She told him to go in the house and get someone and when he got back the seat was wet.

E332.3.3.1 Vanhishing Hitchhiker (c) ghost. . . leaves water spot on automobile seat.

Q. Where did you hear her story and who told you?
A. In the paper.
Q. Have you heard of calling Mary Whales or Mary Worth in the mirror from anyone?
A. Yes.
Q. Have you called her in the mirror yourself?
A. No.

3.
Renea H., 12, questionnaire, Holy Angels, February 8, 1973.

Q.   Have you heard about a dead girl called Mary Whales or Mary Worth?
A.   Yes, I hear she was going to a party when she die.

E332.3.3.1 Vanishing Hitchhiker

Q   Where did you hear her story and who told you?
A.   I hear it three or more [times]. A teacher told me.
Q.   Have you heard of calling Mary Whales or Mary Worth in the mirror?
A.   Yes, at school.
Q.   Have you called her in the mirror yourself?
A.   No.

4.
Carol P., 14, questionnaire, Holy Angels, February 8, 1973.

Q.   Have you heard about a dead girl called Mary Whales or Mary Worth?
A.   I heard that one night she was thumbing a ride and a man picked her up and stopped at the filling station. When he came back she was gone.

E332.3.3.1 Vanishing Hitchhiker

Q.   Where did you hear her story and who told you?
A.   From some girls.
Q.   Have you heard of calling Mary Whales or Mary Worth in the mirror?
A.   From a friend and she said that Mary scratched her face.
Q.   Have you called her in the mirror yourself?
A.   No.

5.
Gregory H., 15½, individual interview, Holy Angels, March 14, 1973.

(His identification of Mary Whales as a mentally-ill woman wishing to become a nun, his report of the litany as negative, and his description of Mary Whales slapping participants are unique.)

JL: And now just tell me again like you did before who the lady was that you called in the mirror?
G: Mary Whales.
JL: It was Mary Whales, Did you ever call her in the mirror yourself?
G: No, no.
JL: Did you hear of other people who did?
G: Ya. [Laughing.]
JL: What did they do? Tell me about it.

G: Well, first they went up to a mirror. They turned the lights out. And then they say, "I don't believe in Mary Whales" about ten times. Then, a, they, they said that she slapped them!

JL: Oh, so she must have come in the mirror then, huh?

G: Ya. They say they can see her ugly face in the mirror. . .

JL: Oh, she was ugly?

G: Uh-huh. And she slapped them.

JL: And she slapped them. Who did she. . . who told you this? Do you remember offhand?

G: It was a boy who used to go to this school named Michael.

JL: Um, he's not here anymore?

G: No.

JL: Oh. And who was Mary Whales supposed to be? Do you remember that?

G: It was a woman, a woman that wanted to become a nun at the, at the rectory, but the, a, father never wouldn't let her and everytime she would come up in church and she asked people, she asked father could she come into the rectory. And, and he say, "No." And then, one night, she climbed up and locked herself in the, in the attic of the church. . .

JL: I heard this.

G: . . . and then everybody started talking like she was a ghost. And then, a, a little later on, they said that she was dead even though she wasn't. That's all.

JL: That's it. What did you think about it when people told you they called her in the mirror?

G: I don't remember.

JL: What did you think about it? Did you believe it?

G: No.

JL: Did you think they believed it?

G: Ya, in a way.

JL: I'm, I'm still wondering why they did it. Did they ever tell you?

G: It just came up. People just started talking about it.

6.

Participants not identified. Edited from Intermediate Boys' group session, Holy Angels, February 21, 1973.

JL: How do you do it?

IB^1:   O.K. Go in the boys' bathroom with us.

[General laughter; dissent.]

JL: I don't think Sister Bridget Ann would like that at all.

IB^2:   Me either!

IB^3:   You mean in the mirror thing?

[General "yes."]

JL: You do need to have a mirror?

IB^4:   You got to be able to see.

IB⁵: Ya, you got to get in the dark.

JL: Well, how come you have to call her in the mirror?

IB⁶: I got something. What I got to tell you is true. It wouldn't come out as bright as it was.

IB⁷: See, you go to a mirror, you go to a mirror—

IB⁶: —and black smoke—

IB⁷: —and you say it about forty, thirty-five times. Call her name. see. "Mary Whales." Like that. About thirty-five or forty times. And then, after you get through saying it about thirty-five or forty times, you go—

IB⁸: You turn out all the lights and do it. And then she'll appear and sometimes she'll scratch you on the—

IB⁷: You're supposed to see a star. And then it starts getting bigger and bigger and then you see it like that. And then her arms be like that. And her feet and her head like that [holding arms out from sides to demonstrate how Mary Whales' head, arms, and feet correspond to the five points of the star first seen in the mirror]. And she comes down like that.

IB⁸: 'Course she had, she had long fingernails.

IB⁹: Here's what happened. Here's what happened. They said a good boy named Rupert was staying—

IB⁸: I'm telling her!

IB⁹: —came out of the bathroom with big old scratches on his face. First, he ran into the bathroom. Ayyyyyyyyy. Crying. Then he came back out with big old scratches on his face. . . "She scratched me!"

IB¹⁰: Girls always do, did it.

IB⁶: You know, Leslie and them was doing it?

IB¹⁰: Almost every day.

IB⁶: He could have run into something [reference to Rupert].

7.

Participants not identified. Edited from Intermediate Boys' group session, Holy Angels, March 21, 1973.

(IB₂, possibly Derrick S., is the only boy who reported trying the calling of Mary Whales at home alone. He reports a negative result.)

IB₁: I never have tried it and I never will.

IB₂: I tried it. I tried it. I went into the bathroom last night. It was kinda early in the morning, about one o'clock, and so I figured that time would be about the best time. And there was a little bitty spot on our mirror. And, you know, it was, somebody had put, it was a little speck or drop of paint. And I turned the lights out and said it. And I was looking at that mirror. My brother put a little bitty drop of glowing paint on there. He didn't know he was doing it. He was, he was trying to sneak it.

[General laughter.]
    And, after that, I started that. And it, and it, and it, and when I got real close up to it, I thought it would get bigger. And so I stepped back and it got real little and I turned on the lights and ran out!

8.

    Frances E., Anna L., Theresa M. Edited from individual interview, Holy Angels, March 14, 1973.

A: Well, yes. [Tape unclear.] Well, we'd just go, we'd just go downstairs.
F: Fourth grade.
A: Oh, that's right. Fourth grade. We'd go downstairs in the lavatory and we'd tell stories about her. and one girl named—this girl [laughing].—
JL: You can name her if you want. . . it's up to you.
F: She doesn't like her that's why she doesn't want to name her.
JL: Oh.
A: This girl, this [tape unclear], was downstairs in the, a, lavatory and she, her and these other girls named Roxanne, well, they looked in the mirror and cut off the light and they had one candle shining—one candle burning—if you don't have one candle burning, Mary Whales won't show—and they, they all had their hands together in the dark. They went downstairs, I mean, they were somewhere. And they were having a seance. And then, after ten seconds, why, Mary Whales scratched one of them.
JL: Who was Mary Whales supposed to be?
F: She was supposed to be a lady who, um, on her way to a dance or something—
A: —a prom—
F: She be, she had on a white dress—
A: Uh-huh. And she *died* or something on the way there or something.
T: And the first time I heard about it was from a boy named Larry [last name not clear]. And he asked us if we ever, you know, cut out the lights and did that. And I said I never heard about it. And then they brought it up in school and we started trying it.
JL: What grade were you in, Theresa, remember? Were you in fourth grade too?
T: Fourth. We were all together.
JL: Oh, you too, Frances? Have you, tell me, a, have any of you called her in the mirror yourself?
A: I was in the bathroom just last night. I was doing that and I went upstairs and got the candle and I was in the bathroom all by myself upstairs. I don't know why anybody'd come up there and my mother was downstairs talking on the phone and everybody else was gone outside. And I was doing, and I was doing it and I put my hands on the mirror. Something tickled me real bad on my fingers. So I jumped up and knocked the candle over! For the good probably. And I turned on the light and went out of the bathroom.
JL: Oh, it's good you tried though. Have you heard about it ever since you were in fourth grade? Or was that just the first time you heard about it?

F: I don't hear about it now.

T: Sometimes I don't hear about it in over a year, sometimes [tape unclear].

F: We just did that last year—

T: Uh-huh. Last year, we did it together last spring.

[All three girls talking together!]

JL: At one of the slumber parties?

F: Unnuh.

T: Unnuh.

A: It was during lunch time when we would always go downstairs.

JL: Oh, to the bathroom downstairs?

A: No, we just go down there to goof off and we didn't try to. . .

JL: Oh, how come, why do you think it has to be in the mirror? Why do you have to call her in the mirror?

F: That's right. That's all I hear, I don't never hear calling her nowhere else.

JL: Ya, me either.

T: So you can probably see her face.

A: They say she'll do something to you.

F: Right.

T: She'll scratch you.

JL: She'll scratch you.

T: Everytime they. . .

F: The first story I heard is about the time that. . .somebody says it's in the newspaper but I didn't hear it from the newspaper, I heard it from somebody in the school that said that she was on the corner. And if you stop for her, [tape unclear] if you, if you pick her up, she'll disappear or something like that—

T: She'll take you to this house or something—

F: —and leave a wet spot.

T: —and she'll tell you to go in the house and do something and when you come back, she won't be there but a wet spot will.

A: Uh-huh.

T: And if you, if you stop and say you not going that way, you'll get killed or something. And that happened one time. One time she. . . one time somebody picked her up and they went to a house, they went to a house. And they went in there, and they said that's the lady we had in the car and she said that was her daughter. She'd been dead for five, ten—I don't know how long.

9.

Debra W., 13, questionnaire, Holy Angels, February 8, 1973.

Q. Have you heard about a dead girl called Mary Whales or Mary Worth?

A. Yes, Mary Whales. Well, they say that Mary Whales was going to a party one night; and after the parties he ask her boyfriend to take her home; and he didn't want to go home right then and they got into an argument. And so she walking home that night in the rain and she crosssed the street and got hit by a car and was killed. And they say that everytime that it rains that she stands on the corner of 38th and Northwestern and hitchhikes a ride and if you don't give her a ride you will crash at the next stop light. And if you do give her a ride she will tell you to take her to a big white house and by the time that you get there she will be gone and the back seat of the car will be wet.

And another way that I hear it is that she went to a party and she ask her boyfriend and she ask her boy to drop her off at the drugstore and so he did. And she was walking home in the rain and she got hit by a car and she died in the hospital and she was buried two days later. And ever since then when it rains she stands on the corner of 38th and Northwestern and hitches a ride. And it has the same ending as the other one.

Q.   Where did you hear her story and who told you?
A.   My friend.
Q.   Have you told her story yourself?
A.   Yes, two weeks ago to a friend.
Q.   Have you heard of calling Mary Whales or Mary Worth in the mirror?
A.   Yes, a long time ago [from] my friend.
Q.   Have you called her in the mirror yourself?
A.   Yes, by myself.

E332.3.3.1 Vanishing Hitchhiker (c) ghost. . . leaves water spot on automobile seat.

10.
Leslie B., 11½, questionnaire, Holy Angels, February 8, 1973.

Q.   Have you heard about a dead girl called Mary Whales or Mary Worth?
A.   Mary Whales. I heard that one night she was going to a party, got to a tree and she ran into it and ran into a river. One day a man seen her and she looked at stopped, they hit a tree and he was knocked unconscious. He found a sweater in the back of the car. It had her address in it so he took it there and her father said, ''Son, my daughter died like that two years ago. Everyday she comes back to try to get home.''

E332.3.3.1 Vanishing Hitchhiker (b) ghostly rider leaves token. . . .

Q.   Where did you hear her story and who told you?
A.   I heard it at school. At school, at home, in the summer. All kind of people.
Q.   Have you told her story yourself?
A.   Yes, I did. At a slumber party. All the girls talked about it.
Q.   Have you heard of calling Mary Worth or Mary Whales in the mirror?
A.   Yes, I have. Everybody told me.

Q. Have you called her in the mirror yourself?
A. Yes! At school, all of the girls called her. Yes, I was [with a group of friends].

11a.
Gia P., 12, individual interview, Psychic Fair, Indianapolis, October 14, 1972.

JL: Now tell me again about Mary Whales, if you remember.
G: There was one time—six years ago she died, Mary Whales, that is—and, a, she, a, got ran over by this truck when she was on the corner of Crown Hill Cemetery.
JL: And this is in Indianapolis?
G: Uh-huh. And so then these two, a young couple, was just driving along and everything. And she was hitchhiking 'cause she was on her way to a party and it was raining that night and so, you know, she was kinda wet and she was bleeding, and she had scratches on her face, so they thought it would be nice to pick her up and things. And so, they, they picked her up. And she told them, she gave them this address. And so. . . they took her there. And when they got there, she was gone! And, a, they went into this house where they had took her. . . the girl got out of the car and the boy did too and they went in this house and her mother was in there and sister. And they were talking and things. And then she looked at the picture and she said, ''Who? We picked a girl up that looked just like her tonight.'' And her mother said, ''Naw, it couldn't have been her. She's been dead for six years.''
    And so then there was another time the same people was riding along and the cops had stopped them. And this girl—Mary Whales—was supposed to be hanging up on top of their car by a rope that wasn't there and she was bleeding and everything.
JL: You told me her neck was bleeding, right?
G: Ya, her neck was bleeding and her head was about to fall. And then them kids at school they talked about it and stuff and got everybody believing it and so, then we went into the bathroom, and we tried it.
JL: Tell exactly what you had to do to call her.
G: Ya, you had to, you could call her ten or a hundred times and call her name and say, ''I do believe in Mary Whales'' and, a, she was supposed to come.
JL: And come in the mirror? That's right?
G: And come in the mirror. And I was back in the corner all by myself. They, they, we said it up to a hundred times and we waited and waited and I closed my eyes and we still waited. And then Leslie said, ''Cut on the lights!'' and they said, she said, ''I saw her, I saw her and you didn't get a chance to see her.'' And so, I went home and I just got through watching a scary movie and I did it in the mirror myself.
JL: And you called her a hundred times?
G: All by myself, I called her a hundred times, and I was saying, ''I do believe in you, I do believe in you.'' And I was by the light switch and she came and her eye started bleeding and then I cut on the light real fast. And then, all that

night, I had a dream about her and I dreamed that she was right by my bed. She was about ready to touch me and I, and I, jumped up and looked around. And I thought that the door was open and I thought I saw something in there. And then I pushed Wendy over and got into bed with her!

JL: When Mary Whales came in the mirror, what was she dressed like? You told me that before.

G: She had on a blue party dress and she was all wet and things. It was horrible.

JL: And when her eye started to bleed. . .

G: I turned on the lights.

11b.

Gia P., 12, questionnaire, Holy Angels, Februay 8, 1973.

Q.   Have you heard about a dead girl called Mary Whales or Mary Worth?

A.   She got hit by a car on a rainy night. Now she comes back to haunt you.

Q.   Where did you hear her story and who told you?

A.   I've heard about her from everybody at school.

Q.   Have you told her story yourself?

A.   Yes. I told Janet at the Fair.

Q.   Have you heard of calling Mary Whales or Mary Worth in the mirror?

A.   Yes, I have heard of calling her in the mirror from my friend Monica.

Q.   Have you called her in the mirror yourself?

A.   Yes I have with the six grade. No [not alone]. Yes, I was with a group.

11c.

Gia P. and her half-sister Connie W. Edited from individual interview, Holy Angels, May 16, 1973.

JL: Well, tell me, how do you both feel? Do you both believe some of the things we've been talking about?

G: I believe in Mary Whales!

C: I do too. I'm scared of her.

JL: Why do you believe in her?

G: It's, it seems true. Too many people who tell of this as true!

JL: Since I've been coming here, have you called her in the mirror at home? At all?

G: Uh-uh. [Shaking head.] No. No.

C: [Shaking head.]

JL: Neither of you have?

G: We leave her alone.

JL: You let her be. Why?

G: 'Cause she might come up one of these nights and we're gonna have to tolerate her and she's gonna get us for messing with her!

JL: Do you think that? Do you think that's possible?

C: Um-hum.

JL: You both think that. So you think it's almost better if. . . if people let her be?

G: Um-hum.

JL: Or do you mean us particularly?

G: Anybody!

JL: Why do you think people called her in the first place?

G: To see if it was true or not.

JL: Ah. You know, Connie, Gia told me where she'd heard, some people at school told her about Mary Whales. Do you remember where you first heard about her?

C: From Gia.

JL: From Gia. How long ago? Do you remember when it was?

G: And Monica also told us.

JL: Who did?

G: Monica. Monica D., you know.

JL: Oh, yes, I do.

G: She, she tell me that. Her and her friend did it and a they, she said that she had to call her name a hundred times.

JL: Ya.

G: And Monica said after she'd said hers a hundred times, she run out of the room [tape unclear] she didn't hear nothing, her friend didn't say anything, you know, and so she said a, "Lucy? You in there?" And Lucy didn't say anything. And she said, "Lucy? You in there!" And she didn't say nothing. And then Lucy screamed and screamed! Monica says that she went in there and Lucy had this scratch on her, you know, and now Lucy calls Monica 'bout every day and asks her: "Have you called Mary Whales yet?"

JL: And, a, and what does Monica say?

G: Monica says, "Noooo, I'm scared." [Laughing.]

JL: Now she's scared too?

G: Um-hum.

JL: Why do you think she's scared?

G: 'Cause the same thing might happen to her!

JL: Oh. In other words, that Mary Whales would scratch her?

G: Um-hum.

JL: Did you tell her [your mother] about Mary Whales?

G: Um-hum.

JL: What did she say?

G: She already knew about it. It was in the paper.

JL: You mean about how she died?

G: And they had a picture of her. She was in the paper. And Mama said that the "Hook" was in the paper.

JL: Tell me a little about your Dad.

G: He just don't believe it, myths and stuff. He thinks they silly!

JL: Does he? Does he think you're silly?

G: He thinks I'm silly for believing in it.

JL: But Mary Whales, you believe in?

G: Ya, ghosts and stuff like that.

JL: Ya, you mentioned too you called back a "The Man With the Blue Shoes"?

G: Ya. I remember you don't have to look in the mirror. We was, we were all girls and we was up there all alone—we was at a slumber party—and that was when this Mary Whales thing was *real big,* and everyone was standing around. . . I didn't know it was going to work because I made it up!

JL: Oh, you did? Oh, Gia!

G: And everybody, and everybody said, "Gia, don't you see it?" And I said, "Where, where?" And it was a blue figure! And I kept it to myself that I made it up [laughing] . . .It was just a big blue thing, just sitting up there.

JL: Good heavens. Now was the "Man With Blue Shoes" anybody in particular?

G: I don't know. It looked to me like blue mist, all blue and stuff, you know, it looked like it was coming after us, you know. I said, "Leslie, Leslie, do you see him down there?" Said, "No!" He was coming over this mirror! I was standing right back there. "No, he's right down there." I said, "Well, I'm getting out!" And everybody ran out, you know, and then—

C: Didn't you all get in trouble for that?

G: Ya, we got in trouble for it.

JL: Why?

G: I don't know.

JL: Making too much noise?

G: Everybody was screaming and stuff trying to get out of there! [Laughing.]

JL: Oh.

G: But then we got into trouble for doing Mary Whales (i.e., calling her back in the mirror) and we had some gym lessons and we was down there (tape unclear) and it was real dark down there. . .

JL: Ooo, yes.

G: . . . calling Mary Whales. And we went down there and did it. And everybody started running out of there! [Laughing.] Everybody got scared!

JL: Well, have you made up any other stories that people believed or—the other ones you made up, wait, the other ones—did people tell you?

G: I told just that one.

JL: Just that one—"The Man with the Blue Shoes."

G: Um-hum.

JL: That was a good one. How do you think about Mary Whales now? Are people still interested in her or has that sort of died down?

G: At school I think it's sort of died down.

JL: What do you think, Connie?

C: *I'm* interested in it.

G: [Laughing.] Well, there was this girl and she was on her way to the party, to a party. And it was up there by Crownhill Cemetery. . . on the corner. Now Crownhill Cemetery's got a lot of corners and I don't know which corner!

[Laughing.] And so, they said she had on a blue dress, a bright blue party dress. It was raining. Had a real bad storm. And, a, she was hitchhiking to the party. And, a, well, anyway, while she was hitchhiking, she got ran over by a semi-trailer. And, a, then they said that she was dead and everything. And so this young couple from out of town didn't know about it, you know, and, a, they saw her hitchiking on the corner. And, a, they picked her up. And, a, she told them to come to this certain address, you know, and she sitting in the back seat and the girl and boy was in the front seat, you know. So they went out there to the father's house. And so the girl came up from her seat to let her out but, a, she wasn't in the back seat. The back seat was just wet and, you know, with mud and stuff.

JL: Um.

G: Where she had been. And so they, they went inside, you know, and they said, "A girl named Mary told us to come here." And he said, I mean the girl said, "There's a picture of her on the piano!" And he said, "She couldn't of told you to come here. She's been dead for three years." And they say if you don't pick her up on the night of her anniversary of her death I guess it is.

JL: Anniversary of her death?

G: Um-hum. If you don't pick her up, you'll have an accident on the next corner.

JL: No.

G: And, a, some of the girls told me that this one lady didn't pick her up and then she had an accident at the next corner.

JL: And when you have the accident, are you killed?

G: They said she was injured.

JL: Oh, she was injured. Well, tell me is Mary supposed to be buried in Crownhill Cemetery?

G: I don't know where she's buried—wherever she is, I hope she stay there!

[All laughing.]

JL: Well, if she, you know, if she did come back, why do you think she is—because people call her or why do you think she kept trying to get home?

G: Could be. . . maybe she wanted revenge on her daddy or something.

JL: Now that's possible. Why, why do you think, why do you think that though?

G: Maybe he didn't give her too much love or nothing.

JL: Ya, you mentioned that earlier. It's possible. Well, you know what, I think I'm just about out of tape. Shall we turn it off or do you still feel like talking about Mary Whales 'cause I'd like to hear everything you have to say but I don't want you to get tired. I don't want to get tired. I've got hours and hours of tape I'm gonna to have to put down with my little old typewriter. See if I can figure out some of these things about Mary Whales.

G: You ever been to her house?

JL: Well, I wish I knew where it was. Have you heard where her house is?

G: No, the only thing I know is it's way out in the country somewhere.

JL: Oh, it is out in the country.

G: Um-hum.

JL: Do you know, Connie, have you heard?

C: [Negative shaking of head]

JL: You don't want to know at all, do you? No? I didn't think so. Now, I don't
        know, I don't know if I would go but I would like to know her house—what
        house, you know, it was supposed to be at. And you had told me once too that
        you had called her in the mirror. Do you want to tell me about that, Gia?

G: Ayyyyy!

JL: Come on.

G: But I don't know when I called her.

JL: Well, anytime. Both times. 'Cause you called her alone too, didn't you? Or
        did you?

G: Ya, when I was home in my bed. We got this big hair, furry rug in my bedroom
        near my bed and one night I hear this noise [Gia made sound of knuckles
        rapping on wood]. And I was all the way back in the bathroom and [tape
        unclear] and I was scared but anyway I did it.

JL: What did you do?

G: I called her, you know.

JL: How many times? Remember?

G: Five hundred the first time I did it.

JL: Oh!

G: [Tape unclear] and I was looking. And I kept looking. But she didn't never
        come! So I turned back on the light and then I turned it off again and tried
        again. [Laughing.] And, you know, I was still looking and I kept looking and I
        think maybe my imagination went wild 'cause [Laughing.] she was looking at
        me right back and she wasn't doing nothing. She was sitting up there looking
        at me and I looked at her. [Laughing.] So then I got scared and clicked on the
        lights!

JL: [Laughing.] Well, tell me, can you tell me what she looked like? I think I can
        sort of see. . . I can sort of picture it but I'd like to know what she was like.

G: O.K. You know how a semi-trailer smashes you!

JL: Oh, she looked like that!

G: Ya, she looked like the way she died.

JL: Oh, my. Did she still have her blue, blue party dress on? You told me.

G: Ya, but she had real long fingernails!

JL: Oh, really?

G: Ya.

JL: Was she bleeding at all or?

G: Um-hum. Monica said she thought her eyes were just ready to *POP* out at her.

JL: No! Who said that?

G: Monica.

JL: Monica. Oh my.

G: If her eyes would have popped out at me, I would have just died.

JL: Ya, I think I would have felt that way too. Well, maybe if we find out about
        Mary Whales we'll let her rest in peace. Maybe that's really what she needs.
        And, when you called her with a whole group of people, you didn't—what
        happened then?

G: When I called her with a whole group of people, I don't think I saw her then.
       Maybe it was too many people.
JL: That, that could be, that could be true. She maybe. . .
G: Maybe she was afraid of too many people. . . .
JL: That's possible. That really is possible.

12.
Leslie B., Gia P. and unidentified participants. Edited from Intermediate Girls'
group session, February 21, 1973.

L: One time we had this seance in our basement. . . in the summertime. Every-
       body was down there. They was about twenty-five people down in our
       basement having a seance.
       [General "oh's."]
          So we was calling back, we was calling back—
IG¹: Who were you calling back?
L: Ah, we called back Mary Lou. That's who we called back. Mary Lou. And we
       said, "Mary Lou, if you're here, knock on the door twice." Nothing hap-
       pened. Everybody said, "Ah, this ain't nothing. You all, this ain't nothing."
       So we said, "Mary Lou, if you're here, open the door." And the door cracked
       a little bit. And everybody said, "Ah, she ain't here yet. You all just doing
       that." O.K. So everybody got together—all the big crowd—and we said,
       "Mary Lou, if you're here, flick a match and flick a candle". . . .And
       everybody was saying, "Mary Lou, if you're here, flick a light." And that
       light flicked on, the door opened, and everybody flew!
       [General laughing, comments.]
JL: Leslie, who's Mary Lou?
L: Oh, just like Mary Whales.
IG²: There's a whole bunch of them. Mary Weatherby or something.
L: Ya, Mary Weatherby.
       [General discussion.]
IG³: Tell the story.
G: It was something about an old man and he always wore blue shoes and things.
       And if you call him back "Old Man in the Blue Shoes" he'll come. . . Janet,
       you know, on Christmas Eve, my—it was, it was in the '60s—my grandfather
       died and my mother had to go home. . . And so she had to leave. And, you
       know, so I was little then. And everybody, you know, was up because they
       was calling everybody. And my daddy, he was asleep. Then I stayed up to wait
       for Santa Claus. And so I was up in the living room waiting for Santa Claus to
       come. And so, but he never did come. That's where I got "The Old, Old Man
       in the Blue, Blue Shoes." 'Cause my grandfather always wore blue shoes.

       [I went with the girls to call Mary Whales in the mirror in the restroom.
       No sooner had we got there, lights off, door closed, than all started
       screaming.]

13a.

Indiana University Folklore Archives. 71:356

> Date collected: Spring 1971
> Place collected: Chi Phi Fraternity, I.U., Bloomington, Indiana.
> Collector's name: Greg Wahlman
> Address: 417 N. Grant St., Bloomington, Indiana.
> Birthplace: East Chicago, Indiana.
> Age: 21
> Race: White, American, Irish- Scandinavian background
> Occupation: Student.
> Religion: Catholic.
>
> Informants name: Robert (Corky) Hovermale.
> Address: 507 S. Fess, Bloomington, Indiana.
> Birthplace: Jamestown, Indiana.
> Age: 20
> Race: White, American, German background.
> Occupation: Student.
> Religion: Protestant.

It was late one week night in the spring of 1971. Corky, my roommate and the informant, and I were sitting alone in our room at the Chi Phi house having a few beers and telling each other the "ghost stories" we knew. After about an hour straight of relating such stories the atmosphere was sort of tense. It was then Corky thought of a story he had heard in a Chicago apartment in a similar story-telling session by two girls in the summer before.

The story comes in kind of a "dare" form in that it is something that one must act out. The performer of the action must enter an entirely dark room alone and lock the door. He must then approach a mirror and put his face about a foot from it. Then he must close his eyes very tight and clasp his hands over his face very tightly. Next he must begin to chant, "I believe in Mary Worth, I believe in Mary Worth. . . ", concentrating completely on those words. After chanting these words about ten times or as many times as it takes to acquire the "right" feeling, then the chanter must pull his hands away and open his eyes simultaneously very quickly. As the legend goes, a woman, Mary Worth by name, comes leaping out of the mirror screaming and lashing out with her long, sharp fingernails and scratching the chanter's face to shreds.

After telling me this story Corky dared me to act it out and I returned the dare. Neither one of us wanted to do it. We finally ended up trying it out, but only with extreme fear. We both knew nothing would happen but we also both admit we were a bit nervous in doing it. Our faces were not scratched.

Corky could give no background to the story. The girls who told him the story could not give any information as to who Mary Worth was or how the story originated. Also neither of us have ever heard the story elsewhere.

13b.

Indiana University Folklore Archives, 71:697

Date of collection: Jan. or Feb. 1968
Place of collection: Salem, Wisc. (southeastern corner of Wisc.)
Collector's Name—Lynne Grams
Address—Rt. 1 Box 39 Salem, Wisc.
Age—19
Race—White
Religion—Lutheran
Occupation—Student

Informant's Name—Heather Morton
Address—Salem
Birthplace—Baton Rouge, Louisiana
Age—16
Race—White
Religion—Unknown
Occupation—Student

A long time ago, there lived an incredibly ugly woman named Mary Worth. Some say she was born that way, and others say she was in a bad accident when she was young. Whichever it was, her face was horribly marred. She was bitter, too, and as time went on she became more and more evil. People stayed away from her for fear of what might happen to them if they went near her. One day, as she looked in a mirror, she could stand her ugliness no more. In a fit of rage and insanity, she put a curse upon the mirror, and shattered it, fatally cutting herself in the process. From that time on, if anyone stares straight into a mirror (providing the room is completely dark), concentrates and says, "Mary Worth, Mary Worth, come to me; come to me!" she will appear. She will come as a distant shadowy figure at first, that gets more distinct as she comes closer. If you continue to watch and look upon her completely, she will shatter the mirror, trying to mar your face as hers was. From then on you will never be able to look into a mirror without her image appearing and coming for you again.

I first heard the Mary Worth legend at a typical girls' pajama party, about three years ago, when I was a junior in high school. It was told by a new friend of mine, who had recently moved to southeastern Wisconsin from Baton Rouge, Louisiana. She was accepted into our group for a number of reasons. She was smart, cute, and could tell some of the best ghost stories ever. Most of what she told us was "positively true," including her tales of various séances she said she had participated in. "Mary Worth" was one of the better ones. Heather vowed that anyone who disbelieved could see Mary's grave anytime, for she was buried in an ancient cemetery down south. To verify her story further, she gave us examples of friends of hers in Baton Rouge who had called into the mirror. One girl tried it and was found by her mother in a state of shock, in a pile of shattered mirror glass, with cuts all over her face, none serious however.

The events leading up to the telling were commonplace to anyone who has ever been to a "P.J." party. Around eleven o'clock or so a few of the girls will retire from the usual topics of school and boys and go off to a quiet corner to discuss the supernatural, or possibly to work a ouija board. The group gets larger until the entire party is either participating or observing in these "mood-setting" events. This is exactly what happened at this party, which, incidently was at Heather's house. Her house must have had a conducive atmosphere for spirits or visitations of the dead if ever there was one. It was an old 19th century model, dark and austere. And we had the whole upstairs to ourselves.

Finally, the inevitable happened—someone suggested a séance, which was also typical of the high school pajama parties I attended. We had one, but nothing really happened. A couple girls started crying, and another almost fainted, but the only "signs" we got from Joan of Arc or Marilyn Monroe were some scratching noises on the roof and the wind rustling the tree branches against the window.

The séance unsuccessful, and the mood for haunting still unsatiated, Heather told us about Mary Worth. A few girls wanted to try it and since the bathroom was the easiest to get completely dark, the bathroom mirror was the one decided upon. It was tried only once. The feeling standing there in the dark calling the dead was uncanny, even with the other girls. The silence and complete darkness created a sensation of total fright that was unbelievable. We could not have stood there more than a few minutes, though it seemed much longer. Suddenly with one consolidated shriek, everyone headed for the door. It was an unorganized and urgent push on everyone's part to get out as soon as possible. With that, the supernatural was put aside for the night, at least on the surface. Underneath, we were uneasy for the rest of the night.

The story was never told at another party that I attended, although I heard about it various times after others tried it. It was still a popular thing to talk about when the topic of the supernatural popped up. But after an initial try or two, most were reluctant to try it again. I knew of no one who stared until Mary appeared completely, but a couple of girls said they saw her image or shadow, then turned on the lights and ran. I have never tried it—I do not believe it, yet do not disbelieve it either. I would rather not take a chance. Also, I have never heard of any boys that have tried it. The appeal was mostly for the girls.

The main things to be gotten from participating in this legend are integration and compensation, as well as entertainment. It integrates those in the special groups in high school, the girls that got invited to the parties and did things together. There was compensation for Heather certainly, for after integrating herself into the group, she got the compensation of being the center of attention while telling her stories. There was also entertainment, which at a party, is essential. It entertained those who heard about it later as well as those who actually participated.

13c.

Indiana University Folklore Archives. 68/148

Miss Brethman also related how to call up the spirit of Mary Johnson and Mary Worth.

22. Everybody sits in the circle and holds hands. The room must be completely dark. you just keep saying "COME, MARY JOHNSON,COME" till in the middle of the circle on the ceiling you see a dim light. If anyone in the circle has any supernatural abilities, the light will move over the 'witch's' head.

23. If you want to see Mary Worth, you stand in front of a mirror in a dark room and say "I believe in Mary Worth." You keep saying this until you see a 'witch' appear in the mirror.

24. Both Mary Worth and Mary Johnson were supposed to have been witches. Both of them were burned after they were convicted in the Salem witch trials. To summon Mary Johnson, everybody should sit in a totally dark room, in a circle, and join hands. Then you repeat together, "Come, Mary Johnson, come!" Eventually a white light will appear in the room, over somebody's head. The person over whose head she appears is said to be the one most like a witch. The light will be bright enough that you will be able to see the faces of all those in the room.

Once, when we were summoning Mary Johnson, there was a rather skeptical girl in the room. Mary Johnson appeared over her head, and she didn't like it. In a rather irritated voice, the girl said "Go jump in a lake, Mary Johnson!" A few seconds later there was a splashing sound, and the girl screamed. We turned on the lights immediately, and the girl was soaking wet—just as though she had had a bucket of water poured over her head!

13d.

Indiana University Folklore Archives. 3338-3352.

This is an old bit of magic that comes down from an ancient African religion. The name is translated from the African language. She is a mullato witch who has many powers. If you go into a very dark, still room, that has a mirror, like that bathroom or something and stare real intently into the mirror and repeat the name Mary Worth 31 times very slowly, you will see this witch appearing in the mirror. She will only do this if you concentrate on seeing her as you say her name. She will appear with a green light around her. She is not a very old witch, and very beautiful, she was burned alive. You can ask her questions, and she will either nod or talk to you, but be careful!

I heard this in Chicago this last July, from a Negro man who was about 24, his name is Bill Byrd. He lives in the ghetto, and says that a lot of times he has seen her appear, but has only talked to her once.She talks real softly so you have to listen real close to what she says. Mara, my informant, said that there was also another boy there with him who had also done this, they talked about it in all seriousness, and were even studying some forms of the different African religions. Mara had never tried this, because she said that she was afraid of the consequences.

This story was collected on November 6, 1967, while Mara and I were going to get something to eat in Bloomington, Indiana.

14.

Denise W. From Junior High Girls' Session, Holy Angels, Feb. 21, 1973.

And we lived in this big old giant, big old giant house. With a long stairs and stuff. And she [Denise's mother] was in her bedroom, in her bedroom getting ready to sleep. And she kept hearing something at the window. And she opened the window up, up. She opened it up and there wasn't nothing out there. And it slammed back down. And she kept opening it and put something under it. And she went to bed. And, then, she turned over on her side and then somebody—she said she could, it felt like somebody's sat the side of her bed. And then, when my father got home, he could see that impression where somebody'd had sit. She was scared! That impression where somebody'd sat on the bed. Wasn't nobody there but her.

15.

David H. From Intermediate Boys' Session, Holy Angels, March 14, 1973.

I got one. One time, one time we was living on Dexter. My mother had waxed, we had the window open. We was living on Dexter, we had moved to Dexter, we had the window open. My mother was, she was just ready to go to sleep and this man stuck his head in our window. My father took his foot— WAM!--he kicked his head, kicked his head. That man took off running.

16.

Clifford B. From Intermediate Boys' Session, Holy Angels, March 14, 1973.

And one time my cousins came over and we pushed the beds beside each other so it was bigger. . . I forgot to close the closet door. And we watched this thing on *Nightmare* called. . . "Horror of the Beach Party." I don't like to see it that much. . . but I like to watch it. And so, I thought I saw the head of it in our closet. . . My mother. . . see, my mother comes home at. . . see, she gets off at 11 o'clock and comes home at 11:30. That's what I like. That's when I be glad.

17.

Elmer E. From Intermediate Boys' Session, Holy Angels, March 21, 1973.

See, one night, I was looking at t.v. And I was the only one up. And, you know, I was spending the night over at my friend's house. We was the only ones up and his cousin came over there. And we was watching Sammy Terry. And so, after he, after he went off, it was about five o'clock in the morning. It was about five o'clock in the morning. And so, all of us got up and we went, 'cause we heard something knocking all over the windows and I was over at a friend's house spending the night. I'm going to have them over to my house, you're not going to see me over there no more! And then, and then we, all of us, got up. It was Vaughn, Brent, and me. And we got up. And so, we looked at the door. It, it looked just like *Nightmare* but he had his make-up off and so, he, he kept coming to the windows, peeking his face in there and knocking all over it. I took that pillow. I hit him against that window. I said WAP! And that man's, that man's eyes just got real big and he *ran!* He had on some big old thick boots with big old heels on them. . . And he came to the window. He was at the window. And the door.

NOTES

1. See, for example, Richard K. Beardsley and Rosalie Hankey, "The Vanishing Hitchhiker," *California Folklore Quarterly* 1 (1942), 303-35; "A History of the Vanishing Hitchhiker," *California Folklore Quarterly* 2 (1943), 13-25; William A. Wilson, " 'The Vanishing Hitchhiker' Among the Mormons," *Indiana Folklore* 8:1-2 (1975), 79-97.

2. Jan Harold Brunvand, *The Study of American Folklore: An Introduction* (New York: W.W. Norton, 1968), 238.

3. See, for example, William Bascom, "The Myth-Ritual Theory," *Journal of American Folklore* 70 (1957): 103-14; Clyde Kluckhohn, "Myths and Rituals: A General Theory," in *Studies on Mythology,* ed. by Robert Georges (Homewood, Ill.: The Dorsey Press, 1968), 137-67; Clifford Geertz, "Religion as a Cultural System," in his *Interpretation of Cultures* (New York, Basic Books, 1973), 87-125; Lord Raglan, "Myth and Ritual," in *Myth: A Symposium,* ed. by Thomas A. Sebeok (Bloomington: Indiana University Press, 1971), 122-35; Victor Turner, *The Forest of Symbols: Aspects of Ndembu Ritual* (Ithaca: Cornell Univeristy Press, 1967) and Anthony F.C. Wallace, *Religion: An Anthropological View* (New York: Random House, 1966).

4. Special thanks to Holy Angels Principal, Sister Bridget Parisi, for permission to interview Intermediate Boys and Girls and Junior High Boys and Girls during their weekly free period, Wednesday, 11:30 a.m.-1:30 p.m. Feb. 7, 21, and March 14, 21, and May 16, 1973. Special thanks to Intermediate and Junior High Girls for their invitation to a slumber party, February 23-24, 1973.

5. Linda Dégh, Personal communication.

6. See Claude Levi-Strauss, "The Structural Study of Myth" in *Myth: A Symposium,* ed. Thomas A. Sebeok (Bloomington, Indiana University Press, 1971), 81-106 and *The Raw and The Cooked* (New York: Harper and Row, 1969) for structural method of analyzing related texts to understand incongruent elements in key texts.

7. See, for example, Aurelio M. Espinosa, "New Mexican Spanish Folklore," *Journal of American Folklore,* 23 (1910), 395; Bacil F. Kirtley, "La

Llorona and Related Themes,'*Western Folklore* 19 (1960), 155-68; Bess Lomax Hawes, "La Llorona in Juvenile Hall," *Western Folklore* 27:3 (1968), 153-70; Soledad Perez, "Mexican Folklore from Austin, Texas," in *The Healer of Los Olmos and Other Mexican Lore,* Texas Folklore Society Publications, 24 (Dallas, 1951); and Stanley L. Robe, "Hispanic Legend Material: Contrasts Between European and American Attitudes," in *American Folk Legend: A Symposium,* ed. by Wayland D. Hand (Berkeley, Los Angeles: University of California Press, 1971), 109-20.

8. Philip George, "The Cline Avenue Ghost," *Indiana Folklore* 5:1 (1972) 56-91.

9. Hawes, 160-61, quoting Renata Adler, "Fly Trans-Love Airways," *New Yorker.*

10. See Max Lüthi, "Aspects of the Märchen and the Legend," *Genre* 2:2 (1969), 162-78 for discussion of the passive participation of legend protagonists in supernatural events.

11. Linda Dégh, "The Haunted Bridges Near Avon and Danville and Their Role in Legend Formation," *Indiana Folklore* 2:1 (1969), 54-89.

12. Kluckhohn, 145-46.

13. David Kaplan and Robert A Manners, *Culture Theory* (Englewood Cliffs, N.J.: Prentice Hall, 1972), 116, n. 44 quoting Melford Spiro's review of Mary Douglas, *Purity and Danger* in *American Anthropologist* 70 (1968), 391-92.

14. Hawes, 169.

15. Kluckhohn, 158.

16. Geertz, 8-125.

17. Wallace, 106.

18. Linda Dégh, "Two Old World Narrators in Urban Setting," *Kontakte und Grenzen: Festschrift für Gerhard Heilfurth* (Gottingen: 1969), 71-86.

19. Kluckhohn, 150-54; Wallace, 30-39.

The Big Tunnel

Gary Hall

Most teenagers know any number of local "haunted" places and legends which verify the existence of the supernatural at these sites. Visits to these "spooky" places are a popular recreation for many Indiana adolescents. One such legend-trip popular with Lawrence County youth is from Bedford to the Big Tunnel, a rail tunnel between Fort Ritner and Tunnelton. Legend-telling is an important part of any visit to this "scary" locale. Accordingly, this paper will first survey legends specifically associated with the Big Tunnel. Next, the legend-trip as a whole will be described and one trip will be analyzed in detail. This analysis both supports previously proposed legend theory and suggests particular influences of the legend-trip context on the process of legend-telling.

On their way to the Tunnel, Bedford teenagers tell legends and horror stories which purportedly review its 116 year history.

A. *The Murdered Watchman and his Lantern*

Perhaps the best known Tunnel legend tells of a watchman who haunts the cavern he walked nightly for years. A tragic, violent death has doomed him to an eternal vigil (Motif E411.10 "Persons who die violent or accidental death cannot rest in grave"). In most variants of this legend the watchman is mysteriously and gruesomely murdered. A1. In what is

*I would like to acknowledge my debt to Susan Holmes, Susan Ikerd, and George Kyme—former students in my Folklore discussion class. These three young people, all from Bedford and frequent visitors to the Tunnel, formed the fieldwork team which so effectively gathered much of the material presented here. The merit of this paper, whatever it may be, owes much to them.

probably the simplest version, the watchman is found murdered and hung by a meat hook at the center of the Tunnel (Told by Larry DeGraff, 18, in Bedford, 1972).[1] Other versions attempt to account for the watchman's death.

A2. There used to be a night watchman at the Tunnel who would walk through the Tunnel every so often to make sure that there wasn't anything on the tracks and that the Tunnel wasn't caving in. After he got through the Tunnel, he would wait at the end for a train to come and would signal with a lantern to the engineer of the train to show that it was OK. One night he was taking some rocks off the track when the train suddenly came through the Tunnel. He didn't have enough time to run to a cubby hole and was sucked underneath the train, and his head was cut off. They didn't get anyone to replace him because they said you could still see him at the end of the Tunnel signaling the train without his head.
    (Told by Jim Craig, 18, in Bedford, 1972.)

Still other versions add a second watchman. A3. Laurie Snyder, a freshman at Indiana University, tells a story about two watchman who walked through the Tunnel and met one another in the middle. One night one of the men screamed. The second watchman went back into the Tunnel and found the other watchman with his head cut off. A long-time resident of the area tells a similar legend.

A4. I think everyone in this county knows, and most believe, the story of the Tunnelton tunnel. The half-mile Tunnel cuts through the mountain near the river. During the Civil War the Tunnel was an ammunition depot and was heavily guarded. There were two guards at each end of the Tunnel and two more inside constantly patroling back and forth from end to end. One night the guards inside failed to report to the guards at the ends for a long time, so the guards at the ends went in to investigate, knowing that no one had gone into the Tunnel. Near the center of the Tunnel they found the two guards with their throats cut, hanging from railroad spikes that had been jammed into the brick walls. The murder was never explained, but the spikes are still there. It's supposed to be disastrous for anyone to touch those spikes, though I don't know exactly what's supposed to happen if you do.
    (Told to Judi Burke by Catherine Grisson, age 53, of Williams. Collected in Bedford, 1972. IUFA IU:2033)

Phyllis Quackenbush Reed, a Bedford housewife, wrote an account of the watchman's death as remembered in her family and submitted it to the Indiana University Folklore Archives in 1969. Her written version follows:

A5. Recently there has been a revival of interest in the tunnel by the young people of the county who have made it the current fad to visit this curiosity. Evidence of these visits can be plainly seen on the interior walls which are inscribed with the usual graffiti and the various names of the more publicity seeking youngsters. There have also been some errie [sic] stories circulating concerning the experiences of the more intrepid ones who chose the hours of darkness for their tour of inspection. It is said that they encounter sights and sounds which should not be present in a supposedly empty tunnel. Vague vaporous forms and noises suspiciously resembling low moans have been the cause of many of the young people's hasty exit. Several have been heard to remark, "When you've seen one tunnel, you've seen them all, and one is enough, thank goodness!"

During a family gathering we were laughing at these fantastic rumors and attributing them to vivid imaginations plus the probable ingenuity of a practical joker. Mother had been listening intently without a comment or smile. When some of the talk had died down she quietly began to tell us the following story:

She told us that she did not know when the original tunnel had been constructed but she did know that it was rebuilt in 1909. During the remolding process it became necessary to hire two guards to prevent the theft of building materials and to stop vandals from strewing debris across the tracks. At designated times throughout the night the two men would meet in the middle of the tunnel to discuss any difficulties they may have encountered and to drink some hot coffee to ward off the chill and dampness.

One of the guards was Henry Dixon, a cousin of mother's. He was a strong man of good character, married and the father of two small boys. One night while patrolling his section of the tunnel, he discovered two rough-necks of the town attempting to assault a young girl whom they had dragged into the tunnel. After assuring himself that the girl had not been seriously harmed, he let the men leave warning them that he would have them prosecuted if he saw them in the tunnel again. Reluctantly the two men left muttering ominous threats under their breath.

A few nights later Henry failed to show up in the middle of the tunnel at the appointed time and the other guard began searching for him. After a long walk through the dark and lonely tunnel he at last found his friend propped up in one of the wall niches seemingly asleep. As he drew nearer and the glow of the lantern was cast upon Henry's face, he saw the glaze of death in the bewildered, staring eyes. The cause of death was immediately apparent as his skull was so badly crushed that a large portion of his brain was exposed.

The terrible news [of Henry's death] was such a terrible shock [to the dead man's sister-in-law] that she began having premature labor pains. In a few hours she gave birth to a son. What should have been a time for rejoicing became a time of horror for the child was born with an exposed brain. The condition of his skull bore a marked similarity to that of the murdered man's fatal wound.

The baby lived for several weeks in this hideous condition and reliable witnesses stated that he continually moaned, "Oh, my God!" until he was mercifully released by death.

Since the night of the murder there have been reports of what could be a lantern gleaming through the long darkness of the tunnel and some folks have heard sounds that could easily be taken for the moans of a dying man.

> (IUFA IU:1563 Mrs. Reed's family has lived in Lawrence County for over 150 years. In later correspondence, she wrote, "my Great-Grandmother did visit the baby before it died. It was she who told of the horrible wound on the baby's head . . . .")

In another closely related variant, the watchman himself is not killed but is so frightened that he is doomed to haunt the Tunnel forever.

A6. There used to be this watchman in there [the Tunnel] all the time. Well, when a watchman was making his rounds one night, he discovered a dead body hanging from a single beam. The man was hung; and he was so scared that the lantern he held was still there, he had clenched it so tight. Now when you walk through the Tunnel, you can see the light of the lantern swaying back and forth. You can also see the beam, it's the only beam in the entire Tunnel. You can see the swaying light when you go through, I've seen it.

(Told by Pat Manis, 19, of Knox, 1972.)

Many Tunnel visitors claim to have seen the watchman's light or at least some mysterious light in the Tunnel. Carol Mathis, a forty-year-old Tunnelton resident, recalls his own experience with the mysterious light in his youth.

A7. I was out hunting around the Tunnel. All of a sudden my dogs took off howling and running in front of me. When I finally caught up with them, they were standing in front of the Tunnel barking. I went up to the entrance and looked in. There was a light swinging back and forth quite aways inside. First I thought it was a bunch of kids but they didn't make any noise and they wouldn't answer when I called out to them. I stood there looking at the light when all of a sudden it disappeared. That was the only time I was ever really scared there since I was a kid.

(Told by Carol Mathis, 40, in Tunnelton, 1972.)

Tunnel visitors today still claim to see the swinging lantern of the dead watchman.

A8. Whatever it is carries á lantern. It's a brakeman's lantern you'll see swinging in the darkness, and when it gets close enough to you it will light up the form of a man dressed in old-time railroad clothes, and you'll see he's carrying his head under his arm.

> (Unidentified informant quoted in the *Bloomington-Bedford Sunday Herald Times*, 26 September, 1971. Motif E422.1.1 "Headless revenant"; E422.1.1.4 "Headless ghost carries head under arm.")

One young Bedford resident, now a junior at Indiana State College, tells of his own experience with the light when he was a junior in high school.

A9. I was out riding with a bunch of guys and we finally ended up at the Tunnel. All of us went in the Tunnel but Mike – – –. He was scared and stayed in the car. The rest of us sneaked up on him once and banged on the car to scare him, but we went back to the Tunnel and started through. When we got back to the car, Mike was laying in the back seat shaking and white as a sheet. He kept saying, "You guys did it, didn't you? Come on, you scared me. At least tell me you did it!" He kept yelling about some light. None of us had any light. When Mike finally realized that, he quit yelling at us and told us what happened. He said that after we'd left, he just sat there listening to the radio. He saw this light coming toward the car and he thought it was us coming back. He said the light kept getting closer and closer and seemed to float. It got right next to the car windows and shone in the car for almost a minute. Then it went back the way it came, just floating along in the air. Some of the guys thought Mike made it up, but he was too scared to have made it up.

> (Name withheld by request: Male, 20, Bedford, 1972.)

A small group of closely related variants tells of a mysterious death—not a watchman's death—in the Tunnel.

Aa1. No one seems to know just how this one fellar was killed. They buried him on Tunnel Hill and after a spell his grave was found open and he was gone.

> (George Horner, 83, of Tunnelton: Quoted in *Bloomington-Bedford Sunday Herald Times*, 26 September 1971.)

Aa2. A dead man was found on the tracks. He had been run over by the train and they buried him in the Tunnel. Sometimes when you walk through the Tunnel you can see the grave.

> (Told by Laurie Snyder, 18, of Bedford, 1972.)

Aa3. A man fell off the back of a caboose and was killed. His ghost haunts the Tunnel as he waves an old lantern in one hand and carries his head under his other arm. This man was buried on the hill above the Tunnel. He haunts the Tunnel because they didn't bury him correctly.
(Told by Jerry Clampit, 18, of Tunnelton, 1972.)

Aa4. A long time ago a man was fishing near Tunnelton and went over to the Tunnel to listen for the train so he could tell what time it was. He put his ear to the track and it stuck there, and he was decapitated by the train. Now his ghost haunts the old Tunnel, walking through sometimes with a lantern but always with his head under his arm.
(Self-collected by Judi Burke, 21, 1972. IUFA IU: 2035)

Both older area residents and young visitors to the Tunnel agree that: 1. watchmen were assigned to the Tunnel, and 2. someone—most say the watchman—was mysteriously murdered in the Tunnel. The young people's legends add that the murdered man now haunts the tube, usually without his head and carrying a lantern.

A watchman was, in fact, employed by the railroad between 1857 and 1908; his function was to walk through the Tunnel after each train and remove any loose rock that had fallen from the walls or ceiling. When the Tunnel was brick-lined in 1908, the watchman was no longer needed and was discharged. It was about this time that Henry Dixon was, in fact, found murdered in the Tunnel.[2]

B. *Mass Murders*

Mass murder is the theme of a second group of Tunnel legends. **B1.** It is said that convicts were impressed to rebuild the Tunnel. They tried to escape and were all killed. They were buried in the Tunnel floor and their graves are the humps still visible there (Told by Pat Manis, 18, of Knox, 1972; Motif R51.4 "Prisoner massacre"). Although the Tunnel was completed before the Civil War, one legend asserts that its construction disturbed the graves of soldiers killed in the war.

B2. A bunch of ex-convicts were sent north on a special mission by the South during the Civil War. Their job was to terrify people by going into towns and killing people. They were ambushed on the hill above the Tunnel and killed. They were buried there. When the Tunnel was built their graves were disturbed and now they haunt the Tunnel. Their screams can be heard as you walk through the Tunnel.
(Told by Jim Craig, 18, of Bedford, 1972. Motif E334.2 "Ghost haunts burial spot"; E402.1.1.3 "Ghost cries and screams.")

B3. Another variant of this legend acknowledges that the Tunnel antedates the War, but like the version above, it tells of a small battle fought near the Tunnel. (See page 155.) Although adolescent narrators tell these Civil War legends as ghost stories, their origin might be traced to southern Indiana's folk history of General John Morgan's Confederate invasion of the state in 1863.[3]

The story of the "Tunnelton Massacre," a mass murder of later date, was first told to the narrator by his father.

B4. It seems there was a gang that was going to rob Alfred Guthrie—a rich man who built a big brick house in Tunnelton. These men were in the saloon at Fort Ritner drinking and talking about their plans to rob Guthrie. Another group of men overheard them and followed them to the Tunnel. They caught them inside the Tunnel and killed every one of them. There were about four of them. These men just dug graves in the ground next to the tracks inside the Tunnel and buried the robbers right there. When I was younger I could see the graves, but I haven't been back for a long time. They're probably worn down by now.

(Told by Carol Mathis, 40, of Tunnelton, 1972.)

This particular legend seems to have a specific historical basis. In 1882 Tunnelton residents ambushed would-be thieves and killed all three. The ambush, however, was in town, not in the Tunnel.[4]

C. *Recent Murders*

A final group of legends tells of recent murders in the Tunnel.

C1. This was supposed to have happened about thirty years ago. A bunch of guys went out to the Tunnel and they were pretty drunk. They all dared this one guy to walk through the Tunnel by himself and kept calling him names until he did it. The rest of the boys sat outside and waited for him to come back but he never did. Finally they went in and found him laying on the railroad tracks; he was dead. He had one of those old fashioned meat hooks through his neck. They all sobered up fast and went looking for the murderers. They never found anyone and no one ever found out what happened in the Tunnel that night.

(Told by John Esary, 20, of Bedford, 1972.)

Similar stories tell of a mysterious death during a teenage visit to the Tunnel, a visit very much like those made today. **C2.** During one of these visits, one boy failed to rejoin the others after the train had passed. The others went back and found him in a manhole dead (Told by Jerry Clampit, 18, of Tunnelton, 1972). **C3.** Another boy abandoned inside the Tunnel by his friends was found dead with a terrified look on his face (Told by Jim Craig, 18, of Bedford, 1972). A common theme underlies these stories: A visitor *alone* in the Tunnel is killed. This doubtless encourages group solidarity during the walk through the dark tube. These stories also serve to validate the presence of mysterious and dangerous forces in the Tunnel. While the danger is identified specifically in other legends (whether that threat be the ghosts of the headless watchman, the buried worker, the massacred convicts or soldiers), in no version of this final legend group is the fatal danger identified.

These three broad groups of legends are characteristic of stories associated with the Big Tunnel site. The texts, albeit isolated from narrative context, are representative of thematic emphases in Tunnel legendry. Typically, the themes of these legends are headless revenants (watchmen), massacres, and mysterious, gruesome murders. While particular Tunnel legends may have their origin in documented historical events, the emphasis during the legend-trip is on the stories' "scare" rather than historical value. The aim of the legend-trip is not to learn local history but to have the fun of a good "scare." Accordingly, any "spooky" story or horror legend is appropriate during the trip. Stories about the Tunnel which suggest the presence of mysterious and malevolent forces in the dark cavern are important to the success of the trip, but are only one segment of a larger and more complex legend event. These Tunnel horror stories are an integral part, but only a part, of the legend-trip.

Legend-trips to "scary" or "haunted" places like the Big Tunnel are common adolescent recreations. Most often they begin informally, almost spontaneously, as "something to do" or "someplace to go." Legend-trips to particular sites involve both legend-telling and activities peculiar to that site. Touching a gravestone, walking in a certain order, or flashing lights a specific number of times might be important parts of trips to a "haunted" place.[5] The Big Tunnel legend-trip is one such traditional or patterned recreation for Bedford youth.

A trip might begin on a summer evening, or after a party, as a carload or two of young people decide to drive to the Big Tunnel. Most everyone in the car has been there before; in fact, a few have driven to the Tunnel as often as once a week during the summer months. Usually boys and girls ride in the same car, but seldom as couples. Someone might have a few cans of beer to pass around, but most often no one gets drunk.

The night drive from Bedford to the Big Tunnel will take about thirty minutes. The winding road will take the teenagers through southern Indiana countryside shrouded almost invariably in dense fog. Once the car has left Bedford and turned onto the country road, someone mentions the Tunnel and the teens review its legendary history. Both individually and cooperatively they re-tell the five or six stories about the Tunnel that nearly everyone knows. They match other "scary" stories, each trying to tell the "scariest"; they tell local legends, modern migratory legends, horror stories from literature or movies and on occasion someone invents a new story. By the time the group is within a few miles of the Tunnel, many of the young people begin to feel the atmosphere of fear which their receptivity to these "scary" stories has generated. The last few miles along the narrow dark road "set" this atmosphere.[6]

To the right of the dirt road that leads the last mile or so to the Tunnel are five or six ramshackle buildings elevated six to eight feet on concrete stilts. Only a short distance away, the White River ensures that these dark buildings are obscured in fog. The weird outlines of these buildings are, the visitors say, a portent of evil. After crossing a small bridge, they stop near a roadside trash pile. A weather-beaten, over-stuffed chair stands beside the footpath leading up the thickly forested hill to the Tunnel. Someone will mention that this is the "Bum's Chair" where hoboes who lurk in the area sit waiting for Tunnel visitors. By now the darkness and almost palpable atmosphere of fear becomes too much for some of the young people. They may refuse to go further or might even insist everyone return to Bedford immediately. Usually, however, almost everyone musters up enough courage to take the footpath up the hill to the railroad and the overwhelming arch of the Tunnel.

The entrance dwarfs the visitors. Its total blackness makes the night seem light by comparison. Without lights, the teenagers—sometimes with hands joined—walk into the Tunnel and feel their way along the right wall. At intervals their hands slip and the wall seems to disappear; manholes, recesses about five feet high and two feet deep built as places of refuge from passing trains, are spaced throughout the Tunnel and are disquieting breaks in the solidity of the wall. To walk through the Tunnel is to walk

"The entrance dwarfs the visitors. Its total blackness makes the night seem light by comparison."   (Photo by John B. Bunch)

through the haunts of headless watchmen, ghosts, and ogres, any of whom might be hidden in one of the manholes. Potential dangers are magnified by perceptual distortions inside the Tunnel. The air is chill and damp; the darkness is so complete that vision seems to fail (visitors most often mention this total darkness in their descriptions of the Tunnel); the walls amplify even the slightest sound—dripping water echoes through the Tunnel.

While some groups leave after their walk through the cavern, others try to time their trip so they will be inside at about ten or twelve o'clock. It is then that night freight trains speed through the Tunnel. To stay inside, crowded in the manholes, while a train rushes through is the high point of the trip. One visitor notes:

All the kids go there. They usually go about the time a train is supposed to go through. They get inside holes in the wall and wait for the train to go through. You are not with it until you go to the Tunnel and stay in it while the train is going through it.
(Comment by D. M.: Female, 22, of Bedford, 1972. IUFA IU: 1979)

Rather than try to characterize the emotional impact of this legend-trip, let me cite two young peoples' own descriptions of their experiences in the Tunnel. The first, written by a frequent Tunnel visitor, is a particularly effective description of the walk through the dark curving tube:

As you walk into the gigantic, man-made cavern, the cool damp air makes you shiver and you suddenly find yourself in unbelievable complete darkness, so dark that you can't even see your hand in front of your face or the person standing next to you. Is there someone next to you? Who is it? You move toward the wall to feel your way. The bricks are cold and you can feel the dirt coming off in your hand, but you drag your hand along it anyway because it gives you a strange sense of security. Suddenly your hand falls into a manhole and you hesitate. Somebody from behind walks into you and swears. You look back and see the Tunnel opening which is rapidly disappearing because of the Tunnel's curve. You walk a little further and neither end is visible. You are now in complete darkness no matter which way you turn. You can't be certain where your companions are, and they sometimes scream or push; you half expect this, so there is no real fear, but still that slight tremor of the spine occurs and the mind grows a little uncertain. A slight rumble is heard and someone yells, "A train!" There is a mad scramble in the dark for the manholes. As many people crowd in, the train's light illuminates the whole interior and its horn blast is deafening. The train brings with it a cold powerful wind and a slight vacuum force. After what seems an eternity, it is gone and everyone scrambles out of their hole, ready to leave. The wind left by the train is strong and cold and it is a good excuse to hurry. It seems that everyone leaves more quickly than they enter.

The ride home is filled with laughing, singing and recollections of the night's events. The pent-up nervousness has been released and the thrill is over.

(Written by George Kyme, 18, of Bedford, 1972.)

The next example is especially interesting. It is an eighteen-year-old girl's oral description of her first visit to the Tunnel; recorded shortly after this visit, her comments describe both activities at the Tunnel and her personal reactions to them.

As we were walking up the hill to the Tunnel, every picture of a tunnel passed through my mind. Then I saw that gigantic opening. I never dreamed it was that big. I wasn't scared before, just curious, but I was scared then. At the top of the hill, we smelled something funny, but no one knew what it was so we just started through the Tunnel. It was so dark inside the Tunnel I thought I was blind until I got to the other end. I couldn't even see the person standing next to me; it could have been the headless watchman for all I know. We used flashlights on the way through, so that all the new people could see what the inside looked like. All kinds of things were painted on the walls and in the cubby holes, like skeletons, ghosts and tombstones. On the way back, we turned off the flashlights until someone tripped on a stick. They turned on the flashlights and saw that the stick was a hobo's knapsack with his clothes wrapped around it. It was really spooky! We wondered why he had taken off so fast and left his clothes behind. I wondered what had scared him off! We hurried through the Tunnel. We stood outside the Tunnel talking when one of the boys discovered what the odd smell was. It was a fire that had been put out recently because it was still hot and smoking. Now we knew someone had been there before us, but we didn't know what had scared him away so suddenly. Then we heard a whistle. Everyone screamed, "A train!" Instead of everyone heading away from the Tunnel, everyone ran straight for the Tunnel to get inside one of those cubby holes. It was crazy! The train was so close to us and so loud! The wind that came along with the train was unbelievable. After the excitement of being in the Tunnel when a train came through, we decided to leave.

(Told by Jamie Gordon, 18, of Logansport, 1972.)

"... we heard a whistle. Everyone screamed, 'A train!' Instead of everyone running away from the Tunnel, everyone ran straight for the Tunnel to get inside one of those cubby holes. It was crazy!" (Photo by John B. Bunch)

The return drive to Bedford is the antithesis of the drive to the Tunnel. The young people joke, sing, and talk about nearly anything.

Although the trip sketched above is representative of most Tunnel trips, it is not meant to be normative. Most trips, it is true, are on summer evenings; however, some groups visit the Tunnel during the spring and fall as well. Although most trips are relatively spontaneous recreations, some are planned to show the "haunted" Tunnel to a new friend or visiting relative. The trip is primarily a group experience, but some individuals drive to the Tunnel on their own simply as "a place to go." This sketch described the trip from Bedford, but this is not to deny that young people from other towns know and visit the Tunnel. In fact, youth from throughout Lawrence County have visited this legend site; graffiti on the Tunnel walls indicate that teenagers from Mitchell have also been frequent visitors.

The popularity of specific legends and legend-trips may vary considerably through time; some may fall into almost total disuse while others may suddenly surface and attain widespread circulation in an amazingly short time. Adolescent legend-trips to the Big Tunnel are a relatively recent development in Lawrence County. It is doubtful whether Bedford youth between 1850 and 1950 visited the Tunnel or believed it was "haunted." Ever since its completion in 1857, the railroad tunnel has been a point of interest for surrounding communities; for residents of Tunnelton and Fort Ritner the Big Tunnel was certainly a local landmark. Although remembered as the site of significant local events, it seems unlikely that nineteenth or early twentieth century area residents believed it was a "scary" place. In fact, residents of Tunnelton and Fort Ritner found the Tunnel a convenient short cut between the two towns. Not until 1960 or 1961 did Bedford teenagers discover the Tunnel as an exciting horror story site. Tunnel graffiti is dated no earlier than 1961; this agrees with recollections of local residents. The development of this legend-trip in the early sixties apparently reflects extended teenage access to the automobile during that decade. The trip increased in popularity through the sixties and reached its peak sometime between 1969 and 1971. Recent years have seen a decline in its popularity. This is not to suggest young people no longer make legend-trips; rather their trips today are more often than not to other sites. Tunnel trips and legends are not on the verge of extinction, nor are they survivals from a bygone age; they are perhaps entering a period of relative disuse only to be rediscovered by another generation of teenagers.[7]

Legend-telling is an important part, although only a part, of the Big Tunnel legend-trip. The milieu of the trip decidedly affects both the process and effectiveness of legend-telling. The horror legend told during the trip is built of bits of narrative and comments contributed by several members of the group. The narrative core (what folklorists usually isolate as text) is expanded and developed through personal experience narratives and specific facts which validate or support the "truth" of the legend. Accordingly the process of legend-telling can be analyzed only through a consideration of the entire event.[8]

With this in mind, I asked a frequent visitor to the Tunnel to record a complete legend-trip to that site. Larry, the student who made the recording, telephoned two friends, Joe and Tim,[9] and explained he would like to record a Tunnel trip as a folklore project. All three young men were then freshmen at Indiana University (Bloomington). All were occasional Tunnel visitors and had been there often that summer. Larry recalls at least twenty trips during high school; perhaps five of these had been with Joe and Tim.

Joe and Tim were born in Bedford and have been good friends since elementary school. Larry's family moved to Bedford when he was eight. He met Joe and Tim in high school and the three became fairly good friends during their junior and senior years. During the two months since they left Bedford, Larry had gotten together with Joe and Tim two or three times before this trip to the Tunnel in early November, 1972.

As he had been so often before, Tim was the driver that night. While they stopped for gas in Bedford, Larry set a portable tape recorder on the dashboard and suspended the microphone from the rear view mirror. As they pulled out of the gas station, the three talked about girls they knew from high school. Leaving Bedford, they talked about friends who lived in the immediate area. Once on the road to Tunnelton, conversation turned to a recent accident along the winding road until Tim began the evening's "scare" with a story about the Tunnel. Larry did not stimulate Tim's comments or any part of the resulting legend event. Although he set up the recorder, it is important to emphasize here that Larry is not an outsider; his comments are not designed to manipulate or direct the event. Rather, he is a complete, active participant in legend-telling; he is an integral member of the small group and a key participant in the evening's activities. There is no outside collector present, only a small recording machine. The three young people were soon oblivious of even its presence;

not one of them thought to check the machine's tape supply until they returned to Bedford much later that night.

That this legend event was minimally affected by recording is evidenced by the success of this particular trip. Legend-telling was so effective, in fact, that by the time they reached the site, an atmosphere of fear and uncertainty so permeated the car that both Joe and Tim refused to leave the car for the walk into the Tunnel. Larry later remarked that this was one of the best Tunnel trips he had ever made. The transcript which follows begins with the first specific mention of the Tunnel as these three begin their drive south through the dark Indiana countryside. While reading the transcript, pay particular attention to interrelationships among the participants and their slowly changing attitudes toward the prospect of a walk into the Big Tunnel.

Tim: What are some of the stories you know about the Tunnel?
Larry: Let's see . . .
Tim: The one I know, besides the fact that everyone goes down there, is the one about the soldiers. I heard there was a Civil War scrimmage, not a major battle. Some of the soldiers were supposed to be buried there. You   5
know the Tunnel is cut off a hill; they're supposed to be buried on top of the Tunnel.
Larry: Was the Tunnel there then?
Tim: Yah.
Larry: I heard it was built by convicts.   10
Joe: That's what I heard.
Tim: It's a mile long, Jesus Christ, can you imagine that!
Larry: I heard they were building it and one of them got trapped inside the walls. That's the first story I heard about it. He was trapped and his spirit haunted it; and what it was, the convicts were building it and one of   15
the convicts was trapped, and when the Tunnel was made bigger in 1910, because the train got bigger, they found this guy's body. Ever since then it's been haunted. Before this it wasn't haunted, but when they found that guy's body it was haunted.
Tim: That's your old Mummy thing.   20
Larry: Yah, that's what I heard.
Tim: It's all brick inside. You know the next thing is people stay in there when trains come through.

Larry: You've been there when a train comes through?

25 *Tim:* Yah, and there's hardly any room.

Joe: I heard that if you look at the sides of the train it will hypnotize you into falling into the train.

Larry: No kidding! I wonder . . . no, I don't think anyone has ever been run over in there.

30 *Tim:* I don't know. . . . .There's no protection there at all, just those little cubby holes you can duck into.

Larry: You know, the most fun I've had going out there was going out there, was going out there and back. When, like I was with Joe and all those guys and we were really drunk, and we were going out here and there was

35 a cow . . .

Joe: I was with you!

Tim: Me too! Both of us.

Larry: Could you believe that cow that was in the road? We chased it too. . . .One time we were coming back from the Chain, Collins was driving.

40 *Tim:* Where's the Chain?

Larry: Over in Orleans. Haven't you been to the Chain?

Tim: Uh-uh.

Larry: It's a tombstone. It's got . . . Haven't you heard the story about it? The guy killed his wife and he died in prison. When they buried him, the

45 day after he was buried, the shadow of a chain formed on the side of the tombstone. Every month another link grows on it. Supposed to be! And if you touch it you have six months of bad luck. Supposed to be if you kiss it you're supposed to die in a year.

We went out there and Jeff and Steve kissed it. I couldn't believe it!

50 And we were coming back, Linda Collins was driving her convertible Nova. We had the top down; it was summer. She said a friend of hers she knew was out there and when she came back, she touched it. When she came back there was a grapevine hanging in the road, and she was in a convertible too. The grapevine caught her by the neck and strangled this

55 girl. And Linda said she knew this girl. So we really got scared and pulled off the road to put the top up. We went around the corner and we were going kind of slow, but before this we were going fast, and we went around the corner and there was another cow in the road. And if we hadn't put the top up we would have run into that mother and killed

60 ourselves!

Joe: When I was young, ghost stories ... when we were out camping at ...

Tim: The worst ghost story I ever heard was true supposedly!

Larry: Well aren't all ghost stories supposedly true?

Tim: Well *this* one is! Actually it isn't a ghost story, but it scares the 65 p——— out of you. Supposedly there was this woman, she was baby-sitting for this little bitty baby.

Joe: I told you that one!

Tim: No, Ronnie Rodgers told me this, and I told you.

Joe: I told your parents then. You didn't tell me.   70

Tim: Well anyway, this woman was baby-sitting and the phone rings so she walks over and answers the telephone and a voice says, "I'm going to kill you in five minutes." So she didn't think a whole lot about it.

Larry: Wait a minute, this is the lady keeping the baby?

Tim: Yah, she was baby-sitting. So she didn't think too much about it. So 75 the guy calls back in two minutes and she answers the phone and the voice says, "I'm going to kill you in three minutes." Now she gets worried and she calls the operator. She told the operator what happened. The operator said, "Well, I don't think it's any big deal but I'll listen in the next time he calls and I can trace the call." So the operator listened in and it was a 80 minute and a half or two minutes later that the guy calls back and says, "I'm going to kill you in thirty seconds." So she was relaxed then. All of a sudden she got a call back and it was the operator.

Larry: She was really relaxed?

Tim: She was relaxed because she thought, "Oh h———, he couldn't get 85 here in thirty seconds." So the operator calls back and she says, "For God's sake get out of there, he's in the house and he's using the extension!" So she runs up to get the baby and the baby had had its head cut off, so she jumped out of the window, and she went and told the police her story. And the next day she woke up and she has been a 90 vegetable ever since and her hair had turned white.

Larry: You mean when she woke up she was ...

Tim: She never came out of it.

Larry: Oh God!

Tim: It was supposed to happen in Minnesota or someplace. Then there is 95 all those stories about people eating babies.

Joe: Here's one! Goes along the same line. There was these newlyweds ...

but not actually newlyweds, it was their first anniversary. They had had a
child one or two months before. They knew this girl that lived down the
100 street so they asked her if she would baby-sit for them. She was a real nice
girl. She came over all the time. So she said she would. So the baby sitter
came and they left. While they were gone she started playing with the
baby, and she thought, "Well I'll just fix them a meal." She fixed all the
stuff to eat and put the main course under the platter. Then the parents
105 came home and she met them at the door and said, "Since it's your
anniversary I fixed your dinner for you, and I've also got candlelight." So
they decided to give her a little extra money. So the man pays her and
gives her five dollars extra. So she leaves and they go in to eat. So they
open up the platter and look at the main course and it was the baby.
110 *Larry:* Oh God! . . .How did she prepare the baby? Did she put an apple
in its mouth?
Joe: Yah, just like a pig.
Larry: I bet they turned into vegetables too.
Joe: No, but the kid turned into meat.
115 *Larry:* Did you hear the story about the Tunnel when the football team
came out here after the last game seven years ago?
Tim: No.
Larry: I can't remember, it was one of the big players that used to be a
lifeguard . . . Ferrel, Tom Ferrel maybe.
120 *Joe:* No, that John's dad.
Larry: There was another Ferrel, he was always at the Boys' Club . . . his
name was Forrill.
Tim: Foddrill?
Larry: Yeah! One time they went there at the end of the football season
125 and they all got drunk. He went in there without a light, way back there.
And they heard him scream and he ran all the way back, and he was scared
s———less, and he has never gone back or anywhere near it. He wouldn't
tell anyone what he saw or what he thought he saw.
Tim: Remember this one time Larry, we were coming down here and
130 went off the d——— road.
Larry: Went off the road?
Tim: Yah. You came around the corner and we were in the dune buggy.
Larry: Oh yah, we were chasing someone, weren't we?
Tim: I don't remember.

Larry: It's right after I got the dune buggy, I think. . . .I read in this book   135
somewhere this baby was born conscious. He was born knowing stuff. He
liked living inside his mother cause he knew what was happening. Well
anyway, after he was born he was p———ed cause he didn't want to be
born, he wanted to be a fetus all his life. So he decided to get his mother
back. His mother started getting scared of him cause he wouldn't sleep at   140
night and babies are supposed to sleep about eighteen or twenty hours a
day, and he only slept twelve hours a day, and so she started getting
worried.

Joe: God d———.

Larry: So she took him to the doctor and the doctor said it was all right   145
cause the kid was healthy and normal. But the doctor couldn't figure out
why he was so co-ordinated.

Tim: Could the baby speak?

Larry: No, the baby couldn't speak or anything but it really concentrated
on those things that hang over a baby's crib. He would watch them a lot.   150
So the mother started really getting scared and she told her husband, and
her husband didn't pay much attention to it. He thought she was
exaggerating. Now the baby is about three months old and he's crawling
around already; it acts like a year old, but it still can't talk.

One night the mother hears the kid crying and she goes in there; and   155
for some reason she thought he wanted her in there, cause the minute she
came in the kid shut up. So she went over to the crib and picked him up
and he didn't pay any attention to her. So one night she walked in there at
two A.M. and the kid was in his crib and he was breathing real heavy, all
tired; and she knew he had crawled back into his crib after being down on   160
the floor. So she kept going in there trying to catch him out of his crib. So
one night she was walking down the hall—she's going to the baby's room
to see if she can catch him out of his crib—and she hears a noise down the
stairs. She starts for the stairs and at the top of the stairs the baby has left
a toy. Accidentally the mother falls down the stairs and breaks her neck   165
and dies. So the father is all upset about it, and he tries to forget his wife's
fears of the baby; so he is treating the baby normal.

One night the father is asleep and the baby crawls into his room and
turns the gas on and closes the door behind him. The doctor comes the
next morning—he was coming to see the baby—and the door was closed   170
and the gas was on so the doctor thought something was wrong, so he

went in and found the man dead. The first thing he thought was the guy killed himself. Then he remembered that the last time he talked to him, the doctor told him the most important thing now was for him to raise the baby. So the father told the doctor, now that his wife was gone that his son was the only thing he was going to live for. So the doctor figured he wouldn't kill himself. So he thought about it for a long time, and he went into the baby's room and the baby was in bed. He went over to the crib and the baby opened his eyes and smiled at him, more or less saying, "I won, I beat them." So the doctor took a pillow and strangled the baby.

Joe: Wow! That was good.

Larry: Here's the road island. You can go around both ways, can't you?

Joe: I've never been around that way.

Larry: Hey Tim!

Tim: Hey what!

Larry: Tell us about your grandmother and her psychic power.

Tim: Actually I've never believed in E.S.P. and all that s——— but she really is psychic. She's proved it. Like when I was born in 1954, and in 1952 she woke up one morning and said that she had seen that my mother was going to have a baby on September 19, 1954. She still has a calendar of 1952 of September 19 where she circled it on the calendar. She told everybody. You know she just told them what happened. My mom wasn't even married; she hadn't even met my dad; she was still in high school.

Larry: She said that in 1952?

Tim: Yah, and I just missed the turn to the Tunnel.

Larry: No you didn't.

Tim: So ah . . . Did I just go through a bridge?

Larry: No.

Tim: Good. I sure the f——— don't remember it. Anyway, so . . .

Joe: Here it is, honk your horn.

(Tim sounds car horn.)

Joe: That's good.

Larry: Oh God.

Tim: Am I on the road to the Tunnel yet?

Joe: Yes.

Tim: How far have I gone?

Joe: You know yourself.

Larry: Anyway, your grandmother said . . .

Tim: Actually Mom got pregnant, and I was born on the nineteenth.

Joe: This is a story my Uncle Danny told me. You know, me and him   2)
always ran around together. He told me him and a girl went out to the
Tunnel one night you know, and they were telling stories. They heard that
there was this pink cloud that floated around out here, and the cloud was
pink and if it ever got in your car, you were sick—like it was a jellyfish.

Larry: It was a cloud?   2)

Joe: It was a cloud, but when it got on something, it turned to jelly. And
they say if you ever see seven vultures on the fence, well, you better stop
right then, cause it meant the cloud was approximately one hundred yards
away.

Larry: What does the cloud do?   22

Joe: It kills them. The cloud has to have things to survive, so this is how it
gets its food, more or less. So when it gets on you, you turn to jelly,
everything turns to jelly.

Tim: Part of the thing about the Tunnel, by the way . . .

Joe: Oh s———, we were out here one time with Joe Allen.   22

Larry: You were out there with Joe Allen one time and what?

Tim: And ah . . .

Larry: He took his clothes off?!

Tim: No . . . he was coming down this road at fifty miles and hour and
missed this turn and we went all the way off in the f———ing field.   23

Larry: No, that was me.

Tim: No, no. You were with me; Bruce was with Beth that night.

Larry: No, it was me and the dune buggy.

Tim: The dune buggy?

Larry: What does Bruce and Beth have to do with Joe going off the road? 23

Tim: They were in the car with him.

Joe: They were on Joe's a——.

Larry: All three of them, sure, I bet.

Joe: Bull————!

Tim: Hey! I think I have a flat tire.   24

Joe: You're crazy!

Tim: I do!

Joe: No you don't.

Tim: It really f———s me up.

Joe: If we get a flat tire here, you just get out and fix it yourself, cause   24
I'm not gonna get out of this f———ing car.

Tim: How far have I gone?
Joe: You know! . . .Hey! You passed it. Oh my God, you passed it!
Tim: Oh shut up Joe! Cool it.
50 *Larry:* Turn around and go back there.
Tim: I'm not going to get out of the car anyway!
Larry: Why not? Come on.
Joe: If we see six vultures, we're sick.
Larry: Let's not chicken out. Let's go back.

For purposes of analysis, this legend-telling event falls roughly into four parts. First, stories and beliefs about the Tunnel are discussed (ll.1-31). Next, other legends are told for their "scare" value (ll.32-134). The stories told here are both local and popular migratory legends. Third, a literary story is adapted into a legend-like tale and is well received (ll.135-204). Fourth, and perhaps most interestingly, one member of the group makes up a "legend" (ll.210-54).

Legends About the Tunnel (ll.1-31)

Once out of Bedford and on the way to the Tunnel, the legend-telling session begins simply enough. Tim asks the others if they know any stories about the Tunnel only to give himself a chance to tell his own story. His brief narrative refers to a supposedly historical event, a Civil War scrimmage fought near the Tunnel. Note that here Tim is emphasizing history and makes no mention of the supernatural. Only after the legend session is well under way does anyone bring up the haunts and horrors found in the Tunnel.

Tim's story of the Civil War massacre reminds Larry of another massacre. He mentions that the Tunnel was supposedly built by impressed convicts and is supported by Joe (l.11). The story that this brief exchange prompts (ll.13-19) is related to widely known legends of the "Foundation sacrifice" (Motif S261). The similarities between this legend and the legend type Linda Dégh has called "The Negro in Concrete" are worth noting.[10] One of the convict crew building the Tunnel is trapped in the construction. Work continues around his body. Dégh observes that in this type of legend the trapped man is often a social outcast or of low social status, and so is ignored by engineers more interested in their construction than in human lives. In Larry's story the trapped convict does not haunt the Tunnel until his corpse is disturbed during reconstruction (related to Motif E235, "Return from dead to punish indignities to corpse"). Tim notes the similarity between Larry's story and the movie Mummy who returns to life when his grave is opened (l.20). His comment, in effect, supports the plausibility of the story.

The conversation now moves from stories about the Tunnel to talk about being inside when a train speeds through (ll.22-31). Joe offers a belief about the near magical power of the train (ll.26-27). Although here in modern guise, this belief (related to beliefs about the Medusa and the hyponotic power of certain animals) is both ancient and widespread. No legend story is offered to support this particular belief. Both the absence of a supporting story, and Tim and Larry's problematic response (ll.28-31) suggest this belief is not a usual part of the Tunnel complex.

Larry reminisces about a particularly good time he had at the Tunnel while he was drunk (ll.32-37). As noted earlier, drinking is not prerequisite to a Tunnel visit. When teenage visitors do drink, it is most often before or after the trip. Notice Larry's emphasis on the drive to and from the Tunnel as the best part of the trip.

Other Scary Stories (ll.32-134)

Larry begins to narrate a personal experience at "The Chain." [11] When he learns to his surprise that Tim has not heard the story of "The Chain" (ll.40-41), he localizes it and tells an abbreviated version of the legend (ll.43-48). Larry only indirectly expresses his own attitude toward "The Chain." Although he does not admit he believes bad luck will follow kissing the stone, his astonished expression when his friends tempt fate ("I couldn't believe it!" l.49) makes his position clear. During trips to the legend site, at least, Larry prefers not to experiment with possible curses of the supernatural.

Larry's complete narrative (including comments and asides, ll.43-69) is particularly interesting because it shows quite clearly what Dégh has called the "dichotomous structure" of the legend. [12] The legend narrative is often a combination of both the legend core and the narrator's (or someone else's) personal experience with the legend subject. After reviewing the basic story of "The Chain," Larry tells about an experience he had at that legend site. He is specific. He names individuals and describes the situation in detail ("Linda Collins was driving her convertible Nova," ll.50-57). While narrating his experience, Larry repeats a legend told at that time about a fatal grapevine (ll.51-55). He repeats the story not as fiction, but fact. He tells how this story warned him and his friends of potential dangers ahead. They heeded the warning and were saved from what surely would have been to Larry's mind a fatal accident (ll.55-60). The dichotomous structure of this narrative might be diagramed as follows:

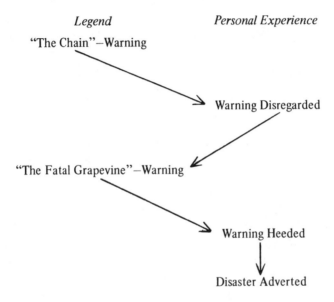

Larry's personal experience thus validates the legend and encourages acceptance of its plausibility and the importance of its warning.

Tim introduces the next story by affirming its truth (ll.63-65). He and Joe attempt to determine its background (ll.68-70) and thus indirectly support its validity. The story's source is not satisfactorily determined, and Tim proceeds to tell the migratory legend of "The Babysitter and the Man Upstairs" (ll.71-95).[13] Larry breaks into Tim's narration at several points to clear up ambiguities in the story (ll.74, 84, 92). The listeners' understanding of the legend seems to be more important than the narrator's style. Accordingly, participants in legend-telling are free to break into the narration *at any point* to ask questions or make comments.

Tim's conclusion of this currently popular legend is unusual. In spite of the operator's warning, the babysitter does not really escape. She runs upstairs, discovers the decapitated baby, and is driven insane with fright. (In other versions she runs outside and escapes the murderer.) Tim closes the story by localizing it and reasserting its veracity (ll.95-96). This story was quite effective; the two others in the car expressed shock.

Tim's legend reminds Joe of a similar story, the widely known legend of "The Hippie Babysitter" (ll.97-114). Although Joe is known to his friends as a good story-teller, he fails to tell this particular legend effectively and it is received poorly. Larry, in fact, makes fun of it (ll.110-11, 113). Joe's version of the story is ineffective because he fails to make it plausible. First, he does not clearly define his characters. He contradicts himself; newlyweds cannot have a baby (ll.97-99). Second, after going to some pains to describe the admirable qualities of the babysitter, he fails to provide a plausible explanation or motivation for her murder of the baby. As he describes her, she is a most unlikely killer. (In other versions of this legend, a weird babysitter cooks the baby while on an L.S.D. trip.) Third, although Joe tries to build narrative tension (ll.104-108), he climaxes the story too brusquely ("... and it was the baby." l.109). Both Tim and Larry have used some sort of denouement to allow the full impact of their stories to settle.

Joe's legend fails to stimulate a similar horror story, and Larry changes the subject back to the Tunnel. His brief narrative supports belief in something mysterious and malevolent at that site (ll.115-28). A football hero known to them all as a big man was "scared s——less" at the Tunnel. Note the attention all three pay to careful and correct identification of the characters (ll.118-24).

A Literary Story Re-told and a Family Memorate (ll.135-214)

Larry's next narrative (ll.135-80), the longest of the evening, is by his own admission taken from a book. As an integral part of this story-telling session, it is an excellent illustration of the close relationship between literary and oral tales. Larry tells his version of the story fairly well; he emphasizes character motivation and consistency, narrative elements which Joe had handled poorly. Although this tale is of little folkloric interest, its reception is worth noting. Both Tim and Joe are interested in the story, interrupt to ask questions, and thoroughly enjoy it.

Joe, in fact, exclaims, "Wow, that was good!" (l.181). That a literary story was told in as informal a situation as this legend event is good indication of the close relationship between written and oral narrative.

By this time—well over two-thirds of the way to the Tunnel—the participants' emotions are beginning to show. They begin to talk loudly and to anticipate the forthcoming walk into the Tunnel as they pass landmarks along the road (ll.182, 195, 197, 204).

Larry again takes the initiative and asks Tim to tell them about his experience with psychic power (l.186). Larry obviously has heard the story before but asks to hear it again. In fact, he makes certain Tim clears up dates and details in the story (ll.194, 208). Tim's brief story is a classic example of the family memorate (ll.187-93). A remarkable family experience has been told through three generations—grandmother, mother, son. It is significant that although Larry is familiar with the story, he asks Tim to tell it. While Tim is present the story is, in effect, his property; it would have been inappropriate for Larry to tell that particular tale. Tim's memorate functions here as yet another story evidencing the role of the supernatural in human life.

An Improvised "Legend" (ll.215-59)

Several of Joe's attempts to participate actively in story-telling this evening have been rebuffed. Early in the session, he began to tell camp ghost stories but was ignored (ll.61-63); his version of "The Hippie Babysitter" was poorly received and stimulated no further comments or stories. At this point he becomes more aggressive. He tries to regain his status as a story-teller by telling a new story, one no one has heard before. Later that evening Joe acknowledged that he had made up this "legend" on the spot. This narrative deserves special attention. Although allegedly original, both its form and content follow traditional patterns.

The story content consists of themes from science fiction and traditonal narrative motifs. The idea of an amorphous being who attacks and dissolves men is closely related to the basic theme of such science fiction movies as "The Blob" and "The Tingler." [14] Specific details of the "legend" are nearly all traditional motifs. Some motifs in the story are: D901 "Magic cloud," D1445.6.1 "Magic cloud burns animals," B147.2.2.6 "Vultures as birds of ill-omen," Z71.5 "Formulistic number: 7," and E253 "Ghost tries to kill person for food."

Moreover, the form of this improvised "legend" follows a pattern common to traditional legends.[15] The narrator: 1. identifies the source of the story (1.210) [In this case the source is fabricated], 2. identifies the characters in the story (1.211), and 3. provides a setting (ll.211-12). 4. The core of this "legend" is the belief that a pink, man-eating cloud exists near the Tunnel. 5. The "legend" has a message or warning for the living and suggests a way in which danger can be adverted (ll.217-18). Larry's question (1.220) elicits 6. the rationale for the cloud's actions (ll.221-22). By providing a more or less rational explanation for his story, Joe supports its plausibility. This improvised narrative illustrates that although the genre of legend is extremely variable, legends do follow a basic form. It was this basic form which Joe unwittingly followed when making up his "legend."

Although this story is dropped from conversation as soon as Joe finishes it, the other two participants thought it was a fine story, one that was really "scary." I suggest two reasons why Larry and Tim accepted this story. First, previous legends had created an atmosphere which made them *particularly receptive* to stories of the supernatural. Second, the form of Joe's "legend" satisfied the listeners' expectations about "scary" stories. *What* Joe said was not as important as *where* and *how* he said it. While it is true that certain motifs and themes are closely associated with legends of the supernatural, the effectiveness of the legend-trip legend depends less upon thematic content than on the legend atmosphere and characteristic legend form which serves to validate the narrative's attestations.

Joe's "legend" will probably never be re-told. In fact, within the next ten minutes the story began to disintegrate. When Joe refers to the story in later conversation (1.253), he has lost count of the vulture omens.

By now the car is rapidly approaching the Tunnel and tension is beginning to show in the little group. Tim and Joe both try unsuccessfully to begin another story (ll.224-25). Conversation becomes brusque and loud. Nonsense comments, bravado, and vulgarity enter the conversation for the first time that evening (ll.225, 230, 239, 244). The three become overtly aggressive toward one another (ll.235-46). I might speculate that such aggression gives the aggressor a sense of strength, strength needed to ward off feelings of fear and insecurity. The possibility that they might have a flat tire and be trapped here on the isolated and dark road occurs to Tim (1.240). Both he and Joe are unnerved by that prospect (ll.241-46). Tim inadvertly drives past the footpath leading up to the Tunnel and is verbally assailed by the others. Forced with a decision, Tim makes it clear that he has no plans to walk through the dark woods or into the even darker Tunnel (1.251). Larry tries to convince him to return to the Tunnel but fails. The transcript ends here. If anything, this legend-telling session had been more effective than most, for it thoroughly frightened its participants. This "fright," however, was remembered by all three as an enjoyable experience.

The dynamics of this legend event suggest several general observations about legends and legend-telling. To state the obvious, the legend event is a group process; narration of one story stimulates others and what begins simply enough may develop into a complex legend-telling session. Which stories will be told during each session will vary with: 1. the time and place (certain situations induce narration of certain legends; the Tunnel legend-trip, for instance, will invariably include something of Tunnel history), 2. group composition and individual personalities (individuals particularly adept at legend-telling, for example, may have a small repetoire of stories which they especially like to tell; further, certain narratives such as family memorates will usually be told only by specific individuals), and 3. chance connections between legends suggested during the session (one legend about baby-sitters, for instance, will almost always suggest other stories about sitters). Novelty is not necessarily a criterion for successful legend-telling. Although new "scary" stories find a receptive audience, most often the group is already familiar with the legends. The story may be so familiar, in fact, that several individuals may participate in its re-telling. Because the "truth" of the legend is more important than individual narrative style, members of the group are free to break into the narrative at any point to ask questions, remove ambiguities, and support specific facts. Further, personal experience narratives may be added to complement and support the legend core. These personal experience stories give legend-telling a dichotomous structure; the legend core or belief narrative is supported by an experience narrative which is detailed and often lengthy. Because the core of the legend is often commonly known to the group, it might not be explicated in detail, and actual narration may concentrate on the more immediate personal experience story.[16]

Style and form are closely related in legend narrative. Although the individual raconteur's style is of secondary importance in legend-telling, it would be a mistake to conclude that narrative style is of no importance.

We must deal with the fact that some narratives are received better than others; the group finds some stories "scarier" than others. The legend event discussed in this paper suggests some tentative observations. Defining style broadly as those elements of narrative which determine whether a story is well or badly received, it is suggested that legend style is intimately bound to form. As used here, form does not imply a certain inevitable thematic progression or underlying structure. Rather, the legend's formal characteristics may be defined as those narrative elements most often present in oral legends; these elements (identification of the source, character definition, setting, a belief core, message or warning, motivation or rationale for activity reported in the legend, and assertion of the legend's validity) do not necessarily appear in any set order nor is each always present in every narrative. [17] Joe's improvised "legend" suggests that these elements are the building blocks of legend construction. That "legend," as previously noted, was made up on the spot. Although its belief core (the existence of a pink, man-eating cloud) was, quite frankly, humorously ridiculous, it was accepted quite positively at the time by both Tim and Larry. It was not the specific thematic content but the form of Joe's "legend" (together with certain typical legend motifs and the legend atmosphere) which was responsible for their acceptance of this "legend." Moreover, because each of these basic formal elements was *well* presented, the legend was "scary," i.e. told with an effective style. By way of contrast, one can refer to Joe's version of "The Hippie Babysitter." This narrative was poorly received not because it is an inherently inferior legend (there is, in fact, no innately ineffective legend; the effectiveness of these narratives is more a matter of form and style than content), but because Joe handled key elements of legend form poorly. He defined his characters poorly and inconsistently, and failed to provide a motive or rationale for the babysitter's apparently inexplicable action. Lacking both plausible characterization and rationale, Joe's version of the legend is patently unbelievable and ineffective. The legend narrative which fails to deal with key elements of form such as character definition, setting and rationale will be ineffective, i.e. badly told. Of course, each raconteur need not include each of these elements in his own narration. Through their comments and questions, others in the group may provide or elicit formal elements not included in the initial narrative. In the complete version of Joe's improvised "legend," for example, Larry's question (1.220) elicits the rationale for the man-eating cloud (ll.221-23).

These observations suggest possibilities for further study of legend form and style. Told in a natural context, not all legend narratives are equally effective. The more effective narratives can be distinguished from the less effective by simple questioning of the legend-telling group after the event; those legends which were "scariest" were stylistically the most effective. Analysis of both effective and ineffective legend narratives should reveal if form is indeed closely related to effective narrative style. Such an analysis must, of course, work from a complete record of the legend event; elements not part of the initial narrative may be included in comments, questions and asides.

As important as form is in legend-telling, the "legend atmosphere" or "general scary condition"[18] is just as crucial to the effectiveness of this type of narrative. More specifically, the "scariness" of the legend-trip is a result of: 1. the foreboding appearance of the legend site, 2. legend-telling, and 3. the atmosphere of tension and uncertainty generated by the trip. During the legend-trip, in fact, the young people cultivate an atmosphere of fear; they try to frighten one another; they seek out contact with the supernatural and attendant dangers.[19] To make the trip "scary" and fun, the adolescents *willingly suspend disbelief* in supernatural haunts and other horrors.[20] One visitor to the Tunnel recalls a particular trip rather glumly. He and his friends invited an acquaintance from another city to join them for a Tunnel trip. The newcomer, however, was a confirmed skeptic; she thought the trip was ridiculous and refused to participate; she was critical of both the stories and the Tunnel. The response of the regular Tunnel visitor is worth noting: "It bummed the whole thing out." Her active disbelief ruined that trip for everyone. The fear generated during an effective legend-trip is not feigned. The bravado and aggression evidenced during the visit of Tim, Joe, and Larry reflect the development of very real apprehensions as they neared the Tunnel. Yet, they and other young people who sense a very real fear as they approach the Tunnel do not all believe—when questioned in another context—that a headless watchman lies in wait there. The "scariness" of the legend-trip does not mean that adolescents necessarily believe in the revenants and assorted horrors of their legendry. Rather, during the legend-trip, during the process of legend-telling, they simply *do not disbelieve*. Questions of actual belief or non-belief are largely irrelevant during the drama and excitement of the trip. An effective horror movie generates emotions of apprehension and alarm in its audience. While in the theatre, the audience temporarily suspends disbelief and cultivates anxiety and terror. The range of actual belief and disbelief among individuals in the theatre is doubtless broad; nonetheless, during the film the audience suspends its skepticism and enjoys collectively shared emotions of apprehension and fear. The dramatic tension of the legend-trip is of a similar nature.

In summary, although adolescents may tell legends and other narratives at parties or in other sedentary contexts, young people very often tell stories as part of a trip to a local "haunted" or "scary" place. Legend-telling is only a part, although an important part, of this legend-trip. The trip itself is often a traditional or patterned adolescent recreation involving specific activities as well as appropriate legends. The function of the legend-trip is primarily recreational; most often each trip begins almost spontaneously as "something to do" or "someplace to go." Although the legend-trip is largely recreational, this is not to imply that it is dysfunctional in adolescent role definition and peer socialization. Questions of psychological and sociological function, however, are best reserved for other studies. Particular adolescent legend-trips rise and fall in popularity through time. Each generation of teenagers may well find its own legend sites and develop its own trips. The "scariness" of the legend-trip is a result not only of legend content, but also of narrative form and style, the forboding appearance of the legend site, and the legend atmosphere. A *willing suspension of disbelief* is crucial to the "scariness" which is so important a part of the legend-trip.

NOTES

1. I have chosen to present only in summary form those legend texts which are incomplete or the accuracy of whose transcription is in doubt.

2. J. M. Guthrie, *Thirty-Three Years in the History of Lawrence County, Indiana, 1884-1917* (Bedford, 1958), 39.

3. The outline of this folk history of Morgan's Raiders is suggested in: Ruth Ann Musick, "Skeletons from a Homespuner's Closet: From the Manuscript of James S. Williams," *Hoosier Folklore* 9:4 (1950), 112-114. Donald A. Bird, "Morgan's Raiders: That's Sure a Good Looking Rifle You Got There," *Indiana Folklore* 2:1 (1969), 124-130. Virginia I. Baker, "Collection of Legends About Morgan's Raiders" (November, 1972), IUFA IU:2109-2115.

4. Guthrie, 29.

5. Linda Dégh, "The Haunted Bridges Near Avon and Danville and Their Role in Legend Formation," *Indiana Folklore* 2:1 (1969), 80.

6. Dégh in "The Haunted Bridges . . ." suggests that a "scary" experience immediately preceding the legend-site creates the "general scary condition." I would note that although the immediate area of the legend-site is certainly important in creating this legend "atmosphere," it does so only when it "sets" or brings to consciousness an atmosphere of fear already developed through legend-telling.

7. For this particular insight I am indebted to Phyllis Quackenbush Reed of Bedford.

8. This is a principle commonly accepted in modern folkloristics. There is nonetheless some disagreement about just how many nuances of the legend event should, for practical reasons, be recorded and included in productive analysis. While some folklorists feel that immediate verbal context is the key to such analysis, others believe that the entire legend event must be recorded in its entirety and any study must account for proxemic and kinesic effects as well as the more commonly analyzed verbal elements of legend-telling.

9. All proper names here and throughout the transcript which follows have been changed.

10. Linda Dégh, "The Negro in Concrete," *Indiana Folklore* 1:1 (1968), 61-67. See also: *Indiana Folklore* 2:1 (1969), 82-83.

11. For discussion of this legend complex, see: William Clements, "The Chain," *Indiana Folklore* 2:1 (1969), 90-96. F. A. de Caro and R. Lunt, "The Face on the Tombstone," *Indiana Folklore* 1:1 (1968), 34-41.

12. Dégh, "The Haunted Bridges . . .," 77-78.

13. This particular legend is currently being studied by W. K. McNeil, doctoral candidate in Folklore at Indiana University.

14. *The Blob*, Irvin Yeaworth, director and Jack Harris, producer. Paramount (Tonylyn Productions), 1958. Reviewed in *New York Times*, 7 November 1958, p. 23. *The Tingler*, William Castle, director and producer. Columbia Productions, 1959. Reviewed in *New York Times*, 10 March 1960, p. 36.

15. Linda Dégh, "Processes of Legend Formation," *International Congress for Folk Narrative Research* (Athens, 1965), 86-87.

16. Dégh, "The Haunted Bridges . . .," 77-78.

17. Dégh, "Processes of Legend Formation," 87-87.

18. Dégh, "The Haunted Bridges . . .," 80.

19. Ibid, 78-80.

20. The phrase "willing suspension of disbelief" was introduced by Samuel Coleridge in *Biographia Literaria* (1817), Chapter 14. Since then the phrase has been widely used in studies of literature and theatre.

"And small links of a chain looks maybe engraved..."

Photo by John E. Nickless

The Chain on the Tombstone

William M. Clements

Q. And, Terry, you were gonna tell me something about the tombstone in Bond's Chapel Cemetery. I wonder what makes this tombstone unusual.

A. Well, the tombstone itself isn't unusual. I mean, it's a small tombstone; but when you get up close, you can see what appears to be a chain. And small links of a chain looks maybe engraved in the tombstone to form a cross. Well, let's see, I think it's a Sarah Pruett; and it's not really an old grave — it's 1930 or '40 or something. But at times the links on the chain will vary. I mean, sometimes there'll be seven or eight; sometimes there'll be up to fifteen or sixteen. And, well, nobody knows why it changes. Some people think maybe it's the weather and something in the stone itself; and other people just think it's psy . . . (whistle) supernatural.

Q. Now what do you know about the person that's buried under there?

A. Well, as I said, it was a Sarah Pruett; and she was supposed to have been killed by her husband with a logging chain. And that's why, you know, they called it the chain and all like that. And, well, she was with her lover; and her husband found her and killed her with a chain. And one of the things about the chain is that if you touch it when it has thirteen links on it, you will be killed by a chain. And so, you know, everybody goes out there and looks at it. If it's got thirteen links on it, you know, they stand back. But if you touch it during the time of a full moon, you're supposed to go insane or lose your mind, you know. And there's been several incidents of people touch it, you know, during full moon; and, well, they get chased by a big bright light all the way back to Orleans. I know we were chased one night; but we didn't believe it, you know. We touched it during full moon and got out into the car and started to leave, and the driver looked in the rear view mirror; and that was all, you know. "Look, there's a white light!" (falsetto) Whoom! We were gone.

Collected by William M. Clements in Bedford, July 14, 1968, from Terry Srygler. The informant was graduated from Bedford High School in 1968 and had been referred to the collector as an "expert" on the legend above.

In *Indiana Folklore* (I, Number 1, pp. 34-41) F.A. de Caro and C. Richard K. Lunt discussed nine variants and related texts of the legend, "The Face on the Tombstone," then filed in the FA IU. In response to the legend's apparent popularity as indicated by the number of texts and to its absence from indices and collections, I did a cursory collecting project of stories pertaining to a single tombstone under the direction of Dr. Dégh during July of 1968. The stated purpose was to trace the legend in the area through as many informants as possible and to obtain related materials in their legend repertoires. The normal bridges to informants such as newspaper reporters, Chambers of Commerce, and local historical societies failed to yield any important leads; but I was directed to sources through the assistance of Miss Judi Burke, an earlier collector of the legend. I then collected seven new texts on tape, including the one given above.

Terry Srygler's text is unique in its contention that the person in the grave is a female. He provides as a rationale for the chain's appearance the death of the woman murdered by a chain. He emphasizes the danger of contact by touching the stone and makes special references to periods when thirteen links appear and there is a full moon. Concerning his own belief in the legend, the informant said, "I know it grows. I'm one of the people that thinks it's weather."

OTHER TEXTS

(1) Told by John Hughes in Tolbert, July 13, 1968. The informant is seventy-one years old and runs a service station and grocery store about a mile south of the Bond's Chapel Cemetery where the tombstone in question is located. While Mr. Hughes told of the addition of links to the chain on the side of the Pruett monument, he gave a rational explanation: when the stone had lain in the quarry, it contacted a rusty chain and bar. The resulting mark had proved ineradicable. "Some kind of dope" had been applied to cover the defect. With time this "dope" had washed away,

and the chain on the stone appeared to grow. When asked about the buried Pruett, Mr. Hughes cited certain "wild stories" in which the Catholic Pruett had either married a Protestant wife or had killed his spouse with a chain. However, the grocer's own recollection was that Pruett died from tuberculosis. Mr. Hughes spoke of the many visitors at the tombstone, observing that "this year it's beginning to die down." (2) Told by David Tolbert in Orleans, July 18, 1968. Mr. Tolbert is in his seventies and had lived in the vicinity of Bond's Chapel Cemetery until about twenty years ago. Mr. Tolbert discounted stories about the chain's growth when he stated, "It's just as long as it was when it first started." Having worked in quarries, he suggested that the mark on the stone was present when it was originally excavated. Mr. Tolbert said Pruett had died of tuberculosis or influenza, but he did mention that Pruett's wife was a Catholic while her husband remained Protestant. (3) Told by Tim Grow in Bedford, July 22, 1968. The informant was graduated from Bedford High School in 1968. He stated that the reason for the chain's existence is Pruett's murder of his wife. He also related that two friends visiting the cemetery had encountered a ragged old man leaving the adjacent church. The old man told the boys to leave, adding that he lived there. The name he gave as his was the same as that on the tombstone. The informant said that touching the chain brought bad luck. (4) Told by Jan Buker, male, 1968 graduate of Bedford High School, in Bedford, July 27, 1968. The informant said the chain was "engraved" on the side of the stone and varied not in length, but in degree of relief from the rest of the stone. On touching it, one is supposed to die "or some honky thing like that which I, of course, don't believe." Nothing was said about Pruett's manner of death, but the informant mentioned that "there's supposed to've been someone hung in there or something, but I don't believe that either." (5) Told by Susan Quackenbush in Bedford, July 27, 1968. The informant graduated from Bedford High School in 1968. The informant stated that the chain gets bigger and smaller because Pruett was strangled with a chain. She had heard that touching the chain brings death; but having touched it herself, she was "still living and perfectly healthy." (6) Told by Spencer Adams, 1968 graduate of Bedford High School, in Bedford, July 28, 1968. After a dance "when we couldn't find anything to do," the informant and others visited Bond's Chapel Cemetery. The chain on the stone was an indentation which increased when a flashlight was shined on it "just like the heat of the light made it grow bigger."

FA variants and related texts:

(7) FA IU: 68/51, collected by Raymond E. Clift from Sandi Root, age twenty-one, from Bedford. The chain is said to add a link every year because the man buried there was beaten to death with a chain. The collector notes that the legend is commonly accepted. (8) FA IU: 69/3, collected by Candace Cunningham from Jill Busick, an eighteen year old student, in Orleans, December 14, 1968. Pruett strangled his wife with a chain. When the moon is full, a link is added to the vertical arm of the chain. (9) FA IU: 68/42, collected by Janis Mellenthin from Gail Webb, a student from Brownsburg. A man is accused of raping a banker's daughter and pleads not guilty. Before his execution, he claims his innocence will be proven when nothing will appear on his tombstone for two years. After two years of fruitless work by stonecutters, the date and "Killed in error" appear on the stone. (10) Collected by James Dow from William J. Dow, age fifty-eight, in Bogalusa, Louisiana, July 6, 1968. Upon the death of a man infamous for his cruelty to animals, the head of a horse which cannot be removed appears on his tombstone. MI Q 285.1. "Cruelty to animals punished," a motif known in India, seems relevant. (11) The *Journal of the Ohio Folklore Society* reports a legend related to "The Chain" (III, 3, 1968, pp. 187-188). The story, collected by Marie Campbell from Karen Dunipace, in Bowling Green, Ohio, March, 1967, is entitled "Murder and the Supernatural." A woman is strangled by her husband, and on her death bed she promises eventually to reveal her murderer. Over the years an etching depicting her husband with his hands around her neck appears on her tombstone. The husband commits suicide, and attempts are made to remove the etching. The etching returns, only to disappear every time a formal investigation is suggested. (12) Another story in the special collection of IU MSU (FN 540) in the FA IU was collected by Beverly

Ann Creig from Mrs. George A. Creig in Detroit, Michigan, May 30, 1956. The story is set in North Carolina. A girl marries a boy whose parents do not like her and treat her harshly. She dies, and on her tombstone appears a picture of herself as a young girl. The boy's parents try to remove the picture with acid, but the picture does not disappear. They even request someone to remove the stone, out most people think that the appearance of the picture is the will of God.

The forms of this legend type have been adequately treated by de Caro and Lunt. My findings concerning the Bedford version seem to indicate a function for the legend among a certain age group to whom the legend is known. John Hughes said that young people are especially interested in seeing and touching the stone, but added that many adults inquire about the chain: "It's human nature to want to be hoodooed or find something that's a little bit out of the routine order of things." Terry Srygler mentioned the situation when narrations of the legend might occur: "Don't have anything to do. It's four o'clock in the morning. And so you go out there. And while you're goin' out there, you're tellin' about the chain and the haunted houses and haunted bridges and everything like that." Tim Grow, who said that almost anyone less than twenty-six years old knew the story, discussed the circumstances in which the story is normally told: "Usually what it is we start out by — we will be ridin' out in the country at night time usually. It's usually always night time. And we'll just start talkin' about things that have happened and things that we've heard. And we just start talkin' different stories that we've heard usually, and this one always gets into it." The same situation (i.e., the visit to the tombstone by youths for something to do) came out in interviews with other informants (Texts, 4, 5, and 6). It seems to be of significance that youthful informants are the only ones to accept any mysterious circumstances surrounding Pruett's death (Texts 1, 3, 5, 7, 8, and Srygler's version). Most of the people in the area of Orleans and Huron know about the alleged growth of the chain, but most are unaware of or reject anything about Pruett's death which would explain the chain's presence.

My conclusion, if not presumptious with so little data, is that a legend has been created among the youth of several southern Indiana counties in order to explain a physical phenomenon as well as to provide a supernatural "thrill" as an escape from boredom.

This latter aspect has been found elsewhere:

Now then, there's another kind of a thing that — of course I ramble all over west Texas here, and I run into these different places and go down to Garden City. And I'm sure you've heard of the glowing tombstone at Garden City. Well, most of the kids here in Big Spring, one time or another, in the evening they say, "Well, what are we gonna do tonight?" You know, "Well, let's go down to Garden City and see the glowing tombstone. There's a tombstone down there that's supposed to glow in the dark." And so many people have been down there to look at it. Of course the Garden City police department, or sheriff's office, is pretty well on the alert because a lot of guys come down there with a six-pack of beer and sit around watching the tombstone glow while they consume large quantities of alcoholic beverages which seem to be somewhat prohibited down that way. But that's a story that I've heard many people say that they've seen it glow. I've never seen it myself — never have gone out there to look at it; but it's supposed to give off an eerie light.

Collected by William M. Clements in Big Spring, Texas, December 23, 1967, from Bruce Frazier. The informant is a local television personality and entrepreneur. He has been an instructor of agriculture at a local junior college.

The use of an allegedly supernatural occurrence for entertainment seems to be a widespread feature of teen-age life. Perhaps in an age where much excitement has to be vicarious, legends and supernatural beliefs provide thrills to a generation brought up to scoff at them.

The Ghost of the Doctor and a Vacant Fraternity House

James Gary Lecocq

In investigating this legend, I have encountered many difficulties and equally many enlightening moments. In chronological order, I will try to remember some of my experiences as well as my feelings while doing them. When I first began research I felt that it would be easy although not particularly interesting work. Since that time I have completely reversed my opinions on the matter.

I first looked rather generally into the matter of deciding whom to contact and what to collect. My first real connection with the house was at the auction held there. The fraternity had disbanded and the furnishings of the house were being sold at public auction. I looked the house over and received some more ideas concerning whom to contact for information and I even bought a bed for my room at that event.

My sister, who had been a little sister[2] at the house, gave me my first variant for the legend and told me more possibilities for doing a project based on it. After talking to her, I visited the house a couple of times to obtain more information about the house in general and to get acquainted with the set up of the house in order to better understand and talk with the Phi Tau members whom I planned to contact.

I next tried to contact Bruce Billman, an acquaintance of my sister's. I finally phoned him but he was rather hesitant on the phone so I told him that I would come over some time. This worked very well because he was quite willing to talk in a more friendly atmosphere. After talking to him, I revisited the house twice more looking for rooms which he described. Next, I contacted Harry Dearing. Harry told me almost nothing, and I sensed that he, like Bruce, was a little hesitant to talk about the legend. At that time I began to wonder if my task would be possible to complete.

I went back to the house and spent the day looking through their files, again coming up almost empty handed. At this time I went back to talk to Bruce. He found an old composite picture of his fraternity, which he gladly sold me for use in finding people.

Next I contacted Peter Kresge, who was, like all the rest, hesitant but somewhat cooperative. I then tried to get in touch with an old alumnus, Gary Smith. He was in graduate school at I.U. but had since moved away and so was unavailable.

My biggest breakthrough came when I called Larry Minnix. He knew more than anyone else about the legend because he had been the last president of the house. He referred me to two alumni in Indianapolis, John Tobin and Charles Hammack, both of whom were in Law School. I called them that night but only John Tobin was home and he gave me my last variant. Since then the university has found a new group to rent the house and this has cut off my direct contact with the house.

A. Wow! You're really getting into a heavy thing. Where do you begin. Yeah, this is the way it began. The way I get it, the man who built the house, more or less just in a fit of insanity, just one night went down to the luggage room, which is a small room in the very corner of the basement, and he shot himself. So the house builder, that's the ghost.

So then the doctor moves in. So he starts with these abortion activities 'cause he was in Bloomington with a lot of sororities and stuff. They say that whatever came out was thrown into this opening in the wall. Because guys say that they hear babies cry at night before, up through vents in the house, up through air ducts, and cats meow things like that. There's these signs. On the wall down in the corner of the basement, arrows pointing to this newly bricked in area in the shape of a cross, in the shape of a distorted cross.

Well, one of the stories I've always heard was a time that somebody had just come back from the summer, and he just walked in the house, and he thought there would be some of the brothers in the house 'cause he saw a couple of cars outside. So he went through the house, and he heard these footsteps. They were starting on the third floor walking across. So he yelled out, "Who's there, who's there." Then he walked in a direction where he would meet the footsteps, so he started walking, and the thing was coming down these stairs, the footsteps were. And he was walking right to the corner that was where the thing would turn just as it came out. So he was just coming around the corner, so all of a sudden, whatever it was came down the stairs and stopped. And he just turned the corner and he looked and there was nothing there and he froze and something touched him right on the shoulder and he went into convulsions. He was taken over to the Health Center. It was Danny Jackson who went through that, a pledge and he freaked out.

I've personally had experiences with it. Oh, one was being drawn into the luggage room—on at least a couple of occasions. Oh just this force kind of like drawing you there. It's kind of hard to explain. And then, one morning I had call duty, and he, the pledge who has call duty, gets up the first person in the house then goes down and unlocks everything. So, I went down and unlocked the kitchen. I was kind of circulating through the house; oh all the lights were off. It was in the middle of the winter and there was nobody was up. It was pitch black. Everything's real silent. And then as I was walking out I kind of like look in the living room and everything was real quiet while in there. And all of a sudden this water was running. It was running in the lady's john. And I walked in and turned the water off. Somebody had turned on the faucet. It's situated in this one corner of the house. And so, it kind of freaked me out because nobody was up and the place was totally dark. And it wasn't on when I went by it. It was just on when I came back by it. So things were getting kind of freaky.

Other times of meeting the ghost were usually after call duty. 'Cause this one person had call duty, and he was walking by this room, and he hears someone dialing the phone. So he looks in and there's nobody in there and the receiver off the hook and the phone must have been dialed but it was just laying there. And the guy just totally freaked out; he couldn't believe it. That's about the brunt of it. People didn't usually meet the ghost who were in groups. Usually the people who met him were those who were isolated either early in the morning or late at night. You know just up by themselves studying or something. And all of a sudden, you'd hear strange noises.

And there was one more. It was about a lot of times I hear babies crying or I several times heard footsteps going through the dorm. And you'd feel this kind of cold like. Things scooting through the door and you'd open your eyes and there'd be nothing there. And it would kind of freak you out 'cause after a while you could see real well in the cold dorm. There was a little bit of light up there. And I think that was about it.

(Told by Larry Minnix, a twenty-year-old college student at Indiana University, in Bloomington, November, 1971. E402.1.1 – "Vocal sounds of ghost of human being"; E402.1.2 – "Footsteps of invisible ghost heard.")

Larry was at his home when the legend was recorded. He was the President of the Phi Kappa Tau house last year before it disbanded. He was extremely cooperative and even eager to tell the legend to me. He believed in it sincerely since he had actually experienced the activities of the ghost.

Larry did not tell this legend to people often. Occasionally, it would come in a conversation, though. Like all ghost stories, this one is a great conversation piece. He most likely used this story to scare visitors as well as impress them with the fact that the Phi Tau house had something which no other house on campus has—a ghost. However, Larry did not tell this to pledges or alumni, unless it happened to come up in some way. This seemed to be a way that Larry and his brothers in the fraternity passed time at night. He did not try to look for the ghost; it seemed to look for him.

Larry communicated a sense of awe and sincerity in his tone of voice which possibly cannot be sensed from his words alone. As collector, it is my judgement that Larry sincerely felt that the supernatural force was actually the doctor or the builder of the house. The trait which separated Larry's story from the others was the detail which he went into when describing the incidents and the deep seriousness which he displayed. He was not embarrassed or in any way ashamed to say he believed that the ghost was actually active in the house. The fact that the legend is practically unknown on campus verifies the fact that the fraternity brothers did not tell it to make a name for themselves.

B. Well, let me see, I guess the place where the legend started was with this doctor who lived there back before World War I. He performed abortions on all the sorority girls illegally and somewhere he slipped up, though, and got arrested. Then the university took over the house and sold it to the Alpha Gams.

They lived there for awhile and when they moved out we took over. Most of the stuff happened the year before we moved in because these idiots used to stay up real late and talk. So, I guess, the ghost used to come out then.

There's a lot of legends about the rooms here that sort of reflects the mystery. The "closet," that room on the second floor right off the staircase, has never had a guy make grades in it. Every guy in there has either flunked out or moved away. We even put two really smart dudes in there last year but they moved out about three weeks before the semester was over. That's just probably because that room is so dark and drabby. The lights are real bad and the window's blocked by a big tree.

But the real stud room is our f———ing coal bin in the basement. If you go down the stairs facing the Health Center you can turn left at the stairs and go all the way back to the steel doors. See, it's really weird 'cause these doors are so thick and all. The brick inside is *really* messed up. It's all really old except for this place in the middle about this high [five feet]. It's where the Doc threw all the s——— after the operations. I had to sleep down there the night before initiation. If they wouldn't have let me out I would have schizzed out.

Minnix used to have seances and stuff down there. Oh, he used to completely scare Haggerty out of his mind. Haggerty used to say, "You guys are crazy going down there." No kidding, he was scared s———less.

Well let's see, is there any more? Yeah there's another room that has a window but there's no way to get in it. This one room and the one next to it are real far apart. The window's way back of the house. Then, you know, everyone always gets to hearing noises too.

Oh, when I was a freshman down here, right before Christmas break, I had a real bad fever and I was laying by the door on the floor. My roommates had just come in. The door handle started turning and I just figured someone wanted to come in so no one went to move. Then, the door moved again so I jumped up really quick since I was kind of sick so I got p———ed off real quick. And there wasn't anyone there and I didn't even hear anyone running away.

Tobin and Haggerty know the most about it though. They're lawyers in Indianapolis.

(Told by Bruce Billman, a 20-year-old college student at Indiana University, October, 1971. E599.11–"Locked doors open at touch of ghosts.")

Legend B is slightly less elaborate than legend A. Like Larry, Bruce was a member of the Phi Kappa Tau fraternity last year. He dated my sister last year and, because of this, he became my closest connection with the house and its legend.

Bruce told this legend to my sister, and it soon became a joke between them watching the brothers hold seances in the basement. Bruce did believe that supernatural events happened since he, too, had been a witness to them; however, he did not believe in the ghost wholeheartedly. Bruce feels that the gloominess of the house was a factor which contributed to the events which the brothers saw.

Bruce spoke freely of the ghost to anyone whom he thought would be interested. He, like Larry Minnix, did not go out of his way, though, to advertise the events. He seemed slightly hesitant to say that he believed in the ghost, even though he had seen events out of the ordinary.

Bruce brought out an important insight when he showed that the "actives" did use the legend to integrate the pledges into their group. By putting them in the coal bin, the "actives" were making them a part of the group which experienced the unusual events of the room. In a way, he was also validating the story of the ghost by relating his personal experience.

C. Well, basically, it started back when I was a sophomore. Well, you know, there were stories before that, but my sophomore year, the Doc really went weird. It was a doctor who lived there . . . that haunted the place. Him and the dude who built the house anyway. Their activities just about drove half the guys out of the house. I guess I've been through as much as anybody—me and Hammack.

Well, let's see, specifically. The first thing I think that happened to me, I guess, was one night when I was sleeping down in the room, and this was the third night I had stayed up for finals and it was really getting to be a hassle. But, anyhow, I was getting about ready to sleep and I started hearing noises over my stereo system. You know, I didn't really think anything of it. Well, I laid there for awhile and finally went over there after it kept going for awhile. And there wasn't anything there. I was looking for a rat or something maybe, and so I went back into bed. And I didn't have any records on or anything. The next morning when I woke up, I found five records were on, and the power was turned on my stereo. And the door was locked, and nobody could've gotten in. And there's no way to sneak in the windows, and nobody said they did anything. But I didn't really think anything of it then. You know, I thought there's gotta be some kind of explanation for it and all. But the same thing happened to Hammack, the guy who lived next door to me then about a week later. So then I started sort of thinking something of it, but I kind of thought he was f— — —ing me over, too.

So I guess that's when it really started hitting then. Everybody almost had something happen to them during that same year. Like at initiation, that too. And the initiation of the fall class my sophomore year, they had a lot of stuff really wild go on, but I guess I probably shouldn't talk about that because they're thinking about starting the fraternity back up. And if this initiation stuff got out, they'd have to change all their rituals and everything, and I know they really wouldn't want to do that. A lot of stuff has happened since then. I mean every year that I was in the house stuff had happened like ghosts just walking through the halls at night and, oh, faucets turning on in the middle of night and stuff like that. It was really a wild place. I don't know, I don't really want to go into all this because it's so long and detailed. And besides, those guys in Bloomington will tell you the same thing.

(Told by John Tobin, a 23-year-old Law student in Indianapolis, November, 1971. E 299.1—"Ghost causes machinery to run unattended.")

John Tobin was the treasurer of the fraternity two years ago, and was at the house when the legend took full force. However, John did not communicate many specific stories which went on during his stay in the house.

John, being older than the other informants, showed that the legend is of relatively recent origin and has been passed on to the newer members of the house. John was basically apathetic toward the topic, neither excited nor bored with the subject. He was not at all nervous and at times he seemed to feel that the story was funny. He supplemented what the members of the fraternity who were still in school had said. He did seem to believe, though, that supernatural events did often occur.

D. Well, I wasn't around when most of this went on but I guess I could tell you some of the stuff the guys told me. The biggest thing that sticks out in my mind is a dude named Robinson fainted one day when he was going to sleep. He was walking up the stairs to the cold dorm and he heard footsteps behind him. When he looked back and nobody was there, he went up the rest of the way and the footsteps went up too. He looked back again and when nobody was there again, he fainted. Then, catch this one, when they told the story to Given, he fainted, too, because he thought he heard something behind him. I'll never forget that.

The only thing that happened to me that was pretty weird was the time when I went down to a seance in the coal bin. We were sitting around for awhile watching some candle and holding hands in a circle. And the flame got this big [one foot] and then just went out like that. The girls were really scared and, well, I guess I was too. The thing is that everybody really thought something was going on. You know, what could have caused it?

But, really, some of the guys who graduated a few years ago would know about things a lot more than I do.

(Told by Peter Kresge, a 19-year-old student at Indiana University, in Bloomington, November, 1971. E402.1.2–"Footsteps of invisible ghost heard.")

Peter Kresge showed that the younger members of the fraternity knew the legend, too. His information had mostly been obtained from the older members of the fraternity. This shows that the story had been passed on in much the same way as it was originally experienced.

Peter was told this information during "rush" at the house. This shows that some of the active brothers did use this as a way to show the rushees the uniqueness of the house. He was integrated into the house by experiencing the fright of the supernatural events. Peter did not really know whether to believe the stories or not since he had not been in the house long enough to experience anything unusual. He was not nervous or unwilling to be interviewed. He was only sorry that he did not have more information about the subject.

Peter did not talk about the legend very often, only when he was with other brothers. Since he did not have much information about the subject, he never went out of his way to advertise the fact that his fraternity house was haunted. Peter did realize, though, that some people in the house sincerely believed in the ghost.

E. I think the way it started was some guy, a doctor, yeah that's right. This doctor used to perform abortion stuff on girls and women, too, I guess before World War II. Well, anyway he used to throw the fetuses into the coal bin, and they didn't die, I think, because people always hear babies cry at night.

Matter of fact, one night I was sitting in my room right after Christmas break. You see, I was studying for finals 'cause I couldn't study at home, and, nobody else was there. So I was sitting at my desk and these shadows were going across my paper, and at first I didn't really understand what was going on. But I looked up at the light, and it was waving back and forth. My windows were closed and everything, and nobody ever did figure out why it happened.

There wasn't anybody in the house who didn't believe some of this stuff. Maybe it was just a spooky place, but I don't know.

(Told by Harry Dearing, a 21-year-old student at Indiana University, in Bloomington, November, 1971. E402.1.1.6–"Ghost sobs.")

Variant E was a short legend told by a brother who did believe in the ghost. Harry seemed a bit honored that I was doing a paper on the legend of his fraternity house. He was very cooperative and even organized his material before telling me his variant of the legend. He was very sincere in telling me his story. He did not seem either bored or embarrassed. It is very interesting that he said that everyone in the house believed in some of the stories.

F. Well let's see, one of the cases was a guy in the restroom real late, about three in the morning, and when he walked in he saw this guy there washing his face or shaving or something. And, he went in and the guy left and he realized he'd never seen the guy before. The guy had started down the stairs so he went to the steps where he was going and there was no one there.

Then another case was about a guy who was walking up the stairs and he heard these footsteps behind him and he would go and they would go then he would stop and they would stop. He just figured it was one of the brothers jacking him around so he finally decided to turn around and see who it was and he did and no one was there. And he went into shock and they had to take him to the Health Center.

And then like supposedly they can hear, sometimes, a baby cry at night.

And another case was about Chambers—that was the president back when I was a freshman—was sleeping during the afternoon up in the cold dorm when hardly anyone's ever there. So he was by himself except for this one dude who was snoring and Chambers told him to shut up and the dude shut up. So he started snoring again and he told the dude to shut up again and he shut up. But it happened again so Chambers decided to go see who it was so he went over to the bed where the snoring was and no one was there and by the time he got to the bed the snoring had stopped.

And another case was about this guy who was sitting in his room reading and the window was shut. Well, the lamp started swinging back and forth and it got going really fast and it almost hit the ceiling and then it just slowed down and stopped.

Most of the activities are done right before the guys are getting ready to go home for vacation or break or something. Like Bruce was sitting in his room one time right before Christmas break when he was a freshman, and the doorknob started shaking and it stopped and it shook again and stopped and it started shaking. So Bruce decided to see who was jacking him around. He opened the door really fast and no one was there.

(Told by Carol Lecocq, a 20-year-old college student at Indiana University and sister of the collector. Carol heard the stories from members of the Phi Kappa Tau fraternity, Bloomington. E402.1.1.5 – "Ghost snores"; E402.1.1.6 – "Ghost sobs"; E402.1.1 – "Footsteps of invisible ghost heard.")

Variant F showed the feelings of a person closely related to the house.

Carol learned about the legend from Bruce Billman and did believe most of the stories. She felt that the true stories had a reason but that some of the experiences were made up. Bruce, in a sense, integrated her into the fraternity by telling her the tales. Thus, she could relate to the house and its members.

Carol was a very good link with the fraternity since she knew most of the members. She knew what the members were talking about and she cleared up problems which I did not understand. She was quite eager to tell me her version of the legend and, of course, was not at all nervous. Carol showed me that the members were very excited about the legend and really believed the stories told to them.

G. Well the way I heard it, before the war, World War II, there was this doctor who performed abortions for some of the not-too-fortunate co-eds of the time. I guess one time, something happened during one of the operations and one of the girls died. I guess he just hid the body somewhere and they didn't find it. The caught him later and put him in jail and he said that accidentally he had killed that one girl. He told them where they could find the body, but they never did.

So the Phi Tau's said that some really weird stuff always happened there. They were a bunch of freaks, though, and I don't know.

(Told by Jon Kubley, an eighteen-year-old student at Indiana University, in Bloomington, December, 1971. Jon heard the story from two of his fraternity brothers.)

Variant G was told by Jon Kubley, a member of the Sigma Chi fraternity. This variant showed that the legend is not only known by the members of the house. Two other members of Jon's fraternity told the legend to him. His legend is quite different from those told by the members of the house. It is an excellent example of the way a legend changes as it is told. Jon told me this variant at the Sigma Chi house.

Since the legend is not extremely widespread, there are not too many variants and a comparison is therefore difficult. One point which is related in variants A, B, E, and G tells of the origin of the ghost. Variant A, in explicit terms, shows that the ghost is the person who built the house and that other happenings arise from the activities of the doctor. Variant B introduces a chronology by stating that the ghost appeared before World War I. The informant also says that the doctor who is the alleged ghost performed abortions on the sorority girls and then was arrested. Variant E changes the time of the doctor's activity to before World War II. Variant G is a compromise between variants B and E in that it takes the time of variant E and agrees with the idea of performing abortions on sorority girls. Variant A is the most unusual in that it contains ideas about the builder of the house who is the ghost rather than the doctor and that he shot himself in the luggage room. No other variants even mention the luggage room in the basement. Variants A and E both mention that the fetuses were thrown into a hole in the basement wall, while variant G tells that one of the girls who was killed in an operation was put there. Variants B and G relate that the doctor was also arrested while variants A and E never tell what happened to the doctor.

Another incident which was related in the narratives of three informants—Larry Minnix, Peter Kresge and Carol Lecocq—was the story about the member who fainted when he heard footsteps but could not see their source. Minnix is very detailed and exact in his description of the event. In this variant, a pledge named Danny Jackson went into convulsions after he was touched on the shoulder. Kresge has the same format but not at all the same details. In his account, "a dude named Robinson" was walking up the same steps as the person in variant A. The ghost, however, was behind him; after he looked back twice without seeing anything he fainted. Variant F tells basically the same story as variant D except that, in this account, the person who was being followed by the ghost went into shock. In variant D, when the story was told to another member of the fraternity, he fainted too.

The house of the Phi Tau's is a very spooky place, both on the outside and the inside. The house is very old, and the lights are placed so that much of the house remains very dark. Trees surround the outside so that almost no light can come in through the windows. Both informants Billman and Dearing suggested that the dreariness of the house perhaps tended to cause some of the experiences. The rooms which these legends speak about actually do exist in much the same way as they were described.

Of Bascom's four basic functions of folklore—compensation, validation, education, and integration—only the compensatory function does not seem to apply to this legend.[3] On the other hand, information is a very prevalent function in the legend. The brothers in the house told each other, as well as some of their friends, about the legend in order to inform them about the experiences which they had gone through. Larry Minnix, being the president of the house, basically educated other people. He was responsible for the image of the house, and obviously there were times when this legend helped to show the true character of the house. He did not advertise this characteristic very often, but at times he did talk about it. Bruce Billman, on the other hand, informed people as well as received information about the ghost. He told my sister about the legend and he himself was told much about the past happenings in the house. Jon Tobin, when he was in the house, did not receive much information since the legend was first building up, but I understand that he made quite a point of telling other people the stories about what went on. He was even supposed to have run an article in the *Indiana Daily Student* about the house but this was never verified. Peter Kresge is the perfect example of one who is informed about the house. The older brothers taught him the stories from the time that he first saw the house. Since he never really had a chance to formulate an opinion, he rarely told the story to anyone else. Harry Dearing, who did not deal with this issue too often, was not really very well informed, nor did he transmit information to other people. Carol Lecocq and Jon Kubley, who were not members of the house, were told these legends by members of the fraternity in order to show then the uniqueness of the house.

Validation of the legend was performed by relating personal experiences and showing other people the unusual aspects of the house. Minnix validated his legend in in two ways: he held seances and showed people around at night when there was nothing better to do. The legend is more believable after seeing the actual locations where the ghost is said to have appeared. Hearing a person say that he has experienced supernatural happenings also helps to stimulate belief in the legend. Billman validated his variant of the legend by showing other people the seriousness with which his fraternity brothers approached the matter. Tobin used the fact that he was there when the legend started to show that his stories were true. By relating how frequently the events happened, he tended to generate a greater belief on the part of the listener. Kresge also used personal experiences as well as the experience of another brother to convince the collector that the legend was true. Dearing used personal experience as well as widespread belief in the stories as his means of validation.

Bascom's function of integration was used on only one of the informants, Bruce Billman. He was integrated into the fraternity by having to sit in the coal bin one night during "Hell Week." There are rumors that two members of Sigma Chi were integrated into the circle of friends of the brothers of Phi Tau by being taken into the basement one night to listen to ghost stories. These two Sigma Chi's are not available for comment. Earlier this year, Bruce Billman and Peter Kresge attempted to integrate a boy and his girl friend into the house. The couple apparently used the house to sleep in quite often since it was vacant. One night when Bruce and Peter went by the house, they saw a car parked there. They went inside the house and scared this couple with some tricks that the ghost supposedly used to play. This prank was tangential to the legend because the boys were really only play-acting at duplicating the activities of the "real" ghost, which may be an indication of their own lack of true belief in the legend itself.

The Phi Kappa Tau fraternity has disbanded and eventually the members who know the legend will graduate and leave Bloomington. Perhaps the legend will remain dormant with the few who will have it passed down to them. It would appear, however, that the legend will not survive because the group who kept the legend alive in oral tradition has ceased to exist. The chain of communication has been broken and with it the means of passing the legend on to others.

NOTES

1. The following collection of variants of a "typical" ghost story cycle involving a haunted fraternity house on the I.U. campus was submitted as a Folklore 101 term paper by Gary Lecocq in 1971 when he was a freshman. The house in question, located at 625 N. Jordan, was the home of the Phi Kappa Tau fraternity at the time this legend was in active but limited circulation. The Beta Lambda chapter was in the process of disbanding at the time this collection was made and the house is now occupied by another fraternity. The variants themselves are excellent examples of how a legend can spread within a group of a select few, i.e. the members if Phi Kappa Tau and their close friends. No attempt has been made to contact any of the people now living in the house to see if the legend has been picked up by them but its continuation is unlikely because the house was vacant for some time before the new fraternity moved in and there was no particular reason for the members of the disbanded fraternity to have had any social contact with the new inhabitants of their house.

The transcripts of the legends are published here verbatim as in Lecocq's term paper. There has been an attempt to preserve the tone and style of the original paper; however, the term paper had to be edited. The succession of the analyses of the texts and their interpretation have been changed and motif numbers have been added.

For information dealing with the texts and telling of other ghost stories among American young people, see: Ronald L. Baker, "Legends about Spook Light Hill," *IF* 3:2 (1970): 163-189; William M. Clements and William E. Lightfoot, "The Legend of Stepp Cemetery," *IF* 5:1 (1972): 92-141; Linda Dégh, "The Haunted Bridges Near Avon and Danville and their Role in Legend Formation," *IF* 2:1 (1969): 54-89; "The House of Blue Lights Revisited," *IF* 2:2 (1969): 11-28; and Carol A. Mitchell, "The White House," *IF* 2:1 (1969): 97-109. [S.A.G.]

2. On the I.U. campus fraternity "little sisters" are usually freshman girls who act as mascots for the fraternity by supporting the group during intra-mural sports events and otherwise participating in house activities. Many little sisters ultimately date fraternity members and join sororities.

3. William R. Bascom, "Four Functions of Folklore," in *The Study of Folklore*, Alan Dundes, editor (Englewood Cliffs: Prentice-Hall, Inc., 1965), pp. 279-298.

The Walking Coffin

William M. Clements

One evening while three teen-agers were walking to a friend's house, they happened to walk by an ol' haunted house. As they passed, they teased each other saying that they were too chicken to spend the night in the haunted house. After many taunts all three of the boys decided to spend the night together in the house to prove to their friends how brave they were. Therefore, during school the next day they told all their friends of their plan; and, of course, all of their friends thought they were crazy. Nevertheless, the three boys were determined to spend the night in the ol' house. So that night, armed with lanterns, bed-rolls, soft drinks, and a rifle, the boys made way to the house. While they were relaxing as best as possible, they heard a noise downstairs. The noise sounded like someone pushing something heavy across an old concrete floor. The noise was a long scratching sound... Fright and curiosity were going through the boys' minds, so they decided to go down the steps, and they did with the lead man holding the gun; the second man had the lantern; and the third man had two empty pop bottles. So down they went; and when they got to the botton floor, the noise started again over in one corner of a large room. The boy with the lantern turned the light to the sound, and they saw a coffin standing on end and scooting itself unassisted across the floor. The boys froze and couldn't move, but the coffin kept getting closer and closer and was only about twenty feet away. Finally, when the coffin was only about three feet away, one of the boys started to react to stop the coffin. Can you guess how he stopped that coffin? Well, he reached into his shirt pocket and pulled out a Smith Brothers cough drop and took it; and he stopped that "coffin" for the time being, so the boys were saved.

279

Collected and told by John William Slavich, a twenty-one year old student from Bloomington.
Baughman E 281."Ghosts haunt house"; E 538.1. "Spectral coffin"; Z 13.4* (j). "Man is chased by coffin."

Stories of nights spent in a haunted house are relatively common, and the text above contains many of the usual elements of such a story. Although it has an incongruous and comic ending, it does possess many of the motifs found in haunted house legends.

FA variants and related texts:

(1) FA IU: 624, collected by Louise Schneiderman from Nancy Hiatt, a twenty year old student, in Speedway. While spending the night in a haunted house, a man hears sounds he thinks are made by rabbits. (2) FA IU: 1015, collected by P. Armstrong from Pam Andres, thirteen years old, in Angola. On three successive nights while staying in a haunted house, a boy hears mysterious footsteps coming up the stairs. On the first two nights the steps retreat before reaching him. On the third he sees a deep fog which dissolves into the shapes of children. The next morning only a cloud of dust is found in his bed. (3) FA IU: 1363, collected by Ruth Breeden from Johnny Cates in Vienna, Illinois. Some girls who are spending the night in a large house hear something approaching from the attic. It comes into their room, and they pull the bed clothes over their heads. After the sound departs, they find the attic door shut; but an investigation in the morning reveals nothing. (4) FA IU: 1410, told by Carol Rhinebarger in Kokomo, 1964. Three boys spend the night in a haunted house with three candles only. Next morning others investigate the first floor of the house and find nothing. In a closet on the second floor one of the boys is found. He has white hair and is gnawing on a severed finger.

"The Walking Coffin" text A seems to be somewhat related to Baughman Z 510., "The fatal fraternity initiation." In his analysis of this motif, "The Fatal Initiation," *Hoosier Folklore* (IV, 3 September, 1945, pp. 49-55), Baughman designates texts of the fatal initiation motif which most closely resemble our text A. This legend may be briefly summarized:

During a fraternity initiation, single pledges are sent into a haunted house with instructions to stay only long enough to leave some proof that they have been there. Although the first pledge to be sent in does not return, the actives of the fraternity send in several others. When none return, an investigation is made. Only one of the pledges is found, and he is in a state of insanity. The affair may result in a curse being brought on the participants in the initiation.

Like variants (1), (2), and (3), "The Walking Coffin" A presents a ghost who makes mysterious sounds. It differs from these variants when it supplements the sounds of the ghost with the appearance of the coffin. The presence of the people in the haunted house as the result of a dare or test is definitely present in (4) and "The Fatal Fraternity Initiation," as it is in "The Walking Coffin" A, and as is hinted in (2) and (3). The suspenseful approach appears in (2), (3), and "The Walking Coffin" A.

B

A man's wife had died and the funeral was to be held in his home. So the coffin was kept upstairs in one of the bedrooms. The coffin was on a cart with wheels. As the man was sitting in the living room late on the night before the funeral he heard a creaking noise upstairs. He could hear the coffin rolling from the back bedroom to the stairway. He heard the wheels bumping slowly one by one down the steps. He heard the coffin creak closer and closer to the living room. So he did the only thing that was left; he got some cough medicine and stopped the coffin.

Collected by Nancy Roach from Richard Hudson of Des Plaines, Illinois, in the IU Commons, May 13, 1968. The collector notes, "The point of the story is the clever play on the word coffin; in the last sentence used to mean coughing." Motifs included are identical with those in text A.

There are many dangers involved in sitting up with a coffin. As in "The Walking Coffin" A, (1), (2), and (3), "The Walking Coffin" B contains a ghost that at least begins to make itself known by means of eerie sounds. The suspenseful approach of the horror is present again, but the presence in the house because of a dare or test is replaced by a husband's waiting for his dead wife's funeral. Although a funeral is planned, the fact that it has not yet occurred seems to make E 412.2., "Dead without proper funeral cannot rest," relevant. The involvement of a coffin of a dead wife in the haunting of a house is a factor in "The House of the Blue Lights," discussed by Magnús Einarsson Mullarký in *Indiana Folklore* (I, 1, 1968, pp. 82-91).

C

This farmer was out in his field plowing one evening when he saw this real spooky-looking guy. He stopped the tractor and asked the guy what he wanted. The spooky guy asked if he could stay the night with the farmer. The farmer told him no and to get off his property.

That night there was a real bad storm and the next morning when the farmer went back out to his field he found the same guy he had talked to yesterday dead. Since he didn't know the guy or who he belonged to, he decided to put him in a coffin and put the coffin in his attic.

Well, every year after this someone in the farmer's family died until there was no one left but the farmer. Then one night the farmer heard a knocking. He searched everywhere trying to find out where it was coming from and finally he came to the attic. When he opened the door he saw that the knocking was coming from the coffin. And then the coffin rose up and started floating towards the farmer. (At this point in the story the teller may make the chase as long as he wishes.) The farmer runs out of the room and down the stairs and when he got to the front door he couldn't get it opened. He turned around and saw the coffin coming at him and then he reached into his pocket and took out a cough drop, ate it, and stopped the coffin.

FA IU: 69/65, collected by Stephen Joseph Daily from Bob Daily, fifteen years old, in Kokomo, December 29, 1968.

MI Q 292 "Inhospitality punished"; E 412.2. "Dead without proper funeral cannot rest"; E 538.1, "Spectral coffin"; Z 13.4*(j)."Man is chased by coffin."

The reason for the coffin's threatening behavior toward the farmer may be his inhospitality, the lack of a proper burial for the corpse, or both. E 412.2., "Dead without proper funeral cannot rest," is more clearly related to "The Walking Coffin" C than to B. The mysterious sounds made by the ghost are again present. As the parenthetical statement in the text indicates, suspense can be created by dwelling on the approach of the coffin. A striking departure from A and B is the deaths which occur before the farmer's encounter with the coffin.

D

Three sisters had inherited a large house from their grandfather. This house was supposed to be haunted, but the three moved into it anyway. One day the oldest sister heard a noise in the attic. She went up the stairs to the attic, opened the door, and walked into the room. Suddenly the door slammed shut behind her. She turned around and screamed. She was so scared by what she saw that she ran across the room and jumped out the third story window. A few days later, the second sister heard a noise in the attic and went up to see what it was. As soon as she walked inside the room, the door slammed shut. She turned around, screamed, and was cut in two by a huge, razor-sharp blade which fell from the ceiling. A few days later, the third sister heard a noise in the attic and went up to find out what it was. When she walked into the room, the door slammed behind her. She turned and saw a coffin floating toward her. She started stepping backwards, but realized that the coffin was trying to force her toward the window that her sister had jumped out of. What did she do? She pulled out a box of Vick's Cough Drops and stopped the coffin.

FA IU: 68/242, collected by Kenneth C. Mumaw from Kathy Ellars, nineteen years old, in Peru, April 3, 1968.
Baughman "Ghosts haunt house"; E 538.1. "Spectral coffin"; Z 13.4* (j). "Man is chased by coffin."

The approach of the coffin is again suspenseful, and the fact that two deaths have already taken place because of the coffin points toward an

exciting climax. Sounds again play a part in the ghost's activities, and the
sisters' presence in the house seems more closely related to A than to B
and C because the sisters may be intruders to a certain degree. Ruth Ann
Musick reports a legend from West Virginia in *The Telltale Lilac Bush and
Other West Virginia Ghost Tales* (University of Kentucky, 1965, pp.
71-72), in which a floating coffin haunts the site of a murder. A variant of
"The Walking Coffin" was collected by Baughman from a twenty year old
student from Aurora, Illinois and published in *HFB* (III, 1944, p. 69).
Although the cough drop motif occurs, the story differs from any of the
texts given above. A middle-aged man lives alone in the city. Staggering
home drunk one night, he finds that he is being pursued by a white coffin.
The coffin bursts through a locked door and smashes a chair that is
thrown at it. The man stops the coffin by using cough drops.

A common element in all these markedly different texts of "The
Walking Coffin" is the laying of the ghost with cough medicine or drops, a
feature which seems incongruous in relation to the rest of the story. The
exorcism of a ghost can be accomplished by means of an object, a ritual,
or an incantation. One FA text possesses this theme: FA IU: 702,
collected by Sally Weibel from Pat Horner in Bloomington, October 1960.
A woman drives away the souls of sinners who harass her at night by
saying, "Jesus, Mary, and Joseph." Robert W. Montgomery cites another
story from Indiana which incorporates the laying of a ghost ("Ghost
Stories from Decatur County," *Midwest Folklore*, XI, 1961, pp. 62-64).
The laying is carried out by lighting a candle and reading the scriptures. In
"The Walking Coffin" the traditional element of the laying of the ghost
has been changed so that the whole atmosphere of the story is
transformed.

Although A, B, C, and D texts are remarkably different in both
formulation and inherent message, they agree in combining mainly two
motifs: E538.1. and Z 13.4* (j).within the framework of different haunted
houses — revenant situations. Probably because of the baffling, dissonant
conclusion, Baughman included this story in the "Catch tales" (MI Z 13.
"The manner of the telling forces the hearer to ask a particular question to
which the teller returns a ridiculous answer,") where it does not seem to
fit very well.

Jan Harold Brunvand ("A Classification for Shaggy Dog Stories," *JAF* LXXVI, 1963, pp. 42-68) considers narratives such as "The Walking Coffin" to be shaggy dog stories. He defines a shaggy dog story as "a nonsensical joke that employs in the punch line a psychological non sequitur, a punning variation of a familiar saying, or a hoax, to trick the listener who expects conventional wit or humor." In his classification, Brunvand includes texts like the one discussed here in section D 500-599, "Hoax Stories told as Real Happenings, Though Not Personal Experiences." "The Walking Coffin," however, is not mentioned.

Although the FA IU follows Brunvand and files this kind of material as a shaggy dog story, it seems possible to consider "The Walking Coffin" a discredited legend, a story which possesses the characteristics of a legend, but substitutes something incongruous for a supernatural climax. Narratives also having such abrupt, humorous conclusions are discussed by Kurt Ranke ("Schwank und Witz als Schwundstufe," *Festschrift für W.E. Peuckert*, München, 1955, pp. 41-59) and by Hermann Bausinger ("Strukturen des alltäglichen Erzählens," *Fabula*, I, 1958, p. 252). Ranke especially sees this phenomenon as a manifestation of the process of disintegration of one type of traditional narratives and the transition into other forms. Bausinger, on the other hand, uses similar examples to prove the close relationship between legends and outlandish jokes. Jokes may be inserted into a legend and transform the legend's atmosphere into the ridiculous. That this is what has occurred in "The Walking Coffin" seems apparent.

Other discredited legends in the FA:

(6) FA IU: 1186, collected by Gerri Bard from Liz Jannach, May 8, 1967. A ship on the ocean is ravaged by starvation, and only two passengers remain alive. They hear a mysterious voice saying, "It floats. It floats." Having asked what floats, they receive the reply: "Dial Soap floats." (7) Collected by Nancy Roach from Paula Schlossberg, nineteen year old student, in Bloomington, May 18, 1968. A man marries a very fastidious wife and murders her. He is haunted by a mysterious voice

which says, "It floats." Finally he asks what floats and is told, "Ivory Soap, stupid!" Bausinger reports a similar story (*op. cit.*). A girl crossing a bridge is hindered by a black hand and by the cry, "Who washes my hands clean?" The answer is "Persil" (a much advertised detergent).

Several reasons may be hypothesized for the telling of a discredited legend. The storyteller may aim to entrap his listeners through his suspenseful building toward a ridiculous climax. There may be an intent to mock the genre of belief legends and horror stories and to express disbelief in the supernatural on the storyteller's part. It should be noted that the rationale may be to divert suspicion of believing in the supernatural from the storyteller. The attempt seems to be to deny with a good laugh the belief conceptions of the legend, the release of fear from the dead and death so naturally human. It is quite remarkable that the story was first noted in 1944 and its peak of popularity, along with similar stories, seems to be very recent in modern urban society.

The Study of Folklore in Indiana
A Bibliography
Nikolai Burlakoff and Carl Lindahl

The present bibliography of Indiana folklore utilized the previously published bibliographies of Donald M. Winkelman and W. K. McNeil as its foundation.[1] Wherever we deemed it necessary, the earlier entries have been corrected or revised. The bibliography has been updated, and over one hundred items have been added.

The earlier Indiana folklore bibliographies listed items according to general subject categories. Rather than continuing this practice (which often requires that a single article be listed under several different headings), we have arranged all entries alphabetically by author. The bibliography draws upon all available pertinent books and journals published by March 1979, but it does not include newspaper articles, tape recordings, video materials, films, or records.[2]

Interested readers should note that there are three archives at Indiana University, Bloomington, which house sizable collections of tapes and unpublished manuscripts. The Indiana University Folklore Archives (510 North Fess Street, Bloomington, IN 47405) contains over 40,000 fieldwork projects, most of which were collected from Indiana residents by folklore students. The Archives of Traditional Music (057 Maxwell Hall, Indiana University, Bloomington, IN 47405) includes hundreds of tapes from Indiana in its massive collection of folk music from around the world. The Archives of Oral History (510 North Fess Street) also contains many items pertinent to Indiana folklore studies. In addition, smaller field collections of Indiana folklore are housed in several universities throughout the state.

Realizing that omissions and errors are inevitable, the authors urge readers to inform the editor of any pertinent additions and corrections.

1. Donald M. Winkelman, "Bibliography of Indiana Folklore," *Midwest Folklore,* 11:2 (1961), 115–124; Donald M. Winkelman, "Bibliography of Indiana Folklore," *Midwest Folklore,* 13:4 (1963–1964), 237–244; W.K. McNeil, "An Annotated Bibliography of Indiana Folklore," *Indiana Folklore,* 6:1 (1973), 100–137.

2. NcNeil includes references to eight records and eleven tape recordings in his bibliography (pp. 132–134); Winkelman indexes one record.

Journal Abbreviations

AMus	*Acta Musicologica*
AS	*American Speech*
CFQ	*California Folklore Quarterly*
DN	*Dialect Notes*
EE	*Ethnologia Europaea*

FF	*Folklore Forum*
FFMA	*Folklore and Folk Music Archivist*
FL	*The Folk-Lorist*
HF	*Hoosier Folklore*
HFB	*Hoosier Folklore Bulletin*
IF	*Indiana Folklore*
IHB	*Indiana History Bulletin*
IMH	*Indiana Magazine of History*
IN	*Indiana Names*
JAF	*Journal of American Folklore*
JFI	*Journal of the Folklore Institute*
JOFS	*Journal of the Ohio Folklore Society*
KFQ	*Keystone Folklore Quarterly*
MF	*Midwest Folklore*
MJLF	*Midwestern Journal of Language and Folklore*
N	*Names*
NYFQ	*New York Folklore Quarterly*
PA	*Pioneer America*
PADS	*Publications of the American Dialect Society*
PMLA	*Publications of the Modern Language Association*
SFQ	*Southern Folklore Quarterly*
WF	*Western Folklore*
YBSIP	*Year Book of the Society of Indiana Pioneers*

1. Adams, Estella. *Songs and Poems of Early Indiana.* Irvington, Indiana, 1916.
2. Adams, Robert Jesse. "Raconteur and Repertoire: A Study of a Southern Indiana Storyteller and His Material." M.A. thesis, Indiana University, 1966. [A well-annotated study of the repertoire of Thomas Sullivan (pseudonym) of Martinsville, Indiana, which considers the use Sullivan makes of his material, his position in the community, and the reactions of his audience. The tapes used in this study are on file in the Indiana University Archives of Traditional Music.]
3. Adler, Elizabeth Mosby. "Problems in the Development of an Outdoor Museum of Folklife." M.A. thesis, Cooperstown, N.Y., 1974. [Discusses the proposed Indiana University Folk Museum.]
4. Adler, Thomas. "Hardware and Software in the Urban Field," *IF,* 10:2 (1977), 113–126.
5. ——. "When Fieldwork Becomes Fieldshock," *FF,* 11:3 (1978), 234–244. [Adler relies on personal fieldwork experience to describe the initial disorientation and eventual adjustment of the collector in the urban field; the setting is the Calumet Region of northwestern Indiana.]
6. Anderson, David D. "Songs and Sayings of the Lakes," *MF,* 12:1 (1962), 5–16. [Great Lakes songs and rhymes: no specific locale is mentioned; no annotation; no mention of informants.]
7. Ashton, John W. "The Indiana University Research Center in Anthropology, Folklore, and Linguistics," *FFMA,* 1:1 (1958), 2.
8. ——. "Popular Wisdom in Indiana in the 1830's," *JOFS,* 3:1 (1968), 41–44. [A discussion and listing of some materials contained in the notes of William Adolphus Ashton, the founder of an unsuccessful cooperative colony in southeastern Indiana in 1834. Among the examples of popular wisdom are quotations from the Bible and other literature, "old saws and wise instances," popular medical beliefs, household hints, and a rule for predicting weather.]
9. ——. "The Vitality of American Folklore," *HF,* 6:3 (1947), 81–87.

10. Attebury, Jennifer Eastman. "Storytelling Style in the Personal Narratives of Homer Spriggs," *JFI*, 14:1–2 (1977), 51–58. [A stylistic analysis of the repertoire of a Monroe County farmer, stressing the teller's use of dialogue and detail.]
11. Baker, Ronald L. "Brown County Place Names," *MJLF*, 2:2 (1976), 64–70.
12. ———. "County Names in Indiana," *IN*, 2:2 (1971), 39–54. [A listing of the names of Indiana's ninety-two counties along with their probable derivations.]
13. ———. "The Face in the Wall," *IF*, 2:2 (1969), 29–46. [Annotated collection and discussion of what may be Terre Haute's most popular legend.]
14. ———. "Hogs are Playing with Sticks—Bound to Be Bad Weather: Folk Belief or Proverb?" *MJLF*, 1:2 (1975), 65–67.
15. ———. "The Indiana Place Name Survey," *IN*, 1:1 (1970), 20. [A brief description of the Committee on Place Names at Indiana State University and an account of its ongoing research.]
16. ———. "The Influence of Mass Culture on Modern Legends," *SFQ*, 40:3–4 (1976), 367–376.
17. ———. "Legends about Lakes Named 'Blue Hole,'" *IN*, 1:2 (1970), 50. [Brief discussion of a legend associated with a small lake near Brazil, Indiana. Baker notes that the name is usually traditional and not official. Therefore, how widespread the name and its accompanying stories are can only be determined by extensive fieldwork throughout Indiana.]
18. ———. "Legends about Spook Light Hill," *IF*, 3:2 (1970), 163–189. [Annotated discussion of legends about a site near Brazil, Indiana.]
19. ———. "Legends about the Naming of Hymera, Indiana," *IN*, 4:2 (1973), 62–63.
20. ———. "Monsterville: a Traditional Place-Name and its Legends," *IN*, 20:3 (1972), 186–192. [Study of the legends surrounding two locales in southern Vermillion County.]
21. ———. "The Phone in the Mausoleum: A Local Legend," *MJLF*, 4:2 (1973), 70–76. [Eleven texts concerning a tomb near Terre Haute, which is said to have been equipped with a telephone in accordance with the owner's deathbed request.]
22. ———. "The Role of Folk Legends in Place-Name Research," *JAF*, 85:338 (1972), 367–373. [Demonstrates, with examples from Indiana, that the study of legendary material can reveal much about a community's cultural values and can also help in the evaluation of the historical worth of data.]
23. ———. "Stiffy Green," *IF*, 3:1 (1970), 113–127. [Legends about a stuffed dog in a mausoleum in a Terre Haute cemetery.]
24. Baker, Ronald L., and Marvin Carmony. *Indiana Place Names*. Bloomington: Indiana University Press, 1975. [2,271 names, primarily of towns and counties, are listed, with short explanations of their origins.]
25. Bastian, Robert W. "Indiana Folk Architecture: A Lower Midwestern Index," *PA*, 9:2 (1977), 115–136. [Detailed survey of house-type distribution in Indiana tests the diffusion model worked out by Kniffen, Lewis, and Glassie. Bastian finds that the model "provides an accurate description of the distributions and probable paths of diffusion" of upright-and-wing and four-over-four dwellings and several barn types. The I-house, and the single level, three-bay barn, however, follow different patterns of diffusion; and Bastian discusses the one-and-one-half story house, previously overlooked by folklife scholars.]
26. Baughman, Ernest W. "An Endless Tale," *HFB*, 4:2 (1945), 37. [Old folktale pattern—"That's tough, what's tough."]
27. ———. "Bobby Hayes, Quarry Worker," *HFB*, 1:3 (1942), 75–77. [Legends concerning the fantastic exploits of a local strong man.]
28. ———. "The Cadaver Arm," *HFB*, 4:2 (1945), 30–32.
29. ———. "The Fatal Initiation," *HFB*, 4:3 (1945), 49–55.
30. ———. "The Hitchhiking Ghost," *HF*, 6:2 (1947), 77–78. [Variant references given.]
31. ———. "The Intelligent Bird Dog," *HFB*, 4:2 (1945), 34–36. [Tall tale.]
32. ———. "Little Moron Stories," *HFB*, 2:1 (1943), 17–18.
33. ———. "Two Tall Tales," *HF*, 7:2 (1948), 55. ["Fighting Snakes" and "Letting out the Cold Air."]

34. Baughman, E.W., and Clayton A. Holaday. "Tall Tales and 'Sells' from Indiana University Students," *HFB*, 3 (1944), 59–70. [Fourteen tales.]
35. Baughman, Frances J. "Queries," *HF*, 6:2 (1947), 78. [Nonsense greeting and cadence count.]
36. Baxter, Ralph C. "With a Ball-Pein Hammer, Hammering Beer," *AS*, 42:4 (1967), 308–309. [Brief note discussing a term used in southern Indiana during the Prohibition Era.]
37. Beard, Anne. "Games and Recreations in the Novels of Edward Eggleston," *MF*, 11:2 (1961), 85–104.
38. Ben-Amos, Dan. "The Americanization of 'The King and the Abbot'," *IF*, 2:1 (1969), 115–123. [A discussion of an American joke related to Aarne-Thompson Type 922, as told by a Jewish narrator in Indianapolis. In Miller's narrative, a Catholic priest has to answer the questions. Thus "the success of the contestant rather than his failure threatens the community."]
39. Bergen, Fanny D. "Popular American Plant Names," *JAF*, 5:17 (1892), 91ff. [Two Indiana references.]
40. ———. "Popular American Plant Names," *JAF*, 6:21 (1893), 136ff. [Four Indiana references.]
41. ———. "Popular American Plant Names," *JAF*, 7:25 (1894), 92ff. [Three Indiana references.]
42. ———. "Popular American Plant Names," *JAF*, 9:34 (1896), 181ff. [Two Indiana references.]
43. ———. "Popular American Plant Names," *JAF*, 10:36 (1897), 50ff. [Two Indiana references.]
44. ———. "Popular American Plant Names," *JAF*, 10:37 (1897), 143ff. [Two Indiana references.]
45. Bergen, Fanny D., and W.W. Newell. "Current Superstitions, II," *JAF*, 2:5 (1889), 105. [No. 6 is a southern Indiana death omen.]
46. Berry, Cecilia Ray, ed. *Folk Songs of Old Vincennes.* Chicago: H.T. Fitzsimmons Company, 1946. [French-American folklore. Contains thirty-eight French songs with translations.]
47. Biebuyck-Goetz, Brunhilde. "'This is the Dyin' Truth': Mechanisms of Lying," *JFI*, 14:1–2 (1977), 73–85. [Study of the tall-tale repertoire of three brothers from Solsberry, Indiana, focusing on the way in which tall tales reflect the brothers' personal environment and experience.]
48. Bird, Donald Allport. "Morgan's Raiders: 'That's Sure a Good Looking Rifle You Got There,'" *IF*, 2:1 (1969), 124–130. [Discussion of a historical legend collected from Benjamin Kuhn of Hartsville, Indiana.]
49. ———. "A Theory for Folklore in Mass Media: Traditional Patterns in the Mass Media," *SFQ*, 40:3–4 (1976), 285–305.
50. Bird, Donald Allport, and James R. Dow. "Benjamin Kuhn: Life and Narratives of a Hoosier Farmer," *IF*, 5:2 (1972), 143–260.
51. Blair, Don. *Harmonist Construction, Principally as Found in the Two-Story Houses Built in Harmonie, Indiana, 1814–1824. Indiana Historical Society Publications,* Vol. 23, no. 2. Indianapolis: Indiana Historical Society, 1964. [A discussion of the folk architecture of the initial settlement of Harmony, Indiana.]
52. Bogardus, Carl R., M.D. *The Lost Silver Mine: A Tale from Indiana. The Ohio Valley Folk Research Project,* N.S., no. 45. Chillicothe, Ohio: The Ross County Historical Society, 1960.
53. Bogle, Victor M. "Reminiscences of a Hillbilly," *IMH*, 61:3 (1965), 205–250. [Autobiography of the late Indiana educator-administrator Paul Van Riper (1876–1944). Included in this and the second installment (item no. 54) are numerous items of folklore including songs, proverbs, and descriptions of customs. Several play-party games are given with music.]
54. ———. "Reminiscences of a Hillbilly," *IMH*, 62:1 (1966), 5–50. [Conclusion of the autobiography of Paul Van Riper. See item no. 53.]
55. Bond, Richmond P. "Animal Comparisons in Indiana," *AS*, 2 (1926–1927), 42–58.

[Similes and other proverbial expressions that tend to associate specific characteristics of human behavior with certain types of animals.]

56. ——. "More Animal Comparisons," *AS*, 4 (1928–1929), 123–124. [See item no. 55.]

57. Bouvy, Jane Faulkner. "Folk Catholicism in Indiana," *IF*, 9:2 (1976), 147–164.

58. Bradunas, Elena. "From the Familiar to the Unknown: A Fieldworker's Progression," *FF*, 11:3 (1978), 273–289. [A collector's description of the personal dimensions of fieldwork, focusing on the Lithuanian-American community in the Calumet Region.]

59. ——. "An Urban Hermit," *IF*, 10:2 (1977), 159–164. [Discussion of an East Chicago local character and his effect on the surrounding community.]

60. Brewster, Paul G. "Additional Observations on Indiana Place-Names," *HFB*, 3:4 (1944), 74–76.

61. ——. "The Archer Gang, Indiana Outlaws," *HF*, 6 (1947), 27–36. [Brief history of the gang.]

62. ——. *Ballads and Songs of Indiana*. Bloomington: Indiana University Publications, Folklore Series, No. 1, 1940.

63. ——. "Folk Beliefs and Practices from Southern Indiana," *HFB*, 2:2 (1943), 23–28.

64. ——. "Folk Cures and Preventives from Southern Indiana," *SFQ*, 3 (1939), 33–43. [Crawford, Dubois, Gibson, Knox, Perry, Pike, Posey, Spencer, Vanderburgh, and Warrick counties are represented.]

65. ——. "Folk 'Sayings' from Indiana," *AS*, 14 (1939), 261–268.

66. ——. "Folksongs from Indiana," *SFQ*, 3 (1939), 201–222.

67. ——. "Folktales from Indiana and Missouri," *Folklore*, 50 (1939), 294–310. [Includes twelve jokes and anecdotes from southern Indiana, most concerning numskulls; in four tales, the Irishman plays the numskull's role; variants of A-T types 1250, 1319, 1697, 1791 included.]

68. ——. "Game-Songs from Southern Indiana," *JAF*, 49:193 (1936), 243.

69. ——. "A Glance at Some Indiana Place-Names," *HFB*, 2:1 (1943), 14–16.

70. ——. "'The Hanging of Sam Archer,' An Indiana Ballad," *HF*, 5 (1946), 125–135. [See also item no. 61.]

71. ——. "Indiana's Representation in the Archives of American Folksong," *HFB*, 4:2 (1945), 25–29. [Gives list of titles and informants.]

72. ——. "More Indiana Ballads and Songs," *SFQ*, 5 (1941), 169–190. [Annotated; no music; from southern Indiana.]

73. ——. "More Indiana Sayings," *AS*, 16:1 (1941), 21–25.

74. ——. "More Songs from Indiana," *SFQ*, 4 (1940), 175–203.

75. ——. "Moses Whitecotton, Hoosier Balladist and Rhymester," *HF*, 8:2–3 (1949), 45–48.

76. ——. "Names of Indiana Quilt Patterns," *CFQ*, 3 (1944), 61. [Southern Indiana.]

77. ——. "Names, Novel and Nonsensical," *HF*, 5 (1946), 157–161.

78. ——. "Riddles from Southern Indiana," *SFQ*, 3 (1939), 93–105. [Seventy-two texts.]

79. ——. "The Romance of Quilt Names," *HF*, 9:2 (1950), 59–62.

80. ——. "Smart Sayings from Indiana," *HF*, 6 (1947), 50–54. [Clever retorts and insults, some of them rhymed; ninety-two entries, no contextual information.]

81. ——. "Some Folksongs from Indiana," *JAF*, 57:226 (1944), 282–287.

82. ——. "Still Another Batch of Indiana Sayings," *AS*, 19 (1944), 155–156.

83. ——. "Stories of the Supernatural from Southern Indiana," *SFQ*, 10 (1946), 227–234.

84. ——. "Traditional Ballads from Indiana," *JAF*, 48:190 (1935), 295–317.

85. Brown, Rollo Walter. "A Word-List from Western Indiana," *DN*, 3:8 (1912), 570–593. [An alphabetically arranged collection of several hundred words with their meanings. Since the author was from Wabash College, the collection was probably made in the vicinity of Crawfordsville. No data about informants is given.]

86. Browne, Ray Broadus, and Egil Ramstad. "The Indian Doctor," *IHB*, 41:3 (1964), 35–36. [An edited version of a book which a Dr. John Williams apparently presented as a souvenir to his patients. The date and place of publication are unknown, "but clearly it is a frontier production, and could as well be from Indiana as from any other state." Most of the cures are of folk provenance, many of them still practiced. Browne

annotates the volume by using the UCLA collection of beliefs and superstitions; *Frank C. Brown Collection of North Carolina Folklore* (7 vols. Durham, N.C.: Duke University Press, 1952–1964), Popular Beliefs and Practices from Alabama; and W. Edson Richmond and Elva Van Winkle's 1958 article, "Is There a Doctor in the House?" *IHB,* 35:9 (1958), 115–135. Ramstad provides pharmacological analyses.]

87. _____. "The Indian Doctor: Part II," *IHB,* 41:4 (1964), 59–70. [The conclusion of John Williams' book, *The Indian Doctor,* most of which was presented in the previous issue of this journal: see item no. 86.]

88. Brunvand, Jan Harold. "An Indiana Storyteller Revisited," *MF,* 11:1 (1961), 5–14. [Brunvand visits a master storyteller seventeen years after Herbert Halpert had recorded stories from the same man; Brunvand notes changes in style and repertoire; tall tales and anecdotes included among the seven texts. See item no. 217.]

89. _____. "The Cars that Went in the River: A Pennsylvania Railroaders' Legend in Indiana," *KFQ,* 5 (1960), 3–5. [Collected by the author in Bloomington.]

90. _____. "A Classification for Shaggy Dog Stories," *JAF,* 76:299 (1963), 42–68. [This index follows the pattern of Thompson's *Motif-Index,* and it includes classifications for 300 Indiana texts, among others.]

91. _____. *A Dictionary of Proverbs and Proverbial Phrases from Books Published by Indiana Authors Before 1890.* Bloomington: Indiana University Press, 1961.

92. _____. "From the Archives: Some Indiana Place-Name Legends," *MF,* 9:4 (1959), 245–248.

93. _____. "Sex in the Classroom," *JAF,* 73:289 (1960), 250–251. [Mostly out of state, but contains one mention of Purdue.]

94. _____. "Some Thoughts on the Ethnic-Regional Riddle Jokes," *IF,* 3:1 (1970), 128–142. [A discussion of jokes that are not necessarily typically Hoosier but "have circulated in Indiana."]

95. _____. "Thor, the Cheechako and the Initiates' Tasks: A Modern Parallel for an Old Jest," *SFQ,* 24 (1960), 235–238. [Contains references from three Indiana texts—all deposited in Indiana University Folklore Archives—of a joke which the author identifies as a thematic relative of the Old Norse story, "Thor and Utgarthr-Loki."]

96. Buckley, Bruce R. "Jump-Rope Rhymes: Suggestions for Classification and Study," *KFQ,* 11:2 (1966), 99–111. [A classification and analysis of six collections of jump-rope rhymes, five of which are from Indiana.]

97. Buehler, Richard Edward. "An Annotated Collection of Contemporary Obscene Humor from the Bloomington Campus of Indiana University." M.A. thesis, Indiana University, 1964. [Material recorded from fourteen students at Indiana University during five sessions conducted from March to December, 1963.]

98. _____. "Looking through the Archives: The Big Cat," *JOFS,* 1:2 (1966), 75–78. [Brief discussion of a story reported in Bloomington, Indiana, and Jacksonville, Illinois, newspapers about a large panther or leopard which has escaped from a circus and cannot be recaptured.]

99. Buley, Roscoe Carlyle. *The Old Northwest: Pioneer Period, 1815–1840.* 2 vols. Bloomington: Indiana University Press, 1962. [The Old Northwest is defined as the connecting region between the Great Lakes-St. Lawrence system and the Mississippi. Chapters 4–6 contain some folklore material.]

100. Buley, Roscoe Carlyle, and Madge Evelyn Pickard. *The Midwest Pioneer: His Ills, Cures, and Doctors.* Crawfordsville, Indiana: R. E. Banta, 1945. ["A non-technical account" of medical practices on the Midwest frontier.]

101. Bundy, Colleen. "A Method for Removing Warts," *JAF,* 59:231 (1946), 70.

102. Burns, Tom. "Folklore in the Mass Media: Television," *FF,* 2:4 (1969), 90–106. [An analysis of the folkloric material used on various Indiana television stations on 15 May 1969. Programs watched were chosen because they seemed to be the ones most likely to contain traditional material. Burns found 101 traditional items or themes, including traditional music and song, folk belief, gesture, narratives, proverbs and proverbial sayings, customs, signs, dance, games, and rhymes.]

103. _____. "A Joke and Its Tellers: A Study of the Functional Variation of a Folklore Item at the Psychological Level." Ph.D. dissertation, Indiana University, 1972. 6 volumes.

Published in condensed form as *Doing the Wash: An Expressive Culture and Personality Study of a Joke and Its Tellers*. Norwood, Pa.: Norwood Editions, 1975. [Very detailed analysis of a "dirty" joke told by eleven white, middle-class college students at Indiana University.]

104. Busse, Ora S. "Indiana Folk Beliefs, Omens, and Signs," *HF*, 6 (1947), 14–26.
105. Butler, Ruby Stainbrook. "Old Man Edmonds," *HF*, 6:4 (1947), 151–152. [Two tall tales attributed to a long-dead narrator who lived near Franklin, Indiana. See following two items.]
106. ———. "Old Man Edmonds," *HF*, 7:2 (1948), 33–38. [Short biography of an Indiana tall-tale teller, accompanied by ten tales told about him forty years after his death.]
107. ———. "Old Man Edmonds," *HF*, 8:2–3 (1949), 48–49. [Four more tales concerning the exploits of a tall-tale teller.]
108. ———. "The Pack Peddler," *HF*, 6:4 (1947), 133–137.
109. ———. "Sassafras George," *HF*, 7 (1948), 124–125. [Description and anecdotes about a peddler in Brown County.]
110. "Cadence Counts," *HFB*, 6:3 (1947), 109–110.
111. Carmony, Donald F. "Flatboat Building on Little Raccoon Creek, Parke County, Indiana," *IMH*, 60:4 (1964), 305–322. [Flatboat building in the 1830s and 1840s, taken from an account written in the 1890s by John Calvin Gilkeson, son of one of Parke County's first settlers.]
112. Carmony, Marvin. "The Americanization of Terre Haute," *IN*, 2:1 (1971), 13–18. [Various accounts of the naming of Terre Haute.]
113. ———. "The Regional Vocabulary of Terre Haute," *MJLF*, 3:1 (1977), 3–34.
114. Carpenter, Inta Gale, ed. *Land of the Millrats: Folklore in the Calumet Region, IF*, 10:2 (1977). [A wide-ranging special issue which deals with the whole complex of modern urban lore as it is found in Gary, Indiana, and surrounding communities. The contents reflect field methodology, questions of folklore theory, politics of doing research under the auspices of the U.S. government and state institutions.]
115. ———. "Coordinating an Urban Folklore Team Project," *IF*, 10:2 (1977), 107–112.
116. Cassagrande, Pamela Mills, and Xenia E. Cord. "An Old Political Joke Reappears," *JAF*, 76:2 (1963), 134. [Anecdote once credited to Abraham Lincoln which reappeared during the 1960 presidential campaign.]
117. Clements, William M. "The Chain," *IF*, 2:1 (1969), 90–96. [Annotated collection of legends about a tombstone in a Bedford, Indiana, cemetery which supposedly shows the weapon with which the person buried there was killed.]
118. ———. *The Types of the Polack Joke. FF: Bibliographical and Special Series*, no. 3. Bloomington, Indiana. [N.d.] [A classification of ethnic riddle-jokes centered on the familiar figure of the Pole, and based on materials deposited at the Indiana University Folklore Archives.]
119. ———. "The Walking Coffin," *IF*, 2:2 (1969), 3–10.
120. Clements, William M., and William E. Lightfoot. "The Legend of Stepp Cemetery," *IF*, 5:1 (1972), 92–141. [Analysis of a legend complex dealing with a grave in the Stepp Cemetery which is located in the Morgan-Monroe State Forest.]
121. Coats, Nellie M. "Children's Rhymes," *HF*, 6:2 (1947), 73–74. [The writer asks for names for eight short rhymes.]
122. Cohen, Anne B. *Poor Pearl, Poor Girl! The Murdered-Girl Stereotype in Ballad and Newspaper*. Austin: University of Texas Press, 1973. *Publications of the American Folklore Society, Memoir Series*, vol. 58. [In a detailed study of "the crime of the nineteenth century," Cohen traces the historic, journalistic, and folksong accounts of the murder to Pearl Bryan, a Greencastle, Indiana, girl whose convicted killers were hanged in 1897.]
123. Cohen, B.B., and Irvin Ehrenpreis. "Tales from Indiana University Students," *HF*, 6 (1947), 57–65. [Tall tales, belief legends, and memorates involving portentous dreams from Indiana University students.]
124. "Conner Prairie Expands," *IHB*, 49:5 (1972), 51–54.
125. Cooley, Gilbert E. "Root Doctors and Psychics in the Region," *IF*, 10:2 (1977), 191–200.

126. ____. "Conversations about Hoodoo," *IF*, 10:2 (1977), 201–215.
127. Cord, Xenia E. "Further Notes on 'The Assailant in the Back Seat'," *IF*, 2:2 (1969), 47–54. [A discussion of eighteen new variants of a legend previously discussed in *Indiana Folklore* by Carlos Drake. See item no. 175.]
128. ____. "Department Store Snakes," *IF*, 2:1 (1969), 110–114. [Legends about shoppers bitten by poisonous snakes hidden in the clothing in a department store.]
129. Crawford, Michael L. "Legends from St. Mary-of-the-Woods College," *IF*, 7:1–2 (1974), 53–76.
130. Cross, Paulette. "Jokes and Black Consciousness," *FF*, 2:6 (1969), 140–161. [In-depth analysis of interviews with three Black American students at Indiana University and of jokes they told "which relate to the black view of white Americans and of some aspects of white culture." This paper is also in Alan Dundes' anthology on Negro folklore, *Mother Wit from the Laughing Barrel* (Englewood Cliffs, N.J.: Prentice-Hall, Inc., 1973).]
131. Daggett, Rowan K. "The Place Names of Chester Township, Wabash County, Indiana," *IN*, 4:1 (1973), 4–30.
132. Danielson, Larry. "The Disappearing Treasure," *IF*, 1:1 (1968), 28–33. [Legends about treasures that disappeared when someone broke a taboo.]
133. ____. "The Revenant Plays the Organ," *IF*, 1:1 (1968), 52–54. [Legends about a dead woman whose spirit returns to play the organ she was fond of playing while alive.]
134. Davidson, Levette J. "Folk Beliefs from Southern Indiana," *WF*, 16:3 (1957), 204.
135. ____. "The Teaching of Folklore," *WF*, 14 (1955), 188.
136. Davidson, Mabel E. *Legend and Lore from America's Crossroads.* Berne, Indiana: Publishers Printing House, 1971. [This booklet is aptly described in the title of its first chapter, "A Bit of This and A Bit of That." Most of the entries deal with nineteenth-century Indiana.]
137. de Caro, F.A. "The Butter Witch," *IF*, 1:1 (1968), 17–20. [Legends about people accused of bewitching milk.]
138. ____. "Finding a Lost Watch," *IF*, 1:1 (1968), 25–27. [Legends about a woman who was believed to have a magic power to see lost things.]
139. ____. "Indiana Miracle Legends: A Survey," *IF*, 2:1 (1969), 36–53. [Concludes that most miracle legends collected in Indiana are from ethnic groups and are not set in America. The "native American" legends are mostly concerned with faith healing.]
140. ____. "The Witch Cat," *IF*, 1:1 (1968), 21–24. [Legends about a male witch who has his hand cut off while he is in the form of a cat.]
141. de Caro, F.A., and C. Richard K. Lunt. "The Face on the Tombstone," *IF*, 1:1 (1968), 34–41. [Legends about tombstones which show the manner in which the murdered persons met their death.]
142. de Caro, F.A., and W. K. McNeil. *American Proverb Literature: A Bibliography. FF: Bibliographical and Special Series,* no. 6 (1976).
143. Dégh, Linda. "Approaches to Folklore Research Among Immigrant Groups," *JAF*, 79:314 (1966), 551–556. [Suggests that the best method of conducting an in-depth investigation among immigrant groups is the multilateral method (i.e., researchers work according to a common plan outlined in a standard fieldwork guide). Illustrates this with examples from fieldwork among Hungarian immigrants in the Calumet region of northern Indiana.]
144. ____. "The Boy Friend's Death," *IF*, 1:1 (1968), 101–106. [Legends about a lovers' lane murder.]
145. ____. "Does Anybody Know About Tharp's Barn?" *IF*, 3:1 (1970), 143–146. [Brief article showing how family reminiscences are of interest to students of folk culture.]
146. ____. "The Haunted Bridges near Avon and Danville and their Role in Legend Formation," *IF*, 2:1 (1969), 54–89. [Legends associated with two southern Indiana bridges.]
147. ____. "The Hook," *IF*, 1:1 (1968), 92–100. [Legends about an escapee from an insane asylum.]
148. ____. "The House of Blue Lights Revisited," *IF*, 2:2 (1969), 11–28. [More information about a mysterious house in Indianapolis and the legends surrounding it. The

subject was previously discussed by Magnus Einarsson-Mullarky. See also item no. 336.]

149. ____. "Importance of Collecting Place-Name Legends in Indiana," *IN*, 1:2 (1970), 34–40. [Suggests that place-name legends are important in the study of onomastics because they provide oral explanations given by local informants which can be compared with other types of name documents. They reveal the folk imagination more adequately than is usually done by place-name collectors and also provide a more complete explanation of the reasons for a place name than is usually given by collectors. Finally, place names stimulate and maintain belief legends which are "the most viable folk-narrative genre in modern Indiana."]

150. ____. "Narratives from Early Indiana ," *IF*, 3:2 (1970), 229–241. [Items of folkloric interest taken from the 1907 volume, *Pioneer History of Indiana, Including Stories, Incidents and Customs of the Early Settlers* by Colonel William Monroe Cockrum.]

151. ____. "The Negro in the Concrete," *IF*, 1:1 (1968), 61–67. [Legends about a bridge haunted by the ghost of a laborer killed during its construction.]

152. ____. "Prepared Comments on Richard M. Dorson's 'Is There a Folk in the City?' " *JAF*, 83:328 (1970), 217–222. [See item no. 169.]

153. ____. "The Roommate's Death and Related Dormitory Stories in Formation," *IF*, 2:2 (1969), 55–74. [Legends about a girl murdered in the dormitory where she and her roommate are staying alone during a school vacation period.]

154. ____. "The Runaway Grandmother," *IF*, 1:1 (1968), 68–77. [Legends about a stolen car which has the body of the family's dead grandmother strapped to the luggage carrier on top.]

155. ____. "Survival and Revival of European Folk Cultures in America," *EE*, 2–3 (1968–1969), 97–107. [Primarily a discussion of fieldwork conducted among Hungarians in the Calumet region of northern Indiana that focused on acculturation and the changes it wrought on Old World traditions.]

156. ____. "The Symbiosis of Joke and Legend: A Case of Conversational Folklore," in *Folklore Today: A Festschrift for Richard M. Dorson*, ed. Linda Dégh, Henry Glassie, and Felix J. Oinas. Bloomington: Indiana University, 1976, pp. 101–122. [Dégh examines the complementary repertoires of a husband and wife, one of whom specializes in humorous narratives, the other in belief legends. The couple are Hungarian immigrants living in the Calumet Region.]

157. ____. "Two Hungarian-American Stereotypes," *NYFQ*, 28:1 (1972), 3–14. [The life histories of Joseph Szabo of East Chicago and Benjamin Varga of Kipling, Canada, which reveal "that the initial attitude of the peasant immigrant acts decisively on his fate, social adjustment, acculturation, language use, and mental development."]

158. ____. "Two Legends about Supernatural Encounters," *IF*, 8:1–2 (1975), 128–133. [Contains two texts: "The Calf-Ghost" and "The Phantom House."]

159. ____. "Two Old World Narrators in Urban Setting," in *Kontakte und Grenzen*. Göttingen: Otto Schwartz & Co., 1969, pp. 71–86. [Study of narrative communication between Mrs. Katie Kis and Mrs. Marge Kovács, both original members of the now dissolved Hungarian ethnic colony in Gary.]

160. D'Haucourt, Genevieve. *La Vie Agricole et Rurale dans L'Etat d'Indiana à L'Epoque Pionnière*. Paris: Mouton & Co., 1956. [Only chapters seven, "La Vie Rurale de la Frontière," and nine, "La Culture et la Vie au Temps de la Frontière," will be of interest to folklorists. The information, however, is available in other sources, notably R. Carlyle Buley's *The Old Northwest: Pioneer Period, 1815–1840*. See item no. 99.]

161. Doering, J. Frederick. "Folk Remedies for Diverse Allergies," *JAF*, 57 (1944), 140–141. [Contains two remedies from Vanderburgh County.]

162. ____. "Folksongs of the Corn Belt," *JAF*, 57:223 (1944), 72. [Contains songs collected in Indiana and Illinois, and in two cases compared to Brewster's versions. See item no. 62.]

163. ____. "Legends from Canada, Indiana and Florida," *SFQ*, 2 (1938), 213–220. [Indian lovers of Brown County; silver horseshoes from Anderson.]

164. Dorson, Richard M. *American Folklore*. Chicago: University of Chicago Press, 1959.

[Chapter seven of this general study of historic and regional trends in American folklore utilizes material from the Indiana University Folklore Archives.]

165. ———. "The Ethnic Research Survey of Northwest Indiana," in *Kontakte und Grenzen.* Göttingen: Otto Schwartz & Co., 1969, pp. 65–69. [Report on a project designed to explore the folklore of urban ethnic groups in Gary and East Chicago, Indiana.]

166. ———. "Folklore and the National Defense Education Act," *JAF,* 75:296 (1962), 160–164. [Discusses folklore studies in the United States with specific reference to Indiana University.]

167. ———. "Folklore in Higher Education," *NYFQ,* 18:1 (1962), 44–54. [A discussion of the Indiana University Folklore Program, including the Folklore Library, Folklore Archives, and Archives of Folk and Primitive Music.]

168. ———. "Hunting Folklore in the Armpit of America," *IF,* 10:2 (1977), 97–106.

169. ———. "Is There a Folk in the City?" *JAF,* 83:328 (1970), 185–216. [The question is answered in the affirmative with the qualification that city folk are different from "the country folk of yesteryear, and the folklorist exploring their ways must drastically revise his own traditional concepts of the folk and their lore." The article is based on fieldwork in Gary and East Chicago, Indiana, and is reprinted in Dorson's *Folklore: Selected Essays.* Bloomington: Indiana University Press, 1972.]

170. ———. "Jewish-American Dialect Stories on Tape," in *Studies in Biblical and Jewish Folklore.* Bloomington: Indiana University Press, 1960, pp. 111–174. [Stories recorded primarily in Indiana and Michigan, many of them from students.]

171. ———. "New Holdings at the Indiana University Folklore Archives," *FFMA,* 1:1 (1958), 2.

172. ———. "The 1958 Folklore Institute of America," *MF,* 9:1 (1959), 39–48. [Description of folklore activities at Indiana University during the 1958 Folklore Institute.]

173. ———. "A Southern Indiana Field Station," *MF,* 11:3 (1961), 133–138.

174. ———. "Team Fieldwork," *FF,* 11:3 (1978), 220–233. [A personal account of the trials and rewards of conducting a team fieldwork project in the Calumet Region.]

175. Drake, Carlos. "The Killer in the Back Seat," *IF,* 1:1 (1968), 107–109. [Annotated collection of legends about how a girl is saved from a murderer. See also item no. 127.]

176. ———. "Traditional Elements in the Cooperage Industry," *KFQ,* 14:2 (1969), 81–95. [A study of the Davis Cooperage in Martinsville, Indiana, based on fieldwork done mainly in January and February, 1968.]

177. Drummond, A.M. "Linguistic Material in David Thomas' 'Travels Through the Western Country'," *AS,* 22 (1947), 207–209.

178. Dundes, Alan. "Brown County Superstitions," *MF,* 11:1 (1961), 25–56.

179. ———. "Some Examples of Infrequently Reported Autograph Verse," *SFQ,* 26:2 (1962), 127–130. [A list of thirteen autograph album verses, five of which are from Indiana.]

180. Dundes, Alan, and Robert A. Georges. "Some Minor Genres of Obscene Folklore," *JAF,* 75:297 (1962), 221–226. [Contains punning rhetorical questions, spooneristic conundrums, wanton daughter puns, confucianisms, depraved definitions, bawdy book titles. Some items are from Indiana; others are compared to material in Indiana University folklore archives.]

181. Dunn, Caroline. "A Civil War Song," *HF,* 6:2 (1947), 69–70. [A song found by the Indiana Historical Society Library which begins, "Ye Unionfolks, I pray,/ Give ear to what I say,/ I will tell you how we give the rebs a training/ From Murfreesboro, Tennessee,/. . .]

182. ———. "Hoosier Dialect Query," *HFB,* 6:3 (1947), 104. [About the word "chincy."]

183. Dunn, Jacob Piatt. *The Word Hoosier. Indiana Historical Society Publications,* Vol. 4, no. 2. Indianapolis: The Bobbs-Merrill Company, 1907. [Attempts to arrive at the origin and meaning of the term used, at least since 1833, to designate the State of Indiana and its people. Surveys various ideas concerning the word's origin and concludes that it is "Anglo-Saxon in form and Anglo-Saxon in ring."]

184. Esarey, Logan. *A History of Indiana from 1850 to the Present.* Indianapolis, 1918. [Contains references to folklife in Indiana, including German-American customs.]

185. Favinger. John J. *"Materia Medica* of Pioneer Indiana," *YBSIP,* (1917), 22–44. [A list of medicinal herbs found in pioneer Indiana and a discussion of their uses.]

186. Fitton, Mary Louise. "College Folklore," *HFB,* 1:2 (1942), 40–41. [Anecdotes from Hanover College, Indiana.]

187. "Five Old-Country Ballads," *JAF,* 25:97 (1912), 171. [Contains "The Gyptian Laddie."]

188. Flanagan, John T. "The Fiction of Jessamyn West," *IMH,* 67:4 (1971), 299–316. [Thesis is that novelist Jessamyn West, who was born in Jennings County, Indiana, excels in creating authentic pictures of rural people's "idiosyncracies, homeliness, honesty, wit and simple humanity." One of the ways she achieves this is through the use of folklore.]

189. Frank, Cliff, as told to B.A. Botkin. "Back Home in Indiana," in *Folk-Say: A Regional Miscellany, 1930.* Norman, Oklahoma: University of Oklahoma Press, 1930, pp. 67–83. [Anecdotes about religious practices and nicknaming in New Amsterdam, Indiana, during the 1850s and 1860s.]

190. Frazer, Timothy C. "South Midland Pronunciation in the North Central States." *AS,* 53:1 (1978), 40–49. [Frazer traces the distribution of six South Midland vowel sounds, finding that southwestern Indiana retains these dialectical features, except in areas settled by Germans. The author cannot explain the prevalence of Northern and North Midland pronunciation among the Germans.]

191. Gary, A.L. "Folklore from Rushville, Indiana," *HF,* 6:1 (1947), 103–104. [Brief anecdotes.]

192. _____. "Proverbs from Rushville, Indiana," *HF,* 6 (1947), 72.

193. _____. "Some Indiana Yarns," *HFB,* 2:2 (1943), 44–45.

194. George, Philip Brandt. "The Ghost of Cline Avenue: 'La Llorona' in the Calumet Region," *IF,* 5:1 (1972), 56–91. [Analysis of a legend complex found among the various ethnic groups in the industrial cities of northern Indiana's Calumet Region. The complex is a combination of the "Vanishing Hitchhiker" legends and the Mexican "La Llorona" legends.]

195. _____. "Reaffirmation of Identity: A Latino Case in East Chicago," *IF,* 10:2 (1977), 139–148.

196. _____. "Tales of a Puerto Rican Storyteller," *IF,* 10:2 (1977), 149–158.

197. Gibbens, V. E. "Notes on Indiana Speech," *AS,* 19 (1944), 204–206.

198. Goldberg, Christine. "Traditional American Witch Legends: A Catalog," *IF,* 7:1–2 (1974), 77–108.

199. Gopalan, Gopalan V., and Bruce Nickerson. "Faith Healing in Indiana and Illinois," *IF,* 6:1 (1973), 33–99.

200. Granger, Byrd Howell. "Indiana and the Place-Name Survey of the United States," *IN,* 2:2 (1971), 55–59. [Discusses ways in which Hoosiers interested in onomastics can help in the proposed United States place-name survey which will be conducted by the American Name Society.]

201. Gray, Harry. "Measuring for Short Growth," *HF,* 7:1 (1948), 15–19. [A series of notes by different authors concerning this folk practice.]

202. Grider, Sylvia. "Dormitory Legend-Telling in Progress: Fall, 1971—Winter, 1973," *IF,* 6:1 (1973), 1–32. [A thorough study of belief legend telling among adolescent women.]

203. _____. "The Supernatural Narratives of Children." Ph.D. dissertation, Indiana University, 1976. [An extensive presentation and analysis of ghost stories as told by sixth graders in Gosport, Indiana, including a detailed discussion of a Halloween celebration. The relationships between the narrators, the stories, and the community are stressed.]

204. Grider, Sylvia Ann, and Barbara Ann Allen. "Howard Taylor, Cane Maker and Handle Shaver," *IF,* 7:1–2 (1974), 5–26.

205. Gutowski, John A. "American Folklore and the Modern American Community Festival: A Case Study of Turtle Days in Churubusco, Indiana." Ph.D. dissertation, Indiana University, 1977. [See item no. 208.]

206. _____. "The Art of Professional Wrestling: Folk Expression in Mass Culture," *KFQ,*

17:2 (1972), 41–50. [Discusses wrestling as a ritual and dramatic event; references to Baron von Rashke (Indianapolis wrestler); description of wrestling event attended in Indianapolis.]

207. ____. "The Gypsies of Gypsy Hill," *IF*, 3:1 (1970), 95–112. [Gypsies in an area in DeKalb County. See item no. 394.]

208. ____. "The Protofestival: Local Guide to American Folk Behavior," *JFI*, 15:2 (1978), 113–132. [A history of the development of a local legend and tall-tale complex surrounding a giant turtle said to haunt a lake near Churubusco, Indiana. Gutowski discusses the "protofestival" which has been created from the legendary materials, and its expression in local contests, business promotions, and popular poetry.]

209. ____. "Traditions of the Devil's Hollows: Relationships Between a Place Name and Its Legends," *IF*, 3:2 (1970), 190–213. [Legends about two separate localities near Fort Wayne.]

210. Hahn, Holly Jane. "The Place-Names of Brown Township, Montgomery County, Indiana," *IN*, 5 (1974), 19–36. [A few place-name legends accompany this survey of the names attached to geographical features, roads, churches, schools, and other architectural and institutional landmarks in an Indiana township.]

211. Hall, Gary. "The Big Tunnel: Legends and Legend-Telling," *IF*, 6:2 (1973), 139–173. [Discusses the relationship of unusual sites (tunnels) to formation and propagation of belief legends.]

212. Hall, Jane Masi. "Homer Spriggs: Chronicler of Brummetts Creek," *JFI*, 14:1–2 (1977), 31–50. [A study of the personal experience narratives of a Monroe County farmer, with several complete texts included.]

213. Halpert, Herbert. "Folktale and Wellerism: A Note," *SFQ*, 7 (1943), 75–76. [Using an Indiana Wellerism, Halpert shows the role of proverbial phrases in the creation of folk narratives and vice versa.]

214. ____. "A Group of Indiana Folksongs," *HFB*, 3:1 (1944), 1–15.

215. ____. "A Group of Indiana Folksongs," *HFB*, 4:4 (1955), 247–248.

216. ____. "Indiana Folktales," *HFB*, 1:1 (1942), 3–34. [With notes and bibliography. Divided into cante fables, tall tales, fools and foolers, work and people, etc.]

217. ____. "Indiana Storyteller," *HFB*, 1:2 (1942), 43–61. [Tales and notes about material from Bloomington, Indiana. See item no. 88.]

218. ____. "Liar's Club Tales," *HFB*, 2:1 (1943), 11–13.

219. ____. "Two Tales from Batesville, Indiana," *HFB*, 2:2 (1943), 47–48.

220. ____. "Witchcraft Stories," *HFB*, 2:1 (1943), 9–10. [Includes a witch tale from Monroe County, Indiana.]

221. Halpert, Herbert, C. B. Mitchell, and D. H. Dickason. "Folktales from Indiana University Students," *HFB*, 1:3 (1942), 85–97.

222. Halpert, Herbert, and Emma Robinson. " 'Oregon' Smith, An Indiana Folk Hero," *SFQ*, 6 (1942), 163–168. [See item no. 262.]

223. Halpert, Violetta Maloney. "Death Beliefs from Indiana," *MF*, 2:4 (1952), 205–219.

224. ____. "Folk Cures from Indiana," *HF*, 9 (1950), 1–12.

225. ____. "Indiana Wart Cures," *HF*, 7:2–3 (1949), 37–43.

226. Hanford, G. L. "Metaphor and Simile in American Folk Speech," *DN*, 5:2 (1922), 149–180. [List of several hundred items most of which are from states east of the Mississippi River, many of them from Indiana. Hanford discusses the following aspects of folk speech: (1) striving for the vigorous and emphatic; (2) tendency toward the jocular; (3) tendency toward disparagement; (4) some illustrative origins; (5) importations from the Old World; and (6) folk proverbs and children's games.]

227. Hanley, O. W. "Dialect Words from Southern Indiana," *DN*, 3:2 (1906), 113–123. [Several hundred words and their meanings which were collected in Vigo County.]

228. Harmeyer, Alice J. "More Folklore from Smithville," *HFB*, 4:1 (1945), 15–18.

229. Hartikka, H. D. "Tales Collected from Indiana University Students," *HF*, 5 (1946), 71–82.

230. Hasse, John. "Field Specifics Learned First-Hand in the City," *FF*, 11:3 (1978), 290–314. [A fieldworker relates his experiences as a collector of Afro-American musical folklore in the Calumet Region.]

231. ____. "The Gary Black Religious Experience: A Photo Essay," *IF*, 10:2 (1977), 165–181.
232. ____. "The Whites Runnin' Because the Blacks are Movin' in: An Interview with Rev. Roosevelt Robinson," *IF*, 10:2 (1977), 183–190.
233. Hayes, Harriett H. "An Indian Death Chant," *FL*, 1:1 (1892), 45–46. [A memorate about an experience of the author's grandfather during the early days of Vincennes.]
234. Heflin, Martha. "Fast Squirrels," *HF*, 6:4 (1947), 156.
235. ____. "Two Stories from Providence," *HF*, 7:2 (1948), 55.
236. Hendricks, Cecelia H. "The Battle of Waterloo," *HFB*, 4:2 (1945), 21–24. [Text supplied by a Bloomington, Indiana, informant.]
237. Henricks, Sylvia. "The Gentle Pastime," *IF*, 11:2 (1978), 161–173. [Turn-of-the-century autograph verse.]
238. Henry, Mellinger E. "Still More Ballads and Folk-Songs from the Southern Highlands," *JAF*, 45:175 (1932), 1–176. ["The Three Ravens" ("The Twa Corbies") with a long introduction; from Terre Haute.]
239. Hickerson, Joseph. "College Songs in the Indiana University Folklore Archives," *FFMA*, 1:2 (1958), 2.
240. ____. "Hoosier Materials in the Indiana University Folklore Archive," *MF*, 11:2 (1961), 75–83.
241. ____. "The Indiana University Folklore Archive Song Index," *FFMA*, 6:1 (1963), 3–6. [Discusses the way in which materials are catalogued.]
242. ____. "Manuscripts of Indiana Folklore in the Indiana University Folklore Archive," *MF*, 13:2 (1963), 105–108. [A listing of fifty-five items arranged alphabetically under genres by collectors, title of collection, number of pages, and place of collection.]
243. Hickerson, Joseph C., and Alan Dundes. "Mother Goose Vice Verse," *JAF*, 75:297 (1962), 249–259. [Rhymes collected in Indiana.]
244. Hines, Donald M. "Some Hoosier Humor from the Maple Grove Neighborhood, Indiana," *SFQ*, 32:1 (1968), 60–65. [Three numskull stories, three racial jokes, and two miscellaneous anecdotes collected from a southern Indiana couple.]
245. Hippensteel, Faith. " 'Sir Hugh,' The Hoosier Contribution to the Ballad," *IF*, 2:2 (1969), 75–140. [Concludes that Indiana has played an active part in the migration of this ballad and also in "the tendency toward localization, condensation, rationalization, and retention of meaningless words and faulty syntax."]
246. Hixson, Jerome C. "Some Approaches to Indiana Place Names," *IN*, 1:1 (1970), 11–19. [Shows how the student of Indiana place names can benefit from the use of the methodologies of history, sociology, literature, language, folklore, and geography.]
247. Hoffmann, Frank A. "Place Names in Brown County," *MF*, 11:1 (1961), 57–62.
248. Hoffmann, Frank A., and Ellen Stekert. "Folklore Materials in the Library and Archive of the Indiana University Institute for Sex Research," *FFMA*, 2:4 (1959), 3.
249. Holaday, Clayton A. "The Bear and His Shadow," *HFB*, 4:2 (1945), 36–37. [Tall tale.]
250. Holaday, Eileen. "Folklore from Smithville, Indiana," *HFB*, 4:1 (1945), 10–15. [Smithville stories collected from ninth grade students.]
251. Holler, Jean. "Place Names of Fayette County, Indiana." *IN*, 5:2 (1974), 43–70.
252. "The Hoosier Folk Festival Enacted on the Floor of the Jeffersonville High School Gymnasium on Nov. 29, 1939," Jeffersonville, Indiana. [1940.] 20 pp. Illustrated. [Detached from 1940 *Cabin Log*, the annual publication of the Jeffersonville High School.]
253. "The Hoosier Folklore Society," *HFB*, 1:1 (1942), 1–2. [Announcement about the founding of the Society.]
254. *Hoosier Tall Stories*. Compiled and written by the Federal Writers' Project in Indiana, Works Progress Administration, 1937.
255. Huntzinger, Mrs. Jennie Catherine. "From the Archives: Cures by 'Powwowing' from My Grandmother's Notebook," *MF*, 10:1 (1960), 55–56.
256. "An Indiana Charm for Bleeding," *FL*, 1:1 (1892), 75–76. [A letter describing a charm used by a man in Indianapolis.]

257. "An Inventory of Bibliographies (Mostly Annotated) Available in the Archives of the Folklore Institute, Indiana University," *FF*, 2:5 (1969), 126–129.
258. Jagendorf, Moritz Adolf. *Sand in the Bag and other Folk Stories of Ohio, Indiana, and Illinois*. New York: Vanguard, 1952.
259. Jakle, John A. *Images of the Ohio Valley: A Historical Geography of Travel, 1740–1860*. New York: Oxford University Press, 1977. [Drawing principally upon the diaries and letters of early travelers in Indiana and adjoining states, Jakle presents exoteric views of folklife in the region.]
260. ___. "Salt-Derived Place Names in the Ohio Valley," *N*, 16:1 (1968), 1–5. [Argues that a rich place-name heritage in Kentucky, Ohio, Indiana, and Illinois derived from the activity of farmers who "search the Valley for the necessary springs from which individual families or even whole neighborhoods could produce a limited salt supply."]
261. Jansen, Violet, and William Hugh Jansen. "Addenda to Smart Sayings from Indiana," *HF*, 6:2 (1947), 54–56.
262. Jansen, William Hugh. *Abraham "Oregon" Smith: Pioneer, Folk Hero and Tale-Teller*. New York: Arno Press, 1977. [Study of Abraham Smith, a nineteenth-century folk hero who lived in Indiana and Illinois and was known by various nicknames including "Oregon," "Sassafras," "Doctor," and "Lying Abe." The first six of the nine chapters deal with the "factual picture of a folk artist and show what can be discovered about a person who has taken on an entirely folk existence and folk coloration." The concluding two chapters discuss Smith's own folk narrative technique and "the technique of others who have aided in preserving the Smith canon. . . ." Reprint of a 1949 Indiana University dissertation.]
263. ___. "Bill Waltz, a Hoosier Folk Character," *HF*, 5 (1946), 38–39. [An "Oregon" Smith type of character who told tall tales.]
264. ___. "Folklore Items from a Teacher's Notebook," *HFB*, 2:1 (1943), 1–8. [Tales from many sections of Indiana. Includes "The Vanishing Hitchhiker," "Coming to Life," "Frozen Flame," "Catching Ducks."]
265. ___. "A Further Note on 'Swapping Song'," *HF*, 4 (1945), 87–89.
266. ___. "Lore of the Tankbuilders," *HFB*, 3:2 (1944), 27–29. [Part III of "Tales from a Steel Town." See items nos. 269 and 270.]
267. ___. "Lying Abe: A Tale Teller and His Reputation," *HF*, VII (1948), 107–124. [Oregon Smith.]
268. ___. "More on 'Oregon Smith'," *HFB*, 3 (1944), 73–74.
269. ___. "Tales from a Steel Town (Part 2)," *HFB*, 1:3 (1942), 78–81.
270. ___. "Tall Tales from a Steel Town," *HFB*, 1:2 (1942), 41–42; 1:3 (1942), 78–81. [Retold tale of the "Wonderful Hunt" from East Chicago, Indiana.]
271. Kahn, Ed. "From the Archives: Practical Poetry, Rhymed Proverbs," *MF*, 8:3 (1958), 239–240. [Proverbial material from the Indianapolis area.]
272. Kellner, Esther. "Token Stories of Indiana," *MF*, 3:4 (1953), 223–230. [Includes forewarnings and omens of death.]
273. Kimball, David A. "The Lincoln Boyhood National Memorial," *Lincoln Herald*, 66 (1964), 15–18. [A description of the outdoor museum in Southern Indiana where the reconstructed farm of Thomas Lincoln stands, and where park employees demonstrate aspects of pioneer folklife to visitors.]
274. Kittredge, G. L. "Ballads and Songs," *JAF*, 30:117 (1917), 301. [Indiana variant of "Love Henry."]
275. Koss, Deborah. "A Collection of Interviews about a Porter County Ghost Hunt," *IF*, 7:1–2 (1975), 100–127.
276. Krueger, John R. "Indiana Limestone Industry Terms," *AS*, 42:4 (1967), 289–296. [Eighty-five terms arranged alphabetically "gathered from reading, from interviews, from films, and from talks with industry executives, quarry and mill workers, and state geologists." Most collected in Bloomington and Bedford, Indiana. An introductory essay includes consideration of pertinent books, periodicals, and films.
277. ___. "More of 'Anymore'," *AS*, 40:2 (1965), 159. [Some examples collected in Bloomington, Indiana, of the use of *anymore* in positive sentences.]
278. ___. "On Pleonastic 'For'," *AS*, 41:1 (1966), 79–80. [Examples of "for" used as

a pleonasm in the Bloomington, Indiana, *Daily Herald-Telephone,* television programs, and at a meeting of the American Association of University Professors.]

279. ____. "Parodies in the Folklore of a Third-Grader," *SFQ,* 32:1 (1968), 66–68. [Parodies of well-known songs collected by the author from his own child.]

280. Kulii, Elon. "Folklore and the Idiosyncratic Make-Up of the Folklorist," *FF,* 11:3 (1978), 265–272. [A fieldworker speaks of personal experiences in collecting folklore from Afro-Americans in urban northwestern Indiana.]

281. Kurtz, Homer H. "Emerald Isle," *CFQ,* 3 (1944), 232–234. [Square dance—music, verses, and explanation of calls.]

282. Lambert, Richard. "The Stretching Harness," *HFB,* 4:2 (1945), 34–35.

283. Langlois, Janet L. "Belle Gunness, the Lady Bluebeard: Community Legend as Metaphor." Ph.D. dissertation, Indiana University, 1977. [See item no. 284.]

284. ____. "Belle Gunness, the Lady Bluebeard: Community Legend as Metaphor," *JFI,* 15:2 (1978), 147–160. [Current legends concerning mass murderess Belle Gunness of LaPorte, Indiana, who flourished in the early twentieth century. Langlois discusses ways in which the legends reflect community values.]

285. ____. "Mary Whales, I Believe in You: Myth and Ritual Subdued," *IF,* 11:1 (1978), 5–34. [Discussion of a legend, accompanied by a ritualistic game, current among adolescent girls in Indianapolis.]

286. Leary, James P. "The Boondocks Monster of Camp Wapehani," *IF,* 6:2 (1973), 174–190. [The legends concerning a summer-camp monster disappear over time; Leary relates the narrative change to social change, particularly to changing attitudes concerning the discipline of children.]

287. ____. "The Boys from the Dome: Folklore of a Modern American Male Group." Ph.D. dissertation, Indiana University, Bloomington, 1977. [A study of the informal get-togethers of a group of Notre Dame alumni, richly documenting their antisocial behavior and suggesting some positive and socially acceptable functions for their actions.]

288. ____. "Fists and Foul Mouths: Fights and Fight Stories in Contemporary Rural American Bars," *JAF,* 89:1 (1976), 27–39. [Leary finds a common structural pattern in eighteen fight stories, told by men in bars; ten were recorded in Bloomington, Indiana.]

289. ____. "Folklore and Photography in a Male Group," *FF, Bibliographical and Special Series,* no. 13 (1975), 45–49. [Leary examines the use of photographs by Indiana college students to enhance certain eccentric aspects of their collective self-image.]

290. ____. "The Notre Dame Man: Christian Athlete or Dirtball?" *JFI,* 15:2 (1978), 133–145. [A discussion of two contradictory images of the Notre Dame student, and the ways in which students play up to the preexisting roles.]

291. ____. "White Guys' Stories of the Night Street," *JFI,* 14:1–2 (1977), 59–71. [Focusing on the male subculture of Bloomington, Indiana, Leary shows how personal experience narratives reveal the most prominent concerns of the group: intoxication, cars, fights, women, "craziness," and "scary" places. Includes references to folk speech, stereotypic notions, and tall tales employed by the group.]

292. Lecocq, James Gary. "The Ghost of the Doctor and a Vacant Fraternity House," *IF,* 6:2 (1973), 191–204.

293. Light, Martin. "Politics in a Jump-Rope Rhyme," *JAF,* 76:300 (1963), 133. [A jump-rope rhyme recorded in West Lafayette, Indiana, shortly after the 1960 presidential election, in which John F. Kennedy and Richard M. Nixon appear as *dramatis personae.*]

294. Lindahl, Carl R., J. Sanford Rikoon, and Elaine Lawless. *A Basic Guide to Fieldwork for Beginning Folklore Students.* Bloomington: Folklore Publications Group, *Monograph Series,* vol. 7, 1979. [This beginner's manual includes many examples of Indiana folklore; chapter seven deals with the resources and potential uses of the Indiana University Folklore Archives.]

295. List, George. "Documenting Recordings," *FFMA,* 3:3 (1960), 2. [Method of documenting recordings placed in the Indiana University Archives of Folk and Primitive Music.]

296. _____. "An Ideal Marriage of Ballad Text and Tune," *MF*, 7:2 (1957), 95–112. [A discussion of "The False Knight upon the Road," including one Indiana variant.]
297. _____. "The Indiana University Archives of Folk and Primitive Music," *FFMA*, 1:1 (1958), 3.
298. _____. "The Indiana University Archives of Folk and Primitive Music," *FFMA*, 2:4, 3:1 (1959, 1960), 1–3; 1–3.
299. Logsdon, Eugene H. "Occupational Folk-Beliefs in Midwest Agriculture." M.A. thesis, Indiana University, 1964. [Annotated collection of 164 occupational folk-beliefs collected in Ohio, Indiana, and Kentucky.]
300. Loomis, Ormond. "The Ford-McCoy Killing: A Look at Folk History," *FF*, 7 (1974), 244–259. [A study of a double-murder which took place in Monroe County in 1907, and which continues to surface in local historical legends. Loomis compares the approaches taken by oral history and literary history toward the same event.]
301. McAtee, W. L. "Gleanings from the Dialect of Grant County, Indiana," *PADS*, 15 (1951), 51–64. [A supplement to three earlier publications on Grant County, Indiana, folk speech and song.]
302. _____. *Grant County, Indiana, Speech and Song.* Privately printed, 1946.
303. _____. "Home Medication in Grant County, Indiana, in the Nineties," *MF*, 5 (1955), 213–216.
304. _____. "Medical Lore in Grant County, Indiana, in the Nineties," *MF*, 8:3 (1958), 151–153.
305. _____. *Rural Dialect of Grant County, Indiana, in the Nineties.* Privately printed, 1942.
306. _____. "Some Folklore of Grant County, Indiana, in the Nineties," *MF*, 1:4 (1951), 243–267. [Various genres included: games, songs, speech, proverbs, and beliefs.]
307. McCulloh, Judith. "Indiana's Treasure Store is a Wealth of Good Old Hoosier Lore," *FF*, 3:5–6 (1970), 135–137. [Brief discussion of items in the Starr sheet-music collection in Indiana University's Lilly Library.]
308. McDavid, Raven I., and Virginia McDavid. "'Cracker' and 'Hoosier'," *N*, 21:3 (1973), 161–167. [Discusses the use of the term "Hoosier" in the southeastern U.S. both as a pejorative for "farmer" and as a nickname for residents of Indiana.]
309. McLean, Irene A. "Rhyme," *HFB*, 2:2 (1943), 46. [Rhyme beginning "I am a little curly head."]
310. McNeil, William K. "Mrs. F.-Little Joe: The Multiple Personality Experience and the Folklorist," *IF*, 4:2 (1971), 216–245. [A study of the psychic experiences of an Indianapolis woman.]
311. McReynolds, F. L. *Play-Party Games: Seventy-Five Musical Games.* Lafayette, Ind.: Purdue University Agricultural Extension Service, n.d.
312. Maddy, Homer Basil, and Loren Phillips. *Ballads of Mountain and Prairie.* Shelbyville, Ind.: Blue River Press, 1941.
313. March, Richard. "How I Became 'The TV Man': Video Fieldwork in the Calumet Region," *FF*, 11:3 (1978), 254–264.
314. _____. "The Tamburitza Tradition in the Calumet Region," *IF*, 10:2 (1977), 127–138.
315. Marckwardt, A.H. "Folkspeech in Indiana and Adjacent States," *IHB*, 17 (1940), 120–140.
316. Marshall, Howard Wight. "Living Microcosm of the Old Northwest: Conner Prairie Pioneer Settlement," *PA*, 9:1 (1977), 90–94. [Short photo essay describing the living museum in Noblesville, Indiana.]
317. _____. "The 'Thousand Acres' Log House, Monroe County, Indiana," *PA*, 3:1 (1971), 48–56. [A detailed folk-architectural examination of a mid-nineteenth century basic Anglo-American log house.]
318. Marshall, Howard Wight, and John Michael Vlach. "Toward a Folklife Approach to American Dialects," *AS*, 48:3–4 (1973), 163–191. [This detailed article, much of which is based on fieldwork in southern Indiana, proposes the use of material culture studies to help "establish dialect boundaries, identify the presence of lexical terms, and further clarify the history of speech patterns."]
319. Mastick, Patricia. "Dry Stone Walling," *IF*, 9:1 (1976), 113–133.

320. Meade, Guthrie T., Jr. "The Sea Crab," *MF,* 8:2 (1958), 91–100. [Contains one Indiana variant of this rarely found ballad.]

321. Meehan, Virginia. " 'Walk-In Restaurant' and 'Temporary Run-Around'," *AS,* 43:2 (1968), 157. [Brief note discussing two colloquial phrases first heard by the author in Indiana.]

322. Mensing, Angela. "Jumping Rope Jingles from Bloomington, Indiana," *HFB,* 2:2 (1943), 48–49.

323. Milanovich, Anthony. "Serbian Tales from Blanford," *IF,* 4:1 (1971), 1–60. [A selection of twelve tales narrated by two Serbian-American narrators, Sava Divjak and Milič Dotlich, of Blanford, Indiana. The narratives are part of a larger collection made by Milanovich in the 1930s, which he later used as a master's thesis at Indiana State University. This selection includes a "Foreword" by Stith Thompson; a brief illustrated article, "Blanford Today," by Yvonne J. Milspaw; "The Collector and the Tellers of the Tales," by Linda Dégh; and notes to the tales by Linda Dégh, Yvonne J. Milspaw, and Milovan Gavazzi.]

324. Miller, William Marion. "Another Indiana Monster Story," *HF,* 6:2 (1947), 71–72.

325. ———. "Another Vanishing Hitchhiker Story," *HF,* 6 (1947), 76.

326. Mitchell, Carol A. "The White House," *IF,* 2:1 (1969), 97–109. [Legends about a strange house in Fort Wayne.]

327. Moe, John F. "Folk Festivals and Community Consciousness: Categories of the Festival Genres," *FF,* 10:2 (1977), 31–40. [There are passing references to the Bean Blossom Bluegrass Festival, the Churubusco Turtle Days Celebration, and other Indiana festivals in this general theoretical discussion of festival types.]

328. Montgomery, Margaret. "Broadcasting a Folklore Project," *HF,* 7 (1948), 39–46. [A project in Indianapolis designed to interest high school students in world folklore.]

329. ———. "A Macedonian Wedding in Indianapolis," *HF,* 7:4 (1948), 101–104.

330. ———. "Slovenian Folklore in Indianapolis," *HF,* 6 (1947), 121–132. [Customs, traditions, and tales.]

331. Montgomery, Pauline. *Indiana Coverlet Weavers and Their Coverlets.* Indianapolis: Hoosier Heritage Press, 1974.

332. ———. "Master Coverlet Weavers of Indiana," *YBSIP,* (1970), 29–34. [Brief discussion of the work of nineteenth-century Indiana coverlet weavers.]

333. Montgomery, Robert W. "Ghost Stories from Decatur County," *MF,* 11:1 (1961), 62–64.

334. ———. "More on the Archer Gang," *MF,* 11:2 (1961), 125–127. [More about "The Hanging of Sam Archer"; see item nos. 61 and 70.]

335. Mullarky, Magnus Einarsson. "The Heavenly Message," *IF,* 1:1 (1968), 49–51. [Legends about people who make a promise to return from the dead and tell the secret of death.]

336. ———. "The House of Blue Lights," *IF,* 1:1 (1968), 82–91. [Legends about a mysterious house in Indianapolis.]

337. ———. "The Mysterious Dog," *IF,* 1:1 (1968), 55–60. [Legends about a dog whose appearance portends death.]

338. ———. "The Warning Light," *IF,* 1:1 (1968), 42–48. [Legends about a light that appears where a person has been murdered.]

339. Mullen, Patrick B. "Department Store Snakes," *IF,* 3:2 (1970), 214–228. [Further discussion of the legend about shoppers in a department store bitten by poisonous snakes hidden in the clothing. Six of the thirty-two variants are from Indiana. See also item no. 128.]

340. Musick, Ruth Ann. "Indiana Witch Tales," *JAF,* 65 (1952), 57–65.

341. ———. "Skeletons from a Homespuner's Closet, from the Manuscript of James S. Williams," *HF,* 9:4 (1950), 111–116.

342. Neal, Mabel Evangeline. "Brown County Songs and Ballads." M.A. thesis, Indiana University, 1926. [One hundred song texts, some with musical notation.]

343. Nettl, Bruno. "The Musical Style of English Ballads Collected in Indiana," *AM,* 27:3–4 (1955), 77–84.

344. Newell, William Wells. "Early American Ballads, II," *JAF,* 13:49 (1900), 105–122. [Contains an Indiana variant of "Springfield Mountain."]
345. Nugent, Walter. "The American People and the Centennial of 1876," *IMH,* 75 (1979), 53–69. [Nugent describes the various ways in which Indiana families and communities celebrated a national holiday; comments on German-American celebrations in southern Indiana are included.]
346. O'Bryant, Jean. "Indiana Folktales," *Folio: A Quarterly of Indiana Writing,* 6:3 (Indiana University, 1941), 40–42. [Introduction by Herbert Halpert. Contains three traditions from southern Indiana.]
347. Ohrn, Karin Becker. "The Photo Flow of Family Life: A Family Photograph Collection," *FF: Bibliographical and Special Series,* no. 13 (1975), 27–36. [Focusing on a Finnish-American family living in Paoli, Indiana, the author discusses the role of family photographs in the transmission and creation of family folklore.]
348. Orth, Donald J. "The Nature of Topographic Terms," *IN,* 3:1 (1972), 5–18. [A survey of the most common topographic terms "found in the generic part of present Indiana place names." Orth suggests that an in-depth study should determine (1) "how local usage of terms differs in meaning compared with place-name applications shown on a map," (2) "development of assemblages of term usage through space and time," (3) "terminology used in ordinary language that is not used in place names," and (4) "how terms and place names influence people and their thinking about the landscape around them."]
349. Parochetti, Joann Stephens. "Scary Stories from Purdue," *KFQ,* 10:1 (1965), 49–57. [A sampling of items from a collection of fifty texts recorded primarily from Purdue University coeds. All the stories are legends, most of them well-known in American tradition.]
350. Peat, Wilbur D. *Pioneer Painters of Indiana.* Indianapolis: Art Association of Indianapolis, 1954. [A book containing materials which border on folk art.]
351. Perrow, E. C. "Songs and Rhymes from the South," *JAF,* 25:96 (1912), 148. [Fragment from southern Indiana.]
352. Pisarski, Sharon. "A Porter County Seer," *IF,* 9:1 (1976), 95–112.
353. Posen, Sheldon, Michael Taft, and Richard S. Tallman. "Index to *Hoosier Folklore Bulletin* (1942–1945) and *Hoosier Folklore* (1946–1950)," *FF: Bibliographical and Special Series,* no. 10, 1973. [The index is arranged by (1) subject, author, and title index; (2) song title index; song first line index; children's rhyme first line index; tale-type index; legend-type index; motif index. Materials from Indiana and other Midwestern states are represented. Foreword by Herbert Halpert.]
354. Power, Richard Lyle. "The Hoosier as an American Folktype," *IMH,* 38 (1942), 107–122.
355. Preston, Dennis R. "Southern Indiana Place-Name Legends as Reflections of Folk History," *IN,* 4 (1973), 50–61. [The author shows how place-name legends in Indiana reflect six different aspects of the past: Indians, pioneers, violence, the Civil War, French settlement, and religious development.]
356. Rabb, Kate Milner. *Indiana Coverlets and Coverlet Weavers. Indiana Historical Society Publications,* Vol. 8, no. 8. Indianapolis: Indiana Historical Society, 1928. [Discusses the processes of coverlet weaving, gives brief biographies of forty men who earned their living as coverlet weavers in nineteenth-century Indiana, and concludes with a short history of coverlet weaving in Switzerland County.]
357. Randall, Dale B. J. "Dialect in the Verse of 'The Hoosier Poet'," *AS,* 35 (1960), 36–50. [Dialect in verse of James Whitcomb Riley.]
358. Rehmer, Rev. R.F. "Sheep without Shepherds: Letters of Two Lutheran Travelling Missionaries, 1835–1837," *IMH,* 71:1 (1975), 21–84. [These letters sent by pioneer preachers document the settlement patterns, folklife, and mores of German-Americans in Indiana.]
359. Rennick, Robert M. "The Folklore of Place Naming in Indiana," *IF,* 3:1 (1970), 35–94. [Discussion of the folklore of Indiana place names, aimed at making Hoosiers 'place-name conscious,' so that they may prove helpful in a proposed study and analysis of Indiana names sponsored by faculty members at Indiana State University.]

360. ——. "Place-Name Derivations Are Not Always What They Seem," *IN*, 2:1 (1971), 19–28.
361. Reuss, Richard. "An Annotated Field Collection of Songs from the American College Student Oral Tradition." M.A. thesis, Indiana University, 1965. [A collection consisting largely of bawdy songs mainly from the repertoires of Indiana University students of 1963–1964.]
362. Richmond, W. Edson. "The Collection of Proverbs in Indiana," *HF*, 5 (1946), 150–156.
363. ——. "From the Archives: Mnemonic Rhymes," *MF*, 9:2 (1959), 127–128.
364. ——. "From the Archives: Some Weather Lore from Indiana," *MF*, 8:3 (1958), 183–184.
365. ——. "The Indiana Issues: An Editorial Comment," *MF*, 11:1 (1961), 24.
366. ——. "Library Resources for the Study of Place Names in the State of Indiana," *IN*, 1:2 (1970), 41–49. [Richmond states that "there is hardly a book which might not be grist for the place-name student's mill." His listing includes journals, bibliographies, works on techniques and methods, basic dictionaries, place-name studies from nearby states, and Indiana place-name studies.]
367. Richmond, W. Edson, and Elva Van Winkle. "Is There a Doctor in the House?" *IHB*, 35:9 (1958), 115–135.
368. Ridlen, Susanne S. "Bank Barns in Cass County, Indiana," *PA*, 4:2 (1972), 25–43. [Discussion of the geographical distribution of the various forms of bank barns in Cass County which also takes into account the location of the barn on the farm. Includes thirty-seven illustrations.]
369. Rikoon, James S. *Guide to the Indiana University Folklore Archives.* Bloomington: Folklore Publications Group, *Monograph Series,* vol. 6, 1979. [A description of the holdings and the classification system of the Indiana University Folklore Archives. Includes a bibliography of published articles which contain materials deposited at the archives.]
370. Roberts, Warren E. "Children's Games and Game Rhymes," *HF*, 8:1 (1949), 7–34. [Games and rhymes collected from students at Indiana University.]
371. ——. "Some Comments on Log Construction in Scandinavia and the United States." In *Folklore Today: A Festschrift for Richard M. Dorson,* ed. Linda Dégh, Henry Glassie, and Felix J. Oinas. Bloomington: Indiana University, 1976, pp. 437–450. [Several Indiana examples are cited in this general discussion of the sources of log construction styles in American folk architecture.]
372. ——. "The Tools Used in Building Log Houses in Indiana," *PA*, 9:1–2 (1977), 30–61. [This study, based primarily on fieldwork, but also on early written accounts of log construction, demonstrates that builders of log houses in early Indiana used a great variety of tools and techniques. Roberts attempts to correct the misconception that early Indiana folklife and folk architecture were "very simple and crude."]
373. ——. "The Whitaker-Waggoner Log House from Morgan County, Indiana," in *American Folklife,* ed. Don Yoder. Austin, Texas: University of Texas Press, 1976, pp. 185–207. [Detailed study of a log house. A much abbreviated version of this article, titled "The Waggoner Log House near Paragon, Indiana," is found in *Forms upon the Frontier,* ed. Austin Fife, Alta Fife, and Henry Glassie. Logan, Utah: Utah State University Press, 1969. *Monograph Series,* 16:2 pp. 28–30.]
374. Robertson, Jerry. *Oil Slanguage.* Evansville, Ind.: Petroleum Publishers, 1954.
375. Rosenberg, Neil V. "Stereotype and Tradition: White Folklore About Blacks." Ph.D. dissertation, Indiana University, 1970. [This lengthy study of exoteric lore concerning blacks draws extensively upon material collected in Indiana and deposited in the I.U. Folklore Archives, Bloomington.]
376. Roy, Nora Leonard. "Maple Sugaring in Southern Indiana: A Descriptive Study of the Technology of Four Maple Syrup Makers," *IF*, 9:2 (1976), 197–234.
377. Schrink, Jeffrey, and Frances Schrink. "Hangman's Crossing," *IF*, 11:1 (1978), 87–97.
378. Schroeder, Marlene. "George De Mayer: Belgian American Wine-Maker," *IF*, 11:2 (1978), 192–200.

379. Schultz, Charles R. "Erasmus Gest's Recollections of Life in the Middle West in the 1830's, "*IMH*, 73:2 (1977), 125–142. [Selections from the journal of a railroad worker in southwestern Indiana.]
380. "The Second Hoosier Festival of the Hoosier Folklore Society, "*MF*, 11:2 (1961), 84. [Program for the 1961 festival.]
381. Seward, Adrienne L. "Gary's Black Self-Image, "*IF*, 10:2 (1977), 217–221.
382. ――――. "Some Dilemmas of Fieldwork: A Personal Statement, "*FF*, 11:3 (1978), 245–253. [A discussion of the human element in fieldwork, derived from collecting experience among Afro-Americans in northwestern Indiana.]
383. ――――. "An Urban Black Philosopher, "*IF*, 10:2 (1977), 223–228.
384. Sharrer, G. T. "Conner Prairie Pioneer Settlement, "*Living Historical Farms Bulletin*, 4:2 (1975), 8–10. [A description of the outdoor museum in Noblesville, Indiana.]
385. Short, O.D. "Origin of the Term 'Hoosier,' "*IMH*, 25 (1929), 101–103.
386. Sinclair, Edna H. "Two Ballad Fragments, "*HF*, 7:2 (1948), 86. [Origin may have been Kentucky.]
387. Sliney, Deanna. "Haunted Sites in Indiana: A Preliminary Survey, "*IF*, 7:1–2 (1974), 27–52. [A listing of various haunted sites, including haunted houses, cemeteries, bridges, and tunnels. Also contains numerous belief legends.]
388. Smith, G. Hubert. "Three Miami Tales, "*JAF*, 52:204 (1939), 194–208. [Three tales recorded by John Dunne from the Mahican Miami chief, Little Turtle, and originally published in the *Transactions* of the Royal Irish Academy (Dublin, 1803), pp. 9, 107–124. The original of Dunne's article, "Notices relative to some of the Native Tribes of North America, " has been strictly adhered to except in instances "where the text would have been obscure if the punctuation had not been modernized."]
389. Smith, Grace Partridge, and Jane Miller. "More Cadence Counts, "*IF*, 7 (1948), 57.
390. Soudek, Lev. "Further Members of the 'Burger' Family, "*AS*, 43:1 (1968), 74–76. [Various usages of the word "burger " which the author has noted in Indiana and other states.]
391. Spear, Louise S. "The Indiana University Archives of Traditional Music: An Interview with George List, "In *Discourse in Ethnomusicology: Essays in Honor of George List*, ed. Caroline Card, John Hasse, Roberta L. Singer, and Ruth Stone. Bloomington, Indiana: Ethnomusicology Publications Group, 1978, 1–40. [Oral history of the archives of traditional music at Indiana University, told by George List, its director for twenty-three years, in this volume of essays honoring his sixtieth birthday.]
392. Stahl, Sandra K.D. "The Oral Personal Narrative in Its Generic Context, "*Fabula*, 18:1–2 (1977), 18–39.
393. ――――. "Style in Written and Oral Narrative, " Bloomington, Indiana: Folklore Publications Group, Preprints Series, 3:1 (1975). [Stahl studies the oral and written repertoire of Larry Scheiber, a joke-teller and local newscolumnist from Huntington, Indiana.]
394. Stiver, Shawn. "Gypsy Hill, "*IF*, 5:1 (1972) 31–55. [Analysis of folklore collected from eighty-nine informants, mostly children, dealing with a DeKalb County site.]
395. Sweeney, Margaret. *Fact, Fiction, and Folklore of Southern Indiana*. New York: Vantage Press, 1967. [Despite the title, this book deals primarily with Clark, Floyd, and Washington counties. The volume is put together from the author's reminiscences and from collections turned in by her students during her many years as a teacher in Jeffersonville High School. Chapters 2, 4–8 have texts and music of some songs. Place names are discussed in chapters 4–5, 7–8, and games in chapters 4–8. Belief legends, historical legends, and oral history are included, as well as descriptions of weddings, customs, and folk cures.]
396. ――――. "New Lamps for Old, "*The Indiana Teacher*, 84:1 (1939), 8, 28, 30. [Use of folklore in high school teaching.]
397. ――――. "Tales and Legends Collected by Jeffersonville Students, "*HFB*, 3:3 (1944), 39–48.
398. Sweterlitsch, Richard. "Jack's Defeat and His Creek, "*IF*, 5:1 (1972), 1–30. [Legends about the origin of the name of a stream in Ellettsville, Indiana.]
399. Sylvester, Lorna Lutes. "Conner Prairie Pioneer Settlement and Museum, "*IMH*, 65

(1969), 1–24. [Brief history of the founding of the original settlement on the site where the Conner Prairie Settlement and Museum is now located, and a discussion of the exhibits on display in 1969. Illustrated with one map and numerous photographs.]

400. ____. " 'Down in the Hills o' Brown County': Photographs by Frank M. Hohenberger," *IMH,* 71:3 (1975), 205–244; 72:1 (1976), 21–62; 72:3 (1976), 189–249. [This series of three annotated photo essays from the Frank M. Hohenberger collection illustrates Brown County folklife during the depression years. Photographs of gold panners, blacksmiths, carpenters, quilters, canners, and farmers at work—as well as many set portraits of rural inhabitants—are accompanied by entries from Hohenberger's diaries.]

401. Taylor, Archer. "Proverbial Materials in Edward Eggleston, *The Hoosier Schoolmaster,*" in *Studies in Folklore* (Bloomington: Indiana University Press, 1957), pp. 262–270.

402. "That Word 'Hoosier' Again," *HFB,* 35:7 (1958), 88–89. [Derivation of name.]

403. Thigpen, Kenneth A., Jr. "Adolescent Legends in Brown County: A Survey," *IF,* 4:2 (1972), 141–215. [A collection of seventy-five legend texts from thirty-seven students at Brown County High School in Nashville, Indiana, and from six former students at the school.]

404. Thompson, Lawrence S. *Bee Lore in the Ohio Valley. The Ohio Valley Folk Research Project,* N. S., no. 83. Chillicothe, Ohio: The Ross County Historical Society, 1961. [Deals mostly with Kentucky but has a few items collected in southern Indiana.]

405. Thompson, Stith. "The Folktale in the Middle West," *HFB,* 1:2 (1942), 39.

406. Tillson, William. "How the Boilermakers Did Not Get Their Name," *MF,* 11:2 (1961), 105–114.

407. ____. "Purdue Classroom Recollection," *NYFQ,* 18:1 (1962), 55–57. [Numerous traditions current at Purdue.]

408. ____. "Purdue Folklore: Planned and Unplanned," *Campus Copy* (published by Purdue University, 1963), pp. 5–6. [Anecdotes and traditions on the Purdue University campus.]

409. "Report to the Hoosier Folklore Society," *MF,* 9:1 (1959), 49–53.

410. Tilney, Philip V. R. "The Immigrant Macedonian Wedding," *IF,* 3:1 (1970), 3–34. [Traditional elements in two Macedonian immigrant weddings in Fort Wayne in 1963 and 1969.]

411. Tolman, Albert H. "Some Songs Traditional in the United States," *JAF,* 29:152 (1916), 155–197. [Songs collected primarily in states east of the Mississippi, many of them from Indiana.]

412. Tolman, Albert H., and Mary O. Eddy. "Traditional Texts and Tunes," *JAF,* 35:138 (1922), 423. [Variant of "Awful! Awful! Awful!" collected in Indiana.]

413. Townsend, Barbara Ann. "String Measurement: Additional Accounts," *IF,* 4:1 (1971), 89–94. [Five accounts of string measurement used in diagnosing or curing children's diseases. See item no. 414.]

414. Townsend, Barbara Ann, and Donald Allport Bird. "The Miracle of String Measurement," *IF,* 3:2 (1970), 147–162. [Ten accounts of Hoosiers who used string measurement to diagnose children's diseases or to cure them or who were familiar with persons who did.]

415. Tucker, Elizabeth G. "Tradition and Creativity in the Storytelling of Pre-Adolescent Girls." Ph.D. dissertation, Indiana University, Bloomington, 1977. [A study of the functions and styles of storytelling among Brownies and Girl Scouts in Monroe County, Indiana.]

416. Tucker, Glen. "Was 'Hoosier' a Headgear?" *IHB,* 35:10 (1958), 141–142. [Derivation of name.]

417. Tullis, C.O. "Folk Beliefs from Mt. Ayr High School," *HF,* 5 (1946), 35–36.

418. ____. "Folklore from the Kankakee Valley," *HFB,* 4:2 (1945), 24–25. [Three tall tales.]

419. "Two Legend Collections," *IF,* 9:2 (1976), 166–196. ["The Legend of Bloody Mary's Grave," collected by Linda McCoy Ray; "The Murder at Franklin College," collected by Gerry Marie Till.]

420. Umble, John. "The Old Order Amish, Their Hymns and Hymn Tunes," *JAF,* 52:203 (1939), 93. [An Amish hymn tune collected in northern Indiana.]
421. Vázsonyi, Andrew. "The *Cicisbeo* and the Magnificent Cuckold: Boardinghouse Life and Lore in Immigrant Communities," *JAF,* 91:2 (1978), 641–656. [Vázsonyi reconstructs boardinghouse customs among Hungarian immigrants in the Calumet Region of Indiana during the early twentieth century. The legendary liaison between the landlord's wife and the "star boarder," her favorite tenant, is discussed as a theme in folklore and as a social reality.]
422. Vlach, John M. "The 'Canada Homestead': A Saddlebag Log House in Monroe County, Indiana," *PA,* 4:2 (1972), 8–17. [History and description of "one of the last traditional log buildings to be built in Monroe County."]
423. ____. "Joseph J. Daniels and Joseph A. Britton: Parke County's Covered Bridge Builders," *IF,* 4:1 (1971), 61–88. [Considers the covered bridges built by Joseph J. Daniels and Joseph A. Britton as folkloristic items.]
424. ____. "One Black Eye and Other Horrors: A Case for the Humorous Anti-Legend," *IF,* 4:2 (1971), 95–140. [A collection of 144 items from fifty-four ten-year-old fifth graders, of which nineteen are what Vlach calls "humorous anti-legends" (a term coined by André Jolles and later used by folklorists Lutz Röhrich and Linda Dégh). The phrase refers to narratives similar in content to legends but told primarily for humor.]
425. Walker, Catherine. "The Well Trained Hunting Dog," *HFB,* 4:1 (1945), 18–19.
426. Waugh, Butler H. "Negro Tales of John Kendry from Indianapolis," *MF,* 8:3 (1958), 125–141.
427. Webb, Hilda E. "Water Witching and Other Folk Talents in the Neighborhood of Bloomington, Indiana." M.A. thesis, Indiana University, 1964. [A study of nine water witches who live in the immediate vicinity of Bloomington. Also includes charm cures.]
428. ____. "Water Witching as Part of Folklife in Southern Indiana," *JFI,* 3:1 (1966), 10–29. [Article based on Mrs. Webb's M.A. thesis.]
429. Weeks, Estella T. "Shakerism in Indiana: Notes on Shaker Life, Customs, and Music," *HFB,* 4 (1945), 59–86.
430. Willets, Jane. "Five Folksongs from Richmond, Indiana," *HF,* 5:1 (1946), 21–28. ["The Sailor Boy," "My Grandmother's Chair," "The Sheriff's Sale," "Crystal Leroy," and "The Stepmother."]
431. Wilson, Ann Scott. "Pearl Bryan," *SFQ,* 3 (1939), 15–19. [West Virginia variants of this ballad, which has been considered to have originated in Indiana.]
432. Wilson, Eddie W. "The Gourd in Hoosier Land," *HF,* 9:2 (1950), 33–36.
433. Winkelman, Donald M. "The Brown County Project," *MF,* 11:1 (1961), 15–23. [A survey, with examples, of the various genres collected in Brown County by Indiana University graduate students.]
434. ____. "Folklore and English in the Secondary School," *Indiana English Leaflet,* 5:4 (1963). [Discussion of folklore and its incorporation into the secondary English curriculum. Contains references to Indiana materials.]
435. Winkle, Edith Walker van. "A Hoosier Folk Game," *HF,* 8 (1949), 35–36.
436. Wolford, Leah Jackson. *The Play-Party in Indiana,* edited and revised by W. Edson Richmond and William Tillson. Indianapolis: Indiana Historical Society, 1959.
437. Woodburn, James Albert. "Local Life and Color in the New Purchase," *IMH,* 9:4 (1913), 215–233. [A brief history of the section of Indiana once known as the "New Purchase," which includes some consideration of customs, folk speech, and folk architecture.]
438. Woodward, Robert H. "Folklore Marginalia in Old Textbooks," *NYFQ,* 18:1 (1962), 24–27. [Several examples of parodies and autograph verse gleaned from a textbook used in the 1980s and which relate to Indiana folklore.]
439. ____. "A Hoosier Folklore Heritage," *MF,* 11:2 (1961), 69–73. [Recollections of beliefs from the author's boyhood.]

Subject Index to the Study of Folklore in Indiana: A Bibliography

(Numbers after the items refer to the numbers in the Bibliography)

ANIMAL TALES: 114, 195, 196, 426.

ARCHITECTURE: 3, 25, 51, 273, 317, 318, 319, 368, 371, 372, 384, 398, 422, 424, 437.

ARCHIVES AND RESEARCH CENTERS: 7, 71, 92, 118, 164, 167, 171, 172, 240, 241, 242, 248, 257, 294, 295, 297, 298, 307, 316, 365, 369, 391.

ART: 76, 79, 331, 350, 399. (See also CRAFT.)

BELIEF LEGEND: 2, 13, 16, 17, 18, 20–23, 28–30, 50, 52, 57, 83, 88, 98, 102, 114, 117, 119, 120, 123, 127–129, 132, 133, 137–141, 144, 146–149, 151, 153, 154, 156, 158, 159, 175, 194–196, 198, 202, 204, 208–212, 217, 220, 228, 229, 233, 258, 264, 272, 275, 285, 286, 291, 292, 324–326, 333, 335–340, 349, 353, 387, 395, 397, 403, 405, 415, 419, 423.

BELIEFS AND CUSTOMS: 8, 14, 45, 53, 54, 63, 86, 87, 99, 102, 104, 134, 160, 178, 184, 189, 199, 201, 202, 220, 223, 272, 275, 299, 306, 330, 352, 363, 395, 404, 408, 410, 413, 414, 417, 427–429, 432, 437, 439. (See also MEDICINE, PLANT LORE, WEATHER LORE.)

CHAIN TALE: 26.

CHILDREN'S LORE: 68, 80, 96, 121, 204, 226, 237, 243, 250, 279, 286, 293, 309, 322, 353, 370, 395, 415.

COLLECTING: 4, 5, 58, 114, 115, 143, 155, 164, 165, 168, 169, 173, 174, 195, 200, 202, 230, 281, 294, 313, 352, 382, 433.

CRAFT: 76, 79, 203, 314, 319, 331, 332, 356, 376, 399. (See also ART.)

DANCE: 102, 280.

DISSERTATIONS AND THESES: 2, 97, 103, 262, 299, 342, 361, 375, 415, 427.

EDUCATION: 93, 114, 135, 166, 167, 172, 228, 252, 341, 395, 396, 434. (See also MASS MEDIA.)

EROTICA: 2, 88, 93, 97, 103, 180, 217, 243, 248, 262, 320, 361.

ETHNIC AND IMMIGRANT LORE: 1) AFRO-AMERICAN: 114, 125, 126, 130, 165, 169, 230–232, 244, 281, 375, 381–383, 426; 2) GERMAN: 53, 184, 190, 345, 358; 3) HISPANIC: 114, 169, 194–196; 4) HUNGARIAN: 143, 155–157, 159, 421; 5) OTHERS: 38, 46, 58, 94, 114, 118, 139, 164, 168–170, 174, 207, 230, 314, 323, 329, 330, 347, 378, 389, 394, 410.

FESTIVALS AND CELEBRATIONS: 204, 205, 208, 252, 327, 329, 345, 395, 410.

FOLK NAMING: 39–44, 65, 76, 77, 79, 92, 183, 189, 308, 385, 402, 406, 416. (See also PLACE NAMES, PLANT LORE, SPEECH.)

FOLKLIFE: 3, 10, 51, 53, 54, 86, 87, 99, 100, 108, 109, 111, 124, 145, 150, 160, 176, 184, 199, 203, 212, 231, 259, 273, 288, 316, 317, 319, 332, 356, 358, 368, 373, 376, 378, 379, 384, 398, 399, 404, 422, 424, 427–429, 432.

FOLKLORE AND LITERATURE: 39, 91, 188, 357, 401.

FOLKLORE AND PHOTOGRAPHY: 4, 114, 125, 230, 231, 289, 313, 316, 347, 399.

FOLKLORE THEORY: 9, 22, 49, 94, 96, 114, 143, 146, 149, 152, 155, 156, 164, 165, 168, 169, 178, 206, 226, 283, 284, 296, 318, 348, 365, 392.

FOODWAYS: 195, 378, 379.

GAMES: 39, 53, 54, 68, 96, 102, 206, 226, 293, 306, 311, 322, 370, 395, 435, 436.

GRAFFITI AND OTHER WRITTEN EXPRESSIONS OF FOLKLORE: 179, 202, 237, 438.

HISTORICAL LEGENDS: 11, 12, 16, 19, 24, 27, 48, 50, 52, 59, 61, 70, 89, 92, 99, 102, 105–107, 109, 131, 132, 145, 149, 150, 163, 189, 207, 210, 211, 233, 247, 251, 255, 283, 284, 300, 334, 341, 353, 355, 377, 394, 395, 397, 400, 431. (See also ORAL HISTORY.)

HOOSIER FOLKLORE SOCIETY: 253, 353, 364, 380, 409.

JOKES AND FOLK HUMOR: 2, 10, 31–35, 65, 67, 77, 88, 90, 94, 95, 97, 102, 103, 114, 116, 118, 119, 130, 136, 156, 159, 170, 180, 191, 195, 196, 202, 208, 213, 216, 217, 221, 229, 244, 250, 262, 279, 287, 289, 290, 375, 393, 405, 408, 423, 426.

MAGIC TALE: 195, 196, 262, 323, 330, 353, 405.

MASS MEDIA: 16, 49, 102, 122, 136, 205, 206, 285, 313, 328, 393.

MEDICINE: 64, 86, 87, 99–101, 114, 125, 126, 136, 161, 185, 199, 224, 225, 255, 256, 299, 303, 304, 367, 395, 412, 414, 427. (See also BELIEFS AND CUSTOMS and PLANT LORE.)

MUSEUMS: 3, 124, 273, 343, 384, 398.

MUSIC: 5, 114, 167, 230, 241, 280, 295, 297, 298, 314, 327, 391, 420. (See also SONG.)

NOVELLA: 38.

OCCUPATIONAL LORE: 1) FARMING: 50, 299; 2) QUARRY WORK: 27, 276; 3) STEEL INDUSTRY: 169, 266, 269, 270; 4) STUDENT: 29, 97, 129, 186, 202, 239, 290, 292, 361, 406, 407; 5) OTHER: 2, 6, 89, 111, 168, 169, 176, 341, 374, 424.

ORAL HISTORY: 50, 111, 145, 176, 288, 300, 317, 347, 394, 395. (See also HISTORICAL LEGENDS and PERSONAL EXPERIENCE NARRATIVE.)

PERSONAL EXPERIENCE NARRATIVE: 10, 47, 50, 53, 54, 57, 108, 109, 114, 145, 196, 212, 232, 250, 288, 291, 310, 314, 347, 352, 427.

PLACE NAMES: 11, 12, 15, 17–20, 22, 24, 60, 69, 92, 112, 131, 149, 207, 209, 210, 246, 247, 251, 260, 348, 355, 359, 360, 365, 377, 394, 395, 400. (See also FOLK NAMING.)

PLANT LORE: 39–44, 185, 203, 432. (See also BELIEFS AND CUSTOMS, FOLK NAMING, and WEATHER LORE.)

PROVERBIAL EXPRESSIONS: 8, 14, 36, 53–56, 65, 72, 80, 82, 91, 102, 136, 142, 192, 213, 226, 261, 271, 306, 362, 401.

QUILTING: 76, 79. (See also CRAFT, FOLKLIFE.)

RELIGION: 57, 114, 125, 126, 139, 189, 199, 231–233, 256, 310, 319, 358, 395, 419, 427, 429.

RHYME: 1, 2, 6, 8, 35, 53, 75, 80, 96, 102, 110, 121, 179, 208, 226, 243, 256, 271, 279, 293, 309, 322, 351, 353, 366, 388, 395, 426, 427, 438.

RIDDLE: 78, 94, 180.

SONG: 1, 2, 6, 8, 46, 53, 54, 62, 66, 68, 70, 71, 73–75, 81, 84, 102, 114, 122, 162, 181, 187, 214, 215, 236, 238, 239, 244, 262, 265, 274, 279, 280, 296, 298, 301, 306, 307, 311, 312, 314, 320, 322, 334, 342–344, 351, 353, 361, 366, 370, 386, 395, 411, 412, 420, 426, 429–431, 436. (See also MUSIC.)

SPEECH: 8, 53, 72, 85, 112–114, 125, 170, 177, 182, 190, 197, 203, 226, 227, 261, 277, 278, 290, 294, 301, 302, 305, 306, 315, 318, 321, 357, 374, 390, 437.

STEREOTYPES: 118, 122, 157, 170, 287, 289–291, 308, 354, 375, 383.

STYLISTICS: 10, 47, 199, 226, 262, 343, 392, 393, 415.

TALL TALES: 2, 27, 31, 33, 34, 47, 88, 105–107, 123, 193, 208, 216–219, 222, 229, 234, 235, 249, 250, 254, 258, 262–264, 267, 268, 270, 282, 291, 346, 393, 395, 397, 405, 418, 425.

URBAN LORE: 4, 5, 58, 59, 114, 115, 125, 126, 143, 155, 156, 159, 165, 168, 169, 174, 194, 195, 230, 231, 270, 281, 285, 313, 329, 330, 381–383, 421, 426.

WEATHER LORE: 8, 14, 50, 299, 363. (See also BELIEFS AND CUSTOMS and PLANT LORE).